我是英语文化书

每天读点世界文化，

主编 王泉 副主编 李笑南

这里是英国

中国水利水电出版社
www.waterpub.com.cn

内容提要

文化大餐，至尊阅读——阅读可以升华人格情操，其更本质、更核心的意义在于培养学习者的兴趣，而兴趣才是一切学习者学习的动力、成功的源泉。

"我是英语文化书"系列正是这样一套让人感觉妙趣横生、受益匪浅的英语读物。本套丛书分为《每天读点世界文化：这里是美国》、《每天读点世界文化：这里是英国》、《每天读点世界文化：这里是澳洲》。本书是一本浓缩世界文化精髓的知识储备书，旨在让读者在品味西方文化魅力的过程中，熟悉英语的逻辑思维和文化背景，从而适应深入沟通和交流的需要，使英语学习事半功倍。

图书在版编目（CIP）数据

每天读点世界文化. 这里是英国：英文 / 王泉主编
. -- 北京：中国水利水电出版社，2012.5（2014.10 重印）
（我是英语文化书）
ISBN 978-7-5084-9629-0

Ⅰ. ①每… Ⅱ. ①王… Ⅲ. ①英语－语言读物②文化
史－英国 Ⅳ. ①H319.4：K

中国版本图书馆CIP数据核字（2012）第065745号

策划编辑：陈 蕾　责任编辑：陈艳蕊　加工编辑：曹亚芳　封面设计：李 佳

书　　名	我是英语文化书 **每天读点世界文化：这里是英国**
作　　者	主编 王泉 副主编 李笑南
出版发行	中国水利水电出版社 （北京市海淀区玉渊潭南路 1 号 D 座 100038） 网　址：www.waterpub.com.cn E-mail：mchannel@263.net（万水） 　　　　sales@waterpub.com.cn 电　话：（010）68367658（发行部）、82562819（万水）
经　　售	北京科水图书销售中心（零售） 电　话：（010）88383994、63202643、68545874 全国各地新华书店和相关出版物销售网点
排　　版	北京万水电子信息有限公司
印　　刷	北京蓝空印刷厂
规　　格	170mm×235mm　16 开本　19 印张　496 千字
版　　次	2012 年 5 月第 1 版　2014 年 10 月第 4 次印刷
印　　数	12001—15000 册
定　　价	38.00 元

前　言

　　全球一体化的进程中，各领域之间都在不断地学习与交流，尤其是在经济全球化和文化全球化浪潮的猛烈冲击下，语言全球化的趋势也越来越明显，英语几乎成为了大多数非英语国家的第一外语。

　　初学英语时，每个月都感觉得到自己的不断进步，每个学期都切实掌握了新的内容。然而进入大学、进入社会后，英语学习越久却再难有很大的进步和突破，买再多的单词书、语法书来看也只能帮助我们通过考试，而对提高我们实际的英语应用水平起不到什么作用。更糟糕的是，我们对英语的热情，也渐渐被这种挫败和迷茫磨灭。我想原因主要有以下三个：缺乏英语的语感，没有英语的语言环境，不熟悉英语的思维逻辑和文化背景。而这三个原因中最重要的就是"对英语思维逻辑和文化背景的不熟悉"。语言是思维的工具，也是思维的轨迹。不同的语言承载着不同的文化，不同文化背景的人们的思维习惯和思维特点也必然存在着差异，而思维方式的差异也造成了文化和语言的差异。

　　若想精通一门语言，没有对其文化背景的深入了解，恐怕永远难登大雅之堂。文化背景的不同，会导致不同国家的人对同一个词、同一句话展开的联想也不尽相同，由此也就产生这样那样的误解。例如"老"与"old"，中国人历来有"尊老敬老"的传统美德，在我们看来，长者不仅是智慧的化身，也是威望的象征，"姜还是老的辣"正是对这一点最好的体现。然而西方国家却极少有人愿意用"old"来形容自己，在他们看来，"old"不仅表示年龄老，更表示能力不济。类似的还有，教师刚上完课在走廊上相遇，中国人可能互相会说"早上好，辛苦你了"等问候，但如果你对欧美教师说"Good morning, you must be tired after the class."，他们会觉得你是怀疑其能力不济，连上一堂课都会觉得累。这就是中西文化背景和思维意识的差异。因此，与外国友人的交流中不仅要注意表达的准确性，还要注意中西文化间的差异。在全球化、国际化的大趋势下，英语学习者如果仍停留在日常生活的层次上，必将难以适应深入沟通和交流的需要。

　　阅读可以升华人格情操，增长知识，提高语言文化的综合素质，其更本质、更核心的意义在于培养学习者的兴趣，而兴趣才是一切学习者的学习动力、成功源泉。"我是英语文化书"系列丛书正是这样一套让人感觉妙趣横生、受益匪浅的英语读物。本套丛书分为《每天读点世界文化：这里是英国》、《每天读点世界文化：这里是美国》、《每天读点世界文化：这里是澳洲》等书，为读者奉上原汁原味的人文阅读精华，读者在学习英语的同时，又能品味西方文化的独特魅力。

编者
2012年4月

使用说明

一本书开启英国之门：政治、经济、历史、地理、文化经典元素全覆盖

1 126个文化现象完美展现

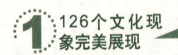

2 "中英双语+精彩图片"同步解读

English languages having equal status. Spoken by 20% of the population, the Welsh language is an important element of Welsh culture, and its use is supported by national policy.

Most parts of Wales are covered by mountains. There are three mountainous regions in particular: Snowdonia in the northwest, the Cambrian Mountains in mid Wales, and the Brecon Beacons in the south. Snowdon in the area of Snowdonia is the highest point in Wales at

独特的文化特征。威尔士的两种官方语言威尔士语与英语地位平等。有20%的威尔士人口讲威尔士语，国家政策也支持其使用，可以说威尔士语是威尔士文化的重要组成部分。

威尔士是多山地形，主要分布在三个区域：西北的斯诺登尼亚地区、威尔士中部的坎布瑞安山脉、南部的布雷肯比肯斯。威尔士最高的山峰斯诺登

3 核心词汇再多学一点

词汇 VOCABULARY

1. retain [ri'tein]
   ☑ 保留，保持，留住；挡住，拦住

2. bilingual [bai'liŋgwəl]
   ☑（能说）两种语言的 ☑ 通两种语言的人

3. mountainous['mauntinəs]
   ☑ 多山的；有山的

4. destination [.desti'neiʃən]
   ☑ 目的地，终点

6. constitutionally [.kɔnsti'tju:ʃənəli]
   ☑ 宪法上，立宪上；本质地，天性地

4 文化超链接再多品一点

背景链接

1. Welsh

威尔士语是威尔士的语言，讲威尔士语的，有六十万人，不到威尔士总人口的四分之一。与通行于爱尔兰与苏格兰部分地区的盖尔语一样，威尔士语是凯尔特语族的语言。作为威尔士的一个殖民地，阿根廷的巴塔哥尼亚也有好一些威尔士语的使用者。

2. Areas of Outstanding Natural Beauty (AONB)

杰出自然风景区。指由英格兰环境保护组织"自然英格兰"（Natural England）选定的位于英格兰、威尔士与北爱尔兰的风景壮丽的自然景区。之所以不包括苏格兰地区是因为苏格兰有自己的国家风景区（National Scenic Areas）。

参编人员（排名不分先后）

董立新	王 迪	袁 丹	武 超	徐永生	胡玲玲	
范 超	王 莹	王 慧	张 静	彭亚平	武 雯	
朱诗晴	徐 晨	沈楠忻	常 成	张晓菲	刘晓芳	
许 文	周 芬	华 巧	曾 莹	徐 焱	宋晓冬	
胡 庆	李月英					

CEOGRAPHY
Part 1 不可错过的英国
地理人文风情

ENTERPRISES
Part 2 正在影响世界的
英国顶级企业

MOVIE & TV
Part 3　英国正在反复热播的影视作品

ARTS
Part 4　英国人正在关注的人文作品

EVENTS
Part 5 英国人正在关注的现代轶事与高频回望的历史事件

PEOPLE
Part 6 英国人正在关注的英国人

GEOGRAPHY

Part 1

不可错过的英国地理人文风情

Unit 1 区域划分

The UK is a unitary state governed under a constitutional monarchy and a parliamentary system. It is made up of four countries: England, Northern Ireland, Scotland and Wales. Each country of the United Kingdom has its own system of administrative and geographic demarcation, which often has origins before the formation of the United Kingdom itself.

In terms of their geographic distribution, we all know that the UK is an island group in Western Europe, islands constituting the island of the Great Britain and the north-eastern part of the island of Ireland and many smaller islands. Britain – the largest island is the location for the separate countries of England, Scotland and Wales. England lies on the southern eastern part of the island of Great Britain. Scotland lies to the north of England, and Wales joins it on the west. Northern Ireland lies across the Irish Sea to the west, sharing the island of Ireland with the Republic of Ireland.

As for the administrative demarcation, there are three devolved national administrations, each with varying powers, situated in Belfast, Cardiff and Edinburgh; the capitals of Northern Ireland, Wales and Scotland respectively.

In this unit we are going to offer more details on the four countries of the UK, namely England, Wales, Scotland and Northern Ireland respectively in terms of their geographic, administrative and cultural features.

英国是在君主立宪制度和议会制度统治下的一个统一的国家。英国由四个部分组成：英格兰、北爱尔兰、苏格兰和威尔士。英国的每个部分都有自己的行政与地理划分区域，这种划分主要形成于联合王国形成之前。

关于地理划分，我们都知道英国是一个西欧的岛国，由大不列颠岛、爱尔兰岛东北部与其他许多小岛组成。其中在面积最大的不列颠岛上，有英格兰、苏格兰与威尔士。英格兰位于大不列颠岛的东南部，苏格兰位于英格兰北部，威尔士位于英格兰西部。北爱尔兰位于爱尔兰海的西部，与爱尔兰共和国共同位于爱尔兰岛上。

至于行政划分，英国有三个国家下放行政权力机构，每个机构权责各不相同，分别位于北爱尔兰的首府贝尔法斯特、威尔士的首府加的夫与苏格兰的首府爱丁堡。

在本单元我们将要为大家详细介绍英国的四个部分：英格兰、威尔士、苏格兰和北爱尔兰，主要介绍这四个地区的地理、行政与文化特征。

001 England

Population (2008) 51,446,000 (UK total 62,008,048)

Area 130,423 km^2 (UK total 241, 752 km^2)

Population Density 395/km^2

The country of England shows dominance over the other three nations in terms of area, population, economy and culture. As a result, it is usually mistakenly used to refer to the UK by foreigners as well as by people in England. But people in the other three nations would always prefer to be called British, Scottish, Irish or Welsh rather than English. So oddly, the English feel the most British and have the weakest sense of themselves as a separate "English" culture as compared with the other three nations.

With regard to geographic view, England consists mostly of lowland terrain which mostly comprises low hills and plains, especially in the central and southern part. However, there are uplands in the north and in the southwest. The upland moors of the Pennine Chain in the north region, known as the "backbone of England", divides northern England into western and eastern sectors. There is no peak in England that is 1,000 m or higher with the highest being 978 m (Scafell Pike). The longest river flowing through England is the Severn (354 km) while Thames is the longest river entirely in England (346 km). There are many lakes in England, the largest being Windermere, within the Lake District in the North West.

As a highly urbanized country, 80% of England's populations live in cities and only 2% working in agriculture. London is situated at the southeast of England. As the capital of the UK, London is also the largest metropolitan area in the United Kingdom and

【小译】

人口 (2008) 51,446,000 （英国共62,008,048）

面积 130,423 km^2 （英国共241,752 km^2）

人口密度 395人/km^2

英格兰是英国四个主要地区中面积最大，人口最多，经济最发达，文化影响力最大的地区。因此很多外国人总是错误地用英格兰来指称整个联合王国，而英格兰人们有时候也犯这种小错误，但是其他三个地区的人们却宁愿被称为不列颠人、苏格兰人、爱尔兰人或者威尔士人，而不是英国人。所以与其他三个地区不同，英格兰文化几乎与英国文化融为一体。

至于地貌特征方面，英格兰中部与南部地区呈低地地形，多低山与平原，而北部与西南部呈高地地貌，北部的高地沼泽奔宁山脉又被称为"英格兰的脊椎"，将北部地区分为东西两部分。英格兰没有1000米以上的高山，最高的斯可费尔峰也只有978米。流经英格兰的最长的河流是塞文河，全长354千米，而泰晤士河是英格兰境内最长的河流，全长346千米。英格兰境内有许多湖泊，其中最大的是位于西北部湖区的温德米尔湖。

英格兰城市化程度很高，拥有约80%的城市人口，只有2%的人口从事农业。伦敦位于英格兰东南部，作为英国的首都，伦敦也是英国乃至欧盟最大的大都市区域。伦敦不仅历史悠

even in the European Union by most measures. With a long history, London is also one of the most bustling financial cities in the world famous for its commercial and manufacturing industries. Other major cities in England also include Birmingham, Manchester, Liverpool and Newcastle.

Today England is governed directly by the Parliament of the United Kingdom, although other countries of the United Kingdom have devolved governments. There exist in England four levels of administrative division today ranging from Region, County, District and Parish; however, such division has only a limited role in public policy. At the highest level, the whole England is divided into nine regions, with London included, that are each made up of a number of counties and districts. The lowest level of parish division is only exercised in parts of England.

久，而且是世界上最繁忙的金融中心之一，并以其发达的商业与制造业闻名于世。英格兰其他主要城市还包括伯明翰、曼彻斯特、利物浦与纽卡斯尔。

和英国其他三个地区不同，英格兰没有自己的地方自治政府，现在直接由英国议会管理。今日的英格兰共有四种不同等级的行政区划，分别是区域等级、郡等级、区等级与教区等级。但是，这种划分方式在实施国家政策方面作用有限。在最高区域等级中，英格兰被分为包括伦敦在内的九个区域，这些区域又被进一步划分为大大小小的郡与区。最低级的教区等级划分只在英格兰的部分地区实施。

词汇 VOCABULARY

1. dominance ['dɒmɪnəns]
   n. 优势；支配（地位），统治（地位）

2. Scottish ['skɒtɪʃ]
   n. 苏格兰人；苏格兰语

3. Irish ['aɪərɪʃ]
   n. 爱尔兰人；爱尔兰语

4. Welsh [welʃ]
   n. 威尔士人；威尔士语

5. terrain ['tereɪn]
   n. 地面；地域；地带；地势

6. metropolitan [metrə'pɒlɪt(ə)n]
   n. 大都市的

7. manufacturing [ˌmænjuˈfæktʃərɪŋ]
   n. 制造业

背景链接 TIPS

Birmingham, Manchester, Liverpool and Newcastle.

伯明翰，位于英格兰中部奔宁山脉南端，东南距伦敦约160公里。现已发展为仅次于伦敦的英国第二大城市。曼彻斯特，英国纺织业中心，位于英格兰西北部的兰开夏郡内，距伦敦西北约290公里，是英国重要的铁路和航空交通枢纽。利物浦，英格兰西北部城市，为英国第二大港口。纽卡斯尔，英国英格兰东北部港市，纽卡斯尔是英格兰北部的政治、商业和文化中心。

002 Scotland

Population (2010) 5,222,100 (UK total 62,008,048)

Area 77,080km^2 (UK total 241, 752 km^2)

Population Density 66/km^2

Situated at the northern region of the UK, Scotland (Gaelic: Alba) is the second largest of the four nations, both in population and in geographic area. Scotland has previously been a unified state independent of the UK for a substantial period of history until 1707; therefore people in Scotland have a strong sense of themselves being "Scottish" and the unique "Scottish" culture. It is well-known in the world for its tartan check, bagpipe, whiskey industry. The official language in Scotland is English and the regional recognized languages include Gaelic and Scots.

Geographically speaking, Scotland is the most rugged part of the UK, with Highlands in both south and north and Lowlands in the middle. The highest peak of the UK – Ben Nevis (1,343m) locates in the northern highlands. The central Lowlands are the location of the Firth of Clyde in the west and the Firth of Forth in the east. The central region is also main farming district in Scotland and boasts several large cities, including Edinburgh and Glasgow, and 90 percent of Scottish population.

Locating in the west of the lowland zone, Glasgow is the largest city in Scotland and the third largest in the UK. With a population of almost 1.2 million, home to nearly a quarter of Scotland's population, it is not only the commercial center of Scotland, but also an art and cultural center with many buildings and museums of the Victoria style. Edinburgh, the capital city and the second biggest city of Scotland, is located at the east of Scotland near the North Sea. As the political,

【小译】

人口 (2010) 5,222,100 （英国共62,008,048）

面积 77,080km^2 （英国共241, 752 km^2）

人口密度 66人/km^2

位于英国北部的苏格兰（盖尔语：Alba）是在人口与面积上均为英国第二的地区。由于苏格兰在1707年之前一直是一个独立自主的国家，因此苏格兰人民族意识很强，拥有独特的苏格兰文化。苏格兰的格子呢、风笛、威士忌世界闻名。虽然苏格兰的官方语言是英语，但是盖尔语和低地苏格兰语也是官方承认的地区语言。

就地貌特征而言，苏格兰是英国最为崎岖不平的地区。北部与南部均为高地，而中部为低地。英国最高的山峰本尼维斯山就位于北部高地，高约1343米。中部低地有西侧的克莱德河湾与东侧的泰河湾。中部低地居住着苏格兰90%的人口，也是苏格兰主要的农业区域，苏格兰最大的城市格拉斯哥与爱丁堡就位于中部低地。

位于低地西部的格拉斯哥是苏格兰最大的城市，也是英国第三大城市，现居人口约120万，占苏格兰总人口的1/4。格拉斯哥不仅是苏格兰的商业中心，也是艺术文化中心，当地有很多维多利亚风格的建筑与博物馆。苏格兰的首府爱丁堡位于苏格兰东部北海附近，也是苏格兰第二大城市。爱丁堡是苏格兰的政治、经济、文化中心，其美丽的风景吸引了超过200万

economical and cultural center of Scotland, the city attracts over 2 million tourists all over the world for its beauty and the annual Edinburgh Festival.

Different from England, Scotland has its own devolved government. It has partial self-government within the United Kingdom as well as representation in the UK Parliament. The Scottish Parliament has legislative authority for Scotland, as well as limited power to vary income tax. As for administrative division, Scotland has been divided into 32 Unitary Authority Regions since 1996. The "Region" in Scotland is similar to the "County" in England in nature.

世界各地的游客。此外，游客来这里也是为了参加每年一度的爱丁堡国际艺术节。

苏格兰与英格兰不同，通过中央权力下放，有自己的自治政府。苏格兰在位于伦敦的联合王国议会有代表权。苏格兰议会拥有立法权和有限的所得税改动权。至于行政区域划分，苏格兰从1996年分为32个统一管理区。苏格兰的"区"与英格兰的"郡"性质接近。

词汇 VOCABULARY

1. previously ['pri:vju:sli]
   ad. 事先；以前

2. substantial [səb'stænʃəl]
   a. 多的；大的；大量的；丰盛的

3. tartan ['tɑ:tən]
   n. 格子呢；方格花纹

4. bagpipe ['bægpaip]
   n. （乐器）风笛

5. whiskey ['(h)wiski]
   n. 威士忌酒

6. legislative ['ledʒis,letiv]
   a. 立法的；有立法权的

7. unitary ['ju:nitəri]
   a. 单一的；统一的；一元的

背景链接 TIPS

1. Gaelic and Scots

盖尔语与低地苏格兰语均是苏格兰除英语之外的官方语言。盖尔语主要用于苏格兰和爱尔兰等凯尔特文化区，发音类似于德语，分为苏格兰盖尔语和爱尔兰盖尔语。苏格兰盖尔语是高地苏格兰人的传统语言。

苏格兰语又称低地苏格兰语，是低地苏格兰人所使用的语言，属于一种日耳曼语族的语言。

2. Edinburgh Festival

爱丁堡艺术节为世界五大综艺节日之一，每年八月举行，为期四周。该节日创立于1947年，为世界上历史最悠久、规模最大的艺术节，所邀请的参展对象包括音乐、舞蹈、戏剧各领域中的顶尖人士以及深具潜力的新秀，也被公认为世界上最具有活力和创新精神的艺术节之一，对推动全球剧场艺术蓬勃发展功不可没。

 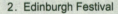

003 Wales

Population (2010) 3,006,400 (UK total 62,008,048)

Area 20,779 km^2 (UK total 241, 752 km^2)

Population Density 140/km^2

Locating at the south west of UK, Wales is the smallest among the three nations of the Great Britain. It is very close to the most densely populated parts of central England and there is no natural boundary between Wales and England, so Wales shares a close political and social history with the rest of Great Britain. Nevertheless, it has retained a distinct cultural identity. Wales is officially bilingual, the Welsh and English languages having equal status. Spoken by 20% of the population, the Welsh language is an important element of Welsh culture, and its use is supported by national policy.

Most parts of Wales are covered by mountains. There are three mountainous regions in particular: Snowdonia in the northwest, the Cambrian Mountains in mid Wales, and the Brecon Beacons in the south. Snowdon in the area of Snowdonia is the highest point in Wales at 1,085m. Wales is much less urbanized as compared with England and has preserved many sites of natural beauty. Wales has three national parks: Snowdonia, Brecon Beacons and Pembrokeshire Coast. It also has five Areas of Outstanding Natural Beauty (AONB).

Cardiff has become the capital city in Wales since 1995, also the youngest capital in Europe. It is the biggest city with around 340 thousand people in Wales and it is Wales' chief commercial centre, the base for

【小译】

人口 (2010) 3,006,400 （英国共62,008,048)

面积 20,779 km^2 （英国共241, 752 km^2)

人口密度 140人/km^2

位于英国西南部的威尔士是大不列颠面积以及人口最小的地区。威尔士紧邻人口密集的英格兰中部地区，与英格兰没有明显界限，因此威尔士在历史上与大不列颠其他地区有着紧密的政治社会联系。然而，威尔士依然有着自己独特的文化特征。威尔士的两种官方语言威尔士语与英语地位平等。有20%的威尔士人口讲威尔士语，国家政策也支持其使用，可以说威尔士语是威尔士文化的重要组成部分。

威尔士是多山地形，主要分布在三个区域：西北的斯诺登尼亚地区、威尔士中部的坎布瑞安山脉、南部的布雷肯比肯斯。威尔士最高的山峰斯诺登山就在斯诺登尼亚地区，高约1085米。与英格兰相比，威尔士乡土气息较重，保存了多处优美的自然风光。威尔士境内有三处国家公园：斯诺登尼亚、布雷肯比肯斯、彭布罗克海岸国家公园，并且有五处杰出的自然风景区。

自1995年起加的夫成为威尔士的首府，也是欧洲最年轻的首府。加的

most national cultural and sporting institutions. Cardiff also has beautiful coastal view and two national parks, so it is a significant tourism centre and the most popular visitor destination in Wales with 18.3 million visitors in 2010.

Wales also has its own devolved government. The Government of Wales Act 1998 established devolution in Wales, and certain executive and legislative powers have been constitutionally delegated to the National Assembly for Wales. The scope of these powers was further widened by the Government of Wales Act 2006. Since 1996 Wales has been divided into 22 unitary authorities including counties, cities and county boroughs.

夫拥有34万人口,是威尔士的主要经济中心,也是大多数威尔士文化与运动机构所在地。加的夫景色秀丽,有两座国家公园,因此也是威尔士最受欢迎的旅游胜地,据统计2010年接待了1830万游客。

威尔士也有自己的自治政府。1998年通过的威尔士政府法案确立了英国在威尔士的权力下放,并将部分行政立法权下放给威尔士国民议会。而相关的权力通过2006年的威尔士政府法案又进一步扩大。从1996年起,威尔士被分为22个一元行政单位,包括郡、市、郡级自治市镇。

词汇 VOCABULARY

1. retain [ri'tein]
   vt 保留,保持;留住;挡住,拦住

2. bilingual [bai'liŋgwəl]
   a (能说) 两种语言的 n 通两种语言的人

3. mountainous['mauntinəs]
   a 多山的;有山的

4. destination [,desti'neiʃən]
   n 目的地,终点

5. constitutionally [,kɔnsti'tju:ʃənəli]
   ad 宪法上,立宪上;本质地,天性地

背景链接

1. Welsh

威尔士语是威尔士的语言,讲威尔士语的,有六十万人,不到威尔士总人口的四分之一。与通行于爱尔兰与苏格兰部分地区的盖尔语一样,威尔士语是凯尔特语族的语言。作为威尔士的一个殖民地,阿根廷的巴塔哥尼亚也有好一些威尔士语的使用者。

2. Areas of Outstanding Natural Beauty (AONB)

杰出自然风景区。指由英格兰环境保护组织"自然英格兰"(Natural England)选定的位于英格兰、威尔士与北爱尔兰的风景壮丽的自然景区。之所以不包括苏格兰地区是因为苏格兰有自己的国家风景区(National Scenic Areas)。

|004 Northern Ireland

Population (2010) 1,789,000 (UK total 62,008,048)

Area 13,483 km^2 (UK total 241, 752 km^2)

Population Density 140/km^2

Northern Ireland (often called "Ulster" after an ancient Irish kingdom which once existed in that part of Ireland) takes up about one-sixth of the island of Ireland and is separated on the east from Scotland by the narrow North Channel. It shares a border with the Republic of Ireland to the southwest – the only land border of the UK. Northern Ireland is the smallest of the four nations both in area and population. Besides English, Irish is also the official language of Northern Ireland.

Geographically speaking, Northern Ireland shapes like a saucer with low central plains surrounded by a ring of coastal mountains. The highest point is Slieve Donard, rising 852m in the southeast. Lough Neagh, which lies near the center of the nation, is the largest freshwater lake in the United Kingdom and one of the largest in Europe. The capital of Northern Ireland is Belfast, which locates at the northeast corner of Northern Ireland with a population of only 350,000. Major industries in Belfast includes ship and airplane constructions, telecommunication, technology and trading. It is also home to the largest shipbuilder in the UK – Harland and Wolff.

Northern Ireland has undergone violent political conflict for many years. The troubles are caused by divisions between nationalists, who are predominantly Roman Catholic, and unionists, who are predominantly Protestant, which takes up the majority of the nation's population. Unionists want Northern Ireland to remain

【小译】

人口 （2010） 1,789,000 （英国共62,008,048）

面积 13,483 km^2 （英国共241, 752 km^2）

人口密度 140人/km^2

北爱尔兰（常被称为"阿尔斯特"——曾位于北爱尔兰的古代国家名）占爱尔兰岛全部面积的1/6，东部的北部海峡将其与苏格兰分开。爱尔兰的西南部与爱尔兰共和国接壤，这也是英格兰唯一的陆地边境。无论从面积还是人口上来说，北爱尔兰都是英国四个地区中最小的。英语、爱尔兰语是北爱尔兰的官方语言。

从地形上看，北爱尔兰很像一个茶托，中间是低的平原，四周被沿海的山脉环绕。境内最高峰是当纳德山，位于北爱尔兰东南部，高852米。内伊湖位于北爱尔兰中部，是英国最大的淡水湖，同时也是欧洲最大的淡水湖之一。北爱尔兰的首府是贝尔法斯特，位于北爱尔兰东北角，仅有35万人口。贝尔法斯特的主要产业有造船业、飞机制造业、无线电通讯、技术与贸易。英国最大的造船厂——哈兰德与沃尔夫就位于贝尔法斯特。

北爱尔兰多年来政治冲突不断。主要争端来自民族派与联合派。大多数爱尔兰人都是民族派，民族派多数是天主教徒，主张与爱尔兰共和国统一；大多数联合派人士是新教徒，主张北爱尔兰继续作为联合王国的一部

as a part of the United Kingdom, while nationalists wish for it to be politically united with the rest of Ireland, independent of British rule. The conflict escalated into armed campaigns between paramilitary groups from 1960s to 1990s. It is not until the signing of the "Good Friday Agreement" in 1998 that the two parties proclaimed to cease fire.

Northern Ireland has devolved government within the United Kingdom. There is a Northern Ireland Executive together with the 108-member Northern Ireland Assembly. As for administrative division, in 1974, Northern Ireland abolished the previous divisions of 6 counties and divided the whole nation into 26 District Council areas.

分，但是民族派认为北爱尔兰在制度上应该有自由权，政治上与爱尔兰其他地区一致。20世纪60年代到90年代间，两派的冲突上升为半军事组织之间的武装冲突。直到1998年，通过签订《受难日协议》，两派才宣布停火。

北爱尔兰也有自治政府，包括北爱尔兰行政部与由108名议员成立的北爱尔兰议会。至于行政区域划分，1974年，北爱尔兰废除原来的6个郡，改设为26个自治区。

词汇 VOCABULARY

1. Saucer ['sɔ:sə]
   n. 茶托；浅碟；（放花盆的）垫盘

2. freshwater ['freʃwɔ:tə(r)]
   adj. 淡水的；内河航行的；无经验的

3. telecommunication ['telikəmju:ni'keiʃən]
   n. 电讯；远程通信；无线电通讯

4. nationalist ['næʃənəlist]
   n. 民族主义者；国家主义者；民族独立主义者

5. unionist ['ju:njənist]
   n. 工会会员；联合主义者

6. escalate ['eskəleit]
   vi. 逐步增强；逐步升高 vt. 使逐步上升

7. paramilitary [ˌpærə'militəri]
   adj. 准军事的；辅助军事的 n. 准军事部队

8. proclaim [prə'kleim]
   vt. 宣告，公布，声明；表明；赞扬

9. abolish [ə'bɔliʃ]
   vt. 废除，废止；取消，革除

背景链接 TIPS

1. Irish

爱尔兰语，即爱尔兰盖尔语，在语言分类上属于印欧语系的凯尔特语族，和同属该语族的布列塔尼语、威尔士语、以及苏格兰盖尔语有相当密切的关系。爱尔兰语是爱尔兰的官方语言，同时也是北爱尔兰官方承认的区域语言，使用人口有26万。

2. Good Friday Agreement

1998年4月10日，包括新芬党在内的北爱尔兰各派在多方多年调停下，终于签订《受难日协议》，宣布停火合作，加强北爱地方自治，负责调停的两名北爱尔兰领袖更得到当年诺贝尔和平奖。

Unit 2 政治体系

The politics of the United Kingdom of Great Britain and Northern Ireland is of a constitutional monarchy with the Monarch as the head of state and the Prime Minister the head of government.

The British monarchy is the oldest institute of government in the world. The Monarch is a king or queen who rules the country. The power of the monarch is believed to come from God and the monarch used to be very powerful. However, since the passing of the Bill of Rights in 1689, the power of the monarch has been greatly reduced. Now, the primary role of the monarchy is to symbolize the tradition and unity of the British State. The current monarch of the state is Elizabeth II.

The British government exercises the executive power. The Prime Minister, the head of government, is assigned by the monarch from the political party that wins the most seats in the General Election. The Legislative power is exercised by two chambers of the Parliament, the House of Lords and the House of the Commons. The House of the Lords consists of the Archbishops and bishops of the Church and barons as well as life peers. The main duty of the House of Lord is to assist and scrutinize the work the other House. The House of Commons are elected through the General Election and responsible for the legislative power, judicial powers and the financial right as well as the supervision right.

The UK is a multi-party system. The two largest political parties are Conservative Party and the Labour Party. The third biggest party, the Liberal Democrats, is not powerful enough to form a government but it is very important in that it has a great impact on determining which of the two biggest party wins.

General Election is a good way for British citizens to participate in the British politics. Every qualified voter can vote for his ideal candidate and party.

大不列颠及北爱尔兰联合王国是一个君主立宪制国家。君主是国家最高的首领，首相是政府首脑。

英国的君主制是世界上最古老的政府机构之一。君主即统治国家的国王或女王。通常人们相信君权神授，因此，古代英国君主的权力很大。从1689年《权利法案》通过之后，君主的权利大大被削减。如今，君主的最主要职责是代表英国的传统与团结。英国的现任君主是伊丽莎白二世。

英国政府行使行政权。而政府的首脑，即首相，是由君主从大选中获得最多席位的政党中任命而产生的。立法权由议会两院行使。议会两院包括上议院和下议院。上议院成员包括大主教，主教，贵族和终身贵族。上议院的主要负责辅助和监督下议院。下议院议员由大选产生，行使立法权、司法权、财政权和监督权。

英国为多党制国家，保守党和工党是英国最大的两个政党。第三大政党自由民主党虽不足以组建政府，但在决定其余两党哪个党在大选中获胜上发挥着极其重要的作用。

英国大选为国民参与英国政治提供了一个很好的平台。每一个具有选举权的公民都可以为自己喜欢的政党和候选人投票。

|005 The Monarchy

The monarchy in Britain is the oldest form of government which could be traced back to the Anglo-Saxon time. The continuity of the monarchy never stops except for once during the years 1649 to 1660 when the Civil War took place in Britain.

It was believed that the power of the monarchy comes directly from God instead of its subject. That is to say, the monarch had the "divine right of kings". Its subjects had no right to interfere or control the power of king.

However, not everyone was satisfied with the sovereign, especially when the king abused his power. There were events in the history of the State for the British people to fight against the power of the monarchs. As a result of these events, the monarchy's absolute power has declined.

In 1215, a group of people from federal barons and the Church fought against King John's abusing of power. Their objection was so powerful that the King was forced to grant them a charter of liberty and political rights, known as Magna Carta (a Latin name). This charter helped limiting the King's abuse of power to some extent.

Another such event occurred in 1688 when King James II governed the country regardless of the opinion of the

【小译】

在英国，君主制是最古老的政府机构，可以追溯到盎格鲁·萨克逊时期。英国的君主只有在1649～1660年英国内战时期终止，除此之外，英国的君主制再也没有中断过。

人们大多相信"君权神授"，即君主的权力来自于上帝而不是臣民，因此，君主的权力是神圣的。臣民无权干涉或阻碍君主行使权力。

然而，并不是所有的君主都能做到顺息民意，尤其是当君主滥用权力的时候。英国历史上就有几次人民反抗君主权力的事件。而君主的权力也由此不断受到限制。

1215年，一群封建贵族和教会成员联合对当时的君主约翰王发起反抗，反对其滥用君权。反抗的力量非常强大，约翰王被迫签署了代表自由和政治权利《大宪章》。《大宪章》大大地削弱了君主的权力。

另一个限制君权的事件发生在1688年。当时，国王詹姆士二世毫不听取议会的意见。一些政治人士和教会首脑联合起来推翻了詹姆士二世的统治，把他的女儿玛丽和女婿奥伦治威廉推上了王位。威廉和玛丽在1689年接受了议会提出

Parliament. The joint effort from politicians and church authorities replaced him with his son-in-Law, William of Orange who accepted more constraints from Parliament than previous monarchs had. In 1689, the Parliament passed the Bill of Rights to limit the power of the monarchy which marked the establishment of the limited constitutional monarchy.

Nowadays, the primary role of the monarchy is to symbolize the tradition and unity of the British State. Other roles of the monarch stated in the Constitution include: She is legally head of the executive, an integral part of the legislature, head of the judiciary, commander in chief of the armed forces and "supreme governor" of the Church of England.

的限制君主的权力的《权利法案》，君主的权力受到了前所未有的削减。《权利法案》标志着英国君主立宪制的形成。

如今，君主的主要角色是代表国家的传统和团结。宪法规定的君主的其他职责还有：她是行政首脑，立法机构的组成部分，司法首脑，全国武装部队总司令，英国国教"至高无上"的领袖。

词汇 VOCABULARY

1. monarchy ['mɔnəki]
   n. 君主政体；君主国；君主政治

2. continuity [ˌkɔnti'nju(:)iti]
   n. 连续性；一连串；分镜头剧本

3. baron ['bærən]
   n. 男爵；大亨；巨头

4. Magna Carta
   n. 大宪章；保障人民权利与自由的法令

5. authority [ɔː'θɔriti]
   n. 权威；权力；当局

6. constitutional [ˌkɔnsti'tju:ʃənəl]
   adj. 宪法的；本质的 *n.* 保健散步；保健运动

7. executive [ig'zekjutiv]
   adj. 行政的；经营的；执行的，经营管理的
   n. 经理；执行委员会；经理主管人员

8. legislature ['ledʒis.leitʃə]
   n. 立法机关；立法机构

9. judiciary [dʒu(:)'diʃiəri]
   n. 司法部；法官；司法制度 法官的；法院的

10. supreme [sju:'pri:m]
    adj. 最高的；至高的；最重要的 *n.* 至高；霸权

背景链接 TIPS

Magna Carta

《大宪章》主要内容有：保障教会选举教职人员的自由；保护贵族和骑士的领地继承权，国王不得违例征收领地继承税；未经由贵族、教士和骑士组成的"王国大会议"的同意，国王不得向直属附庸征派补助金和盾牌钱；取消国王干涉封建主法庭从事司法审判的权利；未经同级贵族的判决，国王不得任意逮捕或监禁任何自由人或没收他们的财产。此外，少数条款涉及城市，如确认城市已享有的权利、保护商业自由、统一度量衡等。大宪章是对王权的限定，国王如违背之，由25名贵族组成的委员会有权对国王使用武力。

006 Houses of Parliament

The United Kingdom Parliament, also known as the Westminster Parliament, is the supreme legislative and judicial authority that is consisted of three parts: the Monarchy, the House of Lords and the House of Commons.

The word "parliament" derives from the word "parley", namely, to negotiate. The original form of Parliament in Britain was the Great Council. The Great Council was a gathering of leading, wealth barons who were assembled by the King to collect money for special needs, such as starting a war. By the 13th century, kings found that the money collected from the barons was not enough, thus they included representatives of counties, cities and towns in the Great Council. Therefore, the group of barons has come to known as the House of Lords while the other group became the House of Commons.

The main duties of the Parliament include passing laws and voting for taxation in order to support the working of the government. The Parliament also plays the role to scrutinize government policy, administration and expenditure and to debate the major issues of the day. It alones has the power to change the Constitution.

The House of Lords nowadays consists of the Archbishops and bishops of the Church, barons and life peers. There are generally two ways to become a member of the House of Lords, one is to inherit from their forefathers and the other is to be appointed by the sovereign for their contribution to the country. The latter are also called life peers who can't pass their title to their offspring. The House of Lords mainly support and scrutinizes the work of the other House. The House of Lords is the highest judicial administrative organ of the State.

【小译】

英国议会或威斯敏斯特议会，是英国最高立法和司法机关。英国议会由三部分组成：君主、上议院和下议院。

Parliament这个单词由parley衍生而来，parley的意思是协商。英国议会的雏形是大议会（the Great Council）。大议会是国王为某些特殊需求，比如征战，筹措资金而召集有名望的富有贵族开的会议。到了13世纪，国王意识到贵族无法满足他们的经济需求，因此，他们把来自不同县市镇的代表也囊括到了大议会中。后来，那部分贵族演变为上议院议员，而那些各个地方的代表则构成了下议院。

议会的主要职责包括通过立法和为政府的正常运作筹措资金。议会同时还有监督政府政策、政府工作和政府支出的职能。议会也是唯一有权修改宪法的机构。

上议院成员包括大主教、主教、贵族和终身贵族。一般来说，能够成为上议院议员的途径有两种，一是继承，二是凭借对国家的巨大贡献被君主授予终身议员的头衔。但是后者的头衔不具有传承性。上议院主要职责

The members of The House of Commons are selected for a five-year term of office. The party that owns the most seats in the House of Commons becomes the party in office. The Prime Minister is appointed by the monarch from this party. The House of Commons owns the legislative power, judicial powers and the financial right as well as the supervision right.

Within the parliament, in terms of representation, the monarch, as the symbol of the country, is non-political and represents each and all; the House of Lords are not elected and therefore are not considered to represent anyone besides themselves; the House of Commons are elected, so they represent for the group of people who vote for them.

是辅助和监督下议院。上议院是国家最高司法机构。

下议院议员由选举产生，任期5年。在大选中获得最多议员席位的政党成为执政党。首相也是君主从该政党中任命产生。下议院行使的主要权利有立法权、司法权、财政权和监督权。

构成议会的不同部分代表不同人的利益。君主作为国家的标志不具有政治性，因此代表英国的所有公民；上议院不是通过选举产生，因此只代表自己；下议院议员都是通过选举产生的，他们代表支持他们的群体的利益。

词汇 VOCABULARY

1. parliament ['pɑ:ləmənt]
   n. 议会，国会

2. scrutinize ['skrutinaiz]
   vt. 细阅；作详细检查 vi. 详细检查；细看
   n. 仔细或彻底检查

3. debate [di'beit]
   vt. 辩论，争论，讨论 vi. 辩论，争论，讨论
   n. 辩论；辩论会

4. Archbishop ['ɑ:tʃ'biʃəp]
   n. [宗]大主教；总教主

5. peer [piə]
   vi. 凝视，窥视 vt. 封为贵族；与…同等
   n. 贵族；同等的人

6. representation [,reprizen'teiʃən]
   n. 代表；表现；表示法；陈述

背景链接 TIPS

1. The Houses of Parliament

依泰晤士河而建的议会大厦（the Houses of Parliament）位于伦敦市中心区的泰晤士河畔，是19世纪中期英国最主要的哥特式建筑。大厦建立在泰晤士河畔一个近于梯形的地段上，面向泰晤士河。议会大厦内有一千间房间，自13世纪以来此处便是英国国会开会之处，也同时兼为国王宫殿。大厦一侧有一座闻名中外的"大本钟"。大本钟每小时报时一次，钟声响起时远近可闻，且是十分准时，英国BBC电视台也是依据此钟报时。

2. Life peers

终身贵族，亦作一代贵族，是英国贵族的一种。与一般贵族不同的是，终身贵族只限于个人，不能让其子女世袭继承。现时的终身贵族由1958年制定的《终身贵族法》所管制，爵位只限于男爵。终身贵族的称呼与勋爵一样，而且都可以成为上议院的议员。成为终身贵族，可以选择封邑，但这个"封邑"只是象征式，并不会为贵族贡献税收。英国著名的终身贵族有彭定康、邓莲如、玛格丽特·希尔达·撒切尔和安德鲁·劳埃德·韦伯。

007 Electoral System

The United Kingdom is the first country in the world to start general election and its election system has a great influence on British representative democratic political system as well as that of other western countries.

All the qualified citizens in Britain can vote. The qualification to vote covers the following aspects:

1. Nationality. People with British nationalities (Irish citizenship and citizenship of the British Commonwealth of Nations are included) can vote.

2. Age. People who are 18 or above can vote.

3. Residential limitation. People who live in the parliamentary constituency for at least 3 months can vote, except for army members who have the right to vote after staying for 1 month.

4. People who cannot vote are those who have mental problems or who serve their terms in prison.

Only after all of the above qualifications are met can a person vote.

The whole state is generally divided into 651 parliamentary constituencies; with each constituency contain a population of around 50,000 people. The voting committee is responsible for balancing the numbers of voters in all the constituencies so that every constituency is of approximately equal voters.

In each constituency, there is a register official assigned by the government to do the registration for the voters door-to-door and work out an "electoral register". "Electoral register" is a list on which all the qualified voters appear. When the voting date is decided, each voter can receive a voting card via mail with detailed information about when and where the voting will take place (The voting date is not fixed

【小译】

英国是世界上第一个实行大选的国家。英国选举制度对英国的代表民主政治体系乃至其他西方国家的政治体系都有很大的影响。

所有符合条件的英国公民都可以参加选举。参与选举的条件包括：

一、国籍。拥有英国国籍的臣民，包括居住在英国的任何英联邦国家和爱尔兰共和国的公民都有选举权。

二、年龄。英国现行法律规定，18岁为选民最低年龄资格条件，不到18岁者无选民资格。

三、居住。普通选民在选区的居住时间限制至少是三个月。军人选民在选区的居住时间限制至少是一个月。

四、因精神问题和刑事问题而丧失投票行为能力和行为资格的人没有选民资格。

只有符合了上面的所有条件才能选举投票。

整个英国被划分为651个选区，每个选区的人数在5万左右。选举委员会负责平衡选区的选举人数从而保证每个选举的选民人数基本一致。

每个选区都有政府指派的注册官员，负责上门进行登记选民并制成"选民登记册"。"选民登记册"上列出所有符合条件的选民。一旦选举日期确定了（英国没有固定的选举日期），每个选民都会收到附有选举卡片的信件。选举卡片上有选举时间和地点的信息。到了

in Britain). When the day comes, the voters go to the voting station and exchange the voting card for another card with names of the candidate on. Every voter has only one vote and is allowed to vote for one candidate. After choosing the candidate, the voter folds the voting card and put it into a sealed box.

The candidates to be voted are mostly from different political parties. The local organization of each party selects the most suitable candidate to represent the party and compete with other candidates. The candidate with the most votes of the constituency wins and the party with the most constituencies wins the election.

All the political parties conduct electoral campaigns to win more votes. There are constituency campaigns and national campaigns. In the campaign, each party uses newspaper advertisement, door-to-door campaign, postal deliveries of leaflets and TV campaigns to "sell" their policies.

The counting begins immediately after the voting and the result of the voting comes out a few hours later. The party with the most constituencies wins the election and forms the new government.

选举日，选民来到选举点，把收到的选举卡片换成另一张上有候选人名字的卡片。每个选民只能为一个候选人投票，而且只能投一次票。选择了候选人之后，选民把卡片折叠并投入一个密封的信箱里。

大多数候选人都来自政党。每个政党在不同地区都有地方组织，负责选出该地区的候选人来与其他政党候选人竞争席位。各选区获得最多票数的候选人赢得该选区，赢得最多选择的政党就是大选的胜利者。

所有的政党都会通过举办竞选活动来赢得更多选票。竞选活动分选区竞选活动和全国竞选活动两种。在竞选活动中，各政党都会通过广告、上门宣传、邮寄竞选传单和电视竞选来"推销"自己的政策主张。

投票一结束，计票就开始了。投票结果在几个小时后之后就揭晓了。赢得最多选区的政党赢得大选并组成新政府。

词汇 VOCABULARY

1. qualification [ˌkwɔlifiˈkeiʃən]
   n. 资格；条件；限制；赋予资格

2. commonwealth [ˈkɔmənwelθ]
   n. 联邦；共和国；国民整体

3. residential [ˌreziˈdenʃəl]
   a. 住宅的；与居住有关的

4. constituency [kənˈstitjuənsi]
   n. （选区的）选民；支持者；（一批）顾客

5. campaign [kæmˈpein]
   vi. 作战；参加竞选；参加活动
   n. 运动；活动；战役

背景链接 TIPS

First-past-the-post election system

简单多数选举制（First-past-the-post election system），即根据一党所占有的议员数量。如果一党拥有绝对多数的议员，则此党将组成下届政府，该党党魁则成为首相。如果没有任何党派拥有绝对多数席位，则合计拥有绝对多数席位的两个或多个政党将组成联合政府（Coalition government），基本上其中最大党党魁将成为首相；或者单独一党成立政府，并通过与其他党派非正式的联盟和协议而得以延续。

GEOGRAPHY

008 Conservative Party and Labour Party

There are two major political parties in Britain: The Conservative party and the Labour party.

The Conservative party was evolved from Tory; a political community first appeared in Charles II's time. In the middle of the 19th century, Tories changed their name into the Conservative party. The Conservative party wins support from land owners, businessmen as well as a majority of farmers. It is a common phenomenon in Britain that the chance for a person to be a conservative increases as he gets older and more prestigious. The Conservative party is mostly favored by the middle class. The main idea of the Conservatives is their belief in "individual enterprise", that is, everyone is capable of building up his own enterprise as long as he works hard and is courageous enough to take risk. Individual ability is highly valued and they commit themselves to protect the individual right and create a better environment which includes a low tax.

However, as the biggest opponent of the Conservative party, the Labour party holds different opinions. Though the Labour party is a relatively young party, it quickly took the place of the Liberal Party as one of the two biggest parties. Since it was created by the trade union movement at the end of the 19th century, it represents the interests of the working class. The Labour party highly doubts the possibility for the tradesmen to serve the best interests of the whole community. They keep reminding people of the miserable life the working class had lived under the exploitation of the employers. As a socialist and more radical party, the Labour party seeks for equality for the working class in economic terms. Therefore, they think

【小译】

保守党和工党是当今英国最主要的两大政党。

保守党的前身是托利党。托利党出现于查理二世在位时期。在十九世纪中期，托利党更名为保守党。保守党的支持者包括土地所有者、商人和大部分的农民。通常，在英国，年纪越大、身份越高的人越有可能属于保守党。支持保守党的群体大部分是中产阶级。保守党的最主要的主张是"私人事业"。他们主张只要有勇气，敢于冒险，每个人都有能力成就一番事业。保守党非常重视个人能力的发挥并致力于保护个人利益，为个人能力的发展创造良好的环境，比如说低税收。

然而，作为保守党最大的竞争对手，工党有着不同的主张。虽然工党的历史没有保守党悠久，但它在出现之后迅速取代了自由党的位置，成为英国两大政党之一。工党是19世纪末期由工会产生的，它代表的是工人阶级的利益。工党不相信商人能够为社会谋福利。他们不断提醒人们以前工人阶级在雇主剥削下苦难的生活。作为一个社会主义政党和一个激进的政党，工党为工人阶级争取经济层面的平等。他们主张政府应该充当资源分配的媒介把财富分配给穷人。对富人征收高额税款来扶持穷人就是他们很重要的一个主张。他们还主张私人企

the government should take the role as a distributive agent to transfer wealth from the richer to the poorer. One way to do so is by collecting high tax from the riches to support the poor. They are also in favor of nationalization by changing the individual enterprise into state-owned ones.

However, the history of the political parties indicates that neither party has stood still, changes in every party is inevitable as time changes. It is important to note that the difference between the two parties is one of degree, not an absolute one.

业的国有化，即把私人企业的性质转化为国有企业。

但是，两党历史政权的交替告诉我们，无论是保守党还是工党，他们都不是一成不变的，他们的主张会随着时间的推移而发生变化。值得一提的是，两个政党的差异是相对的，而不是绝对的。

词汇 VOCABULARY

1. prestigious [,pres'ti:dʒəs] a 有名望的；享有声望的	2. opponent [ə'pəunənt] n 对手；反对者；敌手 a 对立的；敌对的
3. exploitation [,eksplɔi'teiʃən] n 开发，开采；利用；广告推销	4. radical ['rædikəl] a 激进的；根本的；彻底的 n 基础；激进分子；[物化]原子团；[数]根数
5. nationalization [,næʃnəlai'zeiʃən] n 国有化；同化，归化	6. inevitable [in'evitəbl] a 必然的，不可避免的

背景链接 TIPS

1. Conservative Party

保守党以往以"自由火炬"为党的标志，但现今已改为使用一棵绿色的橡树作新标志。另在2005年12月6日，保守党又采用了新的口号，该口号为"以改变迎接胜利——不列颠的胜利"（Change to Win – Win for Britain）。传统上，保守党的官方颜色为红色、白色和蓝色，但蓝色则最为常用，以区别于工党的红色（在坎布里亚部分选区，保守党却会选用黄色，以象征当地朗斯代尔伯爵的家族纹章）。

2. Is Labour Party a communist party?

不是，英国工人运动兴起较早，起初按行业建立了各种工会组织，1868年进一步成立了全国性的统一组织——职工大会（工联），1900年成立了"工人代表委员会"并推选出自己的党选候选人，1906年组织正式改名为工党。工党是由工会、合作社组织和社会主义团体联合组成的，党员都是通过上述组织集体加入。英国工党是比较左倾的政党，以维护工人利益为口号，但还是一个资产阶级政党，不奉行马克思主义。

Unit 3 英国的节日

In Britain, holidays and festivals fall into 3 categories: national holidays, religious holidays and holidays of four nations.

National holidays refer to holidays celebrated throughout the Britain. However, due to different histories and cultures of the 4 nations, it seems rather difficult to have national holidays that could be celebrated by the whole country. Therefore, the Queen's Birthday takes the place and becomes the only national holiday. The present queen, Queen Elizabeth II's official birthday is on the second Saturday of June. On that day, the Queen inspects her troops and a special party is held to celebrate this day.

Britain is basically a Christian nation, although different religions are practiced owing to immigration and belief change. As a result, Christian holidays are celebrated. Two of the most important religious holidays are Christmas and Easter.

For the four nations, different holidays are celebrated at different times for different reasons. The English people celebrate the Bonfire Night or Guy Fawkes Night on 5 December for the successful destruction of the conspirators' intended explosion. The Scottish celebrate Burns Night on 25 January, a day for the remembrance of the great Scottish poet, Robert Burns and also New Year's Eve, or Hogmanay on 31 December and The national holiday in Northern Ireland is the St. Patrick's Day on 17 March. It is St. Patrick, the saint priest, who brought Christianity to Ireland and converted Northern Irish people to Christians. Eisteddfod is held by Welsh people to preserve their culture and language. All the competitions are in Welsh and people participating in Eisteddfod compete for the best essayist, translator and choir.

Nowadays, as a result of culture diversity and change of time, holiday traditions change accordingly. Many holidays are no longer confined by geographical confinement and shared by people throughout the country. Therefore, more and more people have the opportunity to share the rich cultural heritage of the UK.

英国的节日可以大概分为三类：国家节日、宗教节日和不同区域各自的节日。

国家节日指的是全国性庆祝的节日。但是，由于四个国家历史与文化的差异，几乎没有能够全国同时庆祝的节日。因此，女王的生日被视为唯一的全国庆祝的节日。现任女王伊丽莎白二世的官方生日是六月的第二个星期六。在那一天，女王通过检阅部队和举办生日派对来庆祝生日。

由于移民和信仰变化，英国有很多种类的宗教，但绝大多数人信奉基督教。因此，英国人庆祝很多基督教节日。最重要的两个基督教节日是圣诞节和复活节。

英国的四个国家都有本民族自己的节日。因此，不同国家会在不同的时间庆祝不同的节日。英格兰人在12月5日庆祝篝火之夜（也叫盖伊福克斯之夜），以此来庆祝成功挫败阴谋者试图炸议会、谋杀国王的企图。苏格兰人会在1月25日举办彭斯晚餐来纪念苏格兰伟大的诗人罗伯特·彭斯，并在12月31日庆祝新年之夜。北爱尔兰的主要节日在3月17日，这一天是人们为纪念圣贤圣帕特里克而庆祝的节日。相传是圣贤圣帕特里克把基督教带到北爱尔兰并把人们转变为基督教徒。威尔士音乐诗歌节是威尔士人为传承威尔士文化和语言而举办的一年一度的音乐诗歌节。节日里所有的比赛活动都是用威尔士语进行的，最后角逐出最好的散文家、翻译家和合唱队。

如今，随着时间的推移和文化多样性的发展，节日的传统也发生了很大的变化。很多节日不再受到地域的限制而被整个英国的人们庆祝。因此，越来越多的人有机会传承英国丰富的文化遗产。

|009 Christmas

The word "Christmas" is derived from Old English "Cristes Maesse", which means Christ's Mass (Mass means church service). It is the celebration of the birth of Jesus Crist. The first fixed celebration of Christmas held on 25 December was in the year AD 440 by the Christian Church. Most western countries celebrate Christmas.

Before the Christmas, Christmas decorations are put up in homes and churches. Christmas tree is an integral part of the Christmas decorations in most British families. Almost every household has a Christmas tree, be it real tree or plastic and puts up Christmas decorations on it.

At Christmas Eve, Christians go to church to attend a special carol service. During the service, they sing Christmas carols and watch a Nativity performed by children. At the midnight, Christians do a church service to celebrate the coming of Jesus. Christmas Eve is an exciting time for children because the Father Christmas (Santa Clause) will come and stuff their Christmas stockings with gifts and presents.

On Christmas Day, people get together with their families. Many Christians go to churches to sing carols to celebrate the birth of Jesus Christ wearing their new clothes. The number of people going to church on Christmas Day is much more than any other days. The Christmas Dinner is a very important meal for British people. This meal is usually eaten in mid-day of Christmas Day. A traditional British Christmas Dinner includes roast turkey or goose, Brussels sprouts, roast potatoes, pigs in a blanket and etc. Christmas

【小译】

Christmas这个词来源于古英语Cristes Maesse，意思是耶稣的礼拜（Mass是教堂礼拜的意思）。因此，圣诞节就是为了庆祝耶稣基督的诞生。在公元440年，人们第一次在12月25日到教堂庆祝圣诞节。大多数西方国家都会庆祝圣诞节。

人们在圣诞节到来之前用圣诞饰品装饰家庭和教堂。圣诞树在英国是一种必不可少的圣诞装饰品。几乎每家每户都有圣诞树，有的是真树，有的是塑料的。然后人们在圣诞树上挂上各种各样的装饰。

圣诞节前夜，基督徒们会到教堂参加一个特殊的圣诞赞歌礼拜。礼拜包括唱圣诞赞歌和观看孩子们的耶稣诞生表演。午夜时，人们做教堂礼拜迎接耶稣基督的诞生。圣诞夜是孩子们最兴奋的夜晚，因为圣诞老人会到来并在他们的圣诞袜里塞入礼物。

圣诞节也是家人团聚的日子。很多基督徒会穿着新衣服到教堂唱颂歌……稣基督的诞生。在圣诞节当天去教堂的人比其他任何时间都多。圣诞大餐是圣诞节期间最重要的一顿饭。一般在中午吃。传统的圣诞大餐包括烤火鸡或烤鹅、烤土豆、夹有香肠的薄烤饼等。圣诞布丁和圣诞蛋糕是圣诞大

pudding and Christmas cake are inevitable desserts for Christmas Dinner.

At three o'clock in the afternoon, the Queen gives her Christmas message to the nation. The Queen's Christmas speech is one major tradition on Christmas. The message is also broadcasted throughout the British Commonwealth. Another British Christmas tradition is the Christmas Pantomime, a comical musical play in which the main male character is played by a young women. The day after the Christmas day is known as Boxing Day. Different people have different ways of spending this day. Some people go shopping, some go visiting or relaxing.

餐不可缺少的甜点。

在下午3点钟，女王会在电视和广播中对她的臣民们作圣诞演讲。收听女王演讲是英国圣诞节三大传统之一。她的演讲通过广播传送到其他英联邦国家。圣诞节的另一个传统是看圣诞哑剧，它里面的男主角由一个年轻的女演员扮演。圣诞节之后的那一天叫"节礼日"，人们用不同的方式度过这一天，有人去购物，有人拜访别人或去放松一下。

词汇 VOCABULARY

1. integral ['intigrəl]
   a 完整的，整体的；[数学]积分的
   n [数学]积分；部分；完整

2. household ['haushəuld]
   a 家庭的；日常的；王室的
   n 家庭；一家人

3. nativity [nə'tiviti]
   n 出生；出生地；（Nativity）耶稣的诞生

4. stuff [stʌf]
   n 材料；东西 *vt* 填塞 *vi* 吃得过多

5. carol ['kærəl]
   vt 欢乐地歌唱；唱耶诞颂歌 *vi* 欢唱；歌颂
   n 颂歌，赞美诗；欢乐之歌

6. pantomime ['pæntəmaim]
   n 哑剧；手势；舞剧 *vi* 演哑剧；打手势
   vt 打手势；演哑剧

背景链接 TIPS

Santa Clause

法国与圣诞老人类似的形象是Père Noel，他又高又胖，永远挂着微笑，最主要的是他穿的那件棉袄永远是——可口可乐红。

英国的圣诞老人和法国一样也叫Father Christmas（圣诞之父），他的形象比其他圣诞老人更庄严，更清瘦一些。

德国的圣诞老人也带着一个叫做Knecht Ruprecht、Krampus或Pelzebock或是称作"黑彼得"（荷文：Zwarte Piet）的助手，肩上背着个装着礼物的大袋子，手上拿着一根棍子。好孩子可收到他的礼物，顽皮的孩子却要被教训几棍子。

在美国人的传统中，圣诞老人总是快活地在圣诞前夜乘着驯鹿拉的雪橇到来，他从烟囱爬进屋内，留下给孩子们的礼物，并吃掉孩子们为他留下的食物。

010 Easter

Easter is the oldest and the most important holiday for British people. It is the day when people celebrate the resurrection of Jesus Christ three days after his death. In Britain, Easter arrives at different dates every year because the date is observed according to the lunar calendar. It is the first Sunday after the first full moon following the first day of spring in the Northern Hemisphere which means it may arrive at any day between 22 March and 25 April.

The story of Easter is the story of Jesus's death and resurrection. The story is consists of three important days: Maundy Thursday, Good Friday and Easter day. Maundy Thursday is the Thursday before Easter. This day is remembered as the day of Last Supper, which is the last supper Jesus had with his disciples before he died. Good Friday refers the Friday before Easter when Jesus was crucified. Christians go to church to do special Good Friday services to mourn the suffering of Jesus and his death on the cross. On Easter Day, Jesus came back to life and people spend this day on celebrating this.

On Easter, people exchange. Easter egg is a very old tradition for Easter and it is a symbol of spring and hope. The eggs are hard-boiled and painted into bright colors and patterns to represent new life. Besides giving eggs as presents, Easter eggs can also be played in different ways. Egg rolling is a very popular game in England in which hard-boiled eggs are rolled down a hill. The winner is the person whose egg rolls the longest before it cracks. Egg hunt is particularly favored by children. On Easter Day, small chocolate eggs are hidden for children to find. However, more and more people

【小译】

复活节是英国最古老、最重要的节日之一。它是人们庆祝耶稣死后第三天复活的节日。复活节没有固定的日期因为它是根据农历计算的。在北半球,复活节指的是春分月圆后的第一个星期日,可能是3月22日至4月25日中的任何一天。

复活节的故事就是耶稣死亡和复活的故事。这个故事涉及三个重要节日:濯足节、耶稣受难日和圣诞节。濯足节是复活节的前一个星期四。就是在这一天,耶稣和他的门徒们吃了最后的晚餐。耶稣受难日指的是复活节前的那个星期五。这一天人们到教堂做礼拜,哀悼耶稣所受的苦难和他在十字架上的死亡。耶稣在复活节复活,人们为此而庆祝。

在复活节,人们互相赠送复活节彩蛋。复活节彩蛋代表春天和希望,是复活节一个重要的传统。人们把鸡蛋煮熟并在上面涂上鲜艳的颜色和图案,以此来代表新生命。复活节彩蛋除了馈赠以外还可以

replace chocolate eggs for Easter Bunny for this game. Bunny has always been a symbol of fertility and new life.

Easter day, like Christmas, is also connected with special food. Boiled eggs are eaten in the morning to represent people's celebration of new life. Roasted lamb is the traditional meat for the main meal on Easter Day because lamb symbolizes the sacrifice of Jesus. Hot cross bun, an emblem of flesh of Jesus, is also eaten on that day.

用来使大家愉悦。滚彩蛋是英国很受欢迎的一个游戏。人们把彩蛋滚下山坡，谁的彩蛋在碎之前滚的最远谁就赢了。寻彩蛋是孩子们最青睐的游戏。家长在圣诞节时把巧克力彩蛋藏起来让孩子们寻找。现在，越来越多的人用圣诞节兔子来代替巧克力彩蛋，因为兔子一直都是多产和新生的象征。

和圣诞节一样，复活节也有特殊的食物。在复活节早晨，人们吃彩蛋来庆祝新生命。烤羊肉是复活节的一种传统食物因为羔羊象征着耶稣做出的牺牲。十字小面包代表着耶稣的肉体，也是一种传统复活节食物。

词汇 VOCABULARY

1. resurrection [ˌrezəˈrekʃən] *n.* 复活；恢复；复兴	2. lunar [ˈljuːnə] *a.* 月亮的，月球的；阴历的；银的
3. hemisphere [ˈhemisfiə] *n.* 半球	4. Maundy [ˈmɔːndi] *n.* 天主教濯足仪式时分发的救济金
5. pattern [ˈpætən] *n.* 模式；图案；样品 *vt.* 模仿；以图案装饰 *vi.* 形成图案	6. fertility [fəˈtiliti] *n.* 多产，肥沃，[农经] 生产力；丰饶
7. sacrifice [ˈsækrifais] *n.* 牺牲；祭品；供奉 *vt.* 牺牲；献祭；亏本出售 *vi.* 献祭；奉献	8. emblem [ˈembləm] *n.* 象征；徽章；符号 *vt.* 象征；用符号表示；用纹章装饰

背景链接 TIPS

耶稣言论：

1. 神爱世人，甚至将他的独生子赐给他们，叫一切信他的，不致灭亡，反得永生。（约翰福音3章16节）

2. 你们祈求，就给你们；寻找，就寻见；叩门，就给你们开门。因为凡祈求的，就得着；寻找的，就寻见；叩门的，就给他开门。（马太福音7章7—8节）

3. 要爱你们的仇敌，为那逼迫你们的祷告。这样，就可以作你们天父的儿子。因为他叫日头照好人，也照歹人；降雨给义人，也给不义的人。（马太福音5章44—45节）

4. 我是世界的光。跟从我的，就不在黑暗里行走，必要得着生命的光。（约翰福音8章12节）

011 St. Patrick's Day

St. Patrick's Day, as its name indicates, is a day (17 March) when the Irish people celebrate the birth of St Patrick, the patron saint of Ireland who is thought to have introduced Christianity to Ireland.

The story of St. Patrick was legendary. He was born in Wales in AD 385 and remained a pagan until he was 16 years old. At that age, his village was raided by a group of Irish robbers and he was taken to Ireland as a slave. While working as a shepherd, he brought himself close to God. Six years later, he escaped and went to study from a bishop for over twelve years. It was during this period that St. Patrick decided that he would convert the pagans to Christianity. He went back to Ireland as a missionary. St. Patrick did a lot to transform the country. He travelled all across Ireland and built monasteries and set up schools and churches. His mission in Ireland lasted for thirty years. When he died in 17 March in AD 461, people set this day as St. Patrick's Day to commemorate him.

Legend has it that St. Patrick drove all the snakes out of Ireland by doing a sermon. That's why you cannot find any venomous snakes in Ireland.

The story of shamrock is very well known throughout Ireland. In AD 432, St. Patrick went to Ireland to convert pagans. When he landed on Wicklow, the

【小译】

3月17日是爱尔兰人庆祝爱尔兰守护神圣帕特里克诞辰的日子，感谢这位主保圣人把基督教传播到爱尔兰。

圣帕特里克的一生很传奇。公元385年，圣帕特里克出生于威尔士。在16岁之前他一直都是一名异教徒。16岁那年，一群爱尔兰强盗洗劫了他的村庄并把他卖到爱尔兰做奴隶。他在放牧的日子里不断向上帝靠拢。6年后，他逃脱并跟着一位男爵学习了12年。在此期间，圣帕特里克下定了传播基督教的决心。当他再次来到爱尔兰的时候，他已经成为了一名传教士。圣帕特里克在爱尔兰做了很多传教事业。他走遍了爱尔兰，修建了很多修道院、学校和教堂。他在爱尔兰的传教生涯长达30年。圣帕特里克于公元461年3月17日去世后，人们为了纪念他，把每年的这一天命名为圣帕特里克日。

相传圣帕特里克曾通过布道驱走了爱尔兰所有的毒蛇，因此，如今的爱尔兰境内没有毒蛇。

圣帕特里克与三叶草的故事在爱尔兰也被广为流传。公元432年，圣帕特里克到爱尔兰传教。从威克洛上岸后，当地愤怒的异教徒企图用石头将他砸死。圣帕特里克不惧危险，摘下一棵三叶苜蓿阐述了基督教中的天主是"三位一体"的概念。他极具说服力的解释感

angry pagans attempted to kill him by throwing peddles at him. St. Patrick wasn't give up; instead, he picked a three-leaved shamrock and explained calmly how the Trinity of the Father, Son and Holy Spirit could exist as separate parts of the same being. His elaboration was so convincing that people accepted conversion and became Christians. Thereafter, shamrock has been regarded as the symbol of Ireland.

In Ireland, 17 March is a public holiday. It's also the day when most Irish people attend church. Besides, Irish people go on parades on this day, wearing green clothes and drinking Guinness and Baileys.

动了爱尔兰人，接受了基督教洗礼。从此之后，三叶草成为了爱尔兰的标志。

3月17日是爱尔兰的公共假日。这一天也是爱尔兰人去教堂人最多的一天。这一天，爱尔兰人身着绿色服装上街游行，还会喝黑啤酒和百利酒。

词汇 VOCABULARY

1. patron ['peitrən, 'pæ-]
   n 赞助人；保护人；主顾

2. pagan ['peigən]
   a 异教的 n 异教徒，无宗教信仰者

3. missionary ['miʃənəri]
   n 传教的；传教士的 n 传教士

4. monastery ['mɔnəstri]
   n 修道院；僧侣

5. commemorate [kə'meməreit]
   vt. 庆祝，纪念；成为…的纪念

6. shamrock ['ʃæmrɔk]
   n 三叶草（爱尔兰国花）；白花酢浆草

7. trinity ['triniti]
   n 三位一体；三个一组的东西；三倍

8. Guinness ['ginis]
   n 吉尼斯黑啤酒（英国产强性黑啤酒的一种）

9. bailey ['beili]
   n 城壁，外栅；城堡外庭

背景链接 TIPS

1. St. Patrick's Day in America

圣帕特里克日的节庆传统由爱尔兰移民带入美国，于每年的3月17日举行，以纪念传教士圣帕克成功地在爱尔兰传扬基督教。逐渐地该节日演变成一个全美国的绿色节日（Green Day）。所谓绿色节日是指当天所有到街上庆祝的人士及一切节日装饰品都是绿色的，如绿色的衣物、绿色的帽子、绿色的鲜花，你还会发现独特的绿色啤酒，甚至绿色的喷泉。

2. Shamrock

三叶草是爱尔兰的国花，它的生命力很顽强，无论到哪里都可以生根开花。民间总是有这样的传说、如果你找到三叶草、就可以找到幸福。

012 Burns Night

Robert Burns (1759~1796) is a favorite poet for many people. You always have access to Burns even if you don't know much about poetry. For example, you must have heard of the song "Auld Lang Syne" which was written by this great Scottish poet.

Every year, the Scottish people all over the world spend the day 25 January on celebrating Robert Burns, the most beloved national poet by holding a Burns Supper on Burns Night, which is the birthday of Robert Burns (25 January). What makes Burns so dearly loved and adored is that Burns wrote his poems in the Scots dialects and he resorted to Scottish folk songs and stories for the contents of his poems. Burns is said to have created an enduring Scottish identity at a time when the Scots might have been entirely absorbed into a general British culture. It is through Burns and his poems that Scotland showed its peculiarity to the rest of the world. Besides, in his works, Burns also spoke highly of common people which earned himself the title of "common man's poet". The most famous poems of Burns include "My Love is Like a Red, Red Rose", "My heart's on the Highland" and so on.

Burns Supper has been part of the Scottish culture for about 200 years and it is usually celebrated with haggis, whisky and a big party. The common procedure for a Burns Supper goes like this: The chairperson delivers a few welcoming words and the company stand up to receive the haggis during which the poem "Address to a Haggis" is recited emotionally.

【小译】

罗伯特·彭斯（1759～1796）是许多人最爱的诗人。即使你对诗歌了解不多，你也会有认识彭斯的其他途径，比如说，你肯定听过《友谊地久天长》这首歌吧！这首歌就出自这位苏格兰伟大诗人罗伯特·彭斯之手。

每年的1月25日，遍布世界的苏格兰人都会吃彭斯晚餐，以此来纪念苏格兰最受爱戴的伟大诗人罗伯特·彭斯的诞辰。彭斯如此深受爱戴，是因为他的诗歌取材于苏格兰民谣和古老传说，用苏格兰方言创作。彭斯的伟大之处在于在苏格兰的特性几乎被大文化同化时，他用文字描绘出一个本色十足的苏格兰。通过彭斯的作品，全世界的人都领略到了苏格兰的独特风情。同时，罗伯特·彭斯在作品中抒发了他对广大劳动人民的赞美，因此被冠以"平民诗人"的头衔。彭斯最著名的诗歌包括"一朵红红的玫瑰""我的心儿在高原"等等。

彭斯晚宴的传统在苏格兰已经有了200多年的历史并成为苏格兰文化重要的组成部分。

Meanwhile, the haggis is cut open with a knife. Then the company can enjoy their dinner. Later on, an invited guest will give s short speech on the greatness of Burns and the heritage he left for today. Toast to the Lasses follows the speech to express gratitude to the women preparing the food and lasses' response is followed. The climax of Burns Night comes when people begin to sing songs or recite poems of Burns and eventually the night ends with people standing up to hold hands and sing Auld Lang Syne.

人们通过吃肉馅羊肚、喝威士忌和举办晚会来庆祝这一节日。彭斯晚餐的一般程序如下：首先，晚会主席做简短的欢迎词，之后邀请嘉宾朗诵彭斯的诗歌"Address to a Haggis"，朗诵同时，Haggis被切开并被大家分享。紧接着，一位嘉宾受到邀请发表一个关于彭斯或他的诗歌与当今的联系的演讲。在Toast to the Lassies（为女士举杯）环节，男士代表感谢女士们准备丰盛的食物，女士代表给出回应。晚会在诗歌朗诵和歌曲声中达到高潮并在大家手挽手一起歌唱《友谊地久天长》中结束。

词汇 VOCABULARY

1. beloved [bi'lʌvd, bi'lʌvid]
   adj. 心爱的；挚爱的 *n.* 心爱的人；亲爱的教友

2. dialect ['daiəlekt]
   n. 方言，土话；个人用语特征 *adj.* 方言的

3. identity [ai'dentiti]
   n. 身份；同一性，一致；恒等式；特性

4. peculiarity [pi,kju:li'æriti]
   n. 特性；特质；怪癖；奇特

5. haggis ['hægis]
   n. （苏格兰）肉馅羊肚；羊肉杂碎布丁

6. chairperson ['tʃeəpɜ:s(e)n]
   n. 主席；议长

7. heritage ['heritidʒ]
   n. 遗产；传统；继承物；继承权

背景链接 TIPS

A Red, Red Rose	一朵红红的玫瑰
Oh my love is like a red red rose	啊，我的爱人像一朵红红的玫瑰，
That's newly sprung in june:	六月里迎风初开
Oh my love is like the melodie	啊，我的爱人像一曲甜蜜的歌
That's sweetly play'd in tune.	唱得合拍又柔和
As fair art thou, my bonnie lass,	我的好姑娘，多么美丽的人儿！
So deep in love am I	我呀，多么深的爱情！
And I will love thee still, my dear	亲爱的，我永远爱你！
Till a' the seas gang dry	纵使大海干枯水流尽。
Till a' the seas gang dry, my dear	纵使大海干枯水流尽，亲爱的
And the rocks melt wi' the sun	太阳将岩石烧成灰，
I will love thee still, my dear	亲爱的，我永远爱你，
While the sands of life shall run	只要我生命犹存。
And fare thee weel, my only love!	珍重吧，我唯一的爱人。
And fare thee weel a while!	珍重吧，让我们暂时别离。
And I will come again, my love	但我注定要回来。
Though it were ten thousand mile.	哪怕千里万里！

013 The Eisteddfod

While the English celebrate their Bonfire Night and Northern Irish, their St. Patrick's Day; the Scottish, their Burns Night, the Welsh people are proud of their musical and poetic traditions and cherish their native language—the Welsh. The National Eisteddfod of Wales is held annually in the first week of August to preserve the Welsh heritage.

The word "eisteddfod" is a Welsh word means a congress where people recite verses and sing songs. All the competitions in the Eisteddfod are in Welsh language. The uniqueness of this competition also lies in that it visits a different area of Wales each year.

The festival went through ups and downs in the history of Wales. The first Eisteddfod was held in 1176 when Lord Rhys called up musicians all over Wales to his castle to hold a competition. The best poet as well as musician was awarded a chair at the Lord's Table. However, the 18th century saw the decline of popularity for Eisteddfod. The festival was finally revived in the 19th. Since the establishment of the National Eisteddfod Association, the Eisteddfod has been held annually except for 1914 and 1940.

Each year, Welsh people all over the world return to Wales to participate in the Eisteddfod. At the Eisteddfod, tents and pavilions are set up in a big open space. Different competitions are held in different pavilions in which people compete for the best choirs, translators,

essayists and poets. The most exciting scene in Eisteddfod is the "Crowning of the Bard" in which the best poet in the competitions

【小译】

英格兰人有篝火之夜可庆祝，北爱尔兰人有圣帕特里克日，苏格兰人也有他们的彭斯之夜，那么威尔士人庆祝什么呢？他们以他们的音乐诗歌传统以及威尔士语——他们的母语为豪。每年八月第一周举办的威尔士诗歌音乐比赛会就是为了保护威尔士丰厚的文化遗产而举办的。

Eisteddfod是一个威尔士语，意思是一个诵诗唱歌的集会。威尔士诗歌音乐比赛会中的所有比赛都是用威尔士语进行的。该比赛会的另一个特点在于它每年的举办地点都不同。

威尔士诗歌音乐比赛会的历史并非一帆风顺。第一届比赛会是Lord Rhys在1176年举办的。当时，他召集了全威尔士的音乐家到他的城堡进行比赛，最杰出的诗人及音乐家享受与Lord Rhys同桌的殊荣。到了18世纪，比赛会不再流行。这种情况一直持续到19世纪。从国家威尔士诗歌音乐比赛协会（National Eisteddfod Association）成立以来，除1914和1940以外，比赛会每年都会举办。

每年，全球各地的威尔士人都会回到家乡参加比赛。在比赛会上，帐蓬和临时搭建的建筑竖立在一个很大的空地上。各种比赛在不同的帐蓬里举行并最终角逐最好的合唱团、翻译家、散文家和诗人。比赛会最激动人心的时刻要属对最佳诗人的加冕仪式了，这个仪式从第一届比赛会一直延续至今。

is awarded, a tradition passed down from the first Eisteddfod.

One of the saddest things in the history of the Eisteddfod is that the early National Eisteddfod was controlled by the English language. The first National Eisteddfod was literally an English Eisteddfod. The reason for this was that for a long time, the Welsh were living in the shadow of the English dominance. This situation lasted until Hugh Owen came into the story. Hugh Owen devoted himself to establish a national system of education in Wales. In 1862, he added a completely new section, "Social Science Section" to the Eisteddfod and introduced all aspects of life in Wales. The struggle for Walsh to fight for its own culture lasted for nearly a century. Until 1950, Welsh language started to be used in Eisteddfod.

不幸的是，早期的威尔士诗歌音乐比赛会都被英语控制。威尔士诗歌音乐比赛会实际上是英语诗歌音乐比赛会。造成这种局面的原因是威尔士人长期受到英格兰的控制。这种情况一直延续到Hugh Owen的出现。Hugh Owen主张建立国家教育体系并为这个目标而不断奋斗。1862年，他在威尔士诗歌音乐比赛会中增加了一个全新的"社会科学"环节，并在该环节中介绍威尔士的方方面面。威尔士人维护本土文化的斗争持续了一个世纪。直到1950年，威尔士诗歌音乐比赛会才开始使用威尔士语进行。

词汇 VOCABULARY

1. annual ['ænjuəl] adj. 年度的；每年的	2. preserve [pri'zə:v] v. 保存，保护 n. 禁猎地；保护区
3. uniqueness [ju:'ni:knis] n. 独特性；独一无二；单值性	4. popularity [,pɔpju'læriti] n. 普及，流行；名气；受大众欢迎
5. pavilion [pə'viljən] n. 大帐篷；展示馆 v. 搭帐篷；置…于亭中	6. choir ['kwaiə] n. 合唱队；唱诗班；舞蹈队 vt./vi. 合唱
7. crowning ['krauniŋ] adj. 最高的；无比的 n. 加冕 v. 加冕（crown的现在分词）	

背景链接 TIPS

Welsh v.s English

1536年，威尔士被英格兰非正式合并，英语成了官方语言（威尔士已被英格兰控制了几百年），说威尔士语被认为是一件坏事。到了近代19世纪，在威尔士的学校里说威尔士语的学生会受到处罚。威尔士语面临消失的危险，但是威尔士人竭力保护自己的语言，一种方式就是每年的8月在威尔士举行赛诗会，以传承威尔士文化和威尔士语，这也提醒了遍及联合王国的威尔士人不要忘记威尔士的文化遗产。现在有19%的威尔士人讲威尔士语，今后几年，这个数字还会慢慢增长。因为现在的孩子们都在双语学校读书，电视台也用威尔士语，官方活动也采用威尔士语或英语。

014 Halloween

On 31 October, British people celebrate Halloween, an ancient festival which has its origin in the Celtic festival of Samhain. At that time, the Celts celebrated New Year on November 1st, marking the end of summer and the beginning of winter.

British people engage themselves in a lot of Halloween traditions on this day. Trick or Treat is best loved by all the children because they would dress up in costumes and go from door to door to knock the door, or ring the doorbell while yelling 'Trick or treat!' The purpose is for the owner to give them a treat, either sweets or money; otherwise, the children would play a trick on them.

Pumpkin lantern is another necessity for Halloween. First, people scoop out the seeds and any loose flesh in the pumpkin and carve a design onto it, such design include a celebrity face, animals and scenes. Then, they put a light into the hollowed pumpkin to make it into a lantern. The lantern is called Jack o' Lanterns. There's a story behind this name. According to Irish legend, Jack was a mean farmer who tricked the Devil into a tree. He asked the Devil to promise that he would not go to Hell after he died, or he wouldn't let him down. Devil promised. However, when Jack died, he wasn't allowed into Heaven because he did too many bad things on earth. What's worse, Devil kept

【小译】

在每年的10月31日，英国人庆祝西方一个重要的传统节日万圣节。万圣节来源于凯尔特人的夏末节，即夏天正式结束、冬季即将开始的一天。

英国人通过许多万圣节传统庆祝这个节日。孩子们最喜欢的是"不给吃的就捣乱"这一传统，因为他们可以穿上化妆服挨家挨户敲门或按门铃并高声喊"不给吃的就捣乱！"目的是向主人讨些糖果或钱。如果主人不给他们就会捣乱。

南瓜灯是万圣节必不可少的一样物品。要制作一个南瓜灯首先要挖出南瓜籽和瓤并在上面雕刻图案，可以是名人脸，动物或者风景。然后在空心的南瓜里放入一个灯笼。这样，一个南瓜灯就制成了。南瓜灯也叫杰克灯。杰克灯这个名字来自于一个传说。相传在爱尔兰有一个叫杰克的苛刻的农民。他把死神困在树上让死神向他保证不会在他死后让他下地狱，否则就不放他下来。死神答应了。在杰克死后，由于作恶太多而进不了天堂，而死神也信守诺言不许杰克进地狱。于是杰克把蜡烛放在一个挖空的芜菁里制成一个灯笼并无止境地游走于天堂和地狱间寻找一个落脚的地方。这就是杰克的南瓜灯，或者杰克灯。

穿化妆服也是万圣节的一个传统。化妆服种类繁多，有的漂亮

his promise and wouldn't let him into Hell. So, Jack carved out a turnip into a lantern and put a candle in it and began searching for a resting place endlessly. The lantern was known as Jack of the Lantern, or Jack o' Lantern.

Wearing costumes is also a tradition people keep on Halloween. There are a variety of Halloween costumes, some of them are lovely and cute, and some of them are scary and evil. The list of the Top 10 costumes in 2009 for adults include: witch, pirate, vampire, cat, fairy, nurse, Batman, politician, ghost and angel. For children, the Top 10 are: witch, Spiderman, pirate, pumpkin, vampire, Disney princess, Star Wars character, athlete, fairy and Batman.

可爱，有的恐怖邪恶。2009年最受欢迎的十大成人化妆服包括：女巫、海盗、吸血鬼、猫、仙女、护士、蝙蝠侠、政治家、魔鬼和天使。最受欢迎的十大儿童化妆服是：女巫、蜘蛛侠、海盗、南瓜、吸血鬼、迪士尼公主、星球大战人物、运动员、仙子和蜘蛛侠。

词汇 VOCABULARY

1. costume ['kɔstjuːm, -'tjuːm]
   n 服装，装束；戏装 vt. 给…穿上服装

2. scoop [skuːp]
   vt 掘；舀取；搜集 n 勺；铲子；独家新闻

3. hollow ['hɔləu]
   adj 空的；凹的；虚伪的 n 洞；山谷；窟窿 vt / vi 使成为空洞 adv 无用地；彻底地

4. turnip ['təːnip]
   n 芜菁甘蓝，大头菜；萝卜

5. endless ['endlis]
   adj 无止境的, 无穷的

6. vampire ['væmpaiə]
   n 吸血鬼；吸血蝙蝠

背景链接 TIPS

1. Trick or treat

万圣节的一个有趣内容是"不给吃的就捣蛋"，这习俗却并非源自爱尔兰，而是始于公元九世纪的欧洲基督教会。那时的11月2日，被基督徒们称为"ALL SOULS DAY"（万灵之日）。 在这一天，信徒们跋涉于僻壤乡间，挨村挨户乞讨用面粉及葡萄干制成的"灵魂之饼"。据说捐赠糕饼的人家都相信教会僧人的祈祷，期待由此得到上帝的佑护，让死去的亲人早日进入天堂。这种挨家乞讨的传统传至当今竟演变成了孩子们提着南瓜灯笼挨家讨糖吃的游戏。见面时，打扮成鬼精灵模样的孩子们千篇一律地都要发出"不给吃的就捣乱"的威胁，而主人自然不敢怠慢，连声说"请吃！请吃！"同时把糖果放进孩子们随身携带的大口袋里。

2. Why do people dress up like ghosts on Halloween?

凯尔特人相信， 故人的亡魂会在10月31日这天回到故居地在活人身上找寻生灵，借此再生，而且这是人在死后能获得再生的唯一希望。因此，活着的人惧怕死魂来夺生。于是，人们就在这一天熄掉炉火、烛光，让死魂无法找寻活人，又把自己打扮成妖魔鬼怪把死人之魂灵吓走。之后，他们又会把火种烛光重新燃起，开始新的一年的生活。

Unit 4 英国的教育

With its long-standing history, full range of subjects and complete structure, British education has always enjoyed a great international reputation. It has been ranked among the world's best and has attracted students from all over the world on the ground of its strict but flexible teaching method, high quality of the education itself as well as of its graduates. The purpose of British education is not only to provide children with literacy and the other basic skills they will need to become active members of society, it is also to socialize children. Therefore, besides practical skills, schools also teach children the rules and values they need to become good citizens, to participate in the community, and to contribute to the economic prosperity of an advanced industrial economy.

Education background is also an important marker of social class in the UK. To have attended quality universities like Oxford and Cambridge which have been nicknamed as "Oxbridge" – is still the single best way to guarantee a successful career. As early as 1994, three-quarters of the Government executive were graduates of Oxbridge. Most senior civil servants are also Oxbridge graduates. Not only do they dominate government, but they are also very influential in banking, the media, the arts and education. In a word, in the UK, where you are educated is still very important to your future.

英国的教育历史悠久，科目设置全面，结构完整，一直在世界范围内享有盛誉。英国教育严谨而不失灵活教学方法，高质量的教学水平以及培育出的高水平的人才更是让其引领世界一流教育，并且吸引着来自世界各地的学生。英国教育的目的不仅仅是为了教会孩子包括读写在内的一些基本技巧，而且是为了教会他们更好地适应社会生活。因此，除了实用技能，孩子们在学校还能学到价值观与一些基本的社会规则，从而使孩子们能够积极参与社会活动，遵纪守法，为这个发达的工业化国家的经济繁荣奉献自己一份力量。

教育背景在英国是个人社会等级的重要象征。能否到一所诸如"牛桥"（牛津剑桥常被合称为"牛桥"）的优质大学上学是决定你能否有一份成功事业的重要因素。早在1994年，3/4的中央政府行政人员来自牛津与剑桥。英国的大多数高级公务员都是牛津与剑桥毕业生。除了政治领域，这些牛津与剑桥毕业生在银行、媒体与教育这些领域也都影响力颇大。总之，在英国，你的母校依然与你的未来息息相关。

GEOGRAPHY

|015 British Education System

Roughly speaking, education in the UK can be divided into three stages, namely, Compulsory Education, Further Education and Higher Education. The compulsory stage, which usually lasts eleven years, generally covers the periods of primary and secondary education. Children start primary school normally at the age of five. The main goals of primary education are to achieve basic literacy and numeracy and to cultivate their imagination and curiosity of students in order to facilitate their studies in secondary education.

Pupils generally move to a secondary school at the age of eleven or twelve years. In Britain, as many as 90% are studying in the public-funded state schools called "comprehensive School" which offers a wide range of courses for students and are opened to all pupils of the right age, regardless of their aptitude and interest.

After five years of secondary education, British students take their GCSE exams (General Certificate of Secondary Education). GCSEs are the main means of assessing pupils' progress in their final 2 years of compulsory education, based on these results, pupils then decide whether they will quit school to find a job or go for Further Education which provides students with two systems – the "Vocational Route" which lays a solid foundation for those who will get a job and the "Academic Route" for those who will go on studying in colleges and universities. It should be mentioned that Further Education has gradually been overlapping with some Technical Colleges and even secondary schools; therefore it is increasingly inappropriate to take it as a clear-cut stage in the process of education but rather an effective supplement for school education.

Pupils who hope to attend university usually carry on their academic study for two more years and then take A-levels exams (General Certificate of Education-Advanced), which are entry qualifications for universities. For pupils choose vocational route, there is also a

【小译】

英国的教育体制大体上可以分为三个阶段：义务教育、延续教育与高等教育。义务教育历时11年，一般来说分为小学教育与中学教育。英国的孩子一般五岁开始上小学。小学教育主要是为了训练孩子基本的读写与计算能力，培养他们的想象力与好奇心，从而在未来辅助中学阶段的学习。

英国学生一般在11岁到12岁之间上中学。其中90%的学生去公立的综合学校上学，这些学校开设多种不同的课程，所有适龄儿童，不论学习能力如何，兴趣何在，均可去这种综合学校上学。

五年的中学教育结束之后，英国的学生会参加普通中学证书考试。普通中学证书是衡量学生在义务教育最后两年学生成绩的主要途径。学生可以根据考试结果来决定自己应该停止学习开始找工作、还是接受延续教育。延续教育为学生提供两大体系——职业路线与学业路线。其中职业路线为学生今后的工作打下坚实的技能基础，学业路线为学生进一步接受大学教育做准备。不得不提的是今日的继续教育已渐渐与技术学院甚至中学融为一体。因此将其视为英国教育中独立的一个阶段并不太妥当，现今继续教育更像是学校教育的有力补充。

那些想上大学的学生一般需要继续进修两年，然后参加高级水平测试，考试合格者方可进入大学继续深造。对于那些选择职业路线的学生来说，也有与学业路线中的高

vocational equivalent of A-levels – GNVQ (General National Vocational Qualifications) which provide a broadly based preparation for future work.

Higher Education in the UK is highly acclaimed throughout the world. There are about 100 colleges and universities in Britain with various sizes and specialties, providing three-year to six-year teaching programs to the students. After this undergraduate study, they can obtain their bachelor's degree as well as a "degree level" depending on their school performances. The "degree level" is a critical index for reference if you intend to continue your studies as a postgraduate which usually takes not more than one year. After obtaining Master Degree, students will be engaged in one to two year's research, and if satisfactory in progress, can apply for PhD program which may normally requires more than three years for completion.

级水平测试结业证书相平行的资格证书——国家专业资格证书，这一证书为学生未来的工作提供多方面的准备。

英国的高等教育一直在世界范围内广受好评。英国有大约100所不同规模、不同专长的高等学府，为学生提供三年到六年的高等教学。学生毕业之后可以拿到本科学士学位，学位等级评分。这个学位等级评分由学生平时在学校的表现所决定，是学生能否继续进行研究生学习的重要指标。英国的硕士研究生学习一般不超过一年，在获得硕士学位之后，学生可以进行一到两年的科研，如果结果较满意的话就可以申请读博。英国的博士学位一般最少需要三年时间来完成。

词汇 VOCABULARY

1. compulsory [kəm'pʌlsəri] *adj.* 义务的；必修的；被强制的	2. literacy ['litərəsi] *n.* 读写能力；识字；精通文学
3. numeracy ['njumərəsi] *n.* 计算能力，识数	4. cultivate ['kʌltiveit] *vt.* 培养；陶冶；耕作
5. facilitate [fə'siliteit] *vt.* 促进；帮助；使容易	6. vocational [vəu'keiʃənəl] *adj.* 职业的，行业的
7. undergraduate [ʌndə'grædjuit] *n.* 大学生；大学肄业生 *adj.* 大学生的	8. postgraduate['pəust'grædjuit, 'pəust'grædʒuit] *n.* 研究生，研究所学生 *adj.* 大学毕业后的

背景链接 TIPS

A-levels exams (General Certificate of Education-Advanced)

高级水平测试结业证书。16岁的学生通过中学毕业考试后，想继续深造进高等学府，必须通过高级水平测试。从16岁至18岁的两年时间里，学生根据自己想读的大学专业选定3到4门有关课程学习。通过A级水平考试者都可入大学深造。

GNVQ (General National Vocational Qualifications)

国家专业资格证书。这一证书是专为职业技术学校毕业的学生设置的，共分5个级别，这就便于人们按阶梯逐级攀登，根据自己的条件通过实际工作与专业培训由低级向高级发展。获四级国家专业资格证书相当于学士学位；获五级国家专业资格证书相当于研究生水平。

016 Eton College

At the stages of primary and secondary education, there are also some private schools (independent schools) in the UK besides the schools run at public expenses. Although the achievements of the independent schools are outstandingly high compared with the state schools, only a small number of students can afford the expensive tuitions. What is interesting is that some of the most prestigious independent schools are confusingly known as "public schools" in the UK although the "public" only means that it is open to all the pupils regardless of religion, race and region. Most public schools are highly selective on students' former academic performance, financial capacity of their family and probably social connection with the school. In this part we are going to introduce to you the widely recognized most famous public school in the UK – Eton college.

Situated in Eton, near Windsor in England, north of Windsor Castle, Eton College is an independent boarding school for boys aged between 13 and 18 with an annual charge of 26, 490 pound. As one of the oldest schools in the UK, it was founded by Henry IV in 1440 and its initial purpose was to provide free education for pupils from poor families who could not afford private tutors. It gradually developed into an elite school at the 17th century.

The school has cultivated numerous elites in various fields due to the high academic standard and the strict management. It has given birth to 19 British prime ministers with David Cameron as the 19th one and countless figures from the world's royalty including Prince William and Harry. Other notable alumni include writers Henry Fielding, Percy Shelley, George Orwell and economist John Keynes. Among approximately 250 Eton graduates each year, over 70

【小译】

在英国的小学与中学阶段，除了不收学费的公立学校之外，还有私立学校（独立学校）。虽然私立学校的教学成就要比公立学校普遍高很多，但只有少数的学生能支付得起昂贵的学费。有趣的是，英国的很多最有名的私立学校反而被称作"公"学，当然，这个"公"是指学校面向社会上不同信仰，不同种族，来自不同地区的学生"公"开招生。许多公学对学生的学习成绩和家庭的经济能力要求颇高，学生家庭如果与学校有社会联系更好。在这一部分我们将会为您介绍英国公认的最著名的公学——伊顿公学。

伊顿公学位于英格兰温莎的伊顿小镇，温莎城堡以北，是一所仅招收13到18岁男学生的寄宿学校，一年学费26490英磅。伊顿公学由亨利六世于1440年创立，是英国最古老的学校之一，学校创立初衷是为请不起私人家教的贫困学生提供免费教育，到17世纪学校逐渐成为一所名校。

由于高标准的教学与严格的管理，伊顿公学培养了许多不同行业的精英，包括19位英国首相，其中还有现任首相戴维·卡梅伦，还有不计其数的皇室家庭成员也都在这里上过学，像威廉王子与哈里王子。著名作家亨利·菲尔丁、珀西·雪莱、乔治·奥威尔，经济学家约翰·凯恩斯都是从这里毕业的。伊顿

of them go to Oxford and Cambridge and 70% of them are admitted to top universities around the world.

Eton is not only famous for its elite students, but also for the ancient traditions that it has kept for over 600 years. The school uniform, which is first worn as a mourning dress for the death of George III, is made up of a black tailcoat and waistcoat, white shirt, pinstriped trousers and leather shoes. There are also some variations in the school uniform worn by boys in authority as well as award winners. Other old traditions of Eton include ancient sports event like Eton Fields Game, Eton Wall Game and Eton Five.

每年250名左右的毕业生中，70余名进入牛津、剑桥，70%进入世界名校。

伊顿闻名世界不仅仅因为培养出了精英学生，还得益于其保存了600多年的古老传统。伊顿的校服由黑色燕尾服、黑色马甲、白色衬衫、细直条纹的长裤和皮鞋组成，据说伊顿校服最早是乔治三世去世时人们为悼念他而穿的。而高干子弟和获奖者所穿的校服都经过一些改良。其他古老的传统还包括了伊顿野地游戏、伊顿墙球、伊顿五人。

词汇 VOCABULARY

1. outstandingly [aut'stændiŋli] *ad* 醒目地	2. prestigious [pres'ti:dʒəs] *a* 有名望的；享有声望的
3. initial [i'niʃəl] *a* 最初的；字首的	4. alumni [ə'lʌmnaɪ] *n* 男校友；男毕业生（alumnus的复数）
5. mourning ['mɔ:niŋ] *n* 哀痛；服丧	6. tailcoat [tel'kəut] *n* 燕尾服
7. waistcoat ['weistkəut] *n* 背心；[服装] 马甲	8. variation [,vɛəri'eiʃən] *n* 变化；[生物] 变异，变种

背景链接 TIPS

1. Windsor Castle

温莎城堡，位于英格兰东南部区域伯克郡温莎·梅登黑德皇家自治市镇温莎，是世界上有人居住的城堡中最大的一个。与伦敦的白金汉宫、爱丁堡的荷里路德宫一样，温莎城堡也是英国君主主要的行政官邸。现任的英国女王伊丽莎白二世每年有相当多的时间在温莎城堡度过，在这里进行国家或是私人的娱乐活动。

2. Prince William and Harry

威廉王子是当今英国王储威尔士亲王查尔斯和王妃戴安娜的后代。英国王位第二号继承人，排在其父亲之后，以及其弟哈里王子之前，于2011年4月29日迎娶平民王妃凯蒂·米德尔顿。哈里王子现正在皇家陆军第一龙骑兵队担任皇家骑兵侍卫，拥有少尉军阶。

|017 Oxford University

The University of Oxford is situated in a small town known as Oxford which is 85 kilometers away from northwest London. With a history of nine centuries, it is the second oldest surviving university in the world and the oldest in the English-speaking world. Although the exact date of its foundation remains unclear, teaching existed at Oxford in some form in 1096 and developed rapidly after 1167, when Henry II banned English students from attending the University of Paris.

As a collegiate university, Oxford is a federation comprising thirty-eight colleges and six Permanent Private Hall, along with a central administration. Most undergraduate teaching at Oxford is organized around tutorials at self-governed colleges and halls, where 1~4 students spend an hour with an academic once or twice in a week discussing their week's work, usually an essay. These tutorials are complemented by lectures, classes and seminars organized by University faculties and departments. Graduate students are usually instructed through classes and seminars, though there is more focus upon individual research.

Oxford is famous mainly for its social science and humanities, producing numerous prominent political figures including twenty-six British prime ministers and at least 30 other international leaders. Oxford has also

【小译】

牛津大学坐落在一个被称作牛津的小城上，小城位于伦敦西北部约85公里处。牛津大学有九百多年的历史，是世界上第二古老的大学，也是世界上最古老的用英语授课的大学。虽然其准确的创建日期已无法考究，但是于1096年牛津已有教学形式出现，而自从1167年亨利二世禁止英国学生进入巴黎大学学习以后，牛津大学得到迅速发展。

牛津大学是个学院联合体，包括38个学院和6个永久私人公寓和一个中央政府。牛津大学的大部分本科教学是通过由学院组织的"导师制"来进行的，每1到4个学生每个星期与自己的导师见一到两次，每次一个小时，讨论他们这个星期的作业，作业通常是短论文。辅以导师辅导的是由学校不同的系开设的讲座、课堂和研讨会。研究生的教学通常通过课堂和研讨会的形式来进行，虽然重点主要在个人研究上。

牛津主要以社会科学与人文学科而闻名世界，培养了无数的政界显要人物，包括26位英国首相，不少于30

cultivated at least twelve saints and twenty Archbishops of Canterbury. Besides, a large number of famous writers including Samuel Johnson, Oscar Wilde as well as important economists and scientists like Steven Hawking are all alumni of Oxford.

For more than a century, The Rhodes Scholarship selects 80 most outstanding graduate students all over the world to study at Oxford for postgraduates or for a second bachelor's degree at yearly basis. These Rhodes scholars all turned out to be elites in different fields around the world. Oxford consistently ranks in the world's top 10 and is always listed as one of the UK's best universities by the League tables, in regular rivalry with Cambridge, which will be introduced in the next part, for the first place in the tables.

位的国际领导人。牛津还培养了至少12位圣人与20位坎特伯雷大主教。此外，数不胜数的著名作家，包括塞缪尔·约翰逊、奥斯卡·王尔德以及一些著名的经济学家，诸如史蒂芬·霍金的科学家也都是牛津校友。

一百多年来，罗德奖学金每年都在全球选取80名最优秀的大四本科毕业生去牛津大学攻读硕士或第二学位。这些罗德学者之后在全世界都有非常重要的影响力。牛津大学一直是世界排名前十的大学。在英国大学排行榜上，牛津一直在最好大学之列，并常常与剑桥争夺第一的位置。我们将在下一部分为您介绍剑桥大学。

词汇 VOCABULARY

1. surviving [səˈvaiviŋ]
   a 继续存在的 *v* 生存（survive的ing形式）

2. collegiate [kəˈliːdʒiit]
   a 大学的；学院的；大学生的

3. comprise [kəmˈpraiz]
   vt 包含；由…组成

4. tutorial [tjuːˈtɔːriəl]
   a adj. 辅导的；家庭教师的 *n* 个别指导

5. complement [ˈkɔmplimənt]
   n 补语；余角；补足物 *vt* 补足，补助

6. seminar [ˈseminɑː]
   n 讨论会，研讨班

7. rivalry [ˈraivəlri]
   n 竞争；对抗；竞赛

背景链接 TIPS

1. Permanent Private Hall

私人永久公寓，是牛津大学内部的由不同的基督教派建立的教学机构，它们今天依然保留着宗教特征。从规模上来说，私人永久公寓一般要比学院小些，开设的课程也较少。但是，这里的学生与学院的学生是平等的，可使用的学校设施、可参加的学校活动都是一样的。

2. Archbishop of Canterbury

坎特伯雷大主教，又称为坎特伯雷圣座，继承了圣奥古斯丁的使徒统系，为全英格兰的牧首（The Primate of All England）。而约克大主教，是英格兰的牧首（The Primate of England）。坎特伯雷大主教的权威，是因他作为使徒圣奥古斯丁的继承人的事实，令其成为普世圣公宗中的首领。

GEOGRAPHY

018 Cambridge University

Located in the city of Cambridge, in the southeast of central England, Cambridge University is the second oldest university in the UK as well as in the English-speaking world. It was founded in the 13th century and can actually trace its origin from Oxford. It was established when some academics from Oxford fled to Cambridge in 1209 after a dispute with Oxford townsfolk. The two ancient English universities have many common features and are often jointly referred to as Oxbridge.

Similar to Oxford, Cambridge is also a collegiate university made up of central administration and 31 colleges, three of which, Murray Edwards, Newnham and Lucy Cavendish, admit women only. The pedagogical system in Cambridge also resembles the tutorial system in Oxford, only that in Cambridge have a different name "supervision". Typically, students receive between one and four supervisions per week which are usually hour-long sessions in which small groups of students—usually between one and three—meet with a member of the university's teaching staff or a doctoral student and discuss with them about the assignment they have completed ahead of the session, along with any concerns or difficulties they have had with the material presented in that week's lectures. As in Oxford, lectures at Cambridge are often seen as a supplementary to the supervision.

Cambridge has been noted in mathematics and sciences. Graduates of the University have won a total of 61 Nobel Prizes, more than any other universities in the world. Over the course of its history, Cambridge University has built up a considerable number of alumni who are notable in their fields, the most famous figure being Sir Isaac Newton, who spent the majority of his life at the university and Sir Francis Bacon who entered the university when he was just twelve.

【小译】

剑桥大学位于英格兰中部东南方的剑桥市，是英国第二古老的大学，也是英语国家中第二古老的大学。剑桥大学于13世纪建校，与牛津有很深的渊源。1209年，由于与当地人民有些争议，牛津大学的一些学者离开了牛津，来到了剑桥，创立了剑桥大学。这两所英国古老的大学有许多共同点，常常被共称为"牛桥"。

剑桥同牛津一样，也是学院联合体，由中央行政机构和31所学院组成，其中有三所学院——默里爱德华兹学院、纽纳姆学院、露西·卡文迪许学院只招收女学生。剑桥的教学方式也与牛津的导师制相似，只不过叫法略有不同，叫做"指导制"。一般来说，学生第每个月接受一到四次指导，每次指导历时一个小时，通常一到三个学生组成小组，与学校的老师或者是博士生会面，与他们讨论自己在指导之前完成的作业，以及他们对于当周课堂上展示的材料所产生的疑问或遇到的困难。与牛津一样，剑桥的课堂一般仅仅被视为指导的补充。

剑桥大学主要以数学与科学见长，该校毕业生共获得61项诺贝尔奖，居世界所有大学首位。多年来，剑桥也培养了大量的优秀校友，他们都是各个领域显赫的人物，最著名的包括在剑桥度过了大半辈子的艾萨克·牛顿爵士，还有弗朗西斯·培根爵士，12岁就到剑桥上学。

一方面尽管剑桥与牛津有很大的文化历史联系，另一方面它也是牛津

Besides its cultural and historical connections with Oxford, Cambridge is also a formidable rival of the Oxford. As one of the top universities in the world, Cambridge regularly contends with Oxford for first place in UK League tables. In the most recently published ranking of UK universities, published by The Guardian, Cambridge beat Oxford and was ranked first. Competition between the two universities is also shown in their Boat Race, which is held in London at the end of March each year and it has become one of the greatest yearly British sporting events drawing national attention.

有力的竞争对手。剑桥也是世界一流大学，常常在英国大学排行榜上与牛津争夺第一的位置。在英国著名的《卫报》最新刊登的英国大学排行榜上，剑桥打败牛津登上了第一的宝座。两所大学的竞争也显示在它们之间的划船比赛中，比赛每年三月末在伦敦举行，已成为英国每年举国关注的重要体育赛事之一。

词汇 VOCABULARY

1. trace [treis] v. 追溯；沿路走 n. 痕迹，踪迹，微量；缰绳	2. folk [fəuk] n. 人们，亲属（复数），民族
3. pedagogical [pedə'gɔdʒikəl] a. 教育学的；教学法的	4. resemble [ri'zembl] vt. 类似，像
5. supervision [,sju:pə'viʒən] n. 监督，管理；指导	6. assignment [ə'sainmənt] n. 分配；任务；作业；功课
7. supplementary [,sʌpli'mentəri] a. 补充的；追加的 n. 补充者；增补物	8. notable ['nəutəbl] a. 值得注意的，显著的；著名的
9. formidable ['fɔ:midəbl] a. 强大的；可怕的；令人敬畏的；艰难的	10. rival ['raivəl] n. 对手 v. 与…竞争；比得上某人 a. 竞争
11. contend [kən'tend] vi. 竞争；奋斗；斗争；争论	

背景链接 TIPS

1. Sir Francis Bacon

弗兰西斯·培根，英国著名的唯物主义哲学家和科学家。马克思称他是"英国唯物主义和整个现代实验科学的真正始祖。" 代表作《新工具》，在近代哲学史上具有划时代的意义和广泛的影响，哲学家由此把它看成是从古代唯物论向近代唯物论转变的先驱。

2. The Guardian

《卫报》是英国的全国性综合内容日报。一般公众视《卫报》的政治观点为中间偏左，《卫报》重视的领域包括世界主义观点、文艺报道和评论、外国通讯。与《泰晤士报》、《每日电讯报》同为英国三大著名报纸。

GEOGRAPHY

019 London School of Economics

The London School of Economics, the formal name being The London School of Economics and Political Science and abbreviated as LSE, is a constituent college of the federal University of London specializing in the social sciences. Located in Westminster, central London, LSE was founded in 1895 by Fabian Society members Sidney Webb, Beatrice Webb and George Bernard Shaw. It joined the University of London as the university's Faculty of Economics in 1900. LSE is only university in the UK to be dedicated solely to the study and research of social sciences, including accounting and finance, anthropology, economics, geography, history, international relations, law, media and communications, philosophy, politics, psychology, social policy and sociology.

LSE is one of the world's most selective universities at the undergraduate level. According to 2008 UCAS figures, the school received 19,039 applications for 1,299 places, which means that 15 applicants fought for each place, the highest ratio of any university in Britain. Some courses, including Government, Economics and International Relations have more than 20 applicants per place and thus an admissions rate of around 5%.

LSE is also famous for its program of public lectures. Besides leading academics, these lectures are given by prominent national and international figures such as

【小译】

伦敦经济学校的官方称谓叫做伦敦政治经济学院，简称LSE。它是伦敦大学联邦的组成学院之一，专注于社会科学领域。学校位于伦敦中部的威斯敏斯特，于1895年由法比安协会成员西德尼·韦勃、碧翠斯·韦勃与乔治·萧伯纳所建立。1900年学院并入伦敦大学，成为该大学的经济学院。LSE对于社会科学的学术和研究的专注程度在英国的大学中独一无二，其领域包括会计学和金融学、人类学、经济学、地理、历史、国际关系、法律、媒体和交际、哲学、政治、心理学、社会政策和社会学。

对于大学生来说，LSE是世界上最难考入的大学之一。2008年UCAS的统计数据显示，学校该年1299个入学名额，共收到19039份入学申请。这意味着每15个申请者要竞争一个入学名额，这个比率是全英国大学中最高的。其中的一些专业，比如政府政策、经济与国际关系的每个入学名额有超过20个竞争者争夺，录取率低于5%。

LSE的出名还因为它的公共演讲栏目。除了学术上的领先外，这些演讲的主角也都是这个国家以及世界上最杰出的人，比如大使、首席执行官、国会议员以及国家领导人。近年来比较有名的演讲者，如果要列出一小部分，有科菲·安南、托尼·布莱尔、戈登·布朗、大卫·卡梅隆、诺姆·乔姆斯基、

ambassadors, CEOs, members of Parliament as well as heads of state. To name a few recent prominent speakers, Kofi Annan, Tony Blair , Gordon Brown, David Cameron, Noam Chomsky, Bill Clinton.

International students have been an important elements in LSE. There are at one time more countries represented by students in LSE than the UN member countries. LSE has cultivated many notable figures in the fields of law, economics, business, literature and politics. There are currently 16 Nobel Prize winners amongst LSE's alumni and current and former staff, as well as 34 world leaders like former U.S President John F. Kennedy and numerous Pulitzer Prize winners. LSE is one of only four British institutions to have always ranked among the top 10 in any newspaper compiled League table in the UK.

比尔·克林顿。

留学生是LSE的重要组成部分。LSE的在读学生所属的国家一度比英联邦国家还要多。LSE培养了很多法律界、经济界、商界、文学界和政界精英。在LSE的校友以及先前和现在的教职员工中有16人获得了诺贝尔奖；34人成为了国家领导人，例如美国前总统约翰·F·肯尼迪；还有很多的普利策奖获得者。LSE是英国仅有的四个在英国任何报纸编纂的英国高校排行榜上都能稳居前十名的学校。

词汇 VOCABULARY

1. abbreviate [əˈbriːvieit]
   vi 使用缩写词 *vt* 缩写，使省略[(+to)]

2. constituent [kənˈstitjuənt]
   n 成分；组成要素 *a* 构成（全体）的，组成的

3. faculty [ˈfækəlti]
   n （大学的）系，科；院

4. dedicated [ˈdedikeitid]
   vt 献(身)；把(时间、精力等)用于[(+to)]

5. anthropology [ˌænθrəˈpɔlədʒi]
   n 人类学

6. prominent [ˈprɔminənt]
   a 突出的；卓越的；重要的；著名的

7. cultivate [ˈkʌltiveit]
   vt 培养；陶冶

8. notable [ˈnəutəbl]
   a 值得注意的，显著的；著名的

9. alumnus [əˈlʌmnəs]
   n 男校友；男女合校之男女校友

背景链接 TIPS

1. UCAS

Universities and Colleges Admissions Service 的缩写，即"大学和学院招生服务中心"，它是一个公共服务机构，统一为英国所有大学提供招生服务。申请英国大学的本科学位课程，都要通过UCAS进行申请。

2. Pulitzer Prize

普利策奖，也称为普利策新闻奖。 1917年根据美国报业巨头约瑟夫·普利策（Joseph Pulitzer）的遗愿设立，二十世纪七八十年代已经发展成为美国新闻界的一项最高荣誉奖，现在已成为一个全球性的奖项。 约翰·肯尼迪是唯一获得这个奖项的美国总统。

Unit 5 传统体育项目

Britain has a long history in the sports tradition. As a matter of fact, it has given birth to many other world's major sports than any other country in the world including soccer, cricket, snooker, tennis, golf, boxing, rugby, squash, billiards, badminton and curling.

Sports play a crucial role in British life. About 29 million people over the age of 16 in the United Kingdom regularly take part in sports or exercise. Major team sports in the UK include soccer, cricket and rugby. The major sport is soccer except in Northern Ireland where traditional Gaelic games like Gaelic footballs and hurling are the most popular sports and Wales, where rugby union is generally considered as the national sport. Cricket is popular in England and Wales, but is less popular in Scotland and Northern Ireland. Athletics, golf, motorsport and horseracing are major individual sports in the UK. Tennis is the highest profile sport for the two weeks of the Wimbledon Championships, but generally speaking are in decline in the country of its birth. Horseracing also occupies a key place in British sports, probably ranking the top four or five sports with regard to media coverage.

In this chapter, we will give a brief introduction to the most popular team sports in the UK – soccer and cricket and individual sports – horseracing, equestrianism and tennis.

英国的体育传统有着悠久的历史。事实上，在世界上主要的体育项目中，源自英国的体育项目是最多的。其中包括足球、板球、斯诺克、网球、高尔夫、拳击、橄榄球、壁球、撞球、羽毛球和冰壶。

体育在英国人的生活中扮演着重要角色。在英国16岁以上的民众中有大约2900万人定期参加体育锻炼或训练。英国重要的团体项目有足球、板球和橄榄球。在北爱尔兰，传统盖尔人的项目如盖尔足球和曲棍球被视为最流行的体育项目。而在威尔士，橄榄球通常被视为国家体育项目。在英格兰与英格兰，足球都是第一大运动。板球在英格兰和威尔士很流行，但在苏格兰和北爱尔兰却不那么流行。田径、高尔夫、赛车和赛马是英国主要的单人项目。网球因为其为期两周的温布尔登公开赛而成为英国最受世界瞩目的体育项目，但是总体来说，虽然英国是网球的发源地，但这项运动在英国却正在衰落。赛马也在英国最重要的体育项目中占得一席，在媒体所关注的体育项目中大约位列第四或第五位。

在这一章，我们将详细介绍英国最受欢迎的团体项目——足球和板球以及单人项目——赛马、马术和网球。

020 Soccer

Four sports in the United Kingdom operate high profile professional leagues – soccer, rugby, cricket and ice hockey, among which soccer is the most popular sport and is played from August to May. Originated in the UK, soccer is often referred to as association football or football which is a form of sports played by two teams of eleven players with a round ball which may not be handled during play except by the goalkeepers; the object of the game is to score goals by kicking or heading the ball into the opponents' goal. On Oct. 26, 1863, the first official football organization in the world, Football Association (FA) was formed in London, which symbolizes the birth of modern football.

Each of the Home Nations has its own football association, national team and league system. The governing bodies for football in England, Scotland, Wales and Northern Ireland are The Football Association, the Scottish Football Association, the Football Association of Wales and the Irish Football Association respectively. They have however lost a significant amount of power to the professional leagues in recent times.

The English football league system includes hundreds of inter-linked leagues which consists of thousands of clubs, and is topped by four fully professional divisions. At the top

【小译】

英国有四大职业体育联盟——足球、橄榄球、板球和冰球。其中尤以足球最负盛名，其赛季通常是每年八月到第二年的五月。在英国足球通常指的是英式足球，它起源于英国。一场足球比赛有两支队伍参加，每队11个人，围绕着一个圆球展开比赛，其中除守门员外其他队员均不得用手触球。比赛中，每支球队的目标是将球踢入或用头顶入对方的球门。1863年10月26日，世界上第一个正式的足球组织英国足球协会（FA）在伦敦成立，这一天也被视为现代足球运动的诞生日。此后，足球运动在全球广泛传播。

英国的四个地区都有自己的足球协会、国家队以及联赛系统。在英格兰、苏格兰、威尔士和北爱尔兰的足球的官方实体各自分别是英国足球协会、苏格兰足球协会、威尔士足球协会和北爱尔兰足球协会。但近年来这些足协相对于职业联赛，影响力已经显著下降了。

英国的足球联赛系统包括由数千家俱乐部组成的上百个相互交织的联会，通常被分为四个职业层次。处于"金字塔"最顶层的是由20支顶级的英格兰足球俱乐部组成的英格兰足球超级联赛，它也是世界上收视率最高的足球联赛。其他三个"金字塔"中低一些的层次分别是英格兰冠军杯以及分别由

GEOGRAPHY

of the "pyramid" is the FA Premier League with 20 top clubs in England, which is also the football league with the highest audience rating in the world. The other three divisions down the "pyramid" are the Championship, League One and League Two with 24 clubs in each of them.

There are over a hundred fully professional clubs in England, which is considerably more than any other country in Europe. English teams have been successful in European. The most renowned ones are Liverpool, Manchester United, Nottingham Forest and Arsenal, all of which are UEFA (Union of European Football Association) Champions League winners. England has also given birth to lots of world-famous football stars like David Beckham and Michael Owen.

24支球队组成的英格兰足球甲级联赛和英格兰足球乙级联赛。

英格兰拥有超过一百家完全职业的足球俱乐部，比其他欧洲国家都要多。英国的足球队已经在欧洲获得了很大成功，这其中最具声望的有利物浦、曼联、诺丁汉森林和阿森纳队。它们都赢得过欧洲冠军杯或者欧洲足球冠军联赛的冠军。英格兰也诞生过不少世界闻名的足球明星，比如大卫·贝克汉姆和迈克尔·欧文。

词汇 VOCABULARY

1. rugby ['rʌgbi]
   n. 英式橄榄球

2. cricket ['krikit]
   n. [体]板球 vi. 打板球

3. originate [ə'ridʒineit]
   vi. 发源；来自；产生 vt. 创始；发明；创作

4. symbolize ['simbəlaiz]
   vt. 采用象征，使用符号 vi. 象征，标志

5. pyramid ['pirəmid]
   n. 金字塔，角锥形物；角锥形的一堆东西 vt. 成尖塔（或角锥）形 vi. 使成尖塔（或角锥）形

6. professional [prə'feʃənl]
   adj. 职业（上）的；极称职的；高水平的 n. 职业选手

背景链接 TIPS

1. Football Association (FA)

1863年10月26日，英国人在伦敦皇后大街弗里马森旅馆成立了世界第一个足球协会——英格兰足球协会。会上除了宣布英格兰足协正式成立之外，制定和通过了世界第一部较为统一的足球竞赛规则，并以文字形式记载下来。

2. FA Premier League

英格兰足球超级联赛（FA Premier League），是英格兰足总属下的职业足球联赛。由超级联盟负责具体运作。英格兰超级联赛成立于1992年2月20日，其前身是英格兰甲级联赛，是英格兰联赛系统的最高等级联赛。

3. UEFA (Union of European Football Association) Champions League

欧洲冠军联赛（UEFA CHAMPIONS LEAGUE）是欧足联最有声望的一项俱乐部赛事，前身是1955/56赛季创建的欧洲俱乐部冠军杯赛，1992年欧洲足联对这项杯赛的赛制和名称进行了修改。

021 Cricket

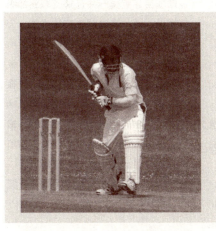

Cricket was invented in southern England in the 16th century. By the end of the 18th century, it had developed into the national sport of England. The expansion of the British Empire led to cricket spreading to the British colonies – to India, Australia and South Africa. By the mid-19th century, the first international matches were held. The great scientist of the 19th century – Charles Darwin mentions seeing Maoris playing cricket in New Zealand. The International Cricket Council (ICC), which is the game's governing body, has ten full members including Australia, England, Bangladesh, India, New Zealand, South Africa and so on.

The England cricket team, which also represents Wales, is the only national team in the UK with test status. It is controlled by the England and Wales Cricket Board. Each summer two foreign national teams visit England to play seven test matches and numerous one-day internationals. In winter the English team tours abroad. The highest profile rival of the England cricket team is the Australian team, with which it competes for The Ashes, one of the most famous trophies in British sport dating back to 1882.

【小译】

板球在16世纪起源于英格兰南部，到18世纪末，发展成为了英格兰的民族体育项目。随着英国大不列颠版图的扩张，板球也发扬到了一些殖民地国家，如印度、澳大利亚、南非等。查尔斯·达尔文——19世纪中叶著名的科学家曾提及新西兰毛利人也玩板球。国际板球理事会是板球运动的主管机构，有十个正式成员国，包括澳大利亚、英格兰、孟加拉国、印度、新西兰、南非等。

英格兰板球队也代表威尔士，是英国唯一一支拥有对抗赛资格的板球队，由英格兰与威尔士板球董事会管理。每年夏天会有两支外国球队来英格兰，进行七场对抗赛、数场国际性单日比赛。冬天英格兰队到国外巡回比赛。英格兰板球队最有力的竞争对手是澳大利亚板球队，两队从1882年起开始争夺"灰烬杯"，"灰烬杯"也是英国体育界最著名的奖杯之一。

板球不论从经济、上座率、报道

GEOGRAPHY

Cricket is by no means equal to football in finance, attendance or coverage, but it has a high profile nonetheless. It is probably the second most widely covered sport in England. There are eighteen professional county clubs, seventeen in England and one in Wales. These clubs are named after the counties where they come from. The clubs are evenly divided into two leagues competing in the first class County Championship in which matches are played over four day. The first match between counties was on 29 June 1790, when Surrey played Kent. These clubs also play the one day National League, a one-day knock out competition called the Friends Provident Trophy, and Twenty20 Cup replaced by Friends Provident 20 in 2010.

率上都无法与足球相提并论，但是板球应该是英格兰第二大被广泛报道的运动项目。英国一共有18支职业郡级板球俱乐部，其中17支在英格兰，一支在威尔士。这些俱乐部都由他们所属的郡命名，被平分为两个联盟，参与甲级郡级锦标赛，甲级锦标赛的板球比赛一般长达四天，历史上第一场郡际比赛于1790年6月29日进行，由萨里对阵肯特。这些俱乐部也参加单日全国联盟比赛——"友诚杯"，以及"2020杯"，于2010年被"友诚20"取代。

词汇 VOCABULARY

1. cricket ['krikit]
   n 板球；蟋蟀

2. Maori ['mɑːri, 'mauri]
   n 毛利人；毛利语 a 毛利人的；毛利语的

3. Bangladesh [,bɑːŋglə'deʃ]
   n 孟加拉共和国

4. trophy ['trəufi]
   n 奖品；战利品；纪念品 v 用战利品装饰

5. attendance [ə'tendəns]
   n 出席；到场；出席人数

6. championship ['tʃæmpjənʃip]
   n 锦标赛；冠军称号；冠军的地位

7. provident ['prɔvidənt]
   a 节俭的；有先见之明的；顾及未来的

背景链接 TIPS

1. test status

对抗赛资格，指国家代表队参加国际板球对抗赛的资格，由国际板球协会（ICC）决定。对抗赛的一场比赛每天进行六小时或六小时以上，并长达五天，每方各打两局；还有许多午餐和饮茶的休息时间。

2. The Ashes

英格兰和澳大利亚之间举行的板球系列对抗赛被称作为"灰烬杯"。此项系列赛的奖杯是一座小而易碎的陶质骨灰瓮。"灰烬杯"起源于1882年，现在每两年举行一次，在英国与澳大利亚轮替举行，是最负盛名的板球国际赛事之一。

022 Horse Racing

Horse racing is a key sport in the UK which enjoys a large audience. It probably ranks in the top four or five sports with regard to media coverage. There are over sixty racecourses in the United Kingdom, and annual racecourse attendance exceeds six million. Horse racing also enjoys a long history. According to historical record, the first race meeting took place during the reign of Henry II at Smithfield, London in 1174 during a horse fair. It is also said that in 1512, the first horse-racing trophy was presented to the winner by the organizers of a fair in Chester, which was a small wooden ball decorated with flowers.

The two main forms of professional horse racing in Great Britain are flat racing, which is unobstructed distances races, and National Hunt Racing, which involves races over fences or over hurdles. Flat racing is a summer sport and National Hunt is a winter sport, but the seasons are very long and they sometimes overlap. Additionally there is another form of racing which is a form of steeplechasing for amateur riders, known as point-to-point racing. Both the two forms of professional horse racing and point to point amateur racing are run under

【小译】

赛马在英国是一项拥有众多观众的关键性的体育项目，它在媒体关注的体育项目中大概位列前四或前五位。英国有超过六十个赛马场，每年参与赛马的人超过六百万。赛马运动拥有悠久的历史。据史料记载，第一场赛马是在亨利二世当政期间的1174年（也有人说是在1512年）于伦敦史密斯菲尔德的一个马市上举行的。第一件赛马比赛的优胜奖品是一个由鲜花装饰成的小木球，它是由一个切斯特集市的组织者授予胜利者的。

英国职业赛马的两种主要形式分别是平地赛马、也就是长距离无障碍的赛马以及包括跨越栅栏或栏杆的障碍赛马。平地赛马是一项夏季运动，而障碍赛马则是冬季运动。但由于赛季很长，它们有时时间上也会重叠。此外还有一种由业余选手参加的，被认为是点对点的

GEOGRAPHY

the auspices of the governing and regulatory body for horse-racing in Great Britain – the British Horseracing Authority. The UK has given birth to some of the greatest jockeys, including Sir Gordon Richards, known as the greatest jockey ever. There are between four and five hundred professional jockeys in the United Kingdom.

Wagering on horseraces is also considered the cornerstone of the British betting industry. It is as old as the sport itself, and in the United Kingdom the links between horseracing and nationwide wagering are very strong. "Betting shops" are common sights in most towns, which can be seen wherever there might be a significant number of people with disposable cash. The last 10 years in the UK, has seen massive growth in online gambling. Punters are now going online to place their bets, where they can get access to a greater amount of information and knowledge.

比赛的越野障碍赛。这两种形式的职业赛马和点对点业余赛事都是在政府或者英国赛马的管理机构——英国赛马管理局的赞助下进行。英国诞生了许多伟大的骑手，比如曾一度被认为是最伟大的骑手的戈登·理查德爵士。英国共有四百到五百名职业骑手。

赛马赌博也被认为是英国博彩业的基石。它与这项运动的历史同样长。英国的赛马与全国范围的赛马赌博的联系非常紧密。在绝大多数城镇中彩票销售点都是一道很普通的风景，大批手握彩票的彩民也随处可见。过去的十年中，在线赌博的人数激增。彩民们现在可以在网上获取大量知识和信息，然后在线下注。

词汇 VOCABULARY

1. coverage ['kʌvəridʒ] n. 新闻报道	2. reign [rein] n. 在位期间，统治时期
3. trophy ['trəufi] n. 战利品；胜利纪念品；奖品	4. fence [fens] n. 栅栏；篱笆 v. 把…用栅（或篱）围起来
5. hurdle ['hə:dl] n. （赛马或赛跑用的）栏；跳栏 v. 跨栏	6. amateur ['æmətə(:), 'æmətjuə] n. 业余从事者 a. 业余的
7. jockey ['dʒɔki] n. 赛马的骑师，骑士	8. punter ['pʌntə] n. 赌马者

背景链接 TIPS

1. National Hunt racing

英国全国障碍赛马，是世界上难度最大的越野障碍赛马，诞生于1839年2月26日。由于两次世界大战等原因，这项赛事一共停办了9次。英国越野障碍赛马国家大赛每年都在4月举行，在比赛中，要在7.2公里的赛道上，穿越难度各异的30道障碍。

2. flat racing

平地赛马是世界上主流赛事的一种，在世界大多数发展赛马的国家都会出现此类型的赛事。通常赛事距离由1000米至2400米，但有时会出现更长或更短的比赛。

023 Tennis

Besides soccer and cricket, tennis is another sports originating from the United Kingdom. Modern tennis was first played in the city of Birmingham between 1859 and 1865 and had two different forms of hard court tennis and lawn tennis since then. The first tennis championship in the UK was held in Wimbledon in 1877 which was the predecessor of the world-famous Wimbledon Championships, the only major tennis tournament still played on grass and one of the four Grand Slam tournaments, the other three being the Australian Open played on hard courts, the French Open played on red clay courts and the US Open played also on hard courts.

As the most prestigious tennis event of the global tennis calendar, the Wimbledon Championships has attracted a large audience around the world and has also brought huge profits to the UK. It takes place over two weeks in late June and early July, culminating with the Ladies' and Gentlemen's Singles Final, scheduled respectively for the second Saturday and Sunday. Each year, five major events are contested, as well as four junior events and three invitational events. Wimbledon traditions include a strict dress code for competitors, the eating of strawberries and cream by the spectators, and Royal patronage. The tournament is also notable for the absence of sponsor advertising around the courts.

However, it seems that tennis has not

【小译】

除了足球和板球以外，网球是另外一项起源于英国的运动。现代网球是于1859年至1865年之间在伯明翰首次出现的，有硬地和草地两种形式。英国第一次网球锦标赛于1877年在温布尔登举行，这就是日后闻名天下的温布尔登网球公开赛的前身。温网也是迄今为止唯一一个仍然在草地球场上进行的大满贯赛事，其他三个大满贯赛事分别是在硬地球场举行的澳大利亚网球公开赛，在红土球场上举行的法国网球公开赛以及同样是在硬地球场举行的美国网球公开赛。

作为国际网坛最具声望的赛事，温布尔登网球公开赛吸引了世界范围内的大量观众，同时也为英国带来了巨大的经济利润。比赛通常在六月底和七月初举行，为期两周，最精彩的比赛当属男子和女子单打决赛，它们分别被安排在比赛第二周的周六和周日。每一年，比赛的五个主要项目，四个青年项目和三个邀请项目竞争都非常激烈。温网的传统包括对参赛选手着装的严格要

flourished in the UK in recent decades besides serving as the location of Wimbledon Championships. No British man has won Wimbledon since 1936 and no British woman since 1977. The governing body of the sport – the Lawn Tennis Association (LTA), invests the vast profits from the tournament in the game in the hope of producing British champions, but a string of revamps of the coaching system have still failed to raise the standard of LTA-trained players.

求，观众们会吃草莓和奶酪，还有来自皇室的赞助。比赛中，场地四周不会有赞助商广告，这同样是比赛的一大特点。

然而，除了在本土举办的温网以外，近年来网球在英国看上去也并不是那么兴盛了。自从1936年以来就没有英国男选手夺得过温网冠军，而英国女选手最后一次摘取此桂冠也是在1977年了。赛事的官方实体——全英草地网球协会(LTA)从赛事中拿出了巨额投资，希望能培养出英国本土冠军，然而不断翻新的训练体制并没有让LTA培养的选手的水平得到提高。

词汇 VOCABULARY

1. lawn [lɔ:n]
   n 草坪，草地

2. tournament ['tuənəmənt]
   n 比赛；锦标赛；联赛

3. prestigious [,pres'ti:dʒəs]
   a 享有声望的，声望很高的

4. culminate ['kʌlmineit]
   v 达到最高点；达到高潮；告终

5. patronage ['pætrənidʒ]
   n 资助，赞助

6. flourish ['flʌriʃ]
   v 繁荣，兴盛

背景链接 TIPS

1. Grand Slam tournaments

大满贯赛事，网球的大满贯赛事包括澳大利亚网球公开赛，法国网球公开赛，美国网球公开赛和温布尔登网球公开赛。这四项赛事无论从规模、历史、奖金、积分和影响力都堪称职业网坛之最。

2. Lawn Tennis Association 全英草地网球协会

ENTERPRISES

Part 2

正在影响世界的英国顶级企业

Unit 6 能源企业

The United Kingdom, owning to its vast crude oil and natural gas reservation, is a major crude oil production country in the Europe. Meanwhile, it is also the biggest producer and exporter among the European Union countries.

Britain has the proved reserves of 5.2 billion barrels of crude oil equivalent, the majority of which is reserved in the North Sea. The major oil fields lie in the northern basin of Scotland situating in the middle of North Sea. The northern part of North Sea also stores a considerable sum of crude oil. The rest of Britain's crude oil are scattered around the North Atlantic area and the western Shetland.

Britain possesses 26.7 TCF gas reserve in the North Sea, most of which is along the coast of the English Channel. The major gas fields include Lemon of British Petroleum Amoco, Brittanie of Chevron and Conoco and Indefatigable and Clipper of Shell.

However, with the continuous consumption of the resources, the output of Britain's crude oil experienced continuous decline and the tendency will still go on. As to the reason of decline, on one hand, it is a result of natural ageing of the oil field which was even accelerated by the application of new technology; on the other hand, the increase in the production cost also affects the output. In view of this tendency, the British governments adjusted the energy and oil strategies by increasing import and decreasing export and putting more emphasis on the exploration of potential resources to ensure the safety of oil supply.

Among several major oil suppliers such as ChevronTexaco and Total Kenya in Britain, the Royal Dutch Shell and the British Petroleum, which will be discussed in this part, are the most prominent ones and make the greatest contribution to Britain's oil and natural gas industry as well as to the world.

得益于其雄厚的原油天然气储量，英国成为目前欧盟最大的原油生产国，同时也是天然气的最大生产国和最大输出国。

英国拥有52亿桶已探明原油储量，大部分都分布在北海区域。主要产区在北海中部的苏格兰东部盆地。北海北部储量也十分可观，另有小储油点分布在北大西洋海域，设得兰群岛西部。

英国北海约有26.7 TCF的天然气储量。大部分气田分布在英吉利海岸，毗邻荷兰北海地区。主要气田有：英国石油公司的莱曼气田、雪佛龙和大陆石油的不列颠合金气田、壳牌公司的INDFATIGABLE和ICLIPPER 气田。

然而，随着能源资源的不断消耗，英国石油日益减产，而这个趋势还可能持续下去。造成减产的主要原因，一方面是油田老化，而新技术的应用加速了油田老化；另一方面是生产成本的增加。这一情况将导致英国调整能源及石油政策，减少出口，增加进口，加大勘探投入，以保证国内石油供应安全。

在诸如雪佛龙德士古、道达尔此类大型石油供应商中，最声名显赫的要算壳牌石油和英国石油了，而他们对英国乃至世界石油天然气做出的贡献也最突出，因此本部分将给予相应介绍。

024 Shell

Royal Dutch Shell, or more commonly referred to as Shell, is a famous multinational oil and gas corporation. As the name indicates, it was merged from two companies, the Dutch Royal Dutch Petroleum Corporation and the British Shell Transport and Trading Co., who were originally rivals. The merger took place in 1907 and thereafter renamed Royal Dutch Shell. With its headquarter situated in London, the company is one of the largest oil in the UK as well as in the world. According to a list issued by Forbes Magazine in 2011, Shell is second only to Exxon Mobil as the largest company in the energy industry and the fifth largest company in the world.

Shell operates its business all over the world with a total number of 44,000 gas stations in 90 countries and has proved reserves of 14.1 billion barrels of oil equivalent. It has the largest retail energy network in the industry.

Shell is active in every area of oil and gas industry and its business is organized into upstream business, downstream business as well as Projects and Technology business. The upstream business includes exploration and production in which crude oil and natural gas is explored and extracted. The downstream

【小译】

荷兰皇家壳牌集团通常被称为壳牌公司，是一家世界著名的大型跨国石油公司。如名字所示，它是通过两家公司的合并组建而成的，这两家公司之前是竞争对手，分别为壳牌运输和贸易有限公司（英国）与荷兰皇家石油公司。两家公司1907年合并更名为现在的荷兰皇家壳牌集团。公司总部设在伦敦，是英国乃至世界最大的石油公司之一。根据福布斯公布的2011年世界企业排名，壳牌公司是仅次于埃克森美孚的世界第二大能源企业，在全球所有企业中排第五位。

壳牌石油在世界90多个国家拥有44000多个加油站，已探测到的石油储量有141亿桶。壳牌拥有行业中最大的能源零售网。

壳牌公司在石油和天然气工业都很活跃。其产业分为3部分：上游产业、下游产业和项目与技术开发。上游产业包括石油勘探和开发，下游产业包括炼油加工、运输及销售。同时，公司还致力于进行一些可再生能

ENTERPRISES

business contains a variety of activities in which crude oil is processed into refined products and is distributed and marketed throughout the world. Besides, some major activates and projects are carried out such as developing renewable energy. Shell has also been seeking diversity in its business besides oil and gas business including nuclear power, coal, mental but were all called off. Shell also entered alternative energy business and invested on solar power, wind power, hydrogen, and forestry but saw no promising future.

Besides its contribution on oil and gas production and services, Shell also boosts economy in UK and the world through taxation and employment. Shell has 8,600 employees in London and totally 97,000 worldwide.

源的开发活动或项目。壳牌曾尝试通过开发核动力、煤炭、金属等其他能源来使公司多元化，降低石油和天然气的主导，但都没有顺利进行下去。壳牌也尝试进入可替换能源产业并在太阳能、风能、氢和林业方面投资，但都没有取得理想的成果。

壳牌除了在石油天然气产品和服务做出贡献之外，还通过税收和提供就业拉动了英国乃至世界的经济。壳牌公司现在英国雇佣职工8,600名，全世界的壳牌公司职工多达97,000名。

词汇 VOCABULARY

1. merger ['məːdʒə]
   n. （企业等的）合并；并购；[法律]吸收（如刑法中重罪吸收轻罪）

2. reserve [ri'zəːv]
   n. 储备，预备队；储备金；自然保护区
   vt. 保留；储备；预约 vi. 预订

3. barrel ['bærəl]
   n. 桶；枪管 vt. 把…装入桶内 vi. 快速移动

4. fiscal ['fiskəl]
   a. 国库的；会计的，财政的

5. upstream ['ʌp'striːm]
   ad. 向上游；逆流地 *a.* 向上游的 *n.* 上游部门

6. downstream ['daunstriːm]
   ad. 下游地；顺流而下 *a.* 下游的；顺流的

7. hydrogen ['haidrəudʒən]
   n. 氢

8. forestry ['fɔristri]
   n. 林学；林业；森林地

背景链接 TIPS

壳牌集团

壳牌集团共有11家服务公司承担着总部的管理和服务职能。这些服务公司既按业务划分，又按地区与职能进行划分，用矩阵式管理方法对全球业务进行组织管理。这11家服务公司分别设在英国和荷兰，它们是：壳牌国际公司、壳牌国际有限公司、壳牌国际勘探和开发公司、壳牌国际石油有限公司、壳牌国际化学公司、壳牌国际化学有限公司、壳牌国际研究公司、壳牌国际石油产品公司、壳牌国际贸易和船运有限公司、壳牌国际天然气公司、壳牌煤炭国际有限公司。

025 British Petroleum

BP, the abbreviation for British Petroleum, is also a major international oil and gas company in the world. It is the third largest oil and natural gas company lining after Exxon Mobil and Royal Dutch Shell.

BP operates its business all over the world in 30 countries and has proved reserves of 18.1 billion barrels of oil equivalent. It also operates 22,400 gas stations worldwide and sells its products in more than 80 countries.

The company was originally founded by William Knox D'Arcy as Anglo-Persian Oil Company, and renamed Anglo-Iranian Oil in 1935. The name BP was acquired in the year 1954. After incorporating Amoco Corporation in 1998, BP is now also known as BP Amoco PLC.

BP is an integrated oil and gas company operating in three major segments: upstream business, downstream business and production of petrochemicals. Similar to Shell, BP's upstream business focuses on the exploration and production of oil and gas in 29 countries; the downstream businesses include refining in its 23 oil refineries, transportation, and marketing and supplying. In the last major segment, they extract substances—petrochemicals from petroleum and apply them to the production of various objects such as packaging and cosmetics. BP obtains sophisticated technologies in

【小译】

BP是英国石油的缩写。英国石油是一家大型全球石油天然气公司，行业排名仅次于埃克森美孚和荷兰皇家壳牌集团。

BP在全球30多个国家拥有业务，已探明石油储量为181亿桶。它在全球拥有22,400加油站，产品销向80多个国家。

BP由威廉·诺克斯·达西创立，最初的名字为Anglo Persian石油公司。1935年改为英（国）伊（朗）石油公司，1954年改为英国石油。1998年在收购阿莫科公司后再次更名为英国石油阿莫科公司。

BP是一家综合性的石油天然气公司，业务主要分为三部分：上游业务、下游业务和石油化学产品的开发。上游业务主要为石油勘探和开发。下游业务有炼油（现拥有23家炼油厂）、运输、营销和销售。在石油化学产品的开发部分，BP提取石油中用于制造其他产品，如包装、化妆品之类的化学产品。BP在

producing aethylenum and polyethylene and produces 10% of them for Western Europe, ranking the second in production capacity.

BP expended its business to China since 1973 and is one of the first investors and also a leading foreign investor in China and actively participated in promoting China's economy.

BP suffered from a huge financial loss and severe criticisms in 2010 as one of its deepwater rigs exploded on 20 April 2010 in the Gulf of Mexico and killed 11 workers. The explosion resulted in the biggest accidental marine oil spill in the history of the petroleum industry. Following the oil spill, BP's stock fell by 52% in 50 days and the total cost of the spill was predicted to be surpassing $100 billion.

乙烯、聚乙烯和醋酸的工艺技术和生产方面有专长。其公司的乙烯、聚乙烯生产能力各占整个西欧的10%，居欧洲第二位。

BP在中国的发展开始于1973年，是中国最早的外资企业之一。它积极地参与并推动了中国经济的发展。

2010年4月20日BP的墨西哥湾深水地平线钻井平台爆炸事件使其在经济和声誉方面都遭受了巨大的损失，爆炸造成11名作业工人死亡。这是迄今为止石油行业发生的最严重的海上漏油事件。事件发生后，BP股票50天内下跌52%，据估计，此次漏油事件将会造成BP1000亿美元的损失。

词汇 VOCABULARY

1. abbreviation [ə,bri:vi'eiʃən]
   n 缩写；缩写词

2. integrated ['intigreitid]
   a 综合的；完整的；互相协调的
   v 整合；使…成整体（integrate的过去分词）

3. petrochemical [,petrəu'kemikəl]
   a 石化的 *n* 石油化学产品

4. refinery [ri'fainəri]
   n 精炼厂；提炼厂；冶炼厂

5. ethene ['eθi:n]
   n 乙烯

6. polyethylene [,pɔli'eθili:n]
   n 聚乙烯

7. gulf [gʌlf]
   n 海湾；深渊；漩涡；分歧 *v* 吞没

背景链接 TIPS

英国石油公司工作服万圣节热销

2010年英国石油公司工程师的一套溅满油污的连衫裤工作服成为美国最热销的万圣节服饰之一。制造商称，工作服热销表明民众仍对这家石油巨头早些时候对"深海地平线"漏油事故的处理耿耿于怀。2010年4月，英国石油公司一个钻井平台爆炸，导致11名工人丧生，据估计另有1.85亿加仑原油泄露进墨西哥湾。制造商承诺将把公司制作工作服的部分收益捐献给一家慈善团体，该团体旨在帮助漏油事故的受害者。

Unit 7 媒体

British media is an inevitable part in British people's daily life. Over 97% of British households own a TV set and everyone has a radio to listen to the programmes.

The most popular TV programmes for the British people are daily News, TV shows, and weather reports. Due to the limitation in the number of TV channels, people often watch the same programmes in the same channel. Therefore, conversations between colleagues, friends and family members are often about the recent popular programmes or TV shows. Anyone who doesn't watch TV might cut himself off from the conversations or even from the latest British popular culture. The British Broadcasting Corporation is a major public service broadcaster in Britain. Originally, BBC had only 2 TV channels and 3 Radio programmes specializing in different types of programmes. Nowadays, BBC has become a multimedia business with a wide range of services providing all over the world.

Besides broadcasting media, newspaper is another important media form. Britain has one of the worlds' oldest established newspaper industries. There are more than 1400 different newspapers to satisfy different needs of different groups of people. There are "quality press" publishing serious political and social issues; there are also "the tabloids" that print the gossip and scandals of famous people.

The British media also has a magic power in bringing the whole country together. By turning on TV or picking up newspapers, British people in different parts of the country can have the same experience to remind them that they are all parts of the same culture and the same country!

媒体是英国人日常生活不可或缺的一部分。超过97%的英国家庭拥有电视机，基本上每个英国人都有一个收听电台节目的收音机。

在英国最受欢迎的电视节目包括新闻、电视剧和天气预报。由于电视节目频道较少，人们通常会同时收看同一个频道的同一个节目。因此，同事、朋友和家人之间的话题经常都是最近人气较高的电视节目。可以说，如果谁不看电视就是把自己隔绝在聊天之外，甚至隔绝在英国流行文化之外。英国广播电台是英国最主要的公共服务广播公司。在成立之初，BBC只有2个电视频道和3个广播频道。每个频道的侧重点和收看或收听对象都不同。如今，BBC已经成为一个综合性媒体，为全球各地提供广泛的服务。

除了广播媒体，报纸在英国也是一种非常重要的媒体类型。英国拥有全世界最古老的报纸行业。英国的报纸种类多达1400种，可以满足不同阅读群体的不同需求。"质报"侧重于报道重大政治社会事件；而"小报"热衷于报道各种花边新闻和名人的丑闻。

在英国，媒体有增加国家凝聚力的神奇魔力。只要打开电视或翻开报纸，不同地区的英国人能够拥有相同的体验，进而产生共同的感受。这些体验与感受时刻提醒每一个英国人，他们都是英国人，感受着相同的文化！

026 The British Broadcasting Corporation

The British Broadcast Corporation, or more familiarly known as BBC, is one of the biggest broadcast media in the world and the biggest in Britain. It has long been regarded as one of the most respectable broadcasting media all over the world.

BBC was founded in 1927 as a public service radio station and later moved into TV area. Before the founding of the Independent Television in 1955 and the Independent Radio Station in 1973, BBC was the only TV and radio company in Britain. It dominated the British TV and radio industry for quite a long time. Presently, BBC becomes a comprehensive corporation providing a wide range of other services, such as book publication, periodicals, English teaching, Internet news service and etc.

BBC is governed by a state-appointed board. However, once the board is appointed, it has complete freedom to operate without any interference from the government. The independent operation is guaranteed by the Royal Charter of Incorporation. The BBC board is consists of 12 members, known as the BBC Trust to make strategies and supervise the work of the BBC Executive Board that is responsible for delivering services.

Traditionally, the BBC has four separate radio channels and two television channels with each channel broadcasting

【小译】
英国广播公司也叫BBC，是英国最大的广播媒体，也是全球最大的广播媒体之一。长期以来，BBC被誉为全球最权威的广播媒体之一。

BBC成立于1927年。最初是一个公共服务电台，后来进军影视业。在1955年独立电视台与1973年独立电台成立之前，BBC是英国唯一一家广播电视公司，主宰着整个英国的电视和电台行业。现如今，BBC已经成为一个提供广泛服务的综合性公司，其他服务包括图书出版服务、杂志服务、英语教学服务及网络新闻服务。

BBC由国家任命的委员会管理。然而，委员会一旦成立了，就可以独立于政府之外而不受到政府的任何干涉。这一独立性受到皇家特许状的保障。BBC委员会，也叫英国广播公司信托，由12名委员组成，主要行使决策并监督BBC行政委员会的工作。BBC行政委员会负责提供服务。

传统的BBC只有4个电台频道和2个电视频道。每个频道的节目侧重点都不同。第1电台播放流行音乐，第2电台广播轻音乐和喜剧，第3电台侧重于严肃音乐和严肃话题。BBC电视台BBC1主要播放有广泛关注度的节目而BBC2侧重于满足部分特

different programme. Radio 1 broadcasts pop music and Radio 2 light music and comedy. Radio 3 provides serious music and serious topic. BBC television channel BBC1 specializes in shows with broad appeal while BBC2 favors those audiences with special interests such as senior and handicapped people and so on.

The fund of BBC comes from license fee. Every family who owns a TV should pay a yearly license fee except for the senior and a few low-income families. The amount of fee is decided by the government and is enforced by the criminal law. Since the BBC is funded by license fees, there are normally no commercials in BBC channels and thus BBC represents the public interest instead of pursuing commercial ends. Besides, BBC is impartial in reporting political news and doesn't favor any particular political party. Consequently, BBC is considered the most unbiased media in the UK and even in the world. There is a wide-spread saying in Britain that the British may not believe the words of British politicians, but they do believe what BBC says.

殊群体的兴趣，比如老年人、残疾人等。

BBC最主要的资金来源是执照费。除了老年人和部分低收入家庭，其他所有拥有电视的家庭都需要每年支付收看费用。费用的多少由政府规定，费用的收取受到刑法的保护。由于BBC的经费来源于执照费，BBC通常都没有广告。因此，BBC不追求商业利益，而是代表公众的利益。BBC在报道政治新闻时保持中立态度，也不会向任何政党靠拢。也正因如此，BBC被认为是英国乃至世界上最公正的媒体。在英国有一种说法：英国人可能不相信英国政治家的言论，但肯定会相信BBC的言论。

词汇 VOCABULARY

1. dominate ['dɔmineit]
   v 支配；控制 vi 处于支配地位；占优势

2. interference [ˌintə'fiərəns]
   n 干涉；干扰，冲突

3. guarantee [ˌgærən'ti:]
   n 保证书；抵押品；保证人 vt 保证；担保

4. specialize ['speʃəlaiz]
   vi 专门从事；详细说明 vt 使专门化

5. license ['laisəns]
   n 执照，许可证；特许 vt 发许可证给

6. impartial [im'pɑ:ʃəl]
   a 不偏不倚的；公平的，公正的

背景链接 TIPS

Independent Television

英国独立电视台，英文缩写ITV。1955年正式开台，是英国最早的商业电视台，也是英国最大的综合电视台之一。它覆盖英国全境，是BBC（英国广播公司）最大的竞争对手。最早为3个频道。现在扩展为6个频道：ITV1、ITV2、ITV3、ITV4、CITV以及"ITV数码频道和ITV游戏频道"等等。在初期，独立电视是由15个营运商组成，有独立的台徽和标志。但是，到2003年为止，只有4个营运商能维持独立的台徽和标志。其他11个营运商已经与"独立电视有限公司"（ITV plc.）合并，成为独立电视第一台（ITV1）。

027 Reuter's News Agency

Reuters News Agency, the oldest News Agency in Britain, is one of the four biggest News Agencies in the world that was founded by Paul Julius Reuter in 1850. It was first founded in Germany and then moved to London the following year. Reuter himself was naturalized as a British subject in 1857.

Reuter News Agency is part of the Reuters Group Limited (or Reuters) and covers 5% of the Reuters' services. Reuter News Agency has been famous for its fastest speed in reporting news scooping from all over the world. Most major events in the world are firstly covered by Reuter News Agency. For example, Reuter News Agency was the first in reporting the assassination of Present Abraham Lincoln in 1865. Its immediacy in reporting world news is a result of the worldwide operation which is now operating in 200 cities in 94 countries in around 20 languages. Besides, Reuter employs several thousand journalists, sometimes at the cost of their lives.

【小译】

保罗·朱利叶斯·路透创办于1859年的路透社是英国最早出现的通讯社，也是全球四大通讯社之一。创办之初的路透社总部位于德国并在次年迁至伦敦。路透本人也于1857年加入英国国籍。

路透社作为路透集团的一部分，占该集团5%的业务比例。长久以来，路透社因其最快的报道速度驰名于世。大部分全球重大事件都是首先由路透社报道的。例如，1865年林肯总统遭遇刺杀的最早的新闻就是出于路透社之手。路透社之所以能够如此及时有效地进行报道，首先要归功于它的全球性的宏观运作。如今，路透社分布于全世界94个国家的200多个城市里，报道语言多达20种。其次，路透社记者团队人数多达几千，有的甚

The Board of directors of Reuter News Agency is consists of 1 chief executive, 2 executive directors and 8 non-executive directors. Every half of a year, the board members hold a meeting to discuss the financial and managing issues of the Agency. The daily administration is taken charge by the executive committee which contains 1 general manager, 2 vice-general managers, 2 assistant vice-general managers as well as 1 chief editor. The chief editor presides over the news work.

In order to preserve the objective reporting tradition, Reuters made a rule that no individual was allowed to possess over 15% of the company share and the rule has been working for many years until 2007 when Canada's The Thomson Corporation merged with Reuters at $17.2 billion. Thereafter, the company was renamed as Thomson Reuters with Thomson controlling about 53% of the company and the acquisition was closed in 17 April 2008.

至为了报道搭上了性命。

路透社采用董事会管理的形式。董事会由1名董事长、2名常务董事和8名非执行董事构成。董事会议每半年一次，会上讨论路透社经济、管理等方面的问题。执行委员会负责日常的行政管理。日常管理由执行委员会进行，其成员包括1名总经理、2名副总经理、2名总经理助理和一名总编辑。总编辑负责日常的新闻工作。

在路透集团有一条规定，那就是任何个人持有的公司股份不得超过15%，以此来维护路透社公正的报道传统。但这条规定终止于2007年。从2007年开始，加拿大汤姆森公司以172亿美元的价格收购了路透集团。合并后公司易称汤姆森路透。汤姆森集团成为该公司最大的股东，持有53%的股份。合并于2008年04月18日正式结束。

词汇 VOCABULARY

1. naturalize ['nætʃərəlaiz]
   vt 移植；使入国籍；采纳 vi 归化；加入国籍

2. assassination [əˌsæsi'neiʃən]
   n 暗杀，行刺

3. immediacy [i'mi:diəsi]
   n 直接；目前；快速

4. preside [pri'zaid]
   vi 主持，担任会议主席 vt 管理

5. merge [mə:dʒ]
   vt 合并；吞没；使合并 vi 合并；融合

6. acquisition [ˌækwi'ziʃən]
   n 获得物，获得

背景链接 TIPS

Three types of News in Reuter

路透社的消息大致有特急快讯、急电和普通电讯三种。这三种电讯的时效按顺序递减，篇幅按顺序递增。特急快讯主要针对商业用户，快讯主要适用于政府机关及电子媒介订户，普通电讯则主要服务于其他新闻媒介订户。特急快讯是路透社播发新闻的一种形式。它可以中断正常的广播优先发出。路透社的特急快讯并不局限于特别重大的国际事件，还包括一切对各类交易市场可能产生重大影响的新闻。

028 The Times

Britain has the oldest newspaper industry in the world and one of the most influential newspapers in Britain and even in the world is The Times, a newspaper that has a long history of 226 years.

Founded by John Walter on January 1, 1785, The Times was originally named The Daily Universal Register. The present name was changed into 3 years after 940 editions on 1 January 1788. Nowadays, there are many newspapers around the world bear the name "Times" such as The New York Times, The Los Angeles Times, The Seattle Times all of which inherit this name from The Times. In fact, in order to distinguish it from other newspapers, The Times is sometimes referred to as "The London Times" or "The Times of London" since its headquarter lies in London. Apart from its huge influence on the naming of newspapers, we should also pay tribute to The Times when using the Times Roman typeface because The Times is also the originator of this typeface.

In its long history of development, the owners of The Times have changed several times. Before 1908, the Walter family ran The Times and made great reputation for the newspaper in not only Britain but also the Europe. It was John Walter Sr., the son of John Walter who brought the newspaper into the first summit. The Times had great

【小译】

英国有全球最古老的报业。英国的《泰晤士报》是全英乃至全世界最有影响力的报纸之一。这份报纸历史悠久，现在已经有超过220年的历史了。

《泰晤士报》由约翰·沃尔特创办于1785年1月1日。创刊之初的名称是《世鉴日报》。《泰晤士报》这个名字是在报纸发行了3年共计940期后的1788年1月1日更改的。当今世界的很多报纸名称都带有时报（Times）这个单词，比如《纽约时报》（New York Times）、《洛杉矶时报》（The Los Angeles Times）和《西雅图时报》（The Seattle Times）等，所有这些Times都来源于《泰晤士报》（The Times）。有时，为了与其他的时报加以区别，《泰晤士报》也被叫做《伦敦时报》（The London Times）因为它的总部设在伦敦。除此之外，我们还应该感谢《泰晤士报》，因为我们经常使用的Times New Roman字体就是来源于该报。

在其悠久的发展历史上，《泰晤士报》屡次易主。1908年之前的《泰晤士报》为沃尔特家族所有，该家族不仅奠定了该报在英国的声誉，也使其在欧洲颇有名气。《泰晤士报》在约翰·沃尔特的儿子小约翰·沃尔特管理时期达到了第一个顶峰。《泰晤士报》在19世纪的很多重大事件中都发挥

influence in many major events of the 19th century, such as in 1815, it was the first newspaper to report Napoleon's defeat in Waterloo. Another example was during the American Civil War, it strongly opposed the slavery system.

In 1908, the newspaper magnate Alfred Harmsworth bought the ownership of The Times. During that time, the newspaper arrived at the second summit in its history of development. However, The Times faced its dark age under the running of the Astor family and Thomson Corporation. After Rupert Murdoch bought the Times in 1981, he introduced many changes into the newspaper including management, technology, style and etc.

The format of The Times is divided into two parts with the first part focusing on news at home and abroad, comment, culture and art and book review and the second part on business, finance, sports, television and entertainment.

了重要的作用。它是第一个登载1815年拿破仑战败滑铁卢消息的报纸。另外，在美国内战期间，《泰晤士报》反对奴隶制的主张也产生了很大的影响。

1908年，报业大亨阿尔佛雷德·哈姆斯沃思购买了《泰晤士报》的所有权并迎来了该报纸第二个顶峰。然而，后继的阿斯特家族和汤姆森公司掌控时期的《泰晤士报》失去了往日耀眼的光彩。1981年鲁珀特·默多克收购了《泰晤士报》并进行了重大的调整。《泰晤士报》在管理、技术、风格等方面都发生了变化。

《泰晤士报》版面分为两部分，一部分是国内外新闻、评论、文艺和书籍评论，另一部分包括商业、金融、体育和电视娱乐内容。

词汇 VOCABULARY

1. distinguish [dis'tiŋgwiʃ]
   vt 辨别；区分；使杰出 vi 区别，区分；辨别

2. headquarter [,hed'kwɔːtə]
   vi [口]设立总部 vt 在…设总部

3. typeface ['taipfeis]
   n 字型，铅字样；打字机字体

4. summit ['sʌmit]
   n 顶点；最高级会议 a 最高级的；政府首脑的

5. defeat [di'fiːt]
   vi 失败；战胜 vt 击败，使…失败；挫败

背景链接 TIPS

1. Name of The Times

《泰晤士报》的英文名称The Times，中文直译过来应该是《时报》。然而它的译名却变成与读音相近、但毫无关联的"泰晤士河"（River Thames）一样。由于约定俗成的关系，错译保留至今。《泰晤士报》是世界上第一张以"Times"命名的报纸。现今世界各地有许多名为Times的报章，如《纽约时报》（The New York Times）等。

2. Feature of The Times

《泰晤士报》一直秉承"独立地、客观地报道事实"、"报道发展中的历史"的宗旨，但纵观其200多年的历史，可见该报的政治倾向基本上是保守的，在历史上历次重大国内及国际事务上支持英国政府的观点。

Unit 8 汽车业

The automotive industry in the United Kingdom has given birth to many world renowned premium and sports car marques including Aston Martin, Bentley, Daimler, Jaguar, Lagonda, Land Rover, Lotus, McLaren, MG, Morgan and Rolls-Royce.

In 2008 the UK automotive manufacturing sector had a turnover of £52.5 billion, generated £26.6 billion of exports and produced around 1.45 million passenger vehicles and 203,000 commercial vehicles. In that year around 180,000 people were directly employed in automotive manufacturing in the UK, with a further 640,000 people employed in automotive supply, retail and servicing.

The origins of the UK automotive industry date back to the final years of the 19th century. By the 1950s the UK was the second-largest manufacturer of cars in the world (after the United States) and the largest exporter. However in subsequent decades the industry experienced considerably lower growth than competitor nations such as France, Germany and Japan and by 2008 the UK was the 12th-largest producer of cars measured by volume. Since the late 1980s many British car marques have become owned by foreign companies including BMW, SAIC, TATA and Volkswagen Group. Rights to many currently dormant brands, including Austen, Riley, Rover and Triumph, are also owned by foreign companies.

英国的汽车业产生了许多世界闻名的高档汽车品牌与跑车品牌，包括阿斯顿·马丁、宾利、戴姆勒、捷豹、拉贡达、美洲豹、陆虎、莲花、麦克拉伦、MG、摩根、劳斯莱斯等。

2008年，英国汽车制造业营业额达525亿英磅，创造266亿英磅出口额，生产了145万辆客车，203,000辆商务车。同年英国汽车业制造业雇佣约18万人，此外还有64万人从事汽车供应、零售与售后行业。

英国汽车业的源头可以追溯到19世纪。到20世纪50年代英国是世界第二大汽车生产国家（美国位列第一），也是世界上最大的汽车出口国。然后在接下来的几十年里，英国汽车业一度低迷，而法国、德国、日本等国的汽车业却后来居上，如日中天。到2008年，按生产量算，英国已经沦落为世界第十二大汽车生产国。从20世纪80年代后期起，许多英国汽车品牌被诸如宝马、上汽、塔塔、大众等外国厂商收购。而许多当前停产的品牌，如奥斯丁、莱利、罗孚和胜利等，其所有权也掌握在外国公司手中。

|029 Rolls-Royce Motor Cars

Rolls-Royce Motor Cars is a global organization, designing and manufacturing luxury automobiles of the highest automobiles, based in the UK. The predecessor of Rolls-Royce Motors was the Rolls-Royce car business, which was demerged from Rolls-Royce Limited in 1973. Due to the financial collapse of the company, the original Rolls-Royce Limited had been nationalized in 1971. In 1973, the British government sold the Rolls-Royce car business to allow Rolls-Royce Limited to concentrate on jet engine manufacture. Since 2003, Rolls-Royce Motor has become a wholly owned subsidiary of the BMW Group.

Rolls-Royce Limited was created over a famous lunch brokered by Henry Edmunds at the Midland Hotel in Manchester on 4 May 1904. Edmunds brought together Henry Royce, a successful engineer and Charles Rolls, the owner of one of the first car dealerships. The meeting led to an agreement that Rolls would exclusively sell as many cars as Royce could produce. By 1907 Royce had created the first Silver Ghost, a car of legendary smoothness that completed a 14,371-mile virtually non-stop run that led a journalist to call it 'the best car in the world'.

The headquarter and manufacturing plant of Rolls-Royce Motor is now based at the Goodwood in West Sussex, England. Creating a spiritual home for Rolls-Royce Motor Cars for the 21st Century meant more than just designing a building to house the headquarters and manufacturing plant. The designer of the building was exerted to make it a symbol of Rolls-Royce's innovative approach – unique, forward-

【小译】

劳斯莱斯汽车公司是一家国际性组织，专门设计和制造高级汽车中的豪华车，总部设在英国。劳斯莱斯汽车公司的前身是劳斯莱斯汽车商业集团，于1973年并入劳斯莱斯有限公司。由于公司的金融危机，原先的劳斯莱斯有限公司于1971年被收归国有。1973年，英国政府出售了劳斯莱斯，使劳斯莱斯公司能专注于航空引擎制造。自2003年起，劳斯莱斯汽车公司完全成为宝马集团的子公司。

劳斯莱斯有限公司的成立得益于一次由中间人亨利·埃德蒙安排的著名的午餐。1904年5月4日在曼彻斯特的米德兰酒店，埃德蒙让成功的工程师亨利·罗伊斯和第一个汽车代理商查尔斯·罗尔斯走到了一起。在这次会面上他们达成了一份协议，由罗伊斯负责制造汽车，而罗尔斯负责独家销售。1907年，罗伊斯制造出了第一辆银色幽灵，它以传说般的流线型设计以及实测14371公里不间断行驶让记者将其称之为"世界上最好的汽车"。

目前劳斯莱斯公司的总部和制造设备设在英格兰西萨塞克斯郡西部的古德伍德。对于建筑师而言，他们不仅仅是要为其总部和制造设备设计一座建筑，更重要的是要为劳斯莱斯汽车公司创造一个面向21世纪的精神家园。建筑设计者们致力于使这座建筑成为劳斯莱斯

ENTERPRISES

thinking. From the outside, you get a tantalizing view of the assembly line through the 'Glass Mile' that runs the length of the building. The interior is naturally-lit from above, giving the assembly line and craft shops a studio-like atmosphere.

Stepping into the 21 century, Rolls-Royce still aims to develop and build the most technologically advanced cars and has invested heavily in labor forces and facilities hoping to develop new models that will continue to make the company's reputation. "'Rolls-Royce' has been a motoring icon for over 100 years. Our task is to ensure it continues to set the pace into the next century." said Torsten Muller-Otvos, present CEO of Rolls-Royce Motor Cars.

创新方法的标志——独一无二的、高瞻远瞩的思维。在外面，你可以透过建筑表层的透明玻璃看到里面流水线的壮观景象。大厦的内里由太阳光线自然照亮，赋予生产线和车间一种摄影棚般的气氛。

迈入21世纪，劳斯莱斯仍然以发展和制造最具技术含量的汽车为目标，在劳动力和设备上投入巨额资金，以期开发出新的模型来继续保持公司的声誉。"劳斯莱斯已是一个有着百年历史的汽车商标。我们的任务就是确保它能在新世纪长盛不衰。"劳斯莱斯汽车公司执行总裁托斯顿·穆勒·奥塔沃斯这样说道。

词汇 VOCABULARY

1. collapse [kə'læps] *n* 倒塌；崩溃 *vi* 垮掉 *vt* 使倒塌；使崩溃	2. subsidiary [səb'sidjəri] *n* 子公司 *a* 隶属的，附设的
3. broker ['brəukə] *n* 经纪人，代理人 *vt* 作为权力经纪人进行谈判 *vt* 以中间人等身份安排…	4. dealership ['di:ləʃip] *n* 代理商
5. exclusively [ik'sklu:sivli] *ad* 专门地；专有地	6. legendary ['ledʒəndəri] *n* 传说集；圣徒传 *a* 传说的，传奇的
7. tantalizing ['tæntəlaiziŋ] *a* 逗人的；惹弄人的；撩人的	

背景链接 TIPS

1. Rolls-Royce Limited—劳斯莱斯汽车有限公司是由亨利·莱斯（F·Henry Royce）和贵族查理·劳斯（C·Rolls）在1906年合作创建的，现为宝马旗下子公司，以生产豪华汽车闻名全球。

2. BMW Group—宝马集团，始创于1916年，总部位于德国慕尼黑，在全球12个国家拥有22个生产和组装厂，员工总数达10.6万人。当今世界最成功和效益最好的高档汽车及摩托车生产商。

3. Goodwood—古德伍德，位于英国西萨塞克斯郡的一个特色小镇，在这里有全世界最富盛名、规模最大的赛车节古德伍德赛车节。同时古德伍德速度节（Goodwood Festival of Speed）也是汽车发烧友的圣地。

030 Lotus Cars

Lotus Cars is a British manufacturer of sports and racing cars based at the former site of RAF (Royal Air Force) in Hethel, a World War II airfield in Norfolk. The company is famous for its design and production of race cars as well as automobiles of light weight and fine handling characteristics.

The company was initially founded as Lotus Engineering Ltd. by engineer Colin Chapman, a graduate of University College, London, in 1952. In the beginning the factory was located in old stables behind the Railway Hotel in North London. Team Lotus was active and competitive in Formula One racing from 1958 to 1994. The Lotus Group of Companies was formed in 1959, comprising Lotus Cars Limited and Lotus Components Limited with the former focused on road cars and the latter on customer competition car production. Since 1966 the company has owned a modern factory and road test facility at Hethel.

Chapman died of a heart attack in 1982 at the age of 54, having begun life an innkeeper's son and ended

【小译】

莲花汽车是一家英国跑车与赛车制造商，其基地位于英国海塞尔，该地也曾是英国皇家空军二战时在诺福克的军用机场所在地。该公司因设计与制造划时代的赛车与生产极度轻量和拥有传奇性操控特色的汽车而著名。

该公司由英国伦敦大学毕业的工程师科林·查普曼于1952年创立，起先为莲花工程有限公司。创立初期，该公司的工厂是一些在伦敦北部的铁道酒店后面的残旧马厩。莲花车队于1958年至1994年在一级方程比赛上表现甚为活跃，竞争力也较强。1959年，莲花集团公司成立，分为莲花汽车有限公司与莲花部件有限公司两部分，其中前者主要专注于公路汽车的生产，后者专注于赛车。自从1966年起莲花开始使用海塞尔的现代工厂与道路测试设备。

ENTERPRISES

a multi-millionaire industrialist in post-war Britain. The car maker built tens of thousands of successful racing and road cars and won the Formula One World Championship seven times.

In 1986, the company was bought by General Motors and in 1993 it was sold by GM for 30 million pound to A.C.B.N. Holdings S.A. of Luxembourg, a company controlled by Italian businessman Romano Artioli. In 1996, a majority share in Lotus was sold to Proton, a Malaysian car company listed on the Kuala Lumpur Stock Exchange.

The company also acts as an engineering consultancy, providing engineering development— particularly of suspension—for other car manufacturers. In 2005 Proton organized the company as Group Lotus, which is divided into Lotus Cars and Lotus Engineering.

查普曼在1982年死于心脏病，享年54岁，从一个旅馆看门人的儿子到死亡时成为一个在战后英国拥有数百万身家的实业家。他制造了无数成功的赛车和汽车，曾在一级方程式世界锦标赛上获得七次胜利。

1986年该公司被通用汽车收购。而1993年通用汽车又以3000万英磅的价格将其出售给卢森堡的A.C.B.N. 控股有限公司.，一家由意大利商人罗马诺·阿蒂奥里控制的公司。1996年大部分莲花的股份出售给宝腾——一家在吉隆坡证券交易所上市的马来西亚汽车公司。

莲花汽车公司也提供工程顾问服务，为其他汽车公司提供工程开发，尤其是悬吊系统开发。2005年马来西亚宝腾公司将莲花组织为莲花集团，将莲花汽车和莲花工程分离。

词汇 VOCABULARY

1.	airfield ['eəfi:ld] n.飞机场，机场（尤指机场的降陆场）	2.	Norfolk ['nɔ:fək] n.诺福克（英格兰东部的郡名）
3.	innkeeper ['inki:pə(r)] n.客栈老板；旅馆主人	4.	industrialist [in'dʌstriəlist] n.实业家；工业家；产业工人
5.	Luxembourg ['luksəm,bə:g] n.卢森堡（西欧大公国）	6.	Malaysian [mə'leiziən] n.马来西亚人（等于Malay）adj.马来西亚的
7.	Kuala Lumpur ['kwɑ:lə 'lumpuə] n.吉隆坡（马来西亚首都）	8.	consultancy [kən'sʌltənsi] n.咨询公司；顾问工作
9.	suspension [səs'penʃən] n.悬浮；暂停；停职			

背景链接 TIPS

Formula One

一级方程式赛车是世界上成本最高、技术等级最顶尖的单座四轮赛车比赛。全名是"一级方程式锦标赛"，主办者是国际汽车联盟（FIA）。F1被很多人认为是赛车界最重要的赛事，同时也是最昂贵的体育运动。F1每年会举办一系列的比赛。

031 MG Rover Group

MG Rover group was established when BMW sold car-making and engine manufacturing assets of the original Rover Group to the Phoenix Consortium in 2000. After the sales, BMW retained ownership of the Rover marque, allowing MG Rover to use it under license. Both Rover and MG has once been a renowned marque in British automobile industry with a long history. MG used to be favored by many prominent British political figures like Winston Churchill, Margaret Thatcher. Queen Elizabeth II also selected MG as her private ride.

MG Rover took control of the remainder of the former Rover Group volume car business, which was consolidated at the Longbridge plant in Birminham. The first new Rover-branded car to be launched after the formation of MG Rover was the estate version of the Rover 75, which went on sale later in 2000. In 2003, MG Rover launched the CityRover, a badge-engineered Tata Indica that served as an entry-level model. Despite high initial expectations, sales were

【小译】

名爵（MG）罗孚集团于2000年由凤凰财团成立，当时宝马汽车公司将属于罗孚集团的汽车与引擎生产资产卖给了凤凰财团。出售之后，宝马依然拥有罗孚商标的所有权，允许名爵罗孚在许可下使用。历史悠久的罗孚曾是英国名噪一时的汽车品牌。MG品牌受到许多政界名流的喜爱，如温斯顿·邱吉尔、玛格丽特·撒切尔。英国女王伊丽莎白二世也选择MG作为自己的私人驾乘。

名爵罗孚集团主要掌控前罗孚集团的批量汽车生产业务，工厂设在伯明翰的长桥。名爵罗孚集团组建之后发行的第一款罗孚牌汽车是旅行车型的罗孚75，于2000年上市。2003年，名爵罗孚集团又通过换牌工程发行了CityRover，以塔塔集团印迪卡轿车为雏形。尽管该车型被寄予厚望，但是

ENTERPRISES

poor. On 15 April 2005, MG Rover production ceased when it was declared insolvent. On 22 July 2005, the physical assets of the collapsed firm were sold to the Nanjing Automobile Group for 53 million pound. On 30 May 2007, Nanjing Automobile Group claimed to have restarted production of MG TF sports cars in the Longbridge plant, the best-selling sports car in British history.

Shanghai Automotive Industry Corporation (SAIC) who bought the intellectual property of Rover 75 car design for 67 million pound before MG Rover collapsed and was also bidding for MG Rover, announced their own version of the Rover 75 in late 2006. In July 2006, SAIC announced their intent to buy the Rover brand name from BMW, who still owned the rights to the Rover marque. However, BMW refused their request. Unable to use the Rover name, SAIC created their own brand with a similar name and badge, known as Roewe. In early 2007, Roewe was eventually launched.

销售量却不尽如人意。2005年4月15日,名爵罗孚集团宣布破产,停止生产。同年6月22日,该公司的实体资产也被南京汽车集团以5300万英磅收购。2007年5月30日,南汽集团宣布英国历史上最畅销的跑车——MG TF跑车在英国长桥工厂重新投入生产。

上汽集团在名爵破产之前以6700万英磅的高价购买了Rover 75的知识产权,并且也竞标收购名爵罗孚集团,宣布于2006年下半年发行新版本的Rover 75。2006年6月,上汽宣布他们打算从宝马处购买罗孚商标,但是遭到了宝马的拒绝。由于无法使用罗孚商标,上汽创建了一个名字与商标相似的品牌——荣威。2007年上半年,荣威终于成功面市。

词汇 VOCABULARY

1. asset ['æset] *n* 资产;优点;有用的东西;有利条件	2. marque [mɑːk] *n* 商品型号
3. remainder [ri'meində] *n* [数] 余数,残余 *a* 剩余的;吃剩的	4. consolidate [kən'sɔlideit] *vt* 巩固,使固定;联合 *vi* 巩固,加强
5. insolvent [in'sɔlvənt] *n* 破产者;无力偿还者 *a* 破产的;无力偿还的	

背景链接 TIPS

1. Winston Churchill

温斯顿·丘吉尔,政治家、画家、演说家、作家以及记者,1953年诺贝尔文学奖得主,曾于1940~1945年及1951~1955年期间两度任英国首相,被认为是20世纪最重要的政治领袖之一,带领英国获得第二次世界大战的胜利。

2. Tata Indica

印迪卡是第一辆印度塔塔汽车公司自己设计并生产的轿车,塔塔汽车公司凭借这款车和其他型号的车成为印度最主要的汽车制造商之一。

Unit 9 饮食业

The food and drink industry in the UK have been increasingly dominated by the domestic suppliers since the 1940s. The main business revolves around bread, cakes and preservation and processing of fruits. Food processing is chiefly located in Yorkshire, South-East England and London while beverage and soft drink are manufactured in Scotland and North England. Beverage accounts for the largest proportion of exports, the equivalent of one-third, followed by biscuits and sweets. The food and drink industry accounts for 15% of the UK's total manufacturing sector by value; and it is an invaluable partner to British agriculture buying two-thirds of what farmers produce.

The Food and Drink Federation (FDF) is a membership organization that represents and advises UK food and drink manufacturers. Its members are companies of all sizes as well as trade associations and groups dealing with specific sectors of the industry. The Federation tackles a range of issues on behalf of its members under the three core areas, namely health and wellbeing, food safety and science, sustainability and competitiveness. Product reformulation has also been another major focus for the Federation, highlighting the industry's ongoing work to reduce salt, trans fats, fat and sugar in food products.

Major food manufacturers in the UK include Premier Foods, Associated British Foods, Northern Foods, Unilever. In this chapter, we will mainly focus on the manufacturer that is closest to our Chinese consumers – Unilever, a large transnational company that owns many of the world's consumer product brands in foods, beverages, cleaning agents and personal care products.

自从二十世纪四十年代起，英国的餐饮业开始逐渐被国内供应商主导。主要产业包括面包、糕点、水果贮存与加工。食品加工点主要集中在约克郡、英格兰东南部与伦敦。而饮料则主要由苏格兰和英格兰北部。饮料占英国食品出口的1/3，位列第一，饼干与糖果次之。饮食业创造的价值占英国制造业总价值的15%。同时英国的饮食业也是农业非常重要的合作伙伴，购买了2/3的农业产品。

饮食联合会（英国）是代表并劝诫英国饮食生产商的会员组织。其成员包括不同规模的公司、贸易协会与组织，它们负责英国饮食业的不同部门。联合会代表其成员处理一系列的事务，主要分为三大核心领域，即健康福利领域、食品安全科技领域以及可持续发展与竞争力部门。产品重新配方也是饮食联合会的主要焦点，重点关注饮食业的食品与饮料中有关降低盐、反式脂肪、脂肪与糖含量的工作进展如何。

英国主要的食品生产商包括第一食品公司、英国联合食品公司、北方食品公司与联合利华公司。在这一章，我们将主要介绍与我们中国消费者关系最为密切的生产商——联合利华。联合利华是一个大型的跨国企业，拥有许多世界性的消费品品牌，除了食品、饮料，还有清洁用品，个人护理用品。

032 Unilever Global Companies

Unilever is a British-Dutch multinational corporation that owns many of the world's consumer product brands largely falling into two categories: Food and Beverages and Home and Personal Care. It has two headquarters located in London, United Kingdom and Rotterdam, Netherlands. Consumers worldwide buy £170 billion Unilever products each year. In 2010, Unilever's worldwide turnover was £44.3 billion.

Unilever was founded on 1 January 1930 which was initially an amalgamation of the operations of British soap maker Lever Brothers and Dutch margarine producer Margarine Unie because palm oil was a major raw material for both margarines and soaps and could be imported more efficiently in larger quantities. After rapid development of about 80 years, Unilever products are now sold in more than 180 countries. More than 167,000 people work for Unilever and more than 50% of Unilever's business is in emerging markets with more than 50 years' experience of working in Brazil, China, India and Indonesia. In 2010, Unilever has launched more than 100 brands into new markets.

From long-established names like Lifebuoy, Sunlight and Pond's to new innovations such as the Pureit affordable water purifier, Unilever's range of brands is as diverse as its worldwide consumer base. Unilever owns more than 400 brands as a result of acquisitions. Each of the top 12 brands of the company enjoys annual sales of more than £1 billion, and the top 20 brands account for 70% of sales. Brands like Dove, Lux,

【小译】

联合利华是一家英国与荷兰合资经营的跨国企业，旗下拥有世界上众多的消费产品的品牌。这些品牌大致分为两类：食品和饮料，以及家庭和个人护理用品。公司有两个总部，分别位于英国的伦敦和荷兰的鹿特丹。每年全世界的消费者都要购买价值1700亿英镑的联合利华的产品，而2010年，联合利华的销售额高达443亿英镑。

联合利华是于1930年1月1日由英国的Lever兄弟香皂公司和荷兰Margarine Unie人造奶油公司合并而成的。当时这项合并主要是因为对于香皂和人造奶油来说，棕榈油都是主要的天然原料，而合并可以使得这种原料更有效率地大量进口。经过80多年的迅速发展，如今联合利华的产品已经畅销180多个国家。超过16.7万员工在为联合利华工作，而在联合利华所有拥有超过50年销售经验的经营项目中，已经有超过一半在诸如巴西、中国、印度和印尼这样的新兴的市场上崭露头角。2010年，联合利华向这些新市场投入了超过100个品牌。

从老字号的品牌爱肤宝、阳光和旁氏到新兴的品牌诸如Pureit水净化装置，联合利华的品牌总能满足全世界不同消费者的需求。联合利华已经拥有了超过400个品牌，其年销售额排在前12位的公司都突破了10亿英镑，而排在前20位的公司的销售额占到总销售的70%以上。像多芬、力士、旁氏和舒耐这样的品牌使得联合利华

Pond's and Rexona have made Unilever global leaders in the deodorant and skin care markets – where the sales grew 7.9% in 2010. Lipton's and Brooke Bond, Ben & Jerry's and Heartbrand are among the brands that have made Unilever global leaders in the ice cream and beverage markets – where volume grew 5.9% in 2010.

As for the logo of the company, obviously the big blue "U" stands for Unilever. But look a little closer and you'll see there's much more to it. The logo was designed to include 24 icons, each of which represents something important to Unilever. From a lock of hair symbolizing Unilever's shampoo brands to a spoon, an ice cream, a jar, a tea leaf, a hand and much more, each little icon has its own meaning.

2010年在清新剂和护肤品市场的销售额增长了7.9%，坐上了全球头把交椅。立顿和Brooke Bond，本杰里和Heartbrand等品牌使得联合利华在饮料和冰激凌市场全球领先——其市场占有率在2010年增长了5.9%。

公司的商标是一个蓝色的大大的U字，代表着联合利华英文的首字母。但是仔细观察，你会发现远不止如此。公司的商标中包含着24个小的图案，每一个都代表着一些对公司至关重要的东西。从一缕代表着公司的洗发水品牌的头发，到勺子、冰激凌、罐子、茶叶，手等等，每一个小图案都有它独特的含义。

词汇 VOCABULARY

1. beverage ['bevə rid3] n 饮料	2. amalgamation [ə,mælgə'meiʃ ən] n 合并，混合
3. margarine [mɑ:dʒə'ri:n, 'mɑ:gərin] n 人造黄油	4. emerging [i'mə:dʒiŋ] a （用作定语）新兴的
5. launch [lɔ:ntʃ, lɑ:ntʃ] n 发行；投放市场 v 开始；积极投入	6. purifier ['pjuərifaiə] n 清洁者，净化器
7. acquisition [,ækwi'ziʃ ən] n 获得，取得	8. deodorant [di:'əudərənt] n 除臭剂
9. volume ['vɔlju:m; (US) -jəm] n （生产，交易等的）量；额	

背景链接 TIPS

1. Pond's

旁氏1864年诞生于美国，是著名的化妆品品牌，1987年被联合利华收购。1988年，旁氏品牌和她的旗舰产品——冷霜一同进入中国。发展至今，旁氏拥有四大系列的产品：美白、抗衰老、基础护理和洁面乳系列。

2. Rexona

舒耐——全球No.1止汗香体品牌。含长效制汗爽身分子，能有效减少腋下汗水。四款淡雅香型，专为中国女人的特质设计，通过各种科学监测和临床实验，安全可靠。ph值亲肤性配方，温和不残留，适合各种肌肤使用。

ENTERPRISES

Unit 10 银行业

The Bank of England is the central bank of Britain. Founded in 1694, it is regarded as the originator of the all the other central banks in the world.

In Britain, there are two kinds of financial institutions, namely, the Recognized Banks and the Licensed Deposit Institutions. The Bank of England is the institution to decide which category a financial institute should belong judging from its size, management and the leadership.

The Recognized Banks are banks that are approved by the Bank of England in view of their trustworthiness, management as well as prudence before being having the accredit to provide highly specialized banking services such as accepting deposits, loan and overdraft, foreign currency exchange, investment management as well as providing financial advice for corporations and individuals and etc.

In contrast, Licensed Deposits institutions provide limited services. The first and foremost role is to accept public deposits. Their qualifications are also evaluated by the Bank of England before the authorizations are given. They are small-scale institutions.

There are basically three types of financial intermediaries in Britain. The Clearing Banks, the discount houses and merchant banks. The Clearing Banks are responsible for the clearing, cash distribution and money transaction. This type of bank includes Barclays Bank, Royal Bank of Scotland, Midland Bank and etc. The discount houses are unique creation of in Britain financial system. Discount houses are the medium for the Bank of England to implement its monetary policies and supervise the banks through discount and rediscount. Merchant banks provide service concerning trade and foreign trade, foreign exchanges.

In this part, four renowned banks in the UK will be introduced as a gateway to access to the banking system in Britain.

英格兰银行是英国的中央银行。它创立于1694年，是全世界公认的中央银行的鼻祖。

在英国有两种金融机构，认可银行和持牌存款银行。一个金融机构属于哪种类型由英格兰银行根据它的规模、管理和领导层来决定的。

认可银行是通过英格兰银行对其信用度、管理和审慎度的认可后被赋予提供高度专业性的银行业务，例如吸收存款、发放贷款和透支业务、外币汇率兑换、投资管理、为企业和个人提供金融建议。

与之相反，持牌存款银行提供较为有限的服务。首要的服务就是吸收公民存款。它们也是在接受英格兰银行的评估后给予授权的。通常这类银行是规模较小的银行机构。

英国有三种金融中介机构：清算银行、贴现商号和商人银行。清算银行负责提供结算、现金支出和转账等业务。该类银行包括巴克莱银行、苏格兰皇家银行、米德兰银行等。贴现商号是英国金融制度的独特产物。贴现商号是英格兰银行向其他银行贯彻货币政策和管制的媒介。这是通过贴现和再贴来实现的。商人银行主要经营贸易和国外贸易相关业务，还办理外汇交易业务。

该部分将介绍四个英国知名银行，作为了解英国银行体系的一种途径。

033 Standard Chartered Bank

Standard Chartered Bank, more familiarly known as Chartered Bank, is a London-based British bank founded in 1853. Standard Chartered PLC is listed on the London Stock Exchange and Hong Kong Exchange as well as Indian Stock Exchanges and is one of the three banks in Hong Kong that has the right to issue bank notes, the other two being Bank of China (Hong Kong) and The Hong Kong and Shanghai Banking Corporation Limited.

Standard Chartered Bank came to being through a merger between Standard Bank and Chartered Bank in 1969 and got its current name since then. Chartered Bank was founded by a Scottish man James Wilson in 1853 under a Royal Charter granted by Queen Victoria. The Standard Bank was established by another Scottish John Paterson in the Port Elizabeth of South Africa in 1862. Both banks developed business in Asia and Africa. The merger was executed with the aim to expand their network in Europe and USA.

With a history of over 150 years of banking, Chartered Bank has extended its business to many

【小译】

标准渣打银行,也被人们习惯地称为渣打银行,建于1853年、总部在伦敦。渣打银行在伦敦证券交易所和香港交易所、印度证券交易所上市,并且是香港的三家发钞银行之一。另外两家分别为中国银行（香港）和汇丰银行。

标准渣打银行是1969年在标准银行和渣打银行合并后形成的,现在的名称就是合并后取的。渣打银行由苏格兰人詹姆士·威尔森在维多利亚女皇的特许下于1853年成立。标准银行于1863年由另一个苏格兰人约翰·帕特森在南非伊丽莎白港建立。两家银行均在亚非洲扩展业务。合并的目的是为了共同开拓欧美市场。

标准渣打银行在其150多年的历史中不断开拓国外市场,并在全球50多个国家开办1700多个支行,雇佣职员达8万人之多,形成了庞大的全球

countries and has developed a global network with over 1700 branches in over 50 countries with around 80,000 employees all over the world. Chartered Bank put its emphasis on developing countries in areas like Asia Pacific Region, South Africa, the Middle East, Africa and Latin America. Consequently, Chartered Bank has a high reputation in developing countries and 90% of its profits come from developing countries while its native market Britain takes up a little percentage in its profit.

The services provided by Standard Chartered Bank include retail banking services like mortgage, investment, credit card service and private loan and business banking services as cash management, equity trading as well as custody and etc.

The first Standard Chartered Bank branch opened in China was in Shanghai in 1858 and thus made it the first foreign bank in China with the longest history. Up to now, Standard Chartered Bank has established branches in 15 Chinese cities and becomes the most wide-spread foreign bank in China.

体系。渣打银行的业务主要集中于亚太、南非、中东、非洲、拉美等地区的发展中国家。因此，它在发展中国家享有很高的声誉。其90%的利润都来自于这些国家，而在英国本土获得的利润只占总利润获的很小份额。

渣打主要业务包括零售银行服务如按揭、投资服务、信用卡及个人贷款等，商业银行服务包括现金管理、贸易融资、托管服务等。

渣打银行自1858年在上海成立第一间分行以来，已成为国内历史最悠久的外资银行。到现在，渣打银行遍布了中国的15个城市，成为在华网络最广的外资银行。

词汇 VOCABULARY

1. merger ['mə:dʒə] *n.* （企业等的）合并；并购；[法律]吸收 （如刑法中重罪吸收轻罪）	2. charter ['tʃɑ:tə] *n.* 特许状；执照；宪章 *v.* 特许；发给特许执照；包租
3. grant [grɑ:nt] *n.* 授予物；拨款 *v.* 授予；承认 *v.* 同意	4. mortgage ['mɔ:gidʒ] *n.* 抵押 *v.* 抵押
5. equity ['ekwiti] *n.* 公平，公正；普通股；抵押资产的净值	6. custody ['kʌstədi] *n.* 保管；拘留；监护；[法]抚养权

034 The Hong Kong and Shanghai Banking Corporation Limited (HSBC)

The Hong Kong and Shanghai Banking Corporation Limited, the largest business bank in Hong Kong was established in Hong Kong in 1864 when Hong Kong was British Empire's colony. HSBC is a founding member of HSBC Group, one of the largest banking and financial services organization in the world that is operating around 10000 branches in 83 countries and regions.

After the Opium Wars, Hong Kong became a colony of British Empire. With the increasing trade between China and Europe, there occurred an urge need for a bank to finance trade. Under this circumstance, a Scottish Thomas Sutherland decided to establish a bank with Scottish banking standards. Therefore, The Hong Kong and Shanghai Banking Corporation Limited was founded on 1 Queen's Road Central, Hong Kong and started business on 3 March 1865. The bank was running in accordance with the Hong Kong and Shanghai Bank Ordinance 1866 and accepted dispensation from the British Treasury in 1866. In the same year, a branch was also opened in Shanghai. Both banks began to release

【小译】

1864年成立于英属殖民地时期的香港上海汇丰银行有限公司是香港最大的商业银行。汇丰有限公司也是世界规模最大的银行及金融服务机构之一的汇丰集团的创始成员之一。汇丰集团在世界83个国家和地区设有超过一万个分支机构。

鸦片战争之后，香港成为英国的殖民地。随着中国和欧洲之间贸易的增长，建立一个融资银行势在必行。在这种情况下，苏格兰人托马斯·萨瑟兰德决定成立一个依照苏格兰银行标准运作的银行。因此，香港上海汇丰银行有限公司于1865年在香港中环皇后大道1号成立，并于当年3月3日开始营业。当时，汇丰银行在1866年香港上海银行条例指导下运行，并在1866年获得英国财政部的减免。同年，汇

local banknotes directed by the local government. Other services at that time included international exchange, deposits and loans and etc. Over the few years, branches opened gradually in Tianjin, Beijing, Hankou, Chongqing and other places. Under the leadership of Sir Thomas Jackson, the Bank became increasingly important in Asia and grew in both size and status.

In its nearly 150 years of operation and development, The Hong Kong and Shanghai Banking Corporation Limited have invested over $5 billion on self-development and in purchasing shares in Chinese financial organizations and became one of the largest investors among the foreign banks to have invested in mainland China. It holds 19% share in Bank of Communications, 16% share in Ping An Insurance and an 8% share in Bank of Shanghai and etc.

On 2 April 2007, Shanghai-based HSBC Bank (China) Company Limited started operation. It was a foreign bank that operated in mainland China. It is also a part of HSBC Group but is wholly owned by The Hong Kong and Shanghai Banking Corporation Limited.

丰银行成立上海支行。两个银行开始发行纸币。除此之外,银行当时的其他业务还有国际汇兑、发行纸币、存贷款业务等。之后没几年,汇丰在天津、北京、汉口、重庆等地也逐渐设立分支。在汤姆森·杰克逊领导时候,汇丰银行在亚洲发挥了越来越重要的作用,规模不断扩大,地位不断提高。

在香港上海汇丰银行有限公司将近150年的运营中,其用于自身发展和入股内地金融机构的支出超过50亿美元。 汇丰银行持有的股份包括入股交通银行19% 的股份、平安保险16% 的股份,以及上海银行8% 的股份等等。

2007年4月2日,总部位于上海的外资银行汇丰银行(中国)有限公司正式开业。该公司由香港上海汇丰银行有限公司全资拥有,是汇丰集团的一部分。

词汇 VOCABULARY

1. colony ['kɔləni]
   n 殖民地;移民队

2. opium ['əupjəm]
   n 鸦片;麻醉剂 a 鸦片的

3. ordinance ['ɔ:dinəns]
   n 条例;法令;[宗]圣餐礼

4. dispensation [,dispen'seiʃən]
   n 分配;免除;豁免;天命

5. share [ʃεə]
   n 股份;份额 vi/vt 分享,分担;分配

背景链接 TIPS

汇丰银行获得奖项:

汇丰的优质服务已获得广泛的认可,所获奖项包括:《金融亚洲》中国最佳外资银行、《资产》中国最佳资金管理银行、《Global Finance》最佳私人银行、《银行家》亚洲与西欧最佳银行、《欧洲货币》评为"中国最佳外资银行"(连续4年)。

035 Royal Bank of Scotland

The Royal Bank of Scotland, a banking subsidiary of The Royal Bank of Scotland Group that was founded in 1727 and headquartered in Edinburg, Scotland, was established in Jersey in 1996. The Royal Bank of Scotland Group is the largest bank in the UK and provides personal and corporate banking services in Britain as well as the world.

Royal Bank of Scotland Group is consisted of The Royal Bank of Scotland, NatWest headquartered in North Ireland and Ulster Bank, Direct Line and Citizens Financial Grouphas headquartered in Rhode Island. Royal Bank of Scotland Group takes the 55th place in the 2011 Fortune 500 released by Fortune Magazine.

Royal Bank of Scotland Group provides eight major types of services to the clients. Company and financial market service is a type of overall financial service provided to national industry and business companies and organizations, added by professional debts and risk management services to the world's clients; retail banking service provided by The Royal Bank of Scotland and Natwest respectively; wealth management service including private banking service and offshore banking service; Retail Direct, an e-bank service provided to the clients through phone and

苏格兰皇家银行是苏格兰皇家银行集团的一个银行分支。该集团成立于1727年，总部设在苏格兰爱丁堡。苏格兰皇家银行成立于1996年，总部在Jersey。苏格兰皇家银行集团，是英国最大的银行，其业务涵盖个人业务和公司业务，业务遍及英国和世界各地。

苏格兰皇家银行集团由苏格兰皇家银行、总部设在北爱尔兰的国民西敏寺银行、阿尔斯特银行、直接在线以及总部设在美国罗德岛的公民金融集团几部分组成。在2011《财富》发布的世界500强企业中，苏格兰皇家银行集团排名第55位。

苏格兰皇家银行集团面对客户的业务单元分为八个：公司和金融市场业务为国内企业和组织提供全面的金融业务以及向国际客户提供专业的债务和风险管理服务；苏格兰皇家银行和国民西敏寺银行各自向客户提供的零售业务；由私人银行业务和离岸银行业务构成的资产管理业务；直接销售，即通过电话、网络直接服务于客

internet; RBS Insurance, Ulster Bank Group and Citizens Bank in America.

Royal Bank of Scotland Group was founded in 1727 as the first bank in the world to offer an overdraft facility. Referred to as the "New Bank" in opposition to the "Old Bank", the Bank of Scotland, Royal Bank of Scotland Group was born a rival to Bank of Scotland and the competition between the two was quite fierce. The competition between the two banks centered on the issue of banknotes. Royal Bank of Scotland began its expansion in Scotland as the first branch office opened in 1783. By 1910, the bank had already got 158 branches all over Scotland. Later on, the bank started its expansion journey to England and the first London branch opened in 1874 and it also acquired various small English banks along the road. Now, it operates over 2000 branches in Scotland and provides services for 15 million clients.

户的电子银行业务；RBS保险；爱尔兰子银行和美国公民金融集团子银行。

成立于1727年的苏格兰皇家银行是全世界第一间有透支服务的银行。它被称为"新银行"，以此与"旧银行"苏格兰银行相对应。两家银行从苏格兰银行刚成立开始就是竞争对手。它们竞争的主要业务是支票业务。苏格兰皇家银行在苏格兰地区的发展壮大开始于1783年，当时在格拉斯哥成立了在苏格兰的第一家分行。截止1910年，苏格兰银行在苏格兰地区的分行开到了158家。后来，苏格兰皇家银行开始扩张到英格兰地区。第一家英格兰地区的分行是1874年在伦敦成立的。在扩张中，它还兼并了部分英格兰的小型银行。如今，苏格兰皇家银行集团在英国和爱尔兰拥有2000多家分行，服务客户多达1500万。

词汇 VOCABULARY

1. subsidiary [səb'sidjəri]
   n 子公司；辅助者 a 辅助的；附属的

2. retail ['ri:teil]
   vt/vi 零售 adv 以零售方式 a 零售的

3. respectively [ri'spektivli]
   adv 分别地；各自地，独自地

4. overdraft ['əuvədra:ft; (US) -dræft]
   n 透支；透支额 vt 透支

5. rival ['raivəl]
   n 竞争者；对手 vt 与…竞争；比得上某人
   vi 竞争 a 竞争的

6. branch [bra:ntʃ]
   vt/vi 分支；出现分歧 n 树枝，分枝；分部

背景链接 TIPS

苏格兰皇家银行的崛起

在2000年以前，苏格兰皇家银行还是一个总部设在英国北部城市爱丁堡的地区性银行，在世界银行排名中处于200名以后。但到2004年6月30日时，苏格兰皇家银行的资本市值已达到了490亿英镑，总资产增加到5190亿英镑，使该行成为拥有2200万客户和12.5万名员工、AA信用评级、英国和欧洲的第二大商业银行，世界上排名第五的大商业银行。从一个名不见经传的地区性商业银行，短短4年多就跻身世界著名商业银行之列，苏格兰皇家银行的确有些大思路。

036 Barclays Bank

Barclays Bank Ltd. or Barclays Bank is one of the four largest commercial banks and the third largest financial organizations in Britain next to only HSBC Bank and the Royal Bank of Scotland. It is also one of the largest global financial services corporations. With a history of over 300 years, Barclays operates some 2,000 domestic branches and nearly 850 international branches in over 60 countries and areas throughout Europe, Africa, the Middle East, and the US. According to Forbe's magazine, Barclays ranked 21st among all the world's largest companies.

The history of Barclays could trace back to as early as 1690 when John Freame and his partner Thomas Gould set up a bank in Lombard, London. The bank didn't acquire the current name Barclays until 1736 when John Freame's son-in-law named the bank after his family name. In 1896, 20 banks in London and other provinces joined together and formed a joint-stock bank under the name Barclays and Co. and then extended its operation in Britain through a series of acquisitions and mergers. Barclays's worldwide started

【小译】

巴克莱银行是英国四大商业银行之一，也是位列汇丰银行和苏格兰皇家银行之后的英国第三大银行。同时它也是世界上最大的全球性金融服务公司之一。巴克莱银行拥有300多年的悠久历史，在英国设有约2000家分行，同时也在欧美、非洲、中东等地区约60个国家和地区拥有近850家分行。根据《福布斯》杂志2011的排行，巴克莱银行是全球第21大企业。

巴克莱银行的历史最早可以追溯到1690年。这一年，John Frame 和他的合作伙伴Thomas Gould在伦敦的Lomnard成立了一家银行。当时这家银行并不叫巴克莱。这个名字是John Freame的女婿在1736年以自己的姓氏命名的。1896年，伦敦和其他省份的20家银行合并成一个股份制的新银行，银行以巴克莱为名。巴克莱银行在全球范围内的业务拓展开始于1925年。这

in 1925 when three of the foreign banks, National Bank of South Africa Ltd., the Anglo-Egyptian D.C.O. and the Colonial merged and later renamed Barclays Bank (D.C.O.)

As a global financial organization, Barclays provides 6 kinds of businesses. Barclays Bank is one of world's largest bank; Barclays Corporate & Investment Banking is a top market-making investment bank; Barclays Wealth Management Company is one of largest international wealth management firm; Barclays Capital is a leading investment bank in the world; Barclaycard owns one of the world's largest credit card circulations; The Global Retail Banking provides banking and retailing services all over the world.

On 12 June 2009, Barclays sold its Global Investors business along with iShare, its exchange traded fund business to BlackRock at the price of $13.5 billion.

一年，南非国家银行、英国一埃及银行和殖民银行合并形成新的巴克莱银行并在后来更名为巴克莱银行（DCO）。

作为一个全球性的金融机构，巴克莱提供的业务主要集中在六个方面：巴克莱银行是世界最大银行之一；巴克莱全球投资者有限公司，是世界上最大的资产经营者之一；巴克莱财富管理公司是一个全球性大型管理机构；巴克莱资本，是全球领先的投资银行；巴克莱信用卡，是最大的全球信用卡发行公司之一；国际零售和商业银行业务在全球范围内位客户提供零售和商业银行业务。

2009年6月12日，巴克莱以135亿的价格将其拥有的全球投资业务和其交易所交易基金iShare业务出售给了贝莱德。

词汇 VOCABULARY

1. domestic [dəˈmestik]
   n 佣人；国货 a 国内的；家庭的

2. joint-stock [dʒɔintstɔk]
   n 股份制的

3. acquisition [ˌækwiˈziʃən]
   n 获得物，获得，合并，兼并

4. colonial [kəˈləunjəl]
   n 殖民地居民 a 殖民地的，殖民的

5. firm [fə:m]
   n 商号；公司 a 坚定的 ad 稳固地
   vt 使牢固；使坚定 vi 变坚实；变稳固

6. circulation [ˌsə:kjuˈleiʃən]
   n 流通，传播；循环；发行量

背景链接 TIPS

巴克莱银行对国内商业银行的启示：

1. 强化分工，在风险管理部门建立分类风险管理团队

2. 建立风险偏好体系，加强风险限额管理，强化经济资本运用

3. 树立资产组合管理理念，对资产进行初步的组合管理

4. 借鉴成熟的市场风险管理经验，加强市场风险管理

5. 重视国家风险，加强国家风险管理研究

6. 强化IT系统的规划整合，增强系统的实时性

Unit 11 电信业

In British Economy, telecommunication industry is one of the sectors with a fastest growth. Until 1982, the main civil telecommunications system in the UK was a state monopoly known as Post Office Telecommunications. In order to encourage new telecom companies to provide various new services and propel market competition, the British government privatlize the Post Office system which had been evolved into British Telecom. Regulation of communications has changed many times during the same period, and most of the bodies have been merged into Ofcom, the independent regulator and competition authority for the UK communications industries.

Now the British government issues around 400 licenses to over 300 service providers. Under government encouragement, British telecom industry has also gone global, providing services to about 170 countries around the world. The British Telecom, Vodafone and Cable and Wireles are the three largest telecom service providers in the UK. Due to limitation of space, we will only give a brief introduction to the first two companies in the following in this chapter.

在英国的经济中，电信业是发展最快的部门之一。在1982年之前，英国主要的民用电信系统供应商一直被国有企业邮局电信垄断。为了鼓励新公司提供各种电信服务，促进市场竞争，英国政府于1984年将垄断性公司英国电信私有化，英国电信的前身即是邮局电信。电信管理部门同期也发生很多变动，最后多家机构合并成为英国通信管理局，该机构对英国电信业拥有独立管理权，也对电信市场竞争进行监管。

现在英国政府为300多家电信服务供应商发放了近400个许可证。在英国政府积极鼓励下，英国电信业也成功国际化，为世界上170多个国家提供服务。英国电信公司、沃达丰、有线与无线电信公司，是英国最大的几个厂家电信服务商。由于篇幅所限，我们在这一章只为大家介绍前两个公司。

037 Vodafone Group Plc

Vodafone Group plc is a global telecommunications company headquartered in London, United Kingdom. It is the world's largest mobile telecommunications company measured by revenues and the world's second-largest measured by subscribers (behind China Mobile), with more than 371 million customers around the world according to the latest statistics. The name Vodafone comes from voice data fone (phone), chosen by the company to "reflect the provision of voice and data services over mobile phones"

Since the first ever mobile call ever was made by Vodafone on 1 January 1985, Vodafone has grown from a small mobile operator in Newbury into a global business and the seventh most valuable brand in the world. It now has a significant presence in more than 30 countries in Europe, the Middle East, Africa, Asia Pacific and the United States through the company's subsidiary undertakings, joint ventures, associated undertakings and investments. It also partners with network operators in over 40 additional countries. On 21 September 1999, Vodafone merged its U.S. wireless assets with those of Bell Atlantic Corp to form Verizon Wireless, the largest mobile telecommunications company in the United States measured by subscribers.

【小译】

沃达丰集团是一个跨国性的电信公司，总部设在英国伦敦，是世界上营业额最多、用户总量第二（仅次于中国移动）的移动电信运营商。据最近的统计，沃达丰在世界上拥有多达3.71亿的用户。沃达丰的名称结合了语音、数据和电话三层含义，是公司为了反映其提供移动电话的数据和语音服务的理念而选择的。

自从1985年1月1日进行史上第一次移动通话以来，沃达丰已经从一个纽布利的小型移动经营商成长为一个国际商业组织，成为全球市场价值第七大品牌。如今公司通过其子公司、合资公司及相关的事业和投资在欧洲、中东、非洲、亚太地区和美国的30多个国家拥有较大的市场占有率，亦在其他40多个国家与网络运营商展开合作。1999年9月21日，沃达丰将它的美国无线通信业务与大西洋贝尔公司兼并，组建了在美国拥有用户数量最多的移动通信公司威瑞森无线。

From its birth on, Vodafone has never ceased the step of delivering useful and inspiring innovation. In 1991 it enabled the world's first international mobile roaming call. In 2002, Vodafone set a new standard for mobile communications with internet access on the move. Fuelled by the desire for sustainable innovation, it recently introduced Vodafone Money Transfer which allows customers in emerging markets to send and receive money safely and easily using their mobile phone.

The primary listing of Vodafone is on the London Stock Exchange and it is a constituent of the FTSE 100 Index. It had a market capitalization of approximately £93 billion as of 9 March 2011, making it the fourth largest company on the London Stock Exchange. It also has a secondary listing on NASDAQ in the U.S.

自诞生之日起，沃达丰从未停止过进行有用的和令人鼓舞的革新。1991年，它实现了世界上第一例国际移动漫游。2002年，沃达丰针对互联网接入移动通信制定了一套全新的标准。在不断创新的渴望的驱动下，沃达丰为新兴市场的用户提供了转帐业务，使得顾客可以简易而又安全地使用手机转移资金。

沃达丰主要在伦敦证券交易所上市，它是英国《金融时报》富时100指数的组成部分。截至到2011年3月9日，沃达丰的市场总值已经达到930亿英镑，这使它成为了伦敦证券交易所的第四大上市公司。同时它在美国纳斯达克股票市场中也有次级上市。

词汇 VOCABULARY

1. telecommunication [ˈtelikəmjuːniˈkeiʃən] *n.* 电信	2. subscriber [sʌbsˈkraibə] *n.* 电话用户
3. provision [prəˈviʒən] *n.* 提供，供应	4. sustainable [səˈsteinəbl] *a.* 能保持的；能保持在一定水平的
5. constituent [kənˈstitjuənt] *n.* 成分，组成的要素 *a.* 构成（全体）的	6. capitalization [kəpitəlaiˈzeiʃən] *n.* 资本化；资本额

背景链接 TIPS

1. FTSE 100 Index

伦敦金融时报100指数（或伦敦金融时报100种股价指数），简称富时100指数。创立于1984年1月3日，是在伦敦证券交易所上市的最大的一百家公司的股票指数。它由伦敦金融时报编制。该指数是英国经济的晴雨表，也是欧洲最重要的股票指数之一。

2. NASDAQ

纳斯达克（Nasdaq）是全美证券商协会自动报价系统（National Association of Securities Dealers Automated Quotations）英文缩写，始建于1971年，是一个完全采用电子交易、为新兴产业提供竞争舞台、自我监管、面向全球的股票市场。纳斯达克是全美也是世界最大的股票电子交易市场。

038 British Telecom

British Telecom is one of the world's leading communications services companies headquartered in London, United Kingdom, serving the needs of customers in the UK and in more than 170 countries. It is a major supplier of telecoms services to corporate and government customers worldwide. As a constituent of the FTSE 100 Index, BT's primary listing is on the London Stock Exchange and its secondary listing is on the New York Stock Exchange.

British Telecom is also the world's oldest telecommunications company. Its origins date back to the establishment of the first telecommunications companies in the United Kingdom. Among them was the first commercial telegraph service, the Electric Telegraph Company, introduced in 1846. As these companies amalgamated and were taken over or collapsed, the survivors were eventually transferred to state control under the Post Office. They later became a privatized company, British Telecommunications plc. AS the forerunner of today's global communications company, BT plc serves customers in 170 countries.

BT runs the telephone exchanges, trunk network and local loop connections for the vast majority

【小译】

英国电信是一个全球领先的电信服务公司，总部设在英国伦敦，为英国及170多个国家的用户提供他们所需的服务。也是全世界范围内企业和政府用户的电信服务的供应商。作为富时100指数的一员，英国电信主要在伦敦证券交易所上市，其次是在纽约证券交易所上市。

英国电信也是世界上历史最悠久的电信公司。它的起源要追溯到英国成立的第一批电信公司，它们中有英国第一个商业电报公司——电子电报公司，成立于1846年。随着这些公司的合并、重组或破产，最后的幸存者转变为了国有的邮局公司。随后他们变成了一个私有化公司，英国电信公共有限公司。作为全球领先的电信巨头，英国电信公共有限公司为170多个国家的客户提供服务。

英国电信为英国绝大多数的固定电话提供电话交换机、主干网络和市内环路连接。目前英国电信负责英国

of British fixed-line telephones. Currently BT is responsible for approximately 28 million telephone lines in the UK. Apart from Kingston Communications, which serves Kingston upon Hull, BT is the only UK telecoms operator to have a Universal Service Obligation (USO) which means it must provide a fixed telephone line to any address in the UK. It is also obliged to provide public call boxes.

BT's businesses are operated under special government regulation by the British telecoms regulator Ofcom (formerly Oftel). In some markets where BT is found to have significant market power, BT is required to comply with additional obligations such as meeting reasonable requests to supply services and not to discriminate.

As well as continuing to provide service in those traditional areas, BT has expanded into more profitable products and services where there is less regulation. These are principally, broadband internet service and bespoke solutions in telecommunications and information technology.

大约2800万的电话线路。除了为赫尔河畔金士敦服务的金士敦电信，英国电信是英国唯一的有普遍服务义务的电信运营商，这意味着它要为英国的任何地址都连接上固定电话线。同时它还负责公共电话亭业务。

英国电信的业务由政府监管，在英国电信监管机构Ofcom英国通信管理局（即以前的OFtel）的特别监管下进行。在一些英国电信拥有巨大市场竞争力的市场，监管机构就会要求英国电信履行一些额外的义务，如满足一些合理的要求来提供无差别的服务。

除了继续在其传统领域内提供服务外，英国电信的势力已经扩展到那些利润更大、监管更宽松的产品和服务中。主要有宽带上网服务，以及为电信和信息领域量身定制的解决方案等。

词汇 VOCABULARY

1. constituent [kən'stitjuənt] *n* 成分，组成的要素 *a* 构成（全体）的	2. forerunner ['fɔː,rʌnə] *n* 先行者，先驱者；先导；前驱
3. discriminate [dis'krimineit] *vt* 区别，辨别；使有区别，区别于 *vi* 区别，辨别；有差别地对待	4. obligation [,ɔbli'geiʃən] *n* （道义上或法律上的）义务；责任
5. bespoke [bi'spəuk] *a* 预定的；定制的	

背景链接 TIPS

1. Universal Service Obligation—普遍服务义务，指电信部门以适当的价格向全国或全地区民众提供基本通用电话或其他电信业务的职责。

2. Ofcom—英国通信管理局（全称Office of Communication），是英国政府许可的广播电信产业监管机构，于2002年成立。根据《2003年通信法案》执行全权。

英国正在反复热播的影视作品

Part 3

Unit 12 电影

The United Kingdom has had a major influence on the development of modern cinema. The first moving pictures developed on celluloid film were made in Hyde Park, London in 1889 by a British inventor who patented the process in 1890.

The U.K is home to many world-famous film artists. The British directors Alfred Hitchcock and David Lean are among the most critically acclaimed of all-time, with other important directors including Charlie Chaplin, Michael Powell, Carol Reed and Ridley Scott. Many British actors have achieved international fame and critical success, including Julie Andrews, Michael Caine, Richard Burton, Sean Connery, Vivien Leigh and Laurence Olivier. There are also a great number of world-renowned currently active British performers like Catherine Zeta-Jones, Jude Law, Kate Winslet, Hugh Grant, Colin Firth, Keira Knightley, Ralph Fiennes, and Orlando Bloom and so on.

Modern British film industry is having active interaction with its American counterpart. Many British films are co-productions with American producers, often using both British and American actors, and British actors feature regularly in Hollywood films. Many successful Hollywood films have been based on British people, stories or events, including Titanic, The Lord of the Rings, and Pirates of the Caribbean.

The British Film Institute has produced a poll ranking what they consider to be the 100 greatest British films of all time, the BFI Top 100 British films. The annual British Academy Film Awards hosted by the British Academy of Film and Television Arts are the British equivalent of the Oscars in the U.S.. In this unit we are going to introduce nine of the most attention grabbing British films around the world in the latest two decades either due to commercial success or awarding-winning experience.

英国电影业对现代电影艺术的发展有着重要的影响。1889年，用电影胶片制作的第一部电影诞生于英国伦敦的海德公园，由一位英国发明家制作，并于1890年申请专利。

英国孕育了许多世界著名的电影艺术家。英国导演阿尔弗雷德·希区柯克与大卫·里恩是世界电影史上广受好评的导演，其他重要导演还包括查理·卓别林、迈克尔·鲍威尔、卡罗尔·里恩与雷德利·斯科特。许多英国电影演员在国际上享有盛誉，包括朱丽·安德鲁丝、迈克尔·凯恩、理查德·伯顿、查理、肖恩·康纳利、费雯·丽与劳伦斯·奥利弗。还有大量的正活跃于国际影坛的英国影星，如凯瑟琳·泽塔琼斯、裘德·洛、凯特·温斯莱特、休·格兰特、科林·费斯、凯拉·奈特莉、拉尔夫·费因斯、奥兰多·布鲁姆等等。

现在英国电影业与美国电影业有许多交集。有许多英国电影是与美国制片人共同制作的，通常由英国与美国演员共同参演。而英国演员也经常出演好莱坞电影。许多成功的好莱坞影片是基于英国人或英国的故事与事件的，如《泰坦尼克》、《指环王》、《加勒比海盗》等。

英国电影协会曾就英国史上最好的100部电影排名进行过一次民意调查，从而得到了英国电影协会百部优秀英国影片排行榜。英国电影学院奖每年由英国电影和电视艺术学院设置颁发，相当于美国的奥斯卡。在接下来的内容我们将介绍9部近20年来拍摄的英国电影，它们有的取得了巨大的商业成功，有的获奖无数奖项，均在国际电影界倍受瞩目。

039 The English Patient (1996)

The English Patient is a 1996 romantic drama film based on the novel of the same name. Adapted for the screen and directed by Anthony Minghella, the film won nine Academy Awards in 1996, including Best Picture.

Set before and during World War II, The English Patient is a story of love, fate, misunderstanding and healing. At the end of the World War II, a critically burned man, at first known only as "the English patient", is being looked after by Hana (Juliette Binoche), a French-Canadian nurse in an abandoned Italian monastery. The patient is reluctant to disclose any personal information but through a series of flashbacks, viewers are allowed into his past. It is slowly revealed that he is in fact a Hungarian geographer, Almásy László de (Ralph Fiennes), who was making a map of the Sahara Desert, and had an affair with a married woman, Katharine Clifton (Kristin Scott Thomas) and was discovered by the latter's husband Geoffrey (Colin Firth), which ultimately brought about his present situation. In addition

【小译】

《英国病人》是一部于1996年根据同名小说改编的爱情剧情电影。安东尼·明格拉是本片的编剧兼导演，该片在1996年一共获得包括最佳影片在内的九项奥斯卡奖项。

电影背景在第二次世界大战前后，是一个有关爱情、命运、误解与原谅的故事。故事开头，一个严重烧伤的男人，开始时被称为"英国病人"，在一个废弃的意大利修道院养病，由一位法裔加拿大护士汉娜（朱丽叶·比诺什饰）照顾。这位病人不愿意透露任何个人信息，但是通过一系列倒叙，人们开始了解他的过去。他实际上是一名匈牙利地理学家，名叫拉斯罗·德·艾马殊（拉尔夫·费因斯 饰），他在为撒哈拉沙漠绘制地图时与一位已婚之妇凯瑟琳·克利夫顿（克里斯汀·斯科特·托马斯 饰）互生情愫，并被凯瑟琳的丈夫（科林·费斯饰）发现，最终导致了他现在的处境。除了艾马殊的故事，影片还穿插了汉娜与一位英国军队中的印度士兵基普（纳威恩·安德鲁斯 饰）的爱情故事，而基普拆弹专家的身份也让他们的爱情故事充满了紧张的氛围。

这部影片是当时各种颁奖典礼上的大赢家，其中包括奥斯

to the patient's story, the film devotes time to Hana and her romance with Kip (Naveen Andrews), an Indian sapper in the British Army, whose position as a bomb defuser makes their romance full of tension.

The movie was a major award winner of at that time; its awards included the Academy Award for Best Picture, the Golden Globe Award and the BAFTA Award for Best Film. Juliette Binoche won the Academy Award for Best Supporting Actress and Anthony Minghella took home the Oscar for Best Director. Kristin Scott Thomas and Ralph Fiennes were nominated for Best Actress and Best Actor. Overall, The English Patient was nominated for 12 Academy Awards and ultimately walked away with 9.

The film also garnered widespread acclaim among film critics. American famous film critic Roger Ebert gave the movie a 4/4 rating, saying "it's the kind of movie you can see twice – first for the questions, the second time for the answers". The New York Times critic Elvis Mitchell praises it as "a stunning feat of literary adaptation as well as a purely cinematic triumph".

卡最佳影片、金球奖最佳影片与英国电影学院奖最佳影片。朱丽叶·比诺什凭借本片获得了奥斯卡最佳女配角奖，安东尼·明格拉获得了奥斯卡最佳导演奖。拉尔夫·费因斯与克里斯汀·斯科特·托马斯也因本片被提名为奥斯卡最佳男女主角。《英国病人》一共获得十二项奥斯卡提名，最后有九项获奖。

这部电影在电影评论家中也广受好评。美国著名的电影评论家罗杰·艾伯特给了电影满分4分，他说："你应该看两次这部电影，第一次为了问题，第二次为了答案"。《纽约时报》评论家埃尔维斯·米切尔称赞这部电影为"技艺高超的文学改编佳作与纯粹的电影艺术奇葩"。

词汇 VOCABULARY

1. monastery ['mɔnəstri] n 修道院；僧侣	2. flashback ['flæʃbæk] n 倒叙；闪回；迷幻药效幻觉重现
3. Hungarian [hʌŋ'gɛəriən] n 匈牙利人；匈牙利语 adj 匈牙利的	4. sapper ['sæpə] n 工兵；坑道工兵；挖掘器
5. defuser [,di:'fjuzə] n 导叶；调解人	6. nominate ['nɔmineit] vt 推荐；提名；任命；指定
7. garner ['gɑ:nə] n 谷仓 vt 获得；储存；把…储入谷仓	

背景链接 TIPS

Academy Awards（美国）电影艺术科学院年奖，即奥斯卡金像奖，由电影艺术与科学学院（Academy of Motion Picture Arts and Sciences）颁发。1928年设立，每年一次，在美国的好莱坞举行。半个多世纪来一直享有盛誉。它不仅反映美国电影艺术的发展进程，而且对世界许多国家的电影艺术有着不可忽视的影响。

040 Pride & Prejudice (2005)

Pride & Prejudice is a 2005 British romance film directed by Joe Wright featuring Keira Knightley and Matthew Macfadyen. It is a film adaptation of Jane Austen's most popular novel of the same name first published in 1813. Although dramatized for television several times (in 1938, 1952, 1967, 1980, and 1995), the classic novel has been a feature film only once before, in 1940, which is famed, but oddly flawed, and is black-and-white. Therefore, in 2005, Europe's leading film production company – Working Title Films decided to put the story back on the big screen. It was widely acclaimed by both audience and many reviewers and was generally considered to have excelled the 1940 film version and to be almost as good as the 1995 BBC television adaptation which is widely regarded the most classic version.

The film portrays life in the genteel rural society of the 19th century, and tells of the initial misunderstandings and later mutual affection between Elizabeth Bennet, whose liveliness and quick wit have often attracted audience and the haughty Fitzwilliam Darcy. The title Pride & Prejudice refers (among other things) to the ways in which Elizabeth and Darcy first view each other.

The movie was released on 16 September 2005, in the UK and took the number one spot in the first

【小译】

《傲慢与偏见》是一部2005年的英国爱情电影，由乔·莱特执导，凯拉·奈特莉与马修·麦克费登主演。电影改编自英国作家简·奥斯汀最受欢迎的同名小说，小说于1813年首次发行。尽管这部小说被多次改编为电视剧搬上荧屏（1938，1952，1967，1980以及 1995年版），但是仅在1940年被改编为电影，这个电影版本虽然小有名气，但是有些古怪的瑕疵，且是黑白版的。因此，2005年，欧洲顶尖的电影制作公司——工作标题电影公司决定将这部小说重新搬上电影大屏幕。2005年的《傲慢与偏见》受到了观众与电影评论家的广泛赞誉，被许多人认为超越了1940年的电影版，甚至与史上公认最经典的1995年BBC电视剧版不相伯仲。

这部电影描绘了19世纪英国上流社会的田园生活图景，讲述了活泼机智、引人注目的伊丽莎白与高傲的菲兹威廉·达西之间由最初互相误解到互相吸引的过程。"傲慢与偏见"指的正是伊丽莎白与达西开始见面时对彼此的看法。

week, earning £2.5 million ($4.5 million) while playing on 400 screens. It stayed on the top spot for two more weeks, earning a total of over £14 million at the UK box office at that time and was played on 1,335 screens at its widest domestic release. The film debuted in the U.S. on 11 November 2005 and was also well-received. In total, the film has grossed over $121 million worldwide at the cinema box office.

Pride & Prejudice garnered a number of nominations in the 2005/2006 film awards season, most notably four nominations in the Academy Awards: Best Actress in a Leading Role for Keira Knightley, Achievement in Art Direction, Achievement in Costume Design and Achievement in Music Written for Motion Pictures (Original Score). It was nominated for five BAFTAs (British Academy of Film and Television Arts) and won the BAFTA Award for Most Promising Newcomer (for Joe Wright, director).

该片于2005年9月16号在英国发行，在四百多家影院上映，首周就获得了票房冠军，收入250万英磅（450万美元），在票房冠军宝座停留了两周之后，该片在英国获得了1400万英磅的票房成绩，最多时候同时在1335家影院上映。该片于2005年11月11日在美国上映，也获得了不斐的票房成绩。《傲慢与偏见》在全球总计获得一亿两千一百万美元的票房成绩。

《傲慢与偏见》在2005/2006年电影颁奖典礼季获得了许多提名，其中最重要的当属奥斯卡的四项提名，包括凯拉·奈特莉的最佳女主角奖、最佳艺术指导奖、最佳服装设计奖与最佳原创音乐奖。此外，该片还获得了五项英国电影电视艺术学院奖提名，导演乔·莱特获得了英国电影与电视学院最有前途新人奖。

词汇 VOCABULARY

1.	dramatize ['dræmətaiz] *vt.* 使戏剧化；编写剧本 *vi.* 戏剧化	2.	flawed [flɔ:d] *a.* 有缺陷的；有瑕疵的；有裂纹的
3.	adaptation [ˌædæp'teiʃən] *n.* 适应；改编；改编本，改写本	4.	portray [pɔ:'trei] *vt.* 描绘；扮演
5.	affection [ə'fekʃən] *n.* 喜爱，感情；影响；感染	6.	haughty ['hɔ:ti] *a.* 傲慢的；自大的
7.	score [skɔ:, skɔə] *n.* 配乐；分数；二十；刻痕		

背景链接 TIPS

Jane Austen

简·奥斯汀（1775～1817）被誉为"地位可与莎士比亚平起平坐的文豪"，"女性中最完美的艺术家"，英国本土最受欢迎的作家，奥斯汀20岁左右开始写作，共发表6部长篇小说：《理智与情感》、《傲慢与偏见》、《曼斯菲尔德庄园》和《爱玛》、《诺桑觉寺》、《劝导》。

MOVIE&TV

041 Bridget Jones's Diary (2001)

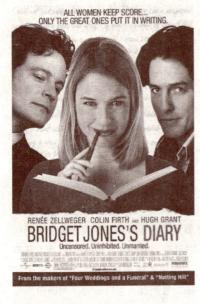

Bridget Jones's Diary is a 2001 British romantic comedy film based on Helen Fielding's novel of the same name. The novel is an international best-seller and won the 1998 British Book of the Year. The adaptation stars American actress Renée Zellweger, British actors Hugh Grant and Colin Firth. A sequel, Bridget Jones: The Edge of Reason was released in 2004.

The film depicts the life of Bridget Jones (Renée Zellweger,), who is an unattached 30-something British woman realizing that she has to change her life to end her single life on a New Year's Eve. She vows that this new year is the one in which she'll get her act together by losing weight, quitting smoking and drinking, and documenting it all in a diary. Complicating everything is Bridget's attraction to her boss, Daniel Cleaver (Hugh Grant), a man of questionable character. They launch an affair and Bridget falls for him head over heels, only to realize later that her feelings aren't reciprocated, when her boss gets engaged to another woman. Thrown into the mix is haughty but honest Mark Darcy (Colin Firth), who admittedly finds Bridget attractive but whom Bridget finds repulsive initially. It won't be until Bridget clearly sees the truth about Daniel, that she also clearly sees Mark for the man he is, and her feelings for him for what they really are.

【小译】

《BJ单身日记》是一部2001年上映的英国浪漫爱情喜剧，根据海伦·菲尔丁的同名小说改编，这部小说是国际畅销书，获得了1998年"英国年度之书"奖。电影版由美国演员芮妮·齐薇格、英国演员休·格兰特、科林·费斯主演。电影续集《BJ单身日记：理性边缘》于2004年上映。

这部电影讲述了30多岁的单身英国剩女布里奇特·琼斯（芮妮·齐薇格 饰）的生活，她在新年的前一个晚上意识到：要想结束自己的单身生活，必须先从改变自己做起。她下定决心在新的一年里要严格自律，减肥、戒烟、戒酒，并把这一切记录在自己的日记里。然而布里奇特被自己的花花公子上司丹尼尔·克里弗（休·格兰特饰）所吸引，一切开始变得复杂，他们不久就在一起了，布里奇特被他迷得神魂颠倒，然而不久就发现自己的感情并没得到回报，她发现丹尼尔其实已经订婚了。卷入这场爱情闹剧的还有高傲却真实的马克·达西（科林·费斯饰），他发现自己不可救药地喜欢上了布里奇特，而布里奇特开始的时候却对他没有好感。直到布里奇特看清丹尼尔的真面目之后，她才开始正视马克，以及自己对马克的潜滋暗长的感情。

在电影上映之前，外界对于

Before the film was released, a considerable amount of controversy surrounded the casting of the American Zellweger as what some saw as a quintessentially British heroine. However, her performance is widely considered to be of a high standard, including her English accent. Renée Zellweger was nominated for the Academy Award for Best Actress for her role in the film.

Fielding, the author of the novel, has stated in many interviews that her novel was based upon both Jane Austen's work Pride & Prejudice and its popular 1995 BBC television adaptation. This was also reflected in the decision to cast Colin Firth as Darcy, since he played the 'real' Mr. Darcy in the BBC adaptation of Pride & Prejudice. This is not the film's only connection to that serial – the screenplay was co-written by Andrew Davies, who had written the adaptation of Austen's novel for the BBC television serial.

让美国人芮妮·齐薇格来饰演典型的英国角色质疑声不断，然而，她出色的表演却被广泛地认为水准很高，包括她的英国口音。芮妮·齐薇格凭借她在电影中的出色表现获得了奥斯卡最佳女主角提名。

《BJ单身日记》的作者菲尔丁在许多访谈中提到她的小说主要基于简·奥斯丁的小说《傲慢与偏见》，与1995年BBC改编的电视剧版《傲慢与偏见》。这也反映在由科林·费斯扮演达西上，他在BBC版的《傲慢与偏见》中扮演了"真正的"达西先生。这部电影与BBC版的电视剧还有其他联系——两部作品的剧本均由安德鲁·戴维斯编写。

词汇 VOCABULARY

1. sequel ['si:kwəl]
   v. 续集；结局；继续；后果

2. unattached ['ʌnə'tætʃt]
   a. 独立的；未订婚的；未被查封的

3. complicate ['kɔmplikeit]
   v. 使复杂化；使恶化；使卷入

4. questionable ['kwestʃənəb(ə)l]
   a. 可疑的；有问题的

5. reciprocate [ri'siprəkeit]
   v. 报答；互换；互给 *v.* 往复运动；酬答

6. admittedly [əd'mitidli]
   ad. 公认地；无可否认地；明白地

7. quintessentially [,kwinti'seʃəli]
   ad. 典型地；标准地

背景链接 TIPS

Renee Zellweger

芮妮·齐薇格，好莱坞喜剧女星，1969年出生于美国德克萨斯州。1996年，芮妮·齐薇格与汤姆·克鲁斯主演《甜心先生》走红影坛。其后，芮妮·齐薇格（Renee Zellweger）先后主演了《BJ单身日记》和《芝加哥》，都为她赢得了奥斯卡提名，最终凭借《冷山》获得了奥斯卡最佳女配角奖。

042 Shakespeare in Love (1998)

Shakespeare in Love is a 1998 British-American romantic comedy film directed by John Madden and written by Marc Norman and Tom Stoppard. The story is fiction, though several of the characters are based on real people like the literary giant William Shakespeare. In addition, many of the characters, lines, and plot devices are references to Shakespeare's plays. The film centers on the forbidden love of the famous playwright, poet – William Shakespeare (Joseph Fiennes) and a noble woman, Viola de Lesseps (Gwyneth Paltrow).

In 1593 London, William Shakespeare is suffering from writer's block when he is writing Romeo and Ethel, the Pirate's Daughter. He is in search of his muse, the woman who will inspire him but all attempts fail him until he meets the beautiful Viola de Lesseps. She loves the theatre and would like nothing more than to take to the stage but is forbidden from doing so as only men can be actors at that time. She is also a great admirer of Shakespeare's works. Dressing as a man and going by the name of Thomas Kent, she auditions and is ideal for a part in his next play. Shakespeare soon see through her disguise and

【小译】

《莎翁情史》是一部1998年上映的英美合拍浪漫爱情喜剧,由约翰·麦登导演,马克·诺曼与汤姆·斯托帕德担任编剧。尽管故事是虚构的,但是其中涉及的一些角色却是基于真人的,如大文豪威廉·莎士比亚。此外,剧中许多角色、台词与情节设置均取自莎士比亚的戏剧。这部电影主要围绕着著名的剧作家、诗人威廉·莎士比亚(约瑟夫·费恩斯 饰)与一个上层社会女子薇奥拉·德·勒沙(格温妮斯·帕特洛 饰)之间的禁忌之爱。

在1593年的伦敦,威廉·莎士比亚在创作《罗密欧与海盗之女埃塞尔》时失去了创作灵感。他在寻找自己的灵感女神,那个能激发她创作灵感的女人,却一直未果,直到他遇上了美丽的薇奥拉·德·勒沙。她热爱戏剧,梦想能上舞台表演,然而这在当时却是被禁止的,因为只有男人才可以当演员。她同时也很仰慕莎士比亚的才华,因此,她打扮成一个男人,给自己取了假名托马斯·肯特,去参加莎士亚新剧的面

they begin a love affair, once they know cannot end happily for them as he is already married and she has been promised to the Lord Wessex (Colin Firth). The forbidden romance provides rich inspiration for William's play leading to the masterpiece – Romeo and Juliet. In the end, Viola and Shakespeare part, resigned to their fate. Shakespeare immortalizes her by making the main character of his new play, Twelfth Night, a strong young woman named Viola who also disguises herself as a boy.

Shakespeare in Love won seven Academy Awards, including Best Picture, Best Actress (for Gwyneth Paltrow), and Best Supporting Actress (for Judi Dench). It is also highly acclaimed by many media reviews. Washington Post comments that "with 'Shakespeare in Love', to see or not to see isn't the question. Where to see, that is the question." The New York Daily News puts it as "inordinately clever, sprightly romantic comedy".

试，并成为新剧一角的理想人选。莎士比亚不久就看穿了她的伪装，虽然他早已结婚，而她已是魏瑟爵士（科林·费斯 饰）的未婚妻，但是他们还是义无反顾地开始了这段不会有结果的感情。他们之间的禁忌之爱为威廉的新剧提供了源源不断的灵感，最终帮助他完成了杰作——《罗密欧与茱丽叶》。最后，莎士比亚与薇奥拉只能屈从于命运的安排而分开。莎士比亚也将薇奥拉命名为新剧《十二夜》中的主角，一个同样喜欢女扮男装的年轻坚强的女子。

《莎翁情史》一共获得七项奥斯卡，包括最佳影片，最佳女主角（格温妮斯·帕特洛），最佳女配角（朱迪·邓奇）。在媒体评论中该片也大受好评，《华盛顿邮报》评论说，"这部片子，问题不在于你去不去看它，而是你去哪看它。"《纽约每日新闻》评价它为"无与伦比地睿智、欢快的爱情喜剧"。

词汇 VOCABULARY

1. disguise [dis'gaiz]
   n 伪装；假装 *vt* 假装；掩饰；隐瞒

2. inspiration [,inspə'reiʃ ən]
   n 灵感；鼓舞；吸气；妙计

3. resign [ri'zain]
   n 辞去职务 *vt* 辞职；放弃 *vi* 辞职

4. immortalize [i'mɔ:təlaiz]
   vt 使不灭；使名垂千古，使不朽

5. inordinately [in'ɔ:dinitli]
   ad 非常地；无度地

6. sprightly ['spraitli]
   a 活泼的；愉快的，*ad* 活泼地

背景链接 TIPS

William Shakespeare

莎士比亚（1564-1616）英国文艺复兴时期杰出的戏剧家和诗人，代表作有四大悲剧《哈姆雷特》《奥赛罗》《李尔王》《麦克白》，喜剧《威尼斯商人》等和一百多首十四行诗。是"英国戏剧之父"，马克思称他为"人类最伟大的天才之一"。被赋予了"人类文学奥林匹克山上的宙斯"。

043 Trainspotting (1996)

Trainspotting is a 1996 British drama film directed by Danny Boyle based on the novel of the same name by a contemporary Scottish novelist Irvine Welsh. The title of the film refers to a hobby of sitting and watching trains pass by and is used as a synonym for 'wasting time'. Beyond drug addiction, other concurrent themes in the film are exploration of the urban poverty and squalor in "culturally rich" Edinburgh.

Set in the late 1980s of Edinburgh, the movie is about the corrupted life of a young Scottish man named Mark Renton and his so-called friends—a bunch of losers, liars, psychos, thieves and junkies. This tragi-comedy charts the disintegration of their friendship as they proceed, seemingly inevitably, towards self-destruction. Mark alone has the insight and opportunity to escape his fate and live a stable and traditional life. But soon after Mark quits heroin, his peaceful life is disturbed by his former friends. This time Mark finally makes a decision to get rid of them entirely.

In Britain, Trainspotting garnered almost universal praise from critics. The Guardian gave

【小译】

《猜火车》是一部1996年上映的英国剧情电影，由丹尼·鲍尔导演，根据苏格兰当代小说家欧文·威尔许的同名小说改编。影片的标题指的是闲坐下来看火车一列列经过的习惯，被用作"浪费时间"的同义词。影片探讨的主题除了毒瘾，还有"文化内涵丰富"的爱丁堡城市的贫穷与肮脏。

故事发生在20世纪80年代的爱丁堡，讲述了苏格兰青年马克·瑞顿和他的朋友们堕落的生活，他们整日无所事事、坑蒙拐骗、精神错乱、吸毒成性。这部悲喜剧描绘了他们似乎不可避免地迈向自我毁灭的过程，同时他们的友情如何分崩离析。马克是几人中最早觉悟的，并有机会逃离自己的命运，过上了稳定而规矩的生活。但是他戒毒不久，平静的生活就又被这帮朋友打破了。这一次马克终于下定决心完全摆脱这帮损友。

在英国，《猜火车》获得了电影评论家们的一致好评。《卫报》称赞了

the film credit for actually tapping into the youth subculture of the time and felt that it was "an extraordinary achievement and a breakthrough in British film history". Empire magazine gave the film five out of five stars and described the film as "something Britain can be proud of and Hollywood must be afraid of". American film critic also speaks highly of the film. Roger Ebert gave the film three out of four stars and praised its portrayal of addicts' experiences with each other.

The film has been ranked 10th spot by the British Film Institute (BFI) in its list of Top 100 British films of all time. In 2004 the professional British film magazine Total Film named it the fourth greatest British film of all time. It was nominated for three British Academy Film Awards in 1995, including John Hodge for Best Adapted Screenplay, Best Film and Best British Film. Hodge won in his category. It also received a nomination for Best Adapted Screenplay in that year's Academy Awards.

这部电影能够深入当时的青年亚文化群体，觉得这是"英国电影史上杰出的进步，伟大的突破"。《帝国》杂志给了这部电影五星的满分，称这是一部"英国人应该感到骄傲，好莱坞应该感到威胁"的好电影。美国电影评论家们也对这部电影评价颇高，罗杰·艾伯特给这部电影打了三星，满分为四星，赞扬了这部电影对于瘾君子之间经历的描绘。

这部电影在英国电影协会选出的百部英国优秀影片中名列第十。2004年英国专业电影杂志《完全电影》将其评选为英国电影史上最好电影的第四位。这部电影在英国电影学院奖中得到三项提名，其中约翰·霍奇获最佳改编剧本提名，还有最佳电影与最佳英国电影。霍奇最终获奖。《猜火车》还在当年的奥斯卡金像奖颁奖典礼上获得最佳改编剧本提名。

词汇 VOCABULARY

1. synonym ['sinənim] *n* 同义词；同义字	2. concurrent [kən'kʌrənt] *a* 并发的；一致的；同时发生的
3. exploration [ˌeksplɔːˈreiʃən] *n* 探测；探究；踏勘	4. squalor ['skwɔlə] *n* 肮脏，悲惨；卑劣；道德败坏
5. junky ['dʒʌŋki] *n* 吸毒者；毒品贩子 *a* 无价值的；质量低劣的	6. disintegration [disˌintiˈgreiʃən] *n* 瓦解，崩溃；分解
7. screenplay ['skriːnplei] *n* 电影剧本；编剧，剧本	

背景链接 TIPS

Irvine Welsh

　　欧文·威尔许，1958年9月27日出生，苏格兰作家，最知名的小说为《猜火车》。作品特色为使用大量的苏格兰方言，以及对爱丁堡现实生活的暴力描述。威尔许除了小说创作，也撰写舞台剧及电影剧本，也导演过短片。他现定居于英国伦敦。

044 The Reader (2008)

The Reader is a 2008 drama film based on the 1995 German novel of the same name by Bernhard Schlink. Although the film is adapted from a German novel and was took in Germany, the director Stephen Daldry and screenwriter David Hare as well as the leading actors Ralph Fiennes and Kate Winslet are all British. Production began in Germany in September 2007, and the film opened in limited release on December 10, 2008.

The story unfolds when Middle aged German lawyer Michael Berg (Ralph Fiennes) recollected to himself his lifelong acquaintance with Hanna Schmitz (Kate Winslet), a relationship with whom he never disclosed to anyone close to him. Michael first met Hanna in 1958, when he was fifteen, she thirty-six. The two had a turbulent summer long love affair and their encounters would begin with him reading to her followed by lovemaking. At the end of the summer Hanna left without notice, left Michael heartbroken.

Michael next encountered Hanna in 1966, when Michael, now a law student, attended the Nazi war crimes trial of six female former concentration camp guards, one of whom is Hanna. Through listening to the testimony, Michael came to realize Hanna's secret which could save Hanna from a life in prison and

【小译】

《生死朗读》是一部2008年上映的剧情电影，根据德国作家本哈德·施林克的同名小说改编。虽然本片改编自德国小说，在德国拍摄，但是导演史蒂芬·戴德利、编剧戴维·黑尔，以及主演拉尔夫·费因斯和凯特·温斯莱特都是英国人。影片于2007年九月开始在德国拍摄，于2008年12月10日开始小范围发行。

影片开始，中年德国律师迈克尔·柏格（拉尔夫·费因斯）开始回忆自己与汉娜·舒密兹（凯特·温斯莱特）相识的过程，这段感情他从来没有向他周围的人提起过。迈克尔在1958年第一次遇到汉娜，当时他只有15岁，汉娜36岁，他们那个夏天发展出一段秘密的情人关系。每次见面，汉娜都让迈克尔先为他朗读，然后才开始做爱。夏末，汉娜不告而别，让迈克尔伤心欲绝。

迈克尔再次看到汉娜是在1966年，当时迈克尔已经是一名法律专业的学生。他在旁听一次对六个纳粹战争集中营女守卫的审判过程中，发现

which she herself was unwilling to disclose: she was illiterate. Hanna received a life sentence and Michael re-established contact with her by reading literary works into a tape recorder and sending the cassettes and another tape recorder to her in prison. Due to regret, Hanna hanged herself before her release and left a tea tin with cash in it with a note asking Michael to give some money to the family of one of the prisoners in the former concentration camp, which was later donated to an organization that combats illiteracy under Michael's suggestion. The film ends with Michael getting back together with his daughter Julia at Hanna's grave and beginning to tell her his story.

The Reader is a story about truth and reconciliation. Kate Winslet received much praise for her excellent performance and won a number of awards for her role, including the Academy Award for Best Actress. The film itself was nominated for several other major awards, including the Academy Award for Best Picture.

汉娜竟然在其中。在旁听审判的过程中，迈克尔发现了汉娜不认识字的秘密，这个秘密可以让汉娜免于牢狱之灾，但是她自己却不愿公开。汉娜被判无期徒刑，迈克尔与他重新建立了联系，将自己朗读的文学作品用录音机录下来，将磁带与另一台录音机送到监狱。出于悔恨，汉娜在刑满释放之前上吊自杀，给迈克尔留下一个字条，请他把装满现金的一个茶叶罐交给曾经在集中营监禁的一家人，在迈克尔的建议下，这些钱后来被捐给了一个扫盲机构。电影的结尾，迈克尔和他的女儿茱丽去汉娜的墓地祭奠汉娜，和茱丽讲起了这段往事。

《生死朗读》是一个有关真相、和解的故事。凯特·温斯莱特在片子表现出色，受到了大量的赞誉，并获得了一系列奖项，包括奥斯卡最佳女主角奖。电影本身也获得几项重要奖项的提名，包括奥斯卡最佳影片奖。

词汇 VOCABULARY

1. acquaintance [ə'kweintəns] *n* 熟人；相识；了解；知道	2. disclose [dis'kləuz] *v* 公开；揭露
3. turbulent ['tə:bjulənt] *a* 骚乱的，混乱的；狂暴的；吵闹的	4. testimony ['testiməni] *n* [法] 证词，证言；证据
5. illiterate [i'litərit] *n* 文盲 *a* 文盲的；不识字的；没受教育的	6. reconciliation [,rekənsili'eiʃən] *n* 和解，调和；和谐；甘愿

背景链接 TIPS

Ralph Fiennes

拉尔夫·费因斯，英国男演员。1962年出生，切尔西学院的艺术设计专业毕业后，进入皇家戏剧艺术学院学习表演，后考入皇家国立剧院，深受剧场训练的扎实功底，在他主演的每部电影中可见一斑。曾出演《辛德勒的名单》、《英国病人》、《哈利波特》、《生死朗读》等众多优秀影片，两获奥斯卡金像奖提名，也是唯一在百老汇剧院以哈姆雷特王子一角获东尼奖的男演员。

045 Love Actually (2003)

Love Actually is a 2003 British romantic comedy film written and directed by Richard Curtis. The film probes into different aspects of love as shown through ten separate stories involving a wide variety of individuals, from the Prime Minister to a rock star, an actor stand-in, a housemaid, and others, many of whom are shown to be interlinked as their tales progress. What is special about the film is that this ensemble cast is predominantly British, like Hugh Grant, Keira Knightley, Colin Firth, and Ralph Fiennes to name a few celebrated ones. Set in London, the film begins five weeks before Christmas and is played out in a weekly countdown until the holiday, followed by an epilogue that takes place one month later.

The central character of the film is the new bachelor prime minister David who cannot express his growing feelings for his new personal assistant Natalie. The prime minister's older sister Karen slowly grows aware of her husband Harry's flirtation with her secretary named Mia. Karen's friend Daniel is a recently widowed writer whose 11-year-old son asks for love advice about a girl he has a crush on. Meanwhile, Jamie is another writer who leaves his girlfriend after catching her cheating on him and travels to France to write a novel where he pursues a possible romance with his non-English speaking Portuguese maid Aurelia. Also, Harry's American colleague Sarah questions a romance she pursues with the office colleague Karl, but her personal family problems get in the way. Other secondary characters involve a photographer who has a crush on his best friend's new wife Juliet; a pair of

【小译】

《真爱至上》是一部2003上映的英国浪漫爱情喜剧，由理查德·柯蒂斯担任编剧与导演。这部电影通过十个独立的爱情故事探讨了爱情的不同方面，这十个爱情故事涉及了各种各样的人群，从首相到包括摇滚歌星、替身演员、女仆在内的各种人，随着电影剧情的发展，人们又发现这些人之间其实又是互相关联的。这部电影的特殊之处在于全体演员班底绝大多数都是英国演员，其中名气较大的有休·格兰特、凯拉·奈特丽、科林·费斯、拉夫·费因斯等。这个故事发生在圣诞节五周前的伦敦，用每周倒计时的形式推进剧情，最后以一个月之后的一段后记结尾。

电影的中心人物是新上任的单身首相大卫，他对自己的个人助理纳塔利渐生情愫，却不知如何开口表白。首相的姐姐凯伦渐渐察觉自己的丈夫哈里与他的秘书米娅感情出轨。凯伦的朋友丹尼尔是一位作家，刚经受丧妻之痛，他11岁的儿子暗恋上了班上的一个女孩，向他寻求感情建议。另一位作家杰米因自己的女朋友偷情而刚刚分手，他旅行来到法国来写小说，在那儿爱上了自己不会讲英语的葡萄牙女仆奥蕾莉亚。同时，哈里的美国同事莎拉一直在犹豫自己要不要与同办公室的卡尔发展恋情，却被她个人的家庭问题妨碍。其他角色还包括：暗恋上自己好朋友的妻子茱莉叶的摄影师；一对名叫约翰与朱迪的电影替身，在一场模拟的床戏中互生情愫；一个好色的年轻小伙子，想去美

movie stand-ins, named John and Judy, who grow closer after their simulated love scenes; a libidinous chum who wants to travel to Wisconsin, USA to get women; and a burned-out former rock star named Billy Mack who is the main connection between all stories involved.

Upon its release, the film received generally positive reviews in both Britain and the United States. BBC awarded it four of a possible five stars and called it a "vibrant romantic comedy... Warm, bittersweet and hilarious, this is lovely, actually. Prepare to be smitten." American famous film critic Roger Ebert gave the film 3.5 out of 4 stars, describing watching it as "a belly-flop into the sea of romantic comedy... The movie's only flaw is also a virtue: It's jammed with characters, stories, warmth and laughs".

国威斯康星得到女人的芳心；以及一个叫做比利·麦克的过气摇滚歌星，他也是将剧中所有爱情故事连接起来的线索人物。

该片从公映之日起就在了美国与英国广受好评。BBC给了这部电影4星，满分5星，称其为"一部充满生机的浪漫爱情喜剧……温暖、苦中有乐而又另人喜不自禁，这部片子事实上很可爱，观众们准备好为他神魂颠倒吧"。美国著名电影评论家罗杰·艾伯特给这部电影打了3.5星，满分四星，描述看这部片子就好像"一头扎入爱情喜剧的海洋……这部电影唯一的缺陷也是一种优点：整部片子充满了角色、故事、温暖与欢笑"。

词汇 VOCABULARY

1. interlink [ˌintə(ː)'liŋk] *n.* 连环 *v.* 连接；把……互相连结	2. countdown ['kaunt‚daun] *n.* 倒数计秒
3. epilogue ['epilɔg] *n.* 结语，收场白；尾声，后记	4. flirtation [fləː'teiʃ(ə)n] *n.* 调情；调戏；挑逗；不认真的考虑
5. stand-in *n.* 替身	6. libidinous [li'bidinəs] *a.* 性欲的；好色的；淫荡的
7. Wisconsin [wis'kɔnsin] *n.* 威斯康星州（美国州名）	8. hilarious [hi'lɛəriəs] *a.* 欢闹的；非常滑稽的；喜不自禁的
9. smite [smait] *v.* 使神魂颠倒；打；重击；毁灭；侵袭	

背景链接 TIPS

Richard Curtis

理查德·柯蒂斯1956年出生于新西兰一个小镇，1978年从牛津大学毕业后他开始写剧本，连续创作了《憨豆先生》、《四个婚礼和一个葬礼》、《诺丁山》、《BJ单身日记》、《真爱至上》(也是他的导演处女作)与《BJ单身日记2：理性边缘》。毫不夸张地说，这几年大受欢迎的英国浪漫爱情片几乎都出自柯蒂斯之手。2009年，理查德的第二部导演(兼编剧)作品《海盗电台》上映，这部明星荟萃的作品同样大受好评。

046 Four Weddings and a Funeral (1994)

Four Weddings and a Funeral is a 1994 British romantic comedy film directed by Mike Newell and written by Richard Curtis. It was the first of the five films by screenwriter Richard Curtis to feature Hugh Grant, the rest being Notting Hill (1999), Bridget Jones's Diary (2001), Love Actually (2003), Bridget Jones: The Edge of Reason (2004).

The film centers on the romance between Charles (Hugh Grant), a debonair but faux pas-prone single Englishman, and an attractive American woman Carrie (Andie MacDowell), whom Charles repeatedly meets at weddings and at a funeral. At the wedding of his friends Angus and Laura where Charles is acting as best man, Charles meets an American woman named Carrie. He falls in love with her at the first sight and she is also attracted to him. Although they spend a memorable evening together, which Charlie only regards as a one-night stand. Over three more successive weddings and one unfortunate funeral, Charlie runs into Carrie, but something always seems to prevent the two from getting together. Finally fate brought

【小译】

《四个婚礼和一个葬礼》是一部1994上映的英国浪漫爱情喜剧，由迈克·内威尔担任导演，理查德·柯蒂斯担任编剧。由理查德编剧，休·格兰特主演的电影共有五部，这是第一部，其他四部分别是1999年的《诺丁山》，2001年的《BJ单身日记》，2003年的《真爱至上》与2004年的《BJ单身日记·理性边缘》。

这部电影主要讲述了温文尔雅但却经常失礼于人的英国单身汉查理（休·格兰特）与迷人的美国姑娘卡丽（安迪·麦克道威尔）之间的故事，他们频繁地在婚礼与葬礼上相遇。在好朋友安格斯与劳拉的婚礼上，查理担当伴郎并遇到了一个叫卡丽的美国姑娘。查理对卡丽一见终情，而卡丽也被查理深深吸引。虽然他们一起度过了难忘的一夜，但是查理却只当作一夜情。在接下来的三个婚礼上与一个不幸的葬礼上，查理均又遇到了卡丽，但是总是有事情阻碍他们在一起。最后查理意识到自己更想要共渡一生的女人其实就是卡丽，在命运的驱使下他们最终走到了一起。

这部电影取得了意想不到的成功，成为当时票房最好的英国电影，全球票房达到两亿四千五百七十万美金，并获得了奥斯卡最佳影片的提名。这部影片还获得了英国电影学院最佳影片奖，

Charles and Carrie together when Charlie realized that the person he would like to spend his life with was Carrie.

The film was an unexpected success, becoming the highest-grossing British film in cinema history at the time, with worldwide box office in excess of $245.7 million, and receiving an Academy Award for Best Picture nomination. It has also won four BAFTA Awards including Best Film, Direction (Mike Newell) Best Actor (Hugh Grant) and Best Supporting Actress (Kristin Scott Thomas). It was voted the 27th greatest comedy film of all time by readers of Total Film in 2000. In 2004, the same magazine named it the 34th greatest British film of all time.

The film was also very well received with critics. Noted film critic Roger Ebert gave the film three-and-a-half stars out of four, calling it "delightful and sly", and directed with "light-hearted enchantment" by Newell. He praised Grant's performance, describing it as a kind of "endearing awkwardness".

最佳导演奖（麦克·内威尔），最佳男主角奖（休·格兰特），最佳女配角奖（克里斯汀·斯科特·托马斯）。2000年，该片在《完全电影》的读者的有史以来最好的喜剧电影评选中位列第27位。2004年，在《完全电影》有史以来最好的英国电影评选中，该片获得第34位。

《四个婚礼一个葬礼》在电影评论家中也广受好评。著名的电影评论家罗杰·艾伯特给电影打了3.5星，满分4星，他称这部电影"可爱而又淘气"，导演内威尔的执导风格有一种"轻松的魅力"，他还称赞了休·格兰特的演技，称其有一种"讨人喜爱的笨拙"。

词汇 VOCABULARY

1. debonair [ˌdebəˈnεə]
   adj. 高兴的，快活的；温文尔雅的；殷勤的

2. faux pas
   （法）失礼，失态

3. memorable [ˈmemərəbl]
   adj. 显著的，难忘的；值得纪念的

4. successive [səkˈsesiv]
   adj. 连续的；继承的；依次的；接替的

5. light-hearted
   adj. 轻松的；无忧无虑的

6. enchantment [inˈtʃɑːntmənt,en-]
   n. 魔法；着迷；妖术；魅力

7. endearing [inˈdiərin]
   adj. 可爱的；引起爱情的；讨人喜欢的

背景链接 TIPS

Hugh Grant

休·格兰特1960年出生于英国伦敦。毕业于牛津大学英文系时，他爱上演戏。在1987年以《墨利斯的情人》一片获得威尼斯影展最佳男演员，在1994年演出《四个婚礼和一个葬礼》受到各方注意，也让他成功打入好莱坞的市场，同时也得到英国皇家学院奖的最佳男主角，令他成为热门影星。1999年他又和茱丽娅·罗伯茨一起主演了《诺丁山》，更是令他大红大紫，成为英国当红小生。

047 Notting Hill (1999)

Notting Hill is a 1999 British romantic comedy film set in Notting Hill, London. It is another work written by screenwriter Richard Curtis, who had written Four Weddings and a Funeral and Love Actually and so on. The film stars Hugh Grant and Julia Roberts. The film was the sixteenth highest grossing film of 1999 and the highest grossing British film that year. As of May 2007 is the 104th highest grossing film of all time.

The film tells a story about a love story between an ordinary guy and an unbelievably famous movie actress. William Thacker, an unsuccessful Notting Hill bookstore owner, comes across Anna Scott, the world's most beautiful woman and best-liked actress in his book shop one day. A little later, William runs into her again—this time spilling orange juice over her. Anna accepts his offer to change in his nearby apartment, and thanks him with a kiss, which seems to surprise her even more than him. Eventually, Anna and William get to know each other better over the months and fall in love with each other. But it is really not easy for William to be together with the world's most wanted woman – neither around his closest friends, nor in front of the all-devouring press.

【小译】

《诺丁山》是1999年上映的英国浪漫爱情喜剧，故事发生在伦敦的诺丁山。这是编剧理查德·柯蒂斯的另一部作品，他的其他作品还包括《四个婚礼一个葬礼》与《真爱至上》等。这部电影由休·格兰特与茱莉娅·罗伯茨主演。《诺丁山》在1999年的全球票房排在第十六位，也是当年票房第一的英国电影。截止2007年五月，《诺丁山》的票房在历史上排第104位。

这个电影主要讲述了一个平常人与一位著名女影星之间的爱情故事。威廉·萨克是诺丁山一家经营不善的书店的店主，一天在他的店里偶遇了世界上最美丽、最受欢迎的女影星安娜·斯科特。不久，威廉又遇到了安娜，并不小心将橘子汁洒到她身上。威廉邀请他到自己附近的公寓换衣服，安娜答应了，并吻了他一下以示谢意，然后这一个吻却在他们之间产生了奇妙的化学反应，尤其是在安娜身上。最终，经过几个月的进一步了解，二人双双坠入了爱河。但是与世界上最令人渴望的女星谈恋爱

Fortunately, they finally get married against all odds after a series of misunderstanding and reconciling and the film concluding with a shot of Will and a pregnant Anna on a park bench in Notting Hill.

The film won the Audience Award for Most Popular Film at BAFTA, and was nominated in two other categories. It also won other awards, including a British Comedy Award and a BRIT Award for the soundtrack. The film was also well received by critics. Roger Ebert commented that "the movie is bright, the dialogue has wit and intelligence, and Roberts and Grant are very easy to like". This film also earns Hugh Grant a considerable international fame and renders him one of the hottest British movie stars.

对于威廉来说确实不容易，他不仅要面对自己最好的朋友，还有铺天盖地的媒体。幸运的是，经过一系列的误会、和解，他们最终还是排除万难、喜结良缘。电影结尾时候的镜头是威廉与已经怀孕的安娜坐在诺丁山某公园长凳上。

这部电影获得了三项英国电影学院项，其中包括最受观众欢迎影片奖。该片还获得了其他奖项，包括英国喜剧奖，其原声大碟也获得了全英音乐奖。《诺丁山》在电影评论家中也大受好评，罗杰·艾伯特评论说，"这部影片很明快，对白充满了机智，罗伯茨与格兰特也很讨人喜欢"。这部电影也让休·格兰特在国际上名声大噪，成为英国当红的一线小生。

词汇 VOCABULARY

1. spill [spil]
   n 溢出，溅出；溢出量；摔下，小塞子
   vt 使溢出，使流出 vi 溢出，流出；摔下

2. reconcile ['rekənsail]
   vt 使一致；使和解；调停，调解；使顺从

3. conclude [kən'klu:d]
   vt 推断；决定，作结论 vi 推断；断定

4. soundtrack
   n 声带；声迹；声道；电影配音

5. intelligence [in'telidʒəns]
   n 智力；理解力；情报工作；情报机关

6. considerable [kən'sidərəbl]
   a 重要的，值得考虑的；相当大的

7. render ['rendə]
   vt 致使；使…成为；实施；着色；以…回报

背景链接 TIPS

1. Julia Roberts

茱莉娅·罗伯茨，美国女演员，于1967年10月28日出生于美国佐治亚州的一个演员之家，在近几年的好莱坞影坛，她仿佛是一支雨后春笋，短短几年之内迅速走红，上升速度既快而且突然，片酬逐年提高，很快成为好莱坞身价最高的女演员。她代表作包括影片《永不妥协》、《风月俏佳人》、《诺丁山》、《我最好朋友的婚礼》。2001年凭借在《永不妥协》中的出色表演获得奥斯卡最佳女演员殊荣。

2. BRIT Award

全英音乐奖，全称British Record Industry Trust Awards，一年举办一次，有"英国的格莱美"之称，是英国最有影响力的音乐奖项。

Unit 13 电视剧

British TV drama or British TV series is a general name for TV dramas produced in the United Kingdom. Similar with American dramas, British TV dramas are also divided into different seasons following the pattern of one season each year. However, different from American TV dramas which usually contain over 20 episodes in one season, British TV dramas have approximately 6 to 8 episodes.

Although American dramas gain more popularity in China such as Prison Break, Lost and so on, Britain, the birthplace of drama, always bring the audience quality TV dramas with original British characteristics. British TV dramas are generally featured by peculiar British humor and humane quality.

British TV dramas fall in a variety of genres, from soap opera to science-fiction to historical dramas and to costume drama. The British TV dramas put emphasis on lives of ordinary people, be it classical dramas like IT Crowd or popular dramas such as Little Britain. The audience could always access to common British people's real life.

The longest British drama is the famous soup opera Coronation Street that has been broadcasted for half a century since its first screening in 1960. It centers on various ordinary people's lives on a fictional street Coronation Street. Most of the British dramas are produced by British Broadcasting Corporation, a worldly famous broadcasting company and broadcasted on BBC TV channels.

British TV dramas may remind many people of classic mini-dramas adapted from classic literature works such as Pride and Prejudice, Sense & Sensibility, Emma, North and South, all of them are highly regarded for their delicate production and faithful representation. However, more and more popular TV dramas branded with "Made in Britain" are warmly received by drama enthusiasts such as Merlin, The Tudors, and Little Britain and so on. In this part, four other most popular British TV dramas to date besides the above mentioned will be given further discussions, namely, The IT Crowd, Hustle, Skins and Black Books.

英国电视剧（英剧）是对在英国制作的电视剧的总称。与美国电视剧（美剧）相似，英国电视剧也分为不同的季，每年一季。然而，美国电视剧一季通常包含20集左右，而英国电视剧每季一般约6到8集。

虽然和英剧相比，美剧在中国更受欢迎，像《越狱》、《迷失》等。但英国，戏剧的故乡，总能带给观众高质量的具有典型英国特色的剧目。英剧一般都具有独特的英国幽默和浓郁的人文气息。

英国电视剧类型多种多样，有肥皂剧、科幻剧、历史剧和古装剧等等。英剧的侧重点通常都放在普通人的生活上，无论是经典剧，比如《IT狂人》还是流行剧像《小不列颠》，都是在描述小人物的生活。观众总是能以此感受到英国人的真实生活。

英国最长的电视剧是著名的肥皂剧《加冕街》，从1960年开播以后，该剧已播放了半个多世纪。该剧讲述的是生活在一个虚构的街——加冕街上的各类人们的生活。大部分英剧都由BBC这家世界著名的广播公司制作并在BBC电视频道播出。

英剧这个名字让很多人联想到BBC拍摄的、由经典名著改编而成的迷你剧，例如《傲慢与偏见》、《理智与情感》、《爱玛》或《北方和南方》之类的英剧。这些迷你剧都因其精致的编排和忠实的再现而享誉盛名。然而，越来越带有"英国制造"品牌的英剧深受电视剧爱好者的广泛推崇，像《梅林》、《都铎王朝》、《小不列颠》。在这一部分，我们除了对上述作品做进一步的介绍，还有另外4部广受欢迎的英剧《IT狂人》、《飞天大盗》、《皮囊》和《布莱克书店》也会涉及到。

048 Merlin

格温(Gwen)
也许只是位女仆
但她心灵高贵
尽管与主人Morgana地位悬殊
仍视她为闺房密友
Gwen是Guinevere
(格温娜维尔，亚瑟王妃）的简称

Merlin is a British television programme produced by an independent production company Shine Limited and was first broadcast in 2008 on BBC One channel. It is a fantasy adventure first scripted by Julian Jones and first directed by James Hawes. The first series received favorable reception from the audience and became the 5th most watched programme on BBC iplayer that year. After the successful first series, the two subsequent series were produced and broadcast and the fourth series have been aired in October 2011.

The Merlin TV series is based on a legendary magician Merlin, a figure in the Arthurian legend and recounts the early life of Merlin and King Arthur in a new perspective. The story of Merlin is mainly about how young Merlin realizes his mission as a magician and his relationship with King Arthur as well as their joint efforts to rescue the magic world. With the development of the plot, many other characters from Arthurian legend also appeared such as King Arthur's Knights of the Round Tables, Great Dragon and etc. The

【小译】

《梅林》是由英国一家独立的制作公司Shine Limited制作，首先在2008年于BBC1台播出。该剧最初由朱利安·琼斯编剧，由詹姆斯·豪维指导，是一部奇幻冒险片。该剧一上映就获得很好的反响，成为当年BBC iplayer排名第五的收看次数最多的节目。随着第一季获得成功，第二季、第三季随之推出，第四季也已于2011年10月上映。

《梅林》系列是根据传奇人物梅林的故事改编。梅林是亚瑟王传说中的一位神奇的魔法师。该剧主要讲述梅林和亚瑟的早期生活，但给这个古老的传说赋予了全新的诠释。故事讲述的是梅林如何认识到他作为一名魔法师的使命、他与亚瑟王先敌后友的关系以及二人他们合力拯救魔法界的故事。随着故事情节的不断展开，亚瑟王传说中的角色也一一登台亮相，比如亚瑟王和他的圆桌骑士们，巨龙等。故事从少年梅林第一次踏进卡梅洛特城开始。根据国王尤瑟

story began as the young Merlin stepped into the kingdom of Camelot, a city where magician was forbidden by the king of the day Uther. Merlin met the last great dragon who told him his future role to protect and assist Arthur to build a great kingdom. However, Merlin disliked Arthur who bullied him all the time. The first series focuses on the two main characters Merlin and Arthur as well as the development of their relationship while the second series gives emphasis to other characters and the maturity of Arthur. In the third series, Merlin and Arthur experiences more enchanted adventures and counter greater evil forces. Merlin is on the way to become the world's greatest magician.

The protagonist Merlin in the TV series is starred by Colin Morgan and Bradley James portrayed Arthur. Other leading stars include Anthony Head, Richard Wilson, Angel Coulby, Katie McGrath and etc.

王的指令，卡梅洛特城不允许存在任何形式的魔法。梅林一次偶遇最后一条巨龙，巨龙告诉梅林，他的使命是协助亚瑟王建造出一个伟大的王国。然而，亚瑟王是梅林很讨厌的一个人，因为他不停地欺负梅林。《梅林》第一季主要介绍梅林和亚瑟王以及他们之间的关系；第二季把重点从两个主角转移向其他人物的故事以及亚瑟王的不断成熟。第三季中，梅林和亚瑟王经历了更多的引人入胜的冒险及他们对抗邪恶势力的斗争。梅林正在走上成为世界上最伟大魔术师的道路。

《梅林》剧集中的主人公梅林由Colin Morgan饰演，亚瑟王的角色由Bradley James承担。剧中其他的主角的扮演者还包括Anthony Head, Richard Wilson, Angel Coulby 和Katie McGrath 等。

词汇 VOCABULARY

1. fantasy [ˈfæntəsi, ˈfæntəzi] *n.* 幻想；幻觉；[心]白日梦 *a.* 虚幻的 *v.* 想像；空想 *n.* 奏幻想曲（等于phantasy）	2. script [skript] *n.* 手迹；脚本；书写用的字母 *vt.* 把…改编为剧本 *vi.* 写电影脚本
3. magician [məˈdʒiʃən] *n.* 魔术师，变戏法的人	4. recount [riˈkaunt] *n.* 重算 *vt.* 叙述；重新计算
5. Arthur [ˈɑːθə] *n.* 亚瑟（男子名）；亚瑟王	6. Uthur *n.* 尤瑟（男子名）；亚瑟王之父

背景链接 TIPS

King Arthur

亚瑟王（King Arthur）是5世纪英格兰最富有传奇色彩的国王。传说中，他是古英格兰的国王，圆桌骑士（Knights of the Round Table）的首领，一位近乎神话般的传奇人物。在罗马帝国瓦解之后，他率领圆桌骑士团统一了不列颠群岛，被后人尊称为亚瑟王。

049 Black Books

Black Books was a hit British situation comedy created by Dylan Moran and Graham Linehan and was co-starred by Dylan Moran portraying Bernard Black, Bill Bailey starring Manny Bianco and Tamsin Greig casting Fran Katzenjammer.

The sitcom Black Books has been had run for 3 series on Channel 4 from 29 September 2000 of the first series to 15 April 2004 when the third series was finished. Like the traditional British TV dramas, each series of Black Books contained 6 episodes and altogether 18 episodes with each episode running 30 minutes. The sitcom closed at the third series, all of which received favorable receptions from the audiences not only in Britain, but also in Singapore, Australia and etc.

The plot of the sitcom centers on the lives of three major characters Bernard, Manny and Gran. Black Books is a shop owned by Bernard Black who might be the most absurd book shop owner in the world. He runs it so terribly as if he doesn't own it and the shop is a mass all the time. He takes no interest in management at all. He avoids contacts with the customers and wishes the books will never be sold so that he wouldn't be bothered to order new ones; he closes the shop whenever he wishes and drives them away rudely. His attitude towards the comers, even to the world is hostile and drives the readers' away whenever he wishes to close the shop. He loathes everything in the outside world including the visitors of his shop. In many cases, the customers are scared away. By accident, he drunkenly hired Manny, an accountant who turns out to be a good helper in the shop. Unlike Bernard, Manny has a sunny and optimistic personality. Another character Fran may be the only person in the world

【小译】

《布莱克书店》是由Dylan Moran 和Graham Linehan编写，由Dylan Moran、Bill Bailey和Tamsin Greig分别扮演Bernard Black、Manny Bianco和 Fran Katzenjammer制成的一部英国热播情景喜剧。

《布莱克书店》第一季在第四频道于2000年9月29日开播，第三季在2004年4月15日播完。该剧继承了英剧普遍的一季六集的模式，共播出了18集，每集30分钟。虽然该剧连续三季都在英国及新加坡、澳大利亚等国家受到了广泛的好评，但依然终结于第三季。

该情景喜剧的情节集中于三个主人公Bernard, Manny 和 Gran的生活。布莱克书店是Bernard Black经营的一家书店。Black估计是世界上最荒唐的书店店主了。他把书店经营得一塌糊涂，就好像那不是他自己的店一样。店里什么时候都是一团糟。他对经营根本不感兴趣。他拒绝跟顾客交流，不愿把书卖光，这样他就省得再订购了。而且他想什么时候关门了，就把顾客都赶出去。他对所有顾客甚至是整个世界都带有一种仇恨的情绪。顾客被他吓走的情况时有发生。在一次偶然的情况下，醉醺醺的Black稀里糊涂地雇佣了Manny。Manny是一名会计而且他后来成了Black一个得力助手。不同于Black，Manny有着阳光、乐观的性格。Fran可能是Black在世界上唯一不讨厌的人，也是他唯

Bernard doesn't hate and the only female friend Bernard maintains. She is more sophisticated than Bernard in communicating with people but unfortunately has a fruitless love life. In many times in the show, Manny and Fran make effort to drag Bernard out of his gloomy world and perceive the world in a friendly way but are frequently influenced by Bernard and sucked in Bernard's dark mental world.

The sitcom is featured by its typical British humor and the absurdity of the plot. If you are a fan of British dramas or classical sitcoms, Black Books is one that is highly recommended.

一的女性朋友。Fran在人际关系方面比Black擅长很多，但是在感情方面总没结果。在剧中很多时候，Manny和Fran都在努力把Black从他黑暗的世界里拉出来，用一种友爱的方式对待世界，而往往却被Black说服，变得和他一样悲观。

该情景剧的特点在于它典型的英式幽默和荒唐的情节。如果你是英剧迷，或者情景剧粉丝，那一定不要错过这部情景喜剧《布莱克书店》。

词汇 VOCABULARY

1. sitcom ['sitkɔm]
   abbr. 情景喜剧（situation comedy）

2. episode ['episəud]
   n. 插曲；插话；一段情节；有趣的事件

3. reception [ri'sepʃən]
   n. 接待；接收；招待会；感受；反应

4. loathe [ləuð]
   v. 讨厌，厌恶

5. optimistic [,ɔpti'mistik]
   a. 乐观的；乐观主义的

6. absurdity [əb'sə:diti]
   n. 荒谬；荒谬的言行；谬论

背景链接 TIPS

情景喜剧（situation comedy or sitcom）是一种喜剧演出形式，这种形式一般认为出现在美国广播黄金时代（1920年代至1950年代），如今在世界范围内被广为接受。在很多国家，情景喜剧都是最受欢迎的电视节目之一。美国的电视剧分类中，情景喜剧、肥皂剧和情节系列剧三者都属于"电视连续剧"的范畴；虽然后两者之间常互相渗透，但情景喜剧和后两者之间的区别很大。除情景喜剧外，其他一些搞笑成分居多的剧集，虽然在内容、表现形式、时间长短上（45分钟左右）和情节系列剧一样，但在参加电视奖项角逐时，通常也会归入喜剧类。

050 Skins

If you need a word to describe a most popular British TV drama Skins, "debauchery" it is the one!

As the name Skins indicates, this drama deals with a kind of hollow lifestyle that no content exists. It centers on the meaningless life of a group of teenagers whose lives are stuffed with nothing but endless drug uses, parties and adolescent sex. They are either pretty or handsome or talented and live comfortable lives since they all come from middle class families. However, every one of them has his or her scars beneath the glamorous "skins". They speak rudely, act violently only to disguise their fragilities. Some of them come from dysfunctional families, some of them suffer from mental illnesses and some even meet with death. They are the representatives of the whole generation.

Made its first appearance on 25 January 2007 on E4, Skins has already broadcast five seasons and the sixth season is still in production. The show introduces one teenage generation every two seasons and the third generation has already been introduced in Season 5 and will still be dealt with in the upcoming season. Therefore, in every two seasons, the audiences meet a total new generation consisting of 8 cast members except for the 2nd generation that owns nine.

One feature of the show Skins is that the cast members are all amateur actors and the script is written by a group

【小译】

如果你想找一个词来形容英国一部热播的电视节目《皮囊》的话，那这个词一定是"纸醉金迷"。

正如题名所示，《皮囊》讲述的是一个空洞的没有内涵的生活方式。剧情围绕一群青少年的虚无的生活展开。充斥着他们生活的只有吸毒、派对和青少年性爱。他很帅气，她很漂亮，他们生活都很富裕，因为他们都来自于中产阶级家庭。然而，每个光鲜的外表下隐藏的都是伤痕。他们出言不逊，飞扬跋扈，为的只是掩饰脆弱。他们中，有人来自不健全的家庭，有的患有精神疾病，有的甚至遭遇死亡。他们是这一代人的代表。

《皮囊》在2007年1月25日首播于E4台，该剧已经制作完成并播放了5季，第六季仍处于制作中。该剧每两季更换一代主角，迄今为止三代年轻人中两代已经被介绍完，而第三代人首次出现于第五季，而且会在下一季继续介绍。也就是说，每两季完成后，我们都会遇到全新的一代年轻人，通常一代人由8个人构成，只有在第二季出现了九名主角。

《皮囊》的一个特点是演员都是均为业

of young writers who have an average age of 21. In order to gather ideas for Season 6, the producer even held an open writing competition in January 2011 in which the winners were invited to the Skins writers' room to work with other Skins Writers besides cash prizes.

The TV show receives lots of positives reviews from audiences and critics alike. It has been described by one critic as "beautiful and sad and poignant and perfectly hurtful" and was awarded many prizes and awards. What's more, Skins introduced a cultural phenomenon known as "skins party", a party night of alcohol and recreational drug use.

余人士，而剧本是由一群平均年龄在21岁的年轻人编写。2011年1月，为了给第六季征集更多的思路，制作人举办了一场写作竞赛。竞赛的前两名不仅得到了奖金，而且获得被邀请与《皮囊》的剧作者们共同进行创作的机会。

观众和评论家对于该剧的评价褒贬不一。它曾被一位批评家形容为"凄美、尖酸且恰到好处的痛心"。《皮囊》也赢得了很多奖项。而且，《皮囊》引起了一种文化现象，称为"皮囊派对"，这是指一种包含酗酒和娱乐性吸毒的派对。

词汇 VOCABULARY

1. debauchery [di'bɔ:tʃəri]
   n 放荡；纵情酒色；堕落

2. teenager ['ti:n.eidʒə]
   n 十三岁到十九岁的少年；十几岁的青少年

3. fragility [frə'dʒiliti]
   n 脆弱；易碎性；虚弱

4. dysfunction [dis'fʌŋkʃən]
   n 功能紊乱；机能障碍 *vt* 功能失调；垮掉

5. cast [kɑ:st]
   n 投掷，抛；铸件，铸型；演员阵容
   vt 投，抛；计算 *vi* 投，抛垂钓鱼钩

6. amateur ['æmətə(:), 'æmətjuə]
   n 爱好者；业余爱好者 *adj* 外行的；业余的

7. phenomenon [fi'nɔminən]
   n 现象；奇迹；杰出的人才

051 Hustle

Created by Tony Jordan and broadcast on BBC One, the crime drama Hustle kept high ratings from the first series straight to the seventh series, with the last series owning the highest average audience of 6.79 million, even in the lowest second series, that number is as high as 5.82 million. The premier of the first episode broadcast on 24 February 2004 on BBC One was an instant success with 6.7 million audiences viewing the show. Owing to its popularity, the rebroadcasting licenses of the first series was bought by 12 other countries before the first series was finished broadcasting and it became an international hit; meanwhile, the second series was commissioned.

As its slogan "the con is on" indicates, the drama specializes in "long cons". The major characters in the drama are a group of elite con artists work as a team who varied a lot in appearance, age and experience. The "long cons" they planned and executed are an extended deception practiced against one mark or marks, the victims or the targets of the cons. "Long con" is different from ordinary tricks in that in long cons, the marks are convinced of a certain situation or a lie and are sent to get money for the con artists. It differs from the ordinary confidence tricks in that it requires longer time, more technological contents and devotions and is also highly rewarded. The team members shoulder different responsibilities in a successful practice of long con. Mickey (portrayed by Adrian Lester) is the group leader and the planner of cons. Albert (portrayed by Robert Vaughn) is a veteran con responsible for spotting the marks and involves them in the con. The designer of the con is Ash (portrayed by Robert Glenister) who decides on the place and equipment and other settings that make the plot so naturally that the

【小译】

《飞天大盗》是由托尼·乔丹创作的在BBC1台播放的一部犯罪剧，第一季到第七季都保持了很高的收视率，收视率最高的一季是第七季，平均收视人数高达679万人次，即使是收视率最低的第二季，平均收视人数也达到了582万人。2004年2月24日，《飞天大盗》第一集在BBC1的首映非常成功，获得了670万观众。由于该剧非常受欢迎，在第一季播放完之前，就有12个国家购买了它的重播许可，《飞天大盗》也因此成为风靡全球的热播剧。第二季也被委托制作。

正如《飞天大盗》的广告语"大骗局开始了！"所说，这部剧专讲"大骗局"。剧中的主要角色是一个由一群诈骗精英组成的诈骗团伙。这些角色在相貌、年龄和经历方面都不尽相同。他们设计实施的"大骗局"是对一个或多个受害人进行的长期欺骗。"大骗局"与普通的骗局不同，因为"大骗局"要求的持续时间更长、技术含量更高、投入的精力更多，相应的回报也更多。团队中每个人都有不同的分工。组长Mickey（Adrian Lester饰）负责部署骗局计划；Albert（Robert Vaughn饰）是一个经验丰富的老千，负责找寻合适的受害人并引导受害人走入骗局；大骗局的设计者Ash（Robert Glenister饰）选择地点、装备和其他道具，他的设计不同寻常，受害者很少会有所怀疑；Stacie（Jaime Murray饰）是

victims fall in without any suspicion. Stacie (portrayed by Jaime Murray), the only female con artist is "the lure" using her feminine attraction. Danny (portrayed by Marc Warren) is the newest member of the group who is included in by Mickey.

Certain misdirection and misguide used in the con is revealed in the end of the story, along with some hidden plots to answer the bewildered and enchanted audiences. The intense and well-organized plots and the final revelation is also a key to the secret of high ratings.

团队唯一的女性，往往用她的性感迷惑对方；Danny（Marc Warren饰）是最晚加入团队的成员，他是被Mickey带入团队。

骗局中使用的误导会在结局中揭晓，同时揭晓的还有一些隐藏的情节，这会使迷惑而惊奇的观众恍然大悟。紧张而安排合理的情节加上结尾的大揭秘也是该剧能够赢得高收视率的一个原因。

词汇 VOCABULARY

1. rating ['reitiŋ]
    n. 等级；等级评定；额定功率
    v. 对…评价（rate的ing形式）

2. premier ['premjə, -miə]
    n. 总理，首相 *adj.* 第一的；最初的

3. slogan ['sləugən]
    n. 标语；呐喊声

4. elite [ei'li:t]
    n. 精英；精华；中坚分子

5. deception [di'sepʃən]
    n. 欺骗，欺诈；骗术

6. lure [ljuə]
    n. 诱惑物；诱惑；饵 *v.* 引诱；诱惑

7. feminine ['feminin]
    adj. 女性的；妇女（似）的；娇柔的；阴性的

背景链接 TIPS

阿德里安·莱斯特（Adrian Lester）

莱斯特出生在英国伯明翰的一个牙买加移民家庭。他10岁就开始在唱诗班表演，并在伯明翰青年剧院演出，后来还参加了伦敦Royal Academy的戏剧学习。他在《United Kingdom》的演出被观众所熟知，并出演了BBC电视剧《飞天大盗》2004-2006年间的三季，还在电影《风起云涌》、《后天》等中扮演了角色，其中在《风起云涌》中的表演为他赢得了芝加哥电影评论协会的最有前途演员奖提名。2005年莱斯特在Channel 4的热播警察剧《影子小队》担任了主要配角，还参演了2007年的《蜘蛛侠3》，不过在最后播出版本中被删减。目前他将在热门电视节目《神秘博士》中扮演第一位黑人医生。

052 The IT Crowd

The IT Crowd is another creation of Graham Linehan after his two other hit sitcoms Father Ted and Black Books. This sitcom follows the usual pattern of six episodes in each series and 25 minutes running for each episode. Four seasons of this show have been broadcast on Channel 4 with the first series premiered on 3 February 2006. The premiere of the show was not an instant hit with only 1.8 million viewers but was increasingly favored by the audience with various awards and nominations coming along.

The story of The IT Crowed revolves around a panel of three IT support team locating at a stinky untidy basement in central London. Two of the team members, Roy Treneman and Maurice Moss are IT geeks or what is described by the third member, the tech-illiterate Jen Barker as "standard nerds". They are put in an awkwardly position as being needed by the whole company for technical problems but at the same time, they are despised and ignored as losers which can be reflected in the environment they work in—basement. They are constantly frustrated by the multitude's ignorant problems and their suggestions are perpetually "Have you tried turning it off and on again?" and "Is it definitely plugged in?". Ironically, their suggestions work all the time. As typical IT technicians, they are highly intelligent but unusually unsophisticated in words and people skills and thus made many jokes in daily life. The only female principle character Jen knows nothing about IT technology but is assigned as the head of the support department which is a funny story to tell. She is lucky to be interviewed by the boss who is more illiterate in IT than she is and

【小译】

《IT狂人》是Graham Linehan 在其两部热播剧《神父特德》和《布莱克书店》之后创作的另一部情景喜剧。这部情景喜剧继承了每季6集，每集25分钟的英剧传统模式。该剧最初由第四频道在2006年2月3日首映，前四季已经全部播完。该部剧的首映没起到轰动效应，只有180万观众观看了首映。然而这部慢热型的喜剧在之后的播放中越来越受到观众的追捧，也囊括了各种奖项提名。

《IT狂人》是围绕伦敦中心位于一个环境恶劣的地下室中的IT支持小组中三名工作人员的故事。其两名小组成员Roy Treneman 和 Maurice Moss是典型的IT狂人，也被第三名成员——一个IT盲称为"标准的呆子"。他们在公司处于一个很尴尬的境地，一方面，他们被很多员工所需要，而另一方面却又被认为是失败者并遭到鄙视和忽视。这从他们的工作环境——地下室就能看出来。他们总是被众多缺乏电脑基本常识的电脑盲的愚蠢问题搞得很崩溃，他们最常给出的建议就是"你试过关机再开机了吗？""你确定插电了吗？"然而，这些建议经常会起作用。作为典型的IT人才，他们智商极高，但在表达方面和人际交往方面很笨拙，因此常常在生活中闹笑话。Jen作为剧中唯一的女性，对电脑一窍不通，却成了IT部门的领导，这里有一个很有意思的故事。面试Jen的面试官同样是个电

gets the job by a narrow superiority than the boss as knowing single clicking and double clicking of the mouse. She is adored by Moss and Roy for her good communication skills. She is also the bridge between the two IT nerds and the outside world but is frequently found herself doing disservices. The humorous performances of the three characters highlight the show and thus is increasingly well-regarded by the viewers.

This popular sitcom has been adapted and imported by some other countries such as America and Germany, both of which, however, are no match for the original one.

脑白痴，Jen凭借自己比面试官多出一点点单击和双击的知识而被录用。她的人际交往能力较强，被Moss和Roy所崇拜。她充当Moss和Roy两个IT狂人与外界之间的桥梁，然后时时发现自己是在帮倒忙。三人的幽默表演成为整部剧的亮点，也受到越来越多的好评。

这部流行的英国情景喜剧被美国、德国等一些国家引入并进行了本土化的改编。然而，改编后都没有原汁原味的更受欢迎。

词汇 VOCABULARY

1. premiere ['premieə(r); (US) pri'mjær]
   n 初次的演出；女主角
   a 首位的；初次的 vt / vi 首次公演；首次露面

2. nomination [nɔmi'neiʃən]
   n 任命，提名；提名权

3. revolve [ri'vɔlv]
   n 旋转，循环；旋转舞台
   vi 旋转；循环出现 vt 使…旋转；反复考虑

4. stinky ['stiŋki]
   n [俚]全景雷达；环视雷达站 a 发恶臭的

5. illiterate [i'litərit]
   n 文盲 a 不识字的；没受教育的；文盲的

6. nerd
   n 讨厌的人；呆子

7. perpetual [pə'petjuəl]
   a 永久的；四季开花的；不断的；无期限的

8. disservice ['dis'sə:vis]
   n 伤害；帮倒忙的行为；不亲切的行为

背景链接 TIPS

社交恐惧症

社交恐惧症（social phobia），又名社交焦虑症，是一种对任何社交或公开场合感到强烈恐惧或忧虑的精神疾病。患者对于在陌生人面前或可能被别人仔细观察的社交或表演场合，有一种显著且持久的恐惧，害怕自己的行为或紧张的表现会引起羞辱或难堪。有些患者对参加聚会、打电话、到商店购物、或询问权威人士都感到困难。在心理学上被诊断为社交焦虑失协症（SAD）。

053 Little Britain

Little Britain is a comedy sketch show created by David William and Matt Lucas who were also the only stars performed in the show. The title Little Britain was a phrase coined by "Little England" and "the Great Britain" as to achieve a comic and sarcastic effect.

The show was initially broadcast on BBC radio and it was a big success. Then, it changed into a television show and was first broadcast on Channel 3 and then switched to Channel 1 to cater for the excessive demand of the audience.

David William and Matt Lucas were the only two leading stars in the show. All the characters in the episodes were starred by the two leading actors through changing costumes and wearing different make-ups. The show was not one complete story but sketches of exaggerated representative of various situations in every aspect of British people's life. The acting was echoed by a narrator to explain as if it serves as the guide for non-British people to understand the British culture. However, most of the situations were familiar only to the native people, thus the foreigners may find them perplexed by their performances due to a lack of personal experience. In Little Britain, a variety of different characters were played by David and Matt including prime minister assistant, teachers, students, mental patients, gays, disabled people and even Scottish people. Their exquisite performances and sidesplitting acting made the audience laughed uproariously all the time. They were literally the British version of Stephen Chow.

Apart from David and Matt's whimsical performances, the show attracted so many

【小译】

《小不列颠》是由David William 和 Matt Lucas创作并出演的一部小品喜剧。标题《小不列颠》是由 "小英格兰" 和 "大不列颠" 这两个词合并而成的，不仅具有喜剧色彩，同时也兼有讽刺意味。

这部剧最初由BBC广播电台播出，后由BBC搬上荧屏。开始在BBC3台播出，大受欢迎，后顺应观众要求改到BBC1台播出。

David William 和Matt Lucas是剧中仅有的两个主要人物。所有的任务中的不同角色都是由两位主演通过更换服装、道具和化妆来完成的。全剧并没有一个完整的故事情节，而是由一个个的英国人熟知、经过夸大的演绎后的生活片段组成的。在两人演绎的过程中会时不时出现旁边的讲解，像是在向非英国人介绍英国。然而，大部分情节取材于英国的现实生活，没有亲身经历过的观众可能时常会迷惑不解。《小不列颠》中David和Matt扮演了很多不同的角色，比如首相秘书、教师、学生、精神病人、同性恋、残疾人甚至苏格兰人。他们的精湛表演和滑稽的动作使观众止不住捧腹大笑。这两人可谓是英国的周

audiences for two other reasons. On one hand, this show was a miniature of the real British life and many audiences shared the same experience with the actors and many people referred to in the show were acquired by the audiences. On the other hand, the two actors were so talented in imitating different accents around the UK, such as London, Welsh, Scottish and the Irish accent. Even Indian English were imitated in the show.

After being staged on BBC for three consecutive series, Little Britain was exported to America and became Little Britain USA.

星驰。

除了David和Matt无厘头的表演之外，该剧受欢迎的原因还有两个。一方面，该剧是英国真实生活的缩影，很多英国人都亲身经历过剧中的情景，因此感同身受；另一方面，两人精湛地模仿了英国的伦敦音、威尔士音、苏格兰音、北爱音，甚至剧中都出现了模仿印度发音的情节。

在BBC连续播放三季之后，《小不列颠》被引入美国，被命名为《小不列颠大美利坚》。

词汇 VOCABULARY

1. cater ['keitə]
   vt 满足需要；投合，迎合；提供饮食及服务

2. perplexed [pə'plekst]
   a 困惑的；不知所措的

3. gay [gei]
   n 同性恋者 a 快乐的；放荡的；艳丽的

4. uproarious [ʌp'rɔːriəs]
   a 骚动的；喧嚣的

5. whimsical ['(h)wimzikəl]
   a 古怪的；异想天开的；反复无常的

6. miniature ['minjətʃə]
   n 缩图；微型画 a 微型的 vt 是…的缩影

背景链接 TIPS

英式幽默vs美式幽默

英国式的幽默举世闻名。与美国式的说话很满、很夸张之后的捧腹大笑比起来，英国式只是点到为止的"莞尔"，一切尽在不言中。美国情境喜剧的喜剧感，常常来自家人朋友之间的"互相吐槽"（对话），英国剧则是通过肢体与表情来体现，憨豆先生便是其中的典型。

054 The Tudors

The Tudors is a historical drama filmed in Ireland by a Canadian. The script was written by Michael Hirst for Showtime. The plot of the show was loosely based on the historical records of a British king from the Tudor dynasty, King Henry VIII of England who was mostly famous for his breaking up with the Roman Catholic Church as well as his cruel treatment of his six wives.

The Tudors is a four-season historical drama broadcast on Showtime from 2007. Its first broadcast was the highest rated Showtime series in 3 years. BBC acquired its broadcasting right in the same year. It ran for four consecutive years with each year debut a new series until the finale was broadcast in 2010.

In Season One, Henry VIII, starred by Jonathan Rhys Myers faced the pressure of fathering a son to secure the Tudor line while his wife Katherine of Aragon, though a dutiful wife, unable to produce a male heir (only a daughter Mary I) and was thus deserted by the king. The lustful king took an interest in an ambitious woman Anne Boelyn. Besides, he was also involved in other affairs and got an illegitimate son who died later. In Season Two, Henry broke with Catholic Church and divorced Katherine in the name of the head of Church of England and married Anne who later gave birth to a daughter Elizabeth I. Failed to produce a son, Anne was destined to meet a tragic end considering Henry's amorous nature and was beheaded by Henry with the charge of infidelity. In Season Three Henry married Jane Seymour who produced a son Edward VI and was divorced by the king. Anne of Cleves became the next queen

【小译】

《都铎王朝》是一部由一名加拿大人制作、在爱尔兰拍摄的历史剧。剧本是Michael Hirst为Showtime编写的。该剧是在英国都铎王朝的亨利八世国王的历史记录的基础上改编而成。亨利八世在英国历史上被人所知一方面是因为他与罗马天主教断绝关系，另一个方面是因为他用极其残酷的手段对待他的六个妻子。

《都铎王朝》一共分为4季。第一季从2007年开始在Showtime台播放，直到第四季终结，这部剧就此画上了句号。《都铎王朝》刚开始播出就创下了Showtime 3年以来最高的收视率。同年，BBC购买了该剧的播放权。《都铎王朝》连续四年每年播放一季，直到2010年第四季终结。

第一季中，Jonathan Rhys Meyers饰演的亨利八世迫切需要生养子嗣继承王位，而妻子阿拉贡的凯瑟琳没有给他生下儿子（仅有一名女儿玛丽一世），因此被国王冷落。贪婪的国王看上了野心勃勃的安妮·博林。同时，他也和其他女性有染并有了一个私生子，但不久就夭折。第二季中，亨利与罗马天主教脱离了关系并以英国国教首领的身份罢黜凯瑟琳、立安妮为皇后，之后生下一女，就是后来的伊丽莎白一世。因为没有为亨利生下儿子，加之亨利多情的特点，安妮也注定下场悲惨，最终被亨利八世以通奸的罪名处死。第三季中，亨利八世娶了简·西摩，终于得到了一个儿子，然而被移情别恋的亨利再次休掉。下一任皇后克里维斯的安妮同样以

but was unfortunately beheaded for infidelity. Also in this season, Henry bettered his relationship with Mary I and Elizabeth I who were renounced by him before. The finale centered on his relationship with Katherine Howard and later Katherine Parr as well as Edward VI's short reign until Mary took the throne.

It was said that the show departed from the real historical events to some extent and was faithful to history to around 85%. This, according to Michael Hirst, was to increase the entertaining effect of the show.

通奸罪被亨利处死。该季中，与亨利一世断绝关系多年的玛丽一世和伊丽莎白一世和父亲化解了矛盾。最后一季主要讲述亨利八世和他最后的两位妻子凯瑟琳·霍华德和凯瑟琳·帕尔的关系，以及爱德华六世的短暂统治和玛丽一世的登基。

据说这部剧中虽然有些情节与历史记载有不同，但超过85%的剧情忠于史书记载。编剧Michael Hirst解释说这是为了提高剧情的观赏性。

词汇 VOCABULARY

1. debut ['debju;'deibju;]
   n 初次登台；开张 *vi* 初次登台

2. dutiful ['dju:tiful]
   a 顺从的；守本分的；忠实的

3. lustful ['lʌstful]
   a 好色的；贪欲的；渴望的

4. infidelity [,infi'deliti]
   n 无信仰，不信神；背信

5. behead [bi'hed]
   vi 砍头；[地质]使河流被夺流

背景链接 TIPS

都铎王朝历任统治者：

亨利七世（亨利·都铎）——亨利六世的侄子（父亲是亨利六世同母异父的弟弟）。

亨利八世——亨利七世次子。

爱德华六世——亨利八世的小儿子。

简·格雷——亨利七世外孙女的女儿 在位只有九天。

玛丽一世——亨利八世的女儿，爱德华六世同父异母的姐姐。

伊丽莎白一世——亨利八世的女儿，玛丽一世同父异母的妹妹。

Unit 14 其他娱乐节目

Speaking of popular British TV shows, almost everyone would cry out a same name Britain's Got Talent. Produced in 2007 by Simon Cowell who is also one of the judges in the show, this television show has attracted numerous audiences who stayed tune from one series to another. With the aim to select the most talented person in Britain, Britain's Got Talent welcomed people with all kinds of talents.

Besides Britain's Got Talent, Simon Cowell also produced another popular Television show X Factor. As the name indicates, this show has a purpose to explore the "factor" in a person that could make him or her next superstar. Although it is a singing competition, but many other aspects are taken into consideration such as appearance and presence and so on. The contestants from 3 categories need to go through 3 phases before enter the live show, namely, the first audition, "bootcamp" and "judges' houses". The show produced several superstars such as Shayne Ward and Leona Lewis and etc.

Another popular TV show in the UK is Strictly Come Dancing, a dancing competition feathered by celebrities and professional dancers competing in Ballroom and Latin dances. First broadcasted in 2004, the show already finished 8th series. Owing to its popularity, Strictly Come Dancing has been exported to 32 other countries including China. Many import counties renamed it Dancing with the Stars.

Big Brother is a show originated from Netherlands and became a world-wide show with other countries making their own versions. The name "Big Brother" took from a line "Big Brother is watching you" from George Orwell's novel 1949. The show casts a group of people living together in a house isolated from the outside world. Their life is recorded by cameras and broadcasts to the audience. The audience vote to evict unpopular ones. The eviction happens on a regular basis and the last survivor is the winner and gets cash prize. Each series lasts for over 3 months.

There are a variety of other popular TV shows in Britain which form an integral part of the British popular culture and enrich the British people's lives.

提起英国选秀节目，几乎每个人都会不约而同地喊出《英国达人秀》。由西蒙·考威尔于2007年制作并在节目中担任一位评委的《英国达人秀》吸引了很多观众的收看，很多人一季接着一季地追随该节目。《英国达人秀》欢迎拥有各种才艺的人参与。

《X元素》是西蒙·考威尔制作的另一档流行选秀节目。该节目的宗旨体现在名称《X元素》中，即发掘选手的成为超级明星的潜能。虽然改节目定位于歌唱选秀节目，但是选手的相貌和舞台表现力等也被纳入选择标准中。选手被分3组，在进入决赛前需要通过三个阶段的筛选，包括海选，"训练营"和"评委之家"环节。这档节目曾捧红了像Shayne Ward、Leona Lewis之类的超级明星。

另一部热播真人秀节目《舞动奇迹》邀请名人和职业舞蹈演员搭配竞赛表演国际交际舞和拉丁

舞等。从2004年首播开始，该节目已经进行了8个赛季。由于大受电视观众的青睐，该节目的版权已经被包括中国在内的全球32个国家购买。在大多数国家，它被叫做《与明星共舞》。

《老大哥》节目起源于荷兰，但由于众多国家推出自己国家的版本，因此它成为一个全球性的选秀节目。这个节目的名字出自乔治·奥威尔著名小说《1984》。节目是关于一群共同生活在一所与外界隔绝的大房子里的选手生活。摄像机一天24小时记录他们的一举一动。观众投票淘汰选出他们最不喜欢的选手。淘汰定期进行，最后没有被淘汰的选手就是冠军并获得现金奖励。该节目每季持续3个多月。

英国还有很多类似的流行电视节目，这些节目共同形成了英国流行文化的一部分，并丰富了英国民众的生活。

| 055 Britain's Got Talent

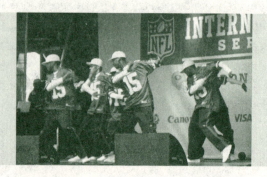

Britain's Got Talent is a popular British television talent show began in June 2007 and is known as one of the biggest television talent shows in Britain. With Simon Cowell as its producer, this show is broadcasted on ITV and TV3 in Ireland as part of the Got Talent series.

The purpose of the show is to select the most talented performer in Britain. Anyone who believes in his or her talent can participate in the show, be it singing or dancing or any other forms of talents. There's literally no limitation for participation. The winner of each series is awarded £100,000 along with the opportunity to perform at the Royal Variety Performance for the Royal family members at Empire Theatre.

The contestants need to perform in front of several producers before getting the chance to perform for the judges on stage and the result of the first audition will

【小译】

《英国达人秀》是2007年6月开播的一档广受欢迎的电视才艺选秀节目，同时也是英国最大的一场选秀节目。作为达人秀系列的一部分，该栏目由西蒙·考威尔制作并在英国ITV和爱尔兰TV3播出。

这档选秀节目的宗旨是挑选英国下一个最具天赋的表演者。任何对自己才能有信心的表演者都可以参加，不管是唱歌、跳舞还是其他任何才艺都可以。该节目基本上没有限制。获胜者不仅得到十万英镑的奖励，还可以参加英国皇家大汇演，在利物浦的帝国剧场上为皇室家族表演。

be given within 2-6 weeks. The contestants who pass the first audition then perform before the judges. Their performances are limited to 1 minute each. Every judge has a button on his or her desk and presses it anytime in the middle to indicate his or her disapproval of the contestant's performance. If all the three judges press their buttons, the contestant should stop the performance immediately and ends his or her journey at BGT. When the performance ends, judges give comments and express their approvals or disapprovals to the contestants. Contestants with two approvals from the judges get through.

The result is revealed in London where the contestants are divided into groups and get the result whether they are admitted to the semifinal competition. The semifinal competition is divided into 3 parts, altogether 24 performances. The judge can end the performance by pressing the buttons. The judges also give comments but it is the audience's votes that decide whether a contestant should stay or leave. The contestant who gains the highest votes in each part rises directly to the final and judge put either 2nd or 3rd through to the final based on their performances. The final competition contains 8 contestants to compete and the contestant receives the highest vote becomes the "Winner of Britain's Got Talent".

There have been four winners to date, namely Paul Potts, George Sampson, Diversity and Spellbound.

选手必须通过几位制作人的海选才能获得在评委面前表演的机会，海选结果在2-6周内被告知。进入下一环节的选手各有1分钟向评委展示的机会。每位评委前面有一个按钮，他们随时可以按下按钮，以此来表示他们对表演的不满意或者否定。如果三个评委都按下按钮，选手必须立即终止表演。评委发表评论并表达他们的立场，同意或否定。

选手们将会被召集至伦敦，分成小组于评委会面。评委会告诉他们，他们是否成功晋级半决赛。半决赛分3场进行，每场8个节目。评委可以在表演中途按钮终止表演。评委在表演完成后给予评论，但比赛结果取决于观众的投票。每场得票最多的选手将自动晋级决赛，评委根据第二三名多选手的表现确定其中一位进入比赛。决赛由8位选手组成进行竞争。获胜者成为《英国达人秀》总冠军。

迄今为止，《英国达人秀》产生的总冠军有Paul Potts，George Sampson, Diversity 和 Spellbound。

词汇 VOCABULARY

1. series ['siəri:z]
   n 系列，连续；丛书；[电]串联；[数]级数

2. audition [ɔ:'diʃən]
   n 试听，听力，听觉 vi 试听，试音
   vt 对…进行面试；让…试唱

3. disapproval [,disə'pru:vəl]
   n 不赞成；不喜欢

4. semifinal['semi'fainl]
   n 半决赛 a 半决赛的

5. vote [vəut]
   n 投票，选举，选票，得票数
   vi 投票决定；公认；提议 vt 选举，投票

056 X Factor

X Factor is another popular Television show originated from Britain. Different from another prevalent TV show Britain's Got Talent which selects talent with a variety of specialty, X Factor focuses on the contestants' singing ability. This show is produced by Simon Cowell and his company Syco Music. The name X Factor refers to an indefinable factor that makes a person becoming a star.

The purpose of the show is to explore the potential superstar. The winner of the year gets the precious chance to release an album. Therefore, a majority of people participate in the show each year with the hope to become the next superstar. Apart from singing ability, a contestant's appearance, personality and presence also affect his or her final results. The show is live and the result is up to audience's votes. The judges' primary duty is to pick the contestants who can attract the audience to vote for them.

The contestants in X Factor are divided into three categories: soloist, age from 16 to 28 and above 28. The competition has four stages: initial televised audition phase and then "bootcamp" where the contestants are further selected and then "judges' houses" where contestants are decided whether they can go further to finale or not, the last stage is the

【小译】

《X元素》是产自英国的另一部热播选秀节目。与另一部火爆选秀节目《英国达人秀》不同，《X元素》不是一个综合性的选秀节目，它注重的是选手的演唱能力。该节目是由西蒙·考威尔和他的公司Syco Music制作推出。节目名称中的X元素指的是能够使人成为明星的一种无法言说的东西。

该档节目的宗旨是发掘潜在的超级明星。节目的年度冠军获得发一张唱片的宝贵机会。因此，每年有无数追逐明星梦的人来参加这档节目，希望自己能够成为未来之星。除了唱功，选手的相貌、个性和舞台表现力也会影响他/她的最终结果。节目是现场录制的，选手的去留由观众投票产生，而裁判的主要任务就是挑选能够吸引观众、赢得观众投票的选手。

《X元素》的选手分三类，独唱选手，16-28岁的选手和28岁以上的选手。比赛分四个阶段进行：海选，训练营（选手们在这个环节面临晋升或者淘汰的选择）。在第三个环节"裁判之家"中，裁判决定选手是否能进入决赛。在最后的现场秀环节，观众投票选出年度冠军。

live show where the final result is revealed and the winner is voted.

Over the years, there have been seven winners coming out of the X Factor. With over 10 million votes in the final competition, Shayne Ward became the 2005 winner whose No. 1 single "That's My Goal" became the top song only four days after its release and made a Guinness World Record for being downloaded the most times in one day. Leona Lewis of the 2006 has the best singing career among all of the winners. Her No. 1 single "A Moment Like this" was downloaded 50, 000 times with half an hour and broke the world's record at that time. Leona's songs have achieved platinum and she has been nominated for Grammy three times and one Golden Globe Awards. The rest of the winners to date are Leon Jackson, Alexandra Joe, McElderry and Matt Cardle all have good performances in their singing careers.

在节目播出的这几年里，《X元素》共产生了7个冠军。Shayne Ward在决赛当天以超过1000万张的投票数赢得了2005年《X元素》的冠军，而他的冠军单曲《That's My Goal》一经发行，4天就登上了单曲冠军宝座，并以有史以来一天之内最多下载次数的歌曲的记录创下了吉尼斯世界纪录。06年冠军Leona Lewis是目前选秀出来发展最好的歌手。她的冠军单曲《A Moment Like This》在30分钟内被下载超过50,000次，打破了当时的世界纪录。现在的她已经是一位拥有多白金销量、身价过亿的歌手，获得过3个格莱美奖提名，1个金球奖提名。其余的各年度冠军Leon Jackson, Alexandra Joe, McElderry和Matt Cardle都在他们自己的音乐生涯中有出色的表现。

词汇 VOCABULARY

1. prevalent ['prevələnt]
   a. 流行的；普遍的，广传的

2. album ['ælbəm]
   n. 相簿；唱片集；集邮簿；签名纪念册

3. presence ['prezns]
   n. 出席；参加；风度；仪态；存在

4. soloist ['səuləuist]
   n. 独唱者；独奏者

5. contestant [kən'testənt]
   n. 竞争者；争辩者

6. platinum ['plætinəm]
   n. 白金；铂；唱片集已售出100万张的

背景链接 TIPS

西蒙·考威尔（Simon Cowell）

西蒙·考威尔，英国人，生于1959年10月7日，他从1979年便开始了自己的流行音乐事业，他和合作伙伴Iain Burton创造属于自己的品牌"Fanfare"。1989年他被BMG公司聘为顾问，由他慧眼识英并一手打造出著名男孩合唱团体Westlife。西蒙堪称是现代流行音乐的开创者。他是著名的电视选秀评审，并为此在英国和美国享有超高人气。这些选秀节目包括Pop Idol, The X Factor, Britain's Got Talent和American Idol。他也是电视制作和音乐出版社Syco的所有者。考威尔以尖刻严厉的"毒舌"著称，他的直率、经常有争议的批评，侮辱参赛者能力的俏皮话具有鲜明的个人特色，也因此受到更多观众推崇。

ARTS

英国人正在关注的人文作品

Part 4

Unit 15 文学作品

The beginning of British literature could be traced back to Anglo-Saxon period. The earliest literature took the form of poetry and passed on orally. The most important literary work at that period was Beowulf about Beowulf defeating monsters.

Geoffrey Chaucer, "the Father of British poetry", was the most important poet before the Renaissance for his The Canterbury Tales as well as his contribution of writing in Modern English and made London dialect the standard speech. English literature flourished in the Renaissance period. Philip Sidney, Edmund Spenser were all great poets of that time. Christopher Marlowe and William Shakespeare made the greatest achievements in drama. English literature in the 17th century was closely related to religious issues. The two representatives were John Milton with his Paradise Lost and John Banyan's The Pilgrim Progress, both stories based on the Bible.

The first half of 18th century English literature was Neo-classicism period in which the classical standards of order, balance, and harmony in literature were promoted. Alexander Pope, Richard. Steele and Joseph Addison were major exponents of the Neo-classical school. The rise of English novel brought with it great novelists like Daniel Defoe, who wrote Robinson Crusoe, Samuel Richardson and Jonathan Swift and Henry Fielding. The 19th century English literature is divided into Romanticism and Realistic novel period. William Blake and Robert Burns were named to Pre-romanticists and the Romanticists included William Wordsworth, George Gordon Byron, Percy Bysshe Shelley and John Keats. In the Realistic novel period, realistic writers strongly criticized the capitalist class and expressed their sympathy for the lower class people. Charles Dickens was such a great writer. At this period, the women writers came to the stage and produced many great works, such as Bronte sisters, Mrs. Gaskell, and George Eliot. Thomas Hardy was the greatest realistic writer at the turn of the 20th century and his most popular works include Tess of the D'urbervilles and Jude the Obscure.

Entering the 20th century, British literature experienced diversity in both themes and writing techniques, such as stream of consciousness, impressionism, cubism and etc.

英国文学最早可以追溯到盎格鲁·萨克逊时期。最早的文学体裁是诗歌，而且大多是通过口头代代相传。早期最重要的一部文学作品是英国史诗《贝奥武夫》，讲述的是贝奥武夫战胜巨兽的故事。

"英国诗歌之父"乔叟是文艺复兴前最重要的作家，他的《坎特伯雷故事集》在民间广为流传。乔叟对英国文学的巨大贡献在于他开启了用现代英语写作的先河，而且用伦敦方言写作。文艺复兴时期的英国文学得到了空前的发展。其中，锡德尼（Philip Sydney）和斯宾塞（Edmund Spenser）都是该时期伟大的诗人。戏剧代表文艺复兴时期英国文学的最高成就。主要戏剧家有马洛（Christopher Marlowe）、莎士比亚（W. Shakespeare）。17世纪的英国最杰出的两个代表作家是弥尔顿和班扬。弥尔顿的代表作《失乐园》和班扬的代表作《天路历程》都取材于《圣经》，具有浓厚的宗教色彩。

18世纪早期，英国文学进入新古典主义时期。新古典主义主张用秩序、平衡、和谐、理性的古典主义标准进行创作。代表作家有诗人蒲伯（Alexander Pope）和期刊随笔的创始人斯梯尔（R. Steele）和艾迪生（J. Addison）。18中期兴起了英国现代小说，出现了大批有影响的小说家，包括《鲁宾逊漂流记》的作者笛福（Danniel Defoe）、理查德（Samuel Richardson）、斯威夫特（Jonathan Swift）以及菲尔丁（Henry Fielding）。18世纪的英国文学可以划分为浪漫主义时期和现实主义时期。早期浪漫主义者有布莱克（William Blake）和彭斯（Robert Burns），鼎盛时期出现了大批优秀的浪漫主义诗人，华兹华斯（William Wordsworth）、拜伦（George Gordon Byron）、雪莱（Percy Bysshe Shelley）和济慈（John Keats）等。现实主义时期的作家抨击资产阶级，同情广大劳苦民众，狄更斯（Charles Dickens）就是其中之一。这一时期也涌现出了很多优秀的女作家，有大家熟知的勃朗特三姐妹（Bronte Sisters）、盖斯凯尔夫人（Mrs. Gaskell）和艾略特（George Eliot）。哈代（Thomas Hardy）是19世纪末20世纪初英国最伟大的现实主义小说家，代表作有《德伯家的苔丝》和《无名的裘德》。

进入20世纪，英国文学在主题和写作技巧上都出现了多样化的特点，涌现出不同的流派，比如意识流、印象派和立体派等。

057 Hamlet

Hamlet, or The Tragedy of Hamlet, Prince of Denmark, is one of the greatest works in the history of British literature. Together with Macbeth, King Lear and Othello, Hamlet is regarded as one of the four greatest tragedies written by William Shakespeare.

This is a play about Prince Hamlet, the prince of Denmark and his revenge of his uncle for murdering his own brother in order to get the throne. The play begins with Hamlet's coming back to Denmark from school in Germany to attend his father's funeral, only to find his mother Gertrude has already wed his uncle Claudius, the dead king's brother. What's more, Claudius made himself the new king despite that Hamlet should be the legal heir. One night, Hamlet's father's ghost visited him and said Claudius murdered him by pouring poison in his ear while he was taking nap.

Prince Hamlet was depressed. On one hand,

【小译】

《哈姆雷特》全称为《丹麦王子哈姆雷特的悲剧》是英国文学史上最伟大的作品之一。《哈姆雷特》同《麦克白》、《李尔王》和《奥赛罗》一起组成莎士比亚的"四大悲剧"。

《哈姆雷特》讲述的是丹麦王子为父复仇的故事，而他的仇人是他的叔叔，一个为了篡夺王位而不择手段谋杀国王的人。故事一开始，哈姆雷特匆匆赶回丹麦参加他的父亲——丹麦国王的葬礼，却发现他的叔叔克莱狄斯非但坐上了本属于哈姆雷特的国王宝座，而且娶了他的母亲乔特鲁德为妻。一天夜里，哈姆雷特遇到了父亲的幽灵并得知父亲是被叔叔、国王的亲弟弟——克莱狄斯从耳朵里滴入毒药杀死的。

哈姆雷特陷入了两难。一方面，

his suspicion of his uncle Claudius started from the moment he came back to Denmark and his father's Ghost confirmed his suspicion; on the other hand, he questioned the Ghost's trustworthiness and feared the ghost was not his father's spirit but a devil to misguide him. In order to testify Claudius, Hamlet seized an opportunity as a troupe of players came to perform and arranged the players to perform a play that recreated the murder scene as the Ghost described. When the play was performed for the new king Claudius, Hamlet observed that Claudius was quite disturbed and left before the play was over. Convinced that Claudius was the murderer of his father, Hamlet resolved to take revenge. However, due to his delay, he missed some good opportunity to kill Claudius.

Claudius sent Queen Gertrude to persuade her son but enraged Hamlet instead. Hamlet accidentally killed an old man Polonius arranged by Claudius to eavesdrop their conversation. This old man happened to be the father of Ophelia, the sweetheart of Hamlet. Distressed by her father's death and Hamlet's behavior, Ophelia went mad and get drowned.

With Polonius' death as excuse, Claudius exiled Hamlet to England while sending a letter to the English king asking him to execute Hamlet. The clever prince discovered the scheme and returned to Denmark before arrived at England. Discovering Hamlet still alive, Claudius provoked Ophelia's brother, Polonius's son Laertes to have a sword fight with Hamlet. In order to kill Hamlet, Claudius put poison on Laertes's sword and then prepared a poisoned cup of wine for Hamlet. In the fight, Hamlet killed Laertes. However, he was also cut by the poisoned sword. At this time, the Queen accidentally drunk the poisoned cup and died. Furious Hamlet stabbed Claudius with the poisoned sword and then met with his death.

他从刚回国就开始怀疑克莱狄斯，而且幽灵也证实了这一点，但另一方面，哈姆雷特担心这不是父亲的幽灵，而是魔鬼作怪，故意误导他。为了试探克莱狄斯，哈姆雷特借助一个戏班子编排了幽灵描述的谋杀场景。在演出之时，哈姆雷特发现新国王局促不安并匆匆离去，证实了克莱狄斯谋杀他父亲的事实。哈姆雷特决定报复，却因为他的犹豫不定而错过了好几个绝佳机会。

克莱狄斯派王后乔特鲁德来当说客，却激怒了哈姆雷特。盛怒之下的哈姆雷特误杀了克莱狄斯派去躲在帷帐后偷听的波洛涅斯。而波洛涅斯恰恰是哈姆雷特心爱的姑娘奥菲莉娅的父亲！可怜的奥菲莉亚接受不了父亲惨死在她所爱恋的王子手里的事实，变得疯疯癫癫，最终溺水而死。

波洛涅斯的死给了克莱狄斯对付哈姆雷特的借口。克莱狄斯以此为借口把哈姆雷特驱逐出境。并写信给英国朝廷编造了一些理由，要他们把哈姆雷特处死。聪明的王子识破了诡计并安全返回丹麦。发现哈姆雷特仍然活着，克莱狄死又唆使奥菲利娅的哥哥雷欧提斯与哈姆雷特决斗，为父亲和妹妹报仇。为置哈姆雷特于死地，克莱狄斯先在雷欧提斯的剑上抹上毒药，然后准备了一杯毒酒。如果哈姆雷特胜利了就把它当庆功酒赐给他。在决战中，哈姆雷特杀死雷欧提斯，自己也被毒剑刺中。与此同时，皇后误喝毒酒身亡。哈姆雷特伤心欲绝，拼起残存的力量把毒剑插进了奸王的胸膛，之后便毒发身亡。

莎士比亚（1564～1616）：英国文艺复兴时期伟大的戏剧家和诗人，人文主义最杰出的代表，近代欧洲文学的奠基者之一。马克思称他是"最伟大的戏剧天才"。本·琼斯称他是"时代的灵魂"。代表作有《哈姆雷特》《奥赛罗》《李尔王》《麦克白》《仲夏夜之梦》《威尼斯商人》等。

词汇 Ｖocabulary

1. revenge [ri'vendʒ]
   n 复仇；报复 vt 替…报仇 vi 报仇；雪耻

2. throne [θrəun]
   n 王座；君主 vt 登上王座 vi 使登王位

3. heir [ɛə]
   n 继承人；后嗣；嗣子

4. testify ['testifai]
   vt 作证；证明，证实 vi 证明；作证

5. delay [di'lei]
   n 耽搁；延期 vt / vi 耽搁；延期

6. eavesdrop ['i:vzdrɔp]
   n 屋檐上流下来的水 vi 偷听，窃听

7. execute ['eksikju:t]
   vt 执行；实行；处死

8. provoke [prə'vəuk]
   vt 激怒；煽动；驱使；惹起

背景链接 Ｔips

名篇名句：

Hamlet: To be, or not to be, that is the question:

Whether 'tis nobler in the mind to suffer

The slings and arrows of outrageous fortune

Or to take arms against a sea of troubles,

And by opposing end them. To die- to sleep.

哈姆雷特：生存或毁灭，这是个必答之问题：

是否应默默忍受坎苛命运之无情打击，

还是应与深如大海之无涯苦难奋然为敌，

并将其克服。

此二抉择，就竟是哪个较崇高？

死即睡眠，它不过如此！

倘若一眠能了结心灵之苦楚与肉体之百患，

那么，此结局是可盼的！

死去，睡去……

058 Robinson Crusoe

As the representative work of the famous British writer Daniel Defoe, Robinson Crusoe is one of the most popular novels in the world and the protagonist Robinson has long been remembered as a model of self-reliant man. Robinson Crusoe ushered a new standard for the English novel by using the first person narration and simple, direct style, and became the favorite for many people, especially young people.

Born as the youngest son of a merchant, Robinson longed for sailing on the sea since he was very little. Therefore, despite of his father's wish of studying law, he went out for sailing. Travelling on the sea was very dangerous. In his first travelling, he met with a big storm which, however, didn't stop him from travelling. In another time, he was enslaved and sold by some Turkey pirates. On a trip to West Africa to gather some slaves, his ship hit rocks which ended up shipwrecked off the coast of Trinidad. All the crews were dead except for Robinson. In order to survive, he returned to the wrecked ship twelve times and got himself guns, powder, food and some other items and began his solitary life on the deserted island.

In order to survive, he built himself a shelter, cultivated lands and grew crops, domesticated wild animals and made clothes with skins of wild animals. Year after year, he overcame the difficulties that other people could not imagine and lived alone. To keep track of time, Robinson made a notch every day on a cross on which his date of arrival was inscribed–1 September 1659. He also kept journal of his activities and his discoveries. During his staying on the island, Robinson experienced a religious illumination and The Bible became the one thing he entirely relied on for his spiritual support. Apart from conquering the

【小译】

《鲁滨逊漂流记》是英国作家丹尼尔·笛福的代表作，也是最受欢迎的英国文学作品之一。书中的主人公鲁滨逊已经成为一个自力更生的楷模。通过采用第一人称的叙述手法和简单明了的写作风格，笛福为英国小说写作创立了一个新标准。而《鲁滨逊漂流记》这本书也成为很多有理想有抱负的年轻人最钟爱的一部文学作品。

鲁滨逊出生于一个商人家庭，从小就对航海产生了极大的兴趣。为此，他忤逆父亲原希望他学法律的想法，踏上了航海的旅程。航海是一件很危险的事情。在他首次出航的时候就遭遇了大风暴。但这并没有使他畏惧。在另一次海航途中，遭遇土耳其海盗的鲁滨逊曾被沦为奴隶。终于，在去西非收集奴隶的航行中，鲁滨逊的船触礁沉没，只有他一人幸存，并只身来到一座荒无人烟的岛上。为了生存，他12次从船的残骸中尽可能多地取得生存物资，有枪、火药、食物和水，然后开始了独立生活。

他在岛上盖了一个房子，拓荒开地，种植食物，驯化动物并用兽皮为自己做衣服。年复一年，他克服了种种常人难以克服的困难独立生活。为了记住他在岛上居住的时间，他把到来的时间，1659年9月1日，刻在一个十字架上，每过一天，他就用小刀刻一道痕。他还用日记记录下他在岛上的生活和新的发现。在岛上的日子也把鲁滨逊带到了上帝的身旁，《圣经》成为他的

harsh environment, he had also to fight with beasts and savages. In the 24th year living alone on the island, he saved a savage and named him "Friday" because Friday was the day of rescuing. Under his education, Friday became a faithful servant to Robinson and helped him a lot in combating severe environment and creating a beautiful home. Robinson spent over 28 years on the island and eventually went back to England with the help of a British ship.

精神寄托。恶劣的生存环境不是鲁滨逊唯一需要克服的，他还不得不与野兽和野人斗争。在独自生存到24个年头的时候，鲁滨逊救了一个野人并给他起名"星期五"（因为鲁滨逊在星期五这一天救了他）。在鲁滨逊的教导下，星期五成了他忠实的仆人并辅助他构造了一个美好的家园。鲁滨逊在岛上生活了28年，最终在一艘英国轮船的救助下回到了文明社会。

作者介绍 Auther

丹尼尔·笛福（1660～1731），英国小说家。出生于伦敦。父亲经营屠宰业，信奉不同于国教的长老会。笛福原姓福，1703年后自称笛福。他受过中等教育，但没有受过大学古典文学教育。他一直保持不同于国教信仰的立场，政治上倾向于辉格党。主要作品有《鲁滨逊漂流记》、《辛格尔顿船长》和《摩尔·弗兰德斯》等。

词汇 Vocabulary

1. protagonist [prəu'tægənist]
   n 主角，主演；主要人物，领导者

2. pirate ['paiərit]
   n 海盗；盗版 vt 掠夺；翻印 vi 做海盗

3. shipwreck ['ʃiprek]
   n 海难；遇难船 vt 使失事，使毁灭

4. notch [nɔtʃ]
   n 刻痕，凹口；峡谷 vt 赢得；在…上刻凹痕

5. inscribed [in'skraibd]
   a 内切的；记名的；有铭刻的
   v 雕刻；题写；内切（inscribe的过去分词）

6. savage['sævidʒ]
   a 残酷的；野蛮的；未开化的 n 粗鲁的人
   vt 乱咬；粗暴地对待

背景链接 Tips

《鲁滨逊漂流记》的魅力

《鲁滨逊漂流记》之所以成为文学史上不朽的名著，还在于它的真实性和不凡的艺术表现力。在他之前，欧洲的长篇小说大都是以帝王将相的业绩或骑士美女的浪漫传奇为主要内容的。笛福开始尝试用日常语言来描写普通人的生活。小说虽是一个虚构的故事，但对鲁滨逊荒岛生活的描写逼真而自然，表现了作者非凡的形象力和艺术表现力。此外，小说通篇采用第一人称的叙述方式，语言明白晓畅，朴素生动，这一切给作品增添了不少魅力。

059 Jane Eyre

Charlotte Bronte, one of the three Bronte sisters, presents to us a most rebellious and strong-minded female character Jane Eyre in the British literature who taught many females how to be independent and persistent in pursuing love.

Jane was an orphan adopted by his uncle since very little. After the death of his uncle, Jane lived in misery because of his aunt's abuse and her cousins' torture. However, Janc's strong character didn't give in; instead, she went against their wishes bravely even if ended up in being beaten. Finally, her aunt sent her to Lowood School, an orphanage. Her life in Lowood was next to intolerable and many students died there but Jane survived. Jane spent altogether 8 years at Lowood, six years as a student and two as a teacher until she accepted a governess position at Thornfield. The new experience changed Jane's life forever. At first arrival, Jane was warmly welcomed by Mrs. Fairfax who presides over the estate. Her student was a little French girl named Adele. One day, on her way back from the post, she helped a man fell off the horse who turned out to be the master Mr. Rochester. In another time, she found out that his bed was on fire and woke him up and helped him to put out the fire which, according to Rochester, was started by a drunken servant Grace Poole. During their contact, Jane found herself secretly fell in love with Rochester. But she was only a governess. Out of

【小译】
"勃朗特三姐妹"之一夏洛特·勃朗特为我们塑造了英国文学史上最叛逆、最独立的一位女性——简·爱。简·爱成为众多女性的楷模,教给女性如何独立、如何追求真爱。

简·爱自小父母双亡,由舅舅抚养。舅舅死后,她受到舅母的虐待,表兄妹的欺凌。但是倔强的简·爱从不屈服,即使挨打也会勇敢地反抗。最终,被舅妈送进了达罗沃德孤儿院。简在达罗沃德孤儿院过着地狱般的生活,很多孩子死在了那里,但是简坚强地活了下来。简在孤儿院度过了8年,6年做学生,2年当老师直到接受了桑费尔德庄园家庭教师的职位。简的命运从此彻底地改变了。刚到了新的环境,简就受到了桑费尔德庄园管家法尔法克斯夫人的热情款待。简的学生是一个叫阿戴尔的法国小女孩。一天,在寄信回来的路上,简帮助了一位坠马的男士。这位男士恰巧是桑菲尔德庄园的主人,也就是简的雇主罗彻斯特。简第二次救罗彻斯特是在一个夜里,简发现罗彻斯特的床着火了,她叫醒他并帮助扑灭了火。罗彻斯特告诉她火是一个喝醉了的仆人雷斯·普尔放的。逐渐地,简发现自己默默地爱上了罗彻斯特。但她告诉自己她只是一个家庭教师,因此不敢奢望太多。殊不知

her expectation, Rochester proved to love her by proposing to her.

On the wedding day, Jane discovered Rochester already had a wife, a woman named Bertha, a mad woman who was the real cause of the fire earlier instead of innocent Grace Poole. Jane left the estate penniless and was taken in by three siblings Mary, Diana and St. John Rivers. St John found a teaching job at a charity school for Jane. During her stay, she inherited a big sum of money from a relative. One day, St. John proposed to Jane because he needed an assistant when travelling to India as a missionary. Jane refused him because she didn't love him at all. Realizing her love for Rochester still remained; she hurried back to Thornfield and discovered the place was burnt down by Bertha who also died in the fire. Rochester lost his eyesight and one hand in saving the servants. Jane found Rochester in his new residence. Jane married him after all of this because she never stopped loving him and finally lived the life she has always been pursuing for.

Jane is a brave woman who knows what she needs and pursues true love despite of every obstacle. It is a merit that many people lack. This is the spirit of Jane Eyre and that's the reason why this book has become a classic and is loved by most people.

罗彻斯特早已爱上了她，并通过求婚证实了对她的爱。

在他们的婚礼上，简得知罗彻斯特早已有了妻子。是一个名叫伯莎·梅森的疯女人。就是这个疯女人之前在罗彻斯特的床上放火想烧死他，雷斯·普尔只不过是个无辜的仆人。因为无法原谅罗彻斯特，简连夜离开了桑菲尔德。身无分文的简被圣约翰和他的两个妹妹玛丽和戴安娜收留。圣约翰为简谋了一份在慈善学校教书的职位。在此期间，简继承了一个亲戚的一笔资产。一天，圣约翰向简求婚，原因是他要去非洲传教需要一个助手，他认为简是最合适的人选。简果断地拒绝了他因为简根本不爱他。意识到自己的爱一直都属于罗彻斯特，简回到桑菲尔德寻找罗彻斯特，却发现桑菲尔德已被烧成一片废墟。原来疯女人伯莎再次放火并把自己也烧死了。罗彻斯特为了救仆人失去了一只胳膊，眼睛也失明了。简找到了罗彻斯特的新住所。经历了这么多，简从来都没有停止爱罗彻斯特，并最终与他结婚，过上了自己一直追寻的生活。

简是一个勇于追求真爱和幸福的女性，她的这种勇气是很多人缺少的。这也是《简·爱》这本书能够成为经典并被无数人喜爱的一个原因。

作者介绍 AUTHER

　　夏洛蒂·勃朗特（1816～1855），英国十九世纪著名的女作家，代表作为《简·爱》。人们普遍认为《简·爱》是夏洛蒂·勃朗特"诗意的生平"的写照，是一部具有自传色彩的作品。夏洛蒂·勃朗特、艾米莉·勃朗特、安妮·勃朗特和勃朗宁夫人获得了那个时代英国妇女最高荣誉。

词汇 VOCABULARY

1. orphan ['ɔːfən]
   n. 孤儿 *a.* 孤儿的；无双亲的 *vt.* 使成孤儿

2. orphanage ['ɔːfənidʒ]
   n. 孤儿院；孤儿身份

3. preside [pri'zaid]
   vi. 主持，担任会议主席 *vt.* 管理

4. sibling ['sibliŋ]
   n. 兄弟姊妹；民族成员

5. residence ['rezidəns]
   n. 居住；住宅，住处

6. pursue [pə'sjuː]
   vt. 从事；追赶；继续 *vi.* 追赶；继续进行

背景链接 TIPS

名篇名句：

Jane: Do you think because I am poor, obscure, plain and little I am soulless and heartless? You think wrong! — I have as much soul as you and fully as much heart. If god has gifted me with beauty and wealth, I should have made it so hard for you to leave me as it is now for me to leave you.

简：你以为我穷，不漂亮，就没有感情吗？如果上帝赐给我美貌和财富，我也会让你无法离开我的！就像我现在无法离开你一样！

|060 Wuthering Heights

When Wuthering Heights was first published in 1847, it was poorly received. Most people found it shocking because of its romantic love and hate under an environment that most works at that time were sentimental. However, as time passes by, more and more people fall in love with this book. Today, Wuthering Heights has secured a position in the canon of world literature.

The story opens with Mr. Earnshaw, the owner of Wuthering Heights, brought home an orphan Heathcliff and raised him with

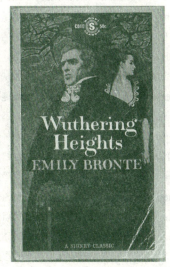

【小译】

《呼啸山庄》在1847年出版之初备受冷落。原因在于艾米莉·勃朗特在书中描写的强烈的爱与恨与当时伤感主义情怀盛行的大环境格格不入。然而，随着时间的流逝，这本书被越来越多的人追捧。如今，《呼啸山庄》当之无愧地成为世界文学经典之一。

一切都源于恩肖先生把孤儿希斯克里夫带回家同自己的儿子辛德雷和女

his own children, Hindley and Catherine. Hindley hated Heathcliff for gaining more preference from his father and abuse Heathcliff whenever there's a chance while Catherine liked him and played with him all the time. Therefore, Mr. Earnshaw sent Hindley to college to prevent him from bullying Heathcliff anymore. Three years later, when Mr. Earnshaw died, Hindley came back with a wife to inherit Wuthering Heights and made Heathcliff a servant and treated him cruelly. Despite of Heathcliff's growing affection to Catherine, she was still engaged to a wealthy young man Edgar Linton for social advancement. Out of resentment, Heathcliff left Wuthering Heights.

Heathcliff returned three years later, shortly after Catherine's marriage with Edgar and began to seek revenge on all the people who treated unfairly. At that time, Hindley became addicted to alcohol after his wife died from giving birth to his son, Hareton. Heathcliff lent money to him with a vast fortune he brought back until Hindley died. When Hindley died, Heathcliff inherited the estate and deliberately raised Hareton into a scoundrel. Another part of his revenge was to marry Elizabeth Linton, Edgar's sister and tortured her cruelly. Soon Catherine died after giving birth to Young Catherine and Elizabeth left Heathcliff with their son Linton. When Elizabeth died, Heathcliff brought back Linton and forced Young Catherine to marry his badly-ill Linton. Till then, Heathcliff took possession of both Wuthering Height and the Linton's property and his revenge was complete. After the death of Young Linton, Young Catherine fell in love with Hindley's son Hareton. At the same time, Heathcliff was haunted by Catherine's ghost and his health declined dramatically. Touched by the true love between Young Catherine and Hareton, Heathcliff finally consent their love before his death.

儿凯瑟琳一起抚养。辛德雷讨厌希斯克里夫因为父亲喜欢他更多于喜欢自己。只要有机会，他都会欺负希斯克里夫。但凯瑟琳喜欢希斯克里夫，所以经常一起玩。恩肖先生把辛德雷送进大学读书，避免希斯克里夫再受欺负。三年后，肖恩先生去世，辛德雷带着妻子回到家继承了呼啸山庄。希斯克里夫被他当做仆人使唤，还得不停忍受他的摆布。凯瑟琳虽然知道希斯克里夫对她的爱意越来越深，但追求名利的虚荣心促使她与富有的年轻人埃德加建立了婚约。希斯克利夫愤而出走。

三年后希斯克里夫致富回乡，凯瑟琳已嫁给了埃德加。希斯克利夫为此开始了疯狂的报复。辛德雷的妻子在生产时死亡，留给他一个儿子哈里顿。辛德雷因为丧妻悲痛无法自拔，染上了酗酒的恶习。希斯克里夫引诱他继续堕落并最终在他死后占有了他的全部家产。哈里顿也被希斯克里夫教唆成了无赖。希斯克里夫报复的第二步是娶埃德加的妹妹伊莎贝拉为妻并不断折磨她。后来，凯瑟琳在女儿小凯瑟琳出生后不久便去世了，伊莎贝拉也无法再忍受希斯克里夫的折磨带着他们的儿子小林顿离家出走。伊莎贝拉死后，希斯克里夫把他病快快的儿子接回了家并强迫小凯瑟琳嫁给他的儿子。至此，希斯克里夫的报复圆满结束了，他占有了两家人的财产。小林顿死后，小凯瑟琳与哈里顿擦出了爱的火花但受到希斯克里夫的阻挠。与此同时，希斯克里夫不断受到凯瑟琳鬼魂的纠缠，身体状况与日剧下。最终，希斯克里夫被小凯瑟琳与哈里顿的爱情感动，决定不再阻挠。对凯瑟琳强烈的爱最终使希斯克里夫郁郁而终。

Though being ignored at first publication for the violent characters and harsh realities described in Wuthering Heights, subsequent audiences are now becoming more and more understanding of the love and hate of this book. The literary value of this book has been increasing over time.

由于书中暴力的角色与残酷的现实，《呼啸山庄》一出版的时候并未得到关注。后来读者们才逐渐理解了书中所表达的爱与恨，从而使得这部作品的文学价值与时俱增。

作者介绍 AUTHER

艾米莉·勃朗待（1818～1848），英国女作家。夏洛蒂·勃朗特之妹，安妮·勃朗特之姐。出生于贫苦的牧师之家。艾米莉性格内向，娴静文雅，从童年时代起就酷爱写诗。1846年，她们三姐妹曾自费出过一本诗集。《呼啸山庄》是她唯一的一部小说，发表于1847年12月。除《呼啸山庄》外，艾米莉还创作了193首诗，被认为是英国一位天才的女作家。

词汇 VOCABULARY

1. sentimental [,senti'mentl]
   a 感伤的；感情脆弱的

2. bully ['buli]
   n 欺凌弱小者 *a* [口]第一流的 *vt* 欺负；威吓

3. resentment [ri'zentmənt]
   n 愤恨，怨恨

4. scoundrel ['skaundrəl]
   n 恶棍；无赖；流氓 *a* 卑鄙的

5. haunted ['hɔːntid]
   a 闹鬼的；反复出现的；受到困扰的
   v 常去（haunt的过去式和过去分词）

6. dramatically [drə'mætikəli]
   a 引人注目地；戏剧地

7. consent [kən'sent]
   n 同意；赞成 *vi* 同意；答应；赞成

8. literary ['litərəri]
   a 文学的；精通文学的；书面的

背景链接 TIPS

哥特小说的影响

19世纪初的女小说家奥斯丁和维多利亚时代的勃朗特姐妹，都受到哥特小说的影响，这主要表现在她们小说所具有的哥特式气氛的布局上。例如《简爱》里的罗彻斯特庄园中的疯女人，夜半闹鬼，庄园焚毁，婚礼受阻等，都具有哥特式的情节。《呼啸山庄》里的呼啸山庄俨如中世纪的城堡，阴森恐怖，充满鬼哭、迫害、复仇、半夜闹鬼、活动窗板等，具有哥特式的神秘恐怖。

061 Sense and Sensibility

As the title indicates, this is a book about the conflict between "sense" and "sensibility" reflected respectively from two sisters, Elinor and Marianne.

When Mr. Henry Dashwood died, his son John Dashwood inherited all the property and the house, Mrs. Dashwood and her three daughters Elinor, Marianne and Margaret were forced to leave the house by John's wife. A distant relative Mr. Middletons took them in and rent them a house within their financial capacity. Upon leaving, Elinor met Edward Ferrars, the brother of John's wife, and got attached to him. At the new house, they met 35 years old Colonel Brandon, a gentleman who fell for Marianne. However, Marianne thought Colonel Brandon was too old and fell in love with a young man Willoughby instead. After courting Marianne openly for some time and made other believe they were engaged, Willoughby announced his departure for London without giving any commitment to Marianne. Meanwhile, Lucy Steele, a relative of the Middletons arrived and met Elinor. Lucy secretly confided to Elinor that she has been engaged to Edward for four years. Elinor was shocked and deeply hurt but still pretended as if nothing had happened.

Later in London, when Marianne was anxious waiting to see Willoughby, the news came that Willoughby has engaged to a rich woman. The sensitive Marianna couldn't bear the news and cried for a long time. Elinor who has been through the same suffering came to comfort Marianne but was accused by Marianne of knowing nothing about how painful she was. Despite of Marianne's ignorance and her history with Willoughby, Colonel Brandon still cared for Marianne very much. He told Elinor that Willoughby has made a 16 years girl pregnant and then deserted her. Marianne was moved by Colonel Brandon and agreed to marry the colonel. Elinor

【小译】

由书名《理智与情感》我们便不难得知这是一个有关"理智"和"情感"的故事。书中的两姐妹埃莉诺和玛丽安就是这两种性格的代表。

在父亲亨利·达什伍德死后，约翰·达什伍德继承了所有遗产，他的妻子刻薄地把他的母亲达什伍德夫人和三个姐妹埃莉诺、玛丽安和玛格丽特赶出了家门。好心的远亲米德尔顿收留了她们，并帮她们租了一处便宜的住所。在临走之前，埃莉诺邂逅约翰妻子的弟弟爱德华·法拉斯并倾心于他。他们刚搬到新住所就迎来了35岁的布兰登上校的登门拜访。布兰登上校对玛丽安产生了好感。然而，追求浪漫的玛丽安嫌弃布兰登上校的年龄，对另一个年轻人威洛比产生了好感。威洛比对玛丽安展开了大胆的追求。当人们以为两人已私定终身之时，威洛比匆忙赶赴伦敦并声称可能不再回来，没给玛丽安任何承诺。与此同时，埃莉诺从露西·斯蒂尔口中得知爱德华已经与露西秘密订婚四年了。一贯理智的埃莉诺把巨大的悲伤藏在心里，并没对任何人倾诉。

后来，姐妹俩陪伴米德尔顿夫人来到伦敦。玛丽安急切地写信告知威洛比并焦急地等待他的到来，却得知威洛比已经与一个贵小姐订婚的消息。情感丰富的玛丽安无法承受，悲伤欲绝。同样承受着被抛弃痛苦的埃莉诺宽慰妹妹，却被不知情的玛丽安指责为无法感受到她的痛苦。而布兰登上校从始至终都没有嫌弃玛丽安，而是对玛丽安更加关心。他告诉埃莉诺威洛比在使一个16岁的女孩怀孕后抛弃了她。玛丽安被布兰

suffered a lot from loving Edward, but she kept all the suffering to herself and remained calm all the time. When Edward's mother discovered Edward's secret engagement to Lucy, she was disappointed and deprived Edward of the right to inherit and all the property would go to his brother Robert. Hearing this, Lucy gave up Edward and eloped with Robert. Edward was free and came to Elinor immediately to ask her forgiveness. Elinor accepted him and everything ended happily.

登上校感动并逐渐与他产生了感情。而埃莉诺因为他对爱德华的爱备受折磨，但从未表现出来。而爱德华的母亲因为他和露西私定终身而剥夺了他继承权，宣布所有的财产都会有他的弟弟罗伯特继承。随后，利益熏心的露西抛弃爱德华与罗伯特私奔。解除了婚约的爱德华回到埃莉诺的身边请求她的原谅并得到了宽恕。最终，姐妹两人都找到了自己的幸福归宿。

作者介绍 AUTHER

简·奥斯汀（Jane Austen，1775年12月16日～1817年7月18日）是英国著名女性小说家，她的作品主要关注乡绅家庭女性的婚姻和生活，以女性特有的细致入微的观察力和活泼风趣的文字真实地描绘了她周围世界的小天地。《理智和情感》是她的处女作，随后又接连发表了《傲慢与偏见》（1813）、《曼斯菲尔德花园》（1814）和《爱玛》（1815）。

词汇 VOCABULARY

1. capacity [kə'pæsiti]
   n 能力；容量；生产力；资格，地位

2. colonel ['kɔ:nl]
   n 陆军上校

3. sensitive ['sensitiv]
   a 敏感的；感光的；灵敏的；易受伤害的

4. pregnant ['pregnənt]
   a 怀孕的；富有意义的

5. deprive [di'praiv]
   vt 使丧失，剥夺

6. elope[i'ləup]
   vt 潜逃；私奔

背景链接 TIPS

英国女小说家产生原因

18世纪最后25年出现大量的女小说家和女读者，与中产阶级妇女的闲逸生活有关。她们发挥才能的机会很少，除了结婚，没有别的办法可以挣钱和补充收入。当时小说刚刚兴起，地位不高，小说家们写小说却瞧不起小说，认为小说只适合妇女和小商人阅读。自尊心强的男作家对写作哥特式小说

和感伤小说不屑一顾。于是，这个领域留给了那些充满奇思异想，不安本分，富有天才的妇女去竞争。和她们处于同一阶层的广大妇女衣食不愁，无所事事，文化有限，却普遍识字，阅读这些女作家写的小说便成了她们主要的精神生活。

062 Great Expectations

Pip was a young orphan living with his bad-tempered sister. Luckily, his brother in-law, Joe Gargery was very nice to him. At one Christmas Eve, Pip met a convict escaping from a prison ship and gave him a file and some food stolen from his sister's house.

One day, Pip visited a strange rich old woman Miss Havishams who was deserted on her wedding day and never took off her wedding gown ever since. She hated all men and wanted to take revenge. In fact, Estella was raised by Miss Havishams as a tool for revenge. She trained Estella to be cruel-hearted so as to use her to break men's hearts. Pip developed a crush on Estella as soon as he met her. But Estella was cold to him and laughed at him. Pip was hurt by Estella's despise and swore to become a gentleman.

Several years later, to his surprise, Pip was given a fortune by a secret benefactor so that he could have a chance to become a gentleman. After some years of undisciplined life in London, Pip got to know the real benefactor was the criminal he helped in his childhood, Magwitch. Upon the discovery, Pip decided to help Magwitch escaping London but failed. Magwitch was put into jail and all his money was gone. It turned out that Magwitch was the father of Estella who has already married. Pip visited and cared for Magwitch until he died in prison.

【小译】

皮普从小失去父母，与性格暴虐的姐姐一起生活。幸运的是，他的姐夫乔很疼爱他。在一个圣诞夜，皮普遇到了越狱犯麦格维奇并从家里偷了锉子和食物给他。

一天，皮普应邀去拜访一个古怪有钱的老女人郝薇香小姐。传说郝薇香小姐在新婚之夜遭到遗弃，从此穿着婚纱从没脱掉过。郝薇香小姐痛恨所有男人并进行报复。她收养了一个漂亮的小女孩艾丝黛拉并把她训练得铁石心肠，用她来伤透男人的心。皮普一见到艾丝黛拉就喜欢上了她。但是傲慢的艾丝黛拉对他很刻薄，还讥笑他衣衫褴褛。皮普自尊心受到伤害并决心把自己改变为一个绅士。

令他吃惊的是，几年之后他意外地受到一个神秘人物的资助，有机会到伦敦学做绅士。皮普在伦敦过着放荡不羁的上流社会生活，几年之后才得知他的资助者竟然是他孩童时帮助过的犯人麦格维奇。得知真相之后，皮普决心帮助麦格维奇逃出伦敦。不幸的是，麦格维奇没有逃脱，被关在了监狱里，财产被没收。一时间，皮普变得一无所有。皮普惊奇地发现麦格维奇是艾丝黛拉的父亲，而此时的艾丝黛拉已经嫁人了。皮普照顾麦格维奇直到他死于狱里。

经过了这一切，皮普"远大前程"的理想幻灭了。他大病一场，姐夫乔一直陪伴在他身边照顾他直到康复。生病期间，皮普重新审视了自

Experiencing the disillusionment of the "great expectation", Pip got very sick and Joe came to take care of him until he recovered. In this period, Pip did some self- reflection and meditation and decided to start over. Pip left to Cairo for 11 years and earned a big fortune. When he returned, he met Estella who divorces years after an abusive marriage. The ending of the book was quite interesting because the original ending was a sad one. However, in order to pacify the angry readers for the sad ending, Dickens changed it into a happy ending. Therefore, the story had two opposite endings.

Great Expectations is an autobiographical novel of Charles Dickens since it bears the marks of his own experience to a large extent. Compared with David Copperfield, the most autobiographical story focusing on acquiring fame and wealth from a humble beginning, Great Expectations went deeper to explore the human heart. In the book, Pip and Dickens both underwent self-examination and self-analysis and realized that fortune cannot replace happiness.

己，决心从头来过。他在开罗待了11年，挣得一笔不小的财富。再次回到家乡的皮普遇到了从失败的婚姻中解脱出来的艾斯黛拉。狄更斯最初给了这本书一个不幸的结局。然而，广大读者对该结局非常不满。为了安抚读者的情绪，狄更斯又给出一个美满的结局。这就是为什么这本书有两个截然不同的结局。

《远大前程》是查尔斯·狄更斯创作的一部自传性质的小说，因为狄更斯在小说中添加了很多自己的经历。与他的另一部自传体小说《大卫·科波菲尔》相比，这本书更深入地挖掘了人的内心，而不是仅仅停留在《大卫·科波菲尔的》描写的白手起家、收获名利的层面。《远大前程》中的皮普和狄更斯本人都进行过自我审视和自我剖析，并领会到财富不等于幸福的生活真谛。

作者介绍 Ａ UTHER

狄更斯（1812~1870），英国现实主义时期作家。狄更斯生活和创作的时间，正是19世纪中叶维多利亚女王时代前期。他主要以写实笔法揭露社会上层和资产阶级的虚伪、贪婪、卑琐、凶残，满怀激愤和深切的同情展示下层社会，特别是妇女、儿童和老人的悲惨处境，并以严肃、审慎的态度描写开始觉醒的劳苦大众的抗争。与此同时，他还以理想主义和浪漫主义的豪情讴歌人性中的真、善、美，憧憬更合理的社会和更美好的人生。主要作品包括《雾都孤儿》《远大前程》《大卫·科波菲尔》《双城记》《艰难时世》等。

词汇 Ｖ OCABULARY

1. convict ['kɔnvikt]
   n. 罪犯　v. 证明…有罪，宣告…有罪

2. crush [krʌʃ]
   v. 压碎，弄皱，使…挤入　v. 挤，被压碎
   n. [俚]迷恋，粉碎，压榨，拥挤的人群

3. benefactor ['benifæktə]
   n. 恩人，捐助者，施主

4. disillusion [,disi'lu:ʒən]
   n. 幻灭，醒悟　v. 使醒悟，使不再抱幻想

5. pacify ['pæsifai]
   v. 使平静，安慰，平定

6. autobiographic [,ɔ:təu,baiəu'græfik]
   a. 自传体的，自传的，自传作家的

自传体小说

自传体小说是传记体小说的一种，是从主人公自述生平经历和事迹角度写成的一种传记体小说。这种小说是在作者亲身经历的真人真事的基础上，运用小说的艺术方法和表达技巧经过虚构、想象、加工而成，它一方面不同于一般的自传和回忆录，另一方面又必须以作者或自述主人公为原型。如：卢梭的《忏悔录》，高尔基的《童年》、《在人间》、《我的大学》等。

063 Treasure Island

Treasure Island, written by Robert Louis Stevenson, is a story about adventure. Being adopted into films several times, this book is now still popular. This book is favored mostly by children who are curious about the outside world and are eager to experience an adventure. The popularity of it can be compared to Journey to the West in Chinese literature. While Journey to the West entertained we Chinese children in our childhood, Treasure Island added colors for most British children's childhood.

The story of Treasure Island is set in the 18th century. The protagonist was a little boy of ten named Jim Hawkings whose parents ran an inn named Admiral

【小译】

罗伯特·路易斯·史蒂文森笔下的《金银岛》是一部寻宝冒险故事。这个故事曾几次被改编成电影。至今仍大受欢迎。这本书最忠实的读者要数那些对外面的世界充满好奇心，富有冒险精神的孩子们了。《金银岛》在西方的受欢迎程度相当于《西游记》在汉语文学中的地位。就像中国孩子从小爱看《西游记》一样，《金银岛》也是一部深受英国小朋友喜爱的作品。

《金银岛》的故事发生在18世

Benbow Inn. One day, the hotel received a strongly-built guest with a scar on his face. This man was Captain Bill. Jim liked to listen to Captain Bill's horror experiences and mysterious sea stories like hanging of the criminal and encountering big storm on the sea. Every time Jim listened to them, he felt scary but excited. However, a few days later, Captain died in the hotel for excessive drinking of alcohol. Jim accidentally found a treasure map on his body. Receiving support from the local rich men, a group of people went on an exploration to the Treasure Island, including Jim and one-legged John Silver. John Silver was a pirate who pretended to be the ship cook with a secret aim to possess the treasure. Besides him, some other pirates also went on board disguised as crew.

In the trip, many things happened. An unexpected malaria killed many people and thrown others in panic; as soon as they arrived at the Treasure Island, they encountered a sailor Bann who has been deserted on the Treasure Island for 3 years; what's more, together with other pirates, John Silver brought up a mutiny against Jim and other crew members and took control. They want to take over this ship and kill the captain. Jim overhears the news. Then Jim and his party fight with these pirates. Finally, Jim and his party win and find the treasure. However, Jim witnessed the people's wickedness and ugliness brought out by the pursuit of money. Back from the adventure, Jim was frequently tortured by bad dreams and swore never to search for treasure anymore.

纪。主人公是一个叫吉姆·霍金斯的小孩。吉姆的父母经营着一家名为"本鲍上将"的小客栈。一天，一个脸上有疤的彪形大汉来到客栈住店。他就是比尔船长。吉姆很喜欢比尔船长给他讲恐怖故事或神秘的海上故事，比如绞死罪犯或海上遭遇暴风雨。每次听到这些故事，吉姆都是既害怕又兴奋。一段日子过后，比尔船长突然酒精中毒身亡。吉姆偶然在他身上发现了一张藏宝图。在当地富人的资助下，包括吉姆在内的一群人踏上了金银岛探险的征程。然而，在这些探险者中潜藏着一些心怀不轨的海盗，他们想霸占宝藏。这群人以独脚水手西尔弗为代表。

航行过程中发生了很多事情。一场突如其来的疟疾杀死了很多人，幸存者不得不在恐慌中度日。在到达金银岛之时，他们遇到了在岛上被困3年的班。独脚水手西尔弗和其他海盗们也开始蠢蠢欲动。他们策划群体叛乱并抢夺宝藏。他们密谋杀死船长、占领航船。他们的计划恰巧被吉姆偶然听到。吉姆和他的跟随者们因此与海盗们展开了激烈的斗争。结果，吉姆方获胜并拿到了宝藏。在此过程中，吉姆看到了金钱利益驱使下人性的丑陋。回到家后，吉姆不断做恶梦，并发誓再也不去寻宝了。

作者介绍 AUTHER

罗伯特·路易斯·史蒂文森 (Robert Louis Stevenson，1850年11月13日～1894年12月3日)出生于苏格兰的爱丁堡。小说家、诗人与旅游作家，也是英国文学新浪漫主义的代表之一。小说《金银岛》 (Treasure Island) （1883年），是其代表作，是关于寻找海盗宝藏的故事，是他的小说中最受欢迎的一部。

1. entertain [,entə'tein]
   ☑ 招待；娱乐；怀抱；容纳 ☑ 款待

2. excessive [ik'sesiv]
   ☑ 过分的；过多的，极度的

3. exploration [,eksplɔ:'reiʃən]
   ☑ 探测；探究；踏勘

4. disguise [dis'gaiz]
   ☑ 伪装；假装 ☑ 假装；掩饰；隐瞒

5. malaria [mə'lɛəriə]
   ☑ 疟疾；瘴气

6. mutiny ['mju:tini]
   ☑ 兵变；叛乱 ☑ 参加叛乱；反叛；暴动

7. wicked ['wikid]
   ☑ 邪恶的；顽皮的；恶劣的；不道德的

名篇名句：

1. We had come so far to find this. Already it had cost the lives of seventeen men from the Hispaniola. And how many others? How many ships had gone to the bottom of the sea? How many brave men had been murdered for this? Perhaps no man alive could tell.

我们远道而来就是为了找到这些。伊斯帕尼奥拉号上已有十七人送了命。此外还有多少人呢？还有多少船沉入了海底？多少勇敢的人为此被人谋杀？恐怕没一个活着的人能讲清楚。

2. I will never return to Treasure Island, but in my worst dreams I still hear the sharp, high scream of Captain Flint the parrot: "Pieces of eight! Pieces of eight!"

我永远不会再回到金银岛上，但在我的噩梦中常常响起那只叫弗林特船长的鹦鹉那尖厉的叫声："八个里亚尔！八个里亚尔！"

|064 Sons and Lovers

Grown up in a coal-mining family, David Herbert Lawrence got much inspiration for writing his masterpiece Sons and Lovers. Written in 1913, as usual, Sons and Lovers dealt with morality and relationship between the opposite sexes.

The book includes two parts, altogether 15 chapters. The first part focuses on the unhappy marriage of protagonist Paul's parents Mr. and Mrs. Morel. Mrs. Morel was a well-educated lady

【小译】

劳伦斯在《儿子与情人》的创作中利用了自己矿工家庭的出身。书中的很多情节的灵感都源于这个背景。《儿子与情人》创作于1913年。与劳伦斯其他的作品一样，这部作品的主题依然涉及道德观和两性关系。

这本书分两部分，共15单元。第一部分主要讲述主人公保罗的父母的不幸婚

from a middle class family while Mr. Morel was a miner. Owning to their difference in personality and class, there were a lot of disagreements between the couple. Mrs. Morel suffered a lot from this marriage and sometimes she was even locked out of the house. The only comfort for Mrs. Morel was her children, especially her sons. After the death of her favorite son William, she put all her love and hopes on her second son Paul. Paul was the only one that can make up for her tragic marriage. Mrs. Morel's love towards Paul was strongly possessive. At the same time, Paul developed the "Oedipus Complex" towards his mother.

When Paul grew up, he fell in love with Miriam Leivers, a farmer's daughter. They had a lot in common and maintained an intimate relationship. However, like Mrs. Morel, Miriam also wanted to possess Paul spiritually. This made her an enemy to Mrs. Morel and she would surely lose the competition. Meanwhile, though Paul loved Miriam, his love towards his mother prevented him from inviting Miriam into his life. Paul met another woman Clara Dawes who was separated with her husband. Both of them found physical comfort in each other. However, their relationship was superficial and could not last long. As a mother, Mrs. Morel was tortured by her relationship with Paul and her heart underwent tremendous emotional struggle until she got very sick. Paul devoted much of his time taking care of her. When Mrs. Morel finally dies, Paul was heart-broken and left his hometown in the end.

This book is quite controversial because it touches upon an unusual relationship, the Oedipus Complex which has always been studying in the literary history.

姻。莫雷尔太太出生于一个中产阶级家庭，受到了良好的教育，而莫雷尔先生是一名矿工。性格上的分歧和阶级的差异使得夫妻二人矛盾不断。莫雷尔太太饱受这段不幸婚姻的种种折磨，有时甚至被粗鲁的丈夫关在门外。孩子们成为莫雷尔太太唯一的慰藉。她把她全部的爱心都倾注在孩子，尤其是两个儿子身上。自从她最疼爱的大儿子威廉死后，莫雷特太太把所有的爱和希望都寄托在二儿子保罗身上。在婚姻中失去的所有，莫雷特都试图从保罗身上找回来。她对保罗的爱带有很强的占有性。同时，保罗也对母亲产生了"恋母情结"。

保罗长大后，爱上了一个农场主的女儿米丽亚姆。两人志趣相投，交往密切。不幸的是，米丽亚姆跟莫雷尔太太一样，希望能从精神上完全占有保罗。如此一来，米丽亚姆为自己树立了一个强劲的敌人，也就是保罗的母亲。两虎相斗必有一伤。而这个受伤的人注定会是米丽亚姆。对保罗来讲，他深爱着米丽亚姆，却因为对母亲的依恋而没有能力接受米丽亚姆。之后，保罗同另一名叫克拉拉的离婚女人保持了肉体关系。二人都灵肉分离，他们的关系也注定无法结出果实。作为母亲的莫雷尔太太不断受到内心的谴责，最终大病一场。期间，保罗守候在母亲身边精心照料。最终，他的母亲因病去世，保罗举步离开了这块伤心之地。

这本书的出版引发了很大的争论，因为它触及的不是一般的关系，而是"俄狄浦斯情节"，或者我们俗称的"恋母情结"。对于这一现象的研究仍在进行中。

戴维·赫伯特·劳伦斯（David Herbert lawrence,1885～1930），英国文学家，诗人。为二十世纪英国最独特和最有争议的作家之一，他笔下有许多脍炙人口的名篇，其中的《查泰莱夫人的情人》（1928），《儿子与情人》，《虹》（1915），《恋爱中的女人》（1921），《误入歧途的女人》等都有中译本。

1. masterpiece ['ma:stəpi:s]
   n. 杰作；绝无仅有的人

2. morality [mɔ'ræliti]
   n. 道德，品行，美德

3. possessive [pə'zesiv]
   n. 所有格 *a.* 所有的；所有格的；占有的

4. Oedipus ['i:dipəs, 'edipəs]
   n. 俄狄浦斯（希腊神话人物）

5. complex ['kɔmpleks]
   n. 复合体；综合设施 *a.* 复杂的；合成的

6. tremendous [tri'mendəs]
   a. 极大的，巨大的；惊人的

俄狄浦斯情结

又称"恋母情结"，是精神分析学的术语。由精神分析学的创始人——西格蒙德·弗洛伊德（Sigmund Freud）提出，儿童在性发展的对象选择时期，开始向外界寻求性对象。对于幼儿，这个对象首先是双亲，男孩以母亲为选择对象而女孩则常以父亲的选择对象。小孩做出如此的选择，一方面是由于自身的"性本能"，同时也是由于双亲的刺激加强了这种倾向，也即是由于母亲偏爱儿子和父亲偏爱女儿促成的。在此情形之下，男孩早就对他的母亲发生了一种特殊的柔情，视母亲为自己的所有物，而把父亲看成是争得此所有物的敌人，并想取代父亲在父母关系中的地位。同理，女孩也以为母亲干扰了自己对父亲的柔情，侵占了她应占的地位。因此，同样也有"恋父情结"。

Unit 16 建筑作品

With a long, rich and vibrant history, the UK today gets the legacy of a large number of architecture works of high aesthetic values and recreational functions throughout Great Britain which attract tourists all over the world. You can literally find anything you want to experience here. If you are fascinated about ancient European buildings, the UK is your best choice. Due to its long history, the UK boasts a large selection of ancient castles, royal palaces and impressive stately homes in various states. There are also some of the world's finest churches, cathedrals, abbeys, temples and other religious sites in the UK. If you want to see some ancient arts collections, Britain is home to many splendid art galleries and museums documenting the history of human culture. If you want to find something that can provide days worth of excitement and entertainment to suit everyone in the family, there are also theme parks or amusement parks. Besides, there are many nature reserves in UK cities including parks, gardens, safari parks and zoos.

Due to the limited space, it is not possible for us to exhaust all these architecture works in the UK. In this unit we will mainly choose some of the most representative sites ranging from ancient castles, royal palaces, museums, landmarks, theme parks and royal parks in the hope of providing a brief glimpse of the spectacular landscape and splendid culture of the UK.

英国悠久的历史、丰富的文化为今天的英国留下了丰富的建筑遗产，这些建筑作品不仅有很高的审美价值，也极具娱乐功能，吸引了世界各地的游客。在这里你几乎可以找到你想要欣赏的任何风景。如果你痴迷于欧洲的古建筑，那英国是你最佳的选择。悠久的历史给这个国家留下了各种各样的古代城堡、皇家宫殿和豪华古宅。这儿还有很多世界上最为精致而又壮观的大教堂、修道院、寺庙等宗教建筑。如果你想看古代艺术展览，英国有许多辉煌的画廊、博物馆，记录了人类文化的历史。如果你想找到一个可以让你们全家都能玩得尽兴的地方，那你可以来主题乐园和游乐场。此外，英国还有许多自然保护区，有公园、花园、野生动物园和动物园等。

由于篇幅所限，我们的介绍不可能将英国所有的建筑作品都囊括在内。我们主要将选择一些最具代表性的建筑进行介绍，包括古城堡、皇家宫殿、博物馆、地标性建筑、主题乐园和皇家公园。我们希望通过这些介绍让大家对英国壮丽的风光和灿烂的文化有一个初步的了解。

065 The Big Ben

The Big Ben, the 320 foot high Clock Tower at the north end of the Palace of Westminster (Houses of Parliament) in London, is one of the most prominent symbols of both London and England, often in the establishing shot of films set in the city. It is the largest four-faced chiming clock and the third-tallest free-standing clock tower in the world.

The name Big Ben actually doesn't refer to the clock-tower itself, but to the bronze bell hung within weighing 13 tons, which was said to have been named after the first commissioner of works, Sir Benjamin Hall. The bell was cast on 10 April 1859 at the Whitechapel Bell Foundry in East London. To this day one of the largest bells they have ever cast. Each clock face is over 7 meters in diameter.

The bell looks most spectacular at night when the clock faces are illuminated. A special light above the

【小译】

大本钟是位于伦敦威斯敏斯特宫（国会大厦）北部的钟楼，是伦敦与英格兰最显著的标志之一，经常在电影中被用来标志伦敦。大本钟是世界上最大的四面报时钟，也是世界第三大独立的钟楼。

大本钟这个名字实际上指的并不是钟楼本身，而是指悬挂在钟楼里重达13吨的铜钟，据说这个铜钟是以建造工程的第一名监督官本杰明爵士的名字命名的。这顶钟于1859年4月10日在伦敦东部的怀特查佩尔铸钟厂铸造成功。是该钟厂迄今为止铸过的最大的钟。铜钟每一面的直径都超过了7米。

大本钟在晚上钟楼四面都亮起

clock faces is also illuminated, letting the public know when parliament is in session. Minutely regulated with a stack of coins placed on the huge pendulum, Big Ben is an excellent timekeeper, which has rarely stopped. During the Second World War in 1941, an incendiary bomb destroyed the Commons chamber of the Houses of Parliament, but the clock tower remained intact and Big Ben continued to keep time. The BBC first broadcast the unique sound of chimes on 31 December 1923 – there is a microphone in the turret connected to Broadcasting House.

There are even cells within the clock tower where Members of Parliament can be imprisoned for a breach of parliamentary privilege, though this is rare; the last recorded case was in 1880. The tower is not open to the general public, but those with a "special interest" may arrange a visit to the top of the Clock Tower through their local (UK) MP (Members of Parliament).

来的时候最为壮观。此外，每当议会召开会议的时候，大钟上方的灯就会点亮，让公众知晓。通过调整放置在钟摆上一些小钱币，大本钟走时精确，鲜有停走的时候。在1941年二战期间，一个燃烧弹将国会大厦的下院议员室炸毁，但是钟楼依然完好无损，大本钟没有受到影响，继续精确计时。英国广播公司从1923年12月31日起开始广播大本钟报时的独特声音——钟楼的角楼中装有麦克风，与BBC广播室相连。

钟楼里还有监狱，可以用来囚禁那些违反国会特权的议员，然而这种情况很少见，最近的一起也是1880年的事了。钟楼内部不对公众开放，那些有"特殊兴趣"的游客可以通过英国当地的国会议员安排到钟楼顶部参观。

词汇 VOCABULARY

1. free-standing adj. 独立的；不需依靠支撑物的	2. illuminate [i'lju:mineit] vt. 阐明，说明；照亮；使灿烂 vi. 照亮
3. timekeeper n. 计时员；钟表；工作时间记录员	4. incendiary [in'sendjəri] n. 燃烧弹；纵火犯 adj. 煽动的；放火的，纵火的
5. chime [tʃaim] n. 一套发谐音的钟；和谐；钟声 vi. 鸣响；和谐 vt. 打钟报时；敲出和谐的声音	6. breach [bri:tʃ] n. 违背，违反；缺口 vt. 打破；违反，破坏

背景链接 TIPS

Palace of Westminster

威斯敏斯特宫，又称国会大厦，位于英国伦敦威斯敏斯特市，是英国国会（包括上议院和下议院）的所在地。威斯敏斯特宫坐落在泰晤士河西岸，是哥特复兴式建筑的代表作之一，1987年被列为世界文化遗产。西北角的钟楼就是著名的大本钟所在地。

066 Buckingham Palace

Buckingham Palace is the official London residence of the British monarch since 1837 and today is the administrative headquarters of the Monarch used to receive and entertain guests on state, ceremonial and official occasions. Located in the City of Westminster between The Green Park, Hyde Park and St. James's Park, the palace has been a focus for the British people at times of national rejoicing and crisis.

Originally a large townhouse known as Buckingham House, it was built for the Duke of Buckingham in 1705. In 1825, George VI commissioned John Nash to remodel the existing house into a palace by adding three wings around a central courtyard, where he could then hold court and conduct official business. Buckingham Palace finally became the official royal palace of the British monarch when in 1837 Queen Victoria took up residence only three weeks after her Accession. The last major structural additions were made in the late 19th and early 20th centuries, including the East front which contains the well-known balcony on which the Royal Family traditionally congregate to greet crowds outside. However, the palace chapel was destroyed by a German bomb in World War II; the Queen's Gallery was built on the site and opened to the public in 1962 to exhibit works of art from the Royal Collection.

Buckingham Palace's 19 state rooms, ballroom and gardens are open to visitors during August and September

【小译】

白金汉宫自1837年起成为英国帝王在伦敦的行宫。而现今，它是女王举行召见、宴请外宾及举行重要的官方活动的行政宅邸。白金汉宫位于威斯敏斯特城，坐落在格林公园、海德公园和圣·詹姆斯公园之间。每当国家有了喜庆或是危急的时刻，这里便是英国民众关注的焦点。

白金汉宫是于1705年为白金汉公爵所建，最早叫做白金汉屋。1825年乔治六世委托建筑师约翰·纳什改变其建筑结构，通过在中央庭院周围加盖三个侧厅使之成为一座宫殿。这样他便可在其中操办法院及官方事务。1837年维多利亚女王继位三周后开始在白金汉宫居住，这里便成了正式的英国皇室的居住地。白金汉宫最近一次改建是在19世纪末20世纪初的时候，其中就包括东侧建有一个著名的阳台的侧楼，按照传统王室成员会聚在那个阳台上向窗外的民众致意。然而，宫内的礼仪厅已于二战时期毁于德国的炮火之中。女王美术馆也建在这里，并于1962年对公众开放，其中陈列着王室珍藏的名贵艺术品。

每年的八九月份女王对巴莫纳进行年度例行访问期间，白金汉宫内的19个国事厅、舞厅和御花园便对公众开放。来访者便可以游览19个国事厅，这些国事厅由王室珍藏的宝物装饰，包括精致的法

while the Queen makes her annual visit to Balmoral. Visitors can tour the nineteen State Rooms, which are decorated with some of the greatest treasures from the Royal Collection, including paintings and the finest French and English furniture.

Particularly popular with visitors is the Changing the Guard ceremony, which takes place in the forecourt of Buckingham Palace at 11:30 a.m. every day in summer, every other day in winter. The New Guard marches to the Palace from Wellington Barracks and the Old Guard hands over in a ceremony during which the sentries are changed and then returns to barracks. The ceremony lasts about 45 minutes and is free to watch.

国和英国的家具和绘画作品。

对于来访者而言，最具吸引力的当属上午11点半在白金汉宫前庭举行的皇家卫队换岗仪式，换岗仪式在夏季每天举行一次，冬季每隔一日一次。在仪式上，新的守卫部队由惠灵顿兵营开进宫内，而原有的卫队则交出防卫，撤下卫兵，然后返回兵营。仪式大约持续45分钟，可以免费观看。

词汇 VOCABULARY

1. commission [kəˈmiʃən] *n.* （权限，任务等的）委任 *vt.* 委任，委托	2. wing [wiŋ] *n.* 侧厅，厢房
3. accession [ækˈseʃən] *n.* 就职；登基；（权力等的）获得	4. congregate [ˈkɔŋgrigeit] *vi.* 聚集，集合 *vt.* 使聚集，使集合
5. chapel [ˈtʃæpəl] *n.* （学校、医院、王宫等的）附属礼拜堂	6. ballroom [ˈbɔːlrum] *n.* 舞厅
7. sentry [ˈsentri] *n.* 站岗；看守，警卫	8. barrack [ˈbærək] *n.* 营房，兵营 *vi.* 住入营房 *vt.* 向…提供营房

背景链接 TIPS

1. Queen Victoria

维多利亚女王（1819年5月24日～1901年1月22日）英国历史上在位时间最长的君主。她是第一个以"大不列颠和北爱尔兰联合王国女王和印度女皇"名号称呼的英国君主。她在位的64年期间（1837～1901年），是英国最强盛的所谓"日不落帝国"时期。她在位的60余年正值英国自由资本主义由方兴未艾到鼎盛、进而过渡到垄断资本主义的转变时期，经济、文化空前繁荣，君主立宪制得到充分发展，使维多利亚女王成了英国和平与繁荣的象征。

2. Changing the Guard ceremony

白金汉宫的皇家卫队每年4～9月时上午11:30至12:00都会举行的换岗仪式，其他月份每两天11:30举行一次，在军乐和口令声中，作各种列队表演，并举行的举枪互致敬礼，一派王室气象，常常吸引路人和游客围观。在每年的8、9月间都对外开放，一般民众就可趁此时进入皇宫。

|067 Westminster Abbey

Westminster Abbey is a large Gothic church in London, part of the Church of England. Located just to the west of the Palace of Westminster, it is more a historical site than a religious site. It was built by Edward the Confessor and opened in 1065. In 1066, it saw its first coronation, that of William the Conqueror. Since then, nearly every king and queen has been coronated there.

Most of the present building dates from 1245 to 1272 when Henry III decided to rebuild the abbey in the gothic style. Large parts were later added: the Chapel of Henry VII was added between 1503 and 1512, while the two West Front Towers date from 1745. The youngest part of the abbey is the North entrance, completed in the 19th century.

The abbey's nave is England's highest. In the nave you find the Grave of the Unknown Warrior, a World War I soldier who died on the battlefields in France and was buried here in French soil. Nearby is a marble memorial stone for Winston Churchill. His body is not, like many fellow prime ministers, buried in the abbey, but in Bladon. The beautiful octagonal Chapter house is one of the largest of its kind in England.

The Henry VII Chapel is one of the most outstanding chapels of its time, with a magnificent vault. The chapel has a large stained glass window, the Battle of Britain memorial window. The window, which dates from 1947 and replaces an original window that was damaged during World War II, commemorates fighter

【小译】

威斯敏斯特大教堂是伦敦一座大型哥特式建筑，属英格兰教会的一部分，西侧毗邻威斯敏斯特皇宫，比起它的宗教作用，它更应算作一座历史遗址。教堂是于1065年由忏悔者爱德华所修建。1066年，教堂举行了第一次加冕仪式，主角是征服者威廉。此后，几乎每个国王和王后都要在此举行加冕。

1245至1272年，亨利三世决定重建哥特风格的大教堂，现今教堂的大部分建筑都建于那个时期。而也有很大一部分是后来加上的：亨利七世礼拜堂建于1503至1512年间，而西侧的两个门塔则建于1745年。整个教堂年代最近的是其北侧入口，建成于19世纪。

教堂的中殿是全英格兰最高的。在中殿内你可以看到一个无名勇士墓，这个士兵死于一战时的法国战场，用法国土壤下葬于此。不远处是一座为温斯顿丘吉尔树立的大理石纪念碑。与其前任首相们不同，丘吉尔的遗体并不是葬在教堂中，而是葬在布拉登。这个漂亮的八角型的房子是英格兰同类建筑中最大的。

亨利七世礼拜堂是同年代最杰出的建筑，有一个富丽堂皇的穹顶。小教堂有一个很大的玻璃窗，用以纪念不列颠战役。原先的窗户已于二战时期被毁坏，新的窗户于1947年建成，为的是纪念1940年不列颠战役中阵亡的战斗机飞行

pilots and crew who died during the Battle of Britain in 1940.

The abbey also serves as the burial ground for numerous politicians, sovereigns and artists. The abbey is stuffed with tombs, statues and monuments. Many coffins even stand upright due to the lack of space. In total approximately 3300 people are buried in the Church and cloisters. The Poet's Corner houses the tombs and memorials of Geoffrey Chaucer, Charles Dickens, John Keats, among many others literary giants. Some famous scientists are also buried here, like Charles Darwin and Sir Isaac Newton.

员以及舰艇船员。

威斯敏斯特大教堂亦被用作政治家、帝王及艺术家的墓地。众多的墓碑、雕像和纪念碑充满其间。有些棺材甚至因为缺乏空间而被直立放置，整个教堂和修道院大约埋葬了3300多人。教堂中的诗人角有许多文学巨将的墓和纪念碑，包括杰佛里·乔叟，查尔斯·狄更斯和约翰·济慈。一些著名的科学家也葬于此，比如查尔斯·达尔文以及伊萨克·牛顿等。

词汇 VOCABULARY

1. confessor [kənˈfesə(r)]
   n 自白者；忏悔者

2. coronation [kɔrəˈneɪʃ(ə)n; (US) kɔːrəˈneɪʃ(ə)n]
   n 加冕典礼

3. accession [ækˈseʃən]
   n 就职；登基；（权力等的）获得

4. abbey [ˈæbi]
   n 属修道院的教堂

5. octagonal [ɔkˈtægənl]
   a 八边形的；八角形的

6. magnificent [mægˈnifisnt]
   a 壮丽的，宏伟的；豪华的；华丽的

7. commemorate [kəˈmeməreit]
   v 庆祝；纪念

8. sovereign [ˈsɔvrin]
   n 君主，元首；最高统治者 *a* 最高统治者的

9. cloister [ˈklɔistə]
   n 修道院 *v* 幽闭于修道院中；使与尘世隔绝

背景链接 TIPS

1. Gothic

哥特式建筑是11世纪下半叶起源于法国、12～15世纪流行于欧洲的一种建筑风格。主要建于天主教堂，也影响到世俗建筑。以尖拱、拱顶、细长柱等为特点。

2. The Henry VII Chapel

亨利七世礼拜堂位于威斯敏斯特教堂（又译为"西敏寺"）的后部，建于16世纪，是英国中世纪建筑的代表作品，装饰华丽，其巨大的扇形垂饰和拱顶设计异常大胆和巧妙。周围还有其他很多献给故去国王的礼拜堂，如英国著名的朝圣地圣爱德华礼拜堂、雕饰繁复的亨利五世礼拜堂等。

068 York Minster

York Minster is a beautiful and imposing Gothic cathedral in York, northern England. It is one of the largest of its kind in Northern Europe alongside Cologne Cathedral. The minster is the seat of the Archbishop of York, the second-highest office of the Church of England, the highest being the Archbishop of Canterbury. The formal title of York Minster is The Cathedral and Metropolitical Church of St Peter in York. The title "Minster" is attributed to churches established in the Anglo Saxon period as missionary teaching churches, and serves now as an honorific title.

York Minster incorporates all the major stages of Gothic architectural development in England. It has an extra-wide Decorated Gothic nave (1275~1290), a Decorated Gothic chapter house (1275~1290), a Perpendicular Gothic choir, and Early English north and south transepts (1220~1255). The west towers, west front and central tower were built in the Perpendicular style (1470~1472).

The nave is extra wide and tall, and is roofed in wood made to look like stone. At the west end is the Great West Window, constructed in 1338, which featuring delicate stone tracery that forms a heart in the top center. There are several other fine windows along the nave walls, dating from the early 14th century. The Great East Window (1408) towers over the Lady Chapel in the east end. It is the largest medieval stained glass window in the world. Its colorful panes depict Biblical scenes from Genesis and Revelation: the beginning and end of the world. The 13th-century chapter house is considered an excellent example of the Decorated style. It contains no central pillar, and beneath great stained glass windows are more than 200 carved heads and figures — including humans, animals and foliage.

【小译】

约克大教堂是位于英格兰北部约克郡的一座漂亮而壮观的哥特式教堂。它与科隆大教堂都是北欧同类建筑中最庞大的。该教堂是英格兰教会的第二把交椅约克郡大主教的座堂，而教会中地位最高的则是坎特伯雷大主教。约克大教堂的正式称谓叫做约克郡圣彼得座堂和大主教教堂。大教堂的称谓主要赐予那些在盎格鲁撒克逊时期作为教会的传教之所而建立的教学，而时至今日，这是一个尊贵的称呼。

约克大教堂体现了哥特式建筑在英格兰发展所经历的所有重要阶段。教堂有一个外扩的哥特式装饰的中殿（1275～1290），一个哥特式装饰的牧师礼堂（1275～1290），一个垂直的哥特式的唱诗圣坛，早期英格兰北部和南部风格的十字翼（1220～1255），而西侧塔楼，西大门以及中央塔楼皆以垂直风格建造（1470～1472）。

教堂的中殿格外宽敞和高大，其房顶是由木材制成，看上去却像是石制的。西侧的尽头是大西窗，建于1338年，于顶部中央以精致的石制窗格形成一个心型。沿中殿的墙壁还另有其他一些源于14世纪的精美的窗户。大东窗（1408）远高出东侧的圣母堂，是世界上最大的中世纪彩色玻璃窗。其丰富多彩的窗格绘画描绘着《圣经》中从《创世纪》开始的景象：世界的起源和末日。13世纪的牧师礼堂被认为是哥特尖拱式建筑样式

From the south transept, you can pay an additional fee to climb 275 narrow steps to the central tower, or descend a few steps to the undercroft. The undercroft displays archaeological finds from the 1967 repair of the Minster's foundations, including both Roman and Norman ruins. Also down here is the treasury, featuring 11th-century artifacts and relics from the graves of medieval archbishops, and the crypt, with the cathedral's only font and numerous medieval stone carvings.

的杰出代表。它没有中央立柱,其下庞大的彩色窗格中雕刻着超过200幅图案——包括人类、动物和树叶。

从教堂南侧的十字翼部,你可以额外支付些费用来攀登通向中央塔楼的275级狭窄的台阶,或者下台阶到达地下室。地下室展示着1967年修复的教堂根基的考古学发现,包括罗马及诺曼时期的废墟。再往下是金库,里面有中世纪大主教的墓中出土的11世纪的古器物和遗迹,以及地下土窖,伴着教堂特有字体以及很多中世纪石雕。

词汇 VOCABULARY

1. imposing [im'pəuziŋ]
   a.（建筑物等）壮观的;（仪表）堂堂的

2. cathedral [kə'θi:drəl]
   n. 大教堂

3. archbishop ['ɑ:tʃ'biʃəp]
   n. 大主教;总教主

4. missionary ['miʃənəri]
   n. 传教士 a. 传教的;传教士的

5. honorific [,ɔnə'rifik]
   a. 尊敬的;敬称的

6. perpendicular [,pə:pən'dikjulə]
   n. 垂线 a. 垂直的,正交的;直立的;陡峭的

7. transept ['trænsept]
   n. 教堂的十字型翼部

8. delicate ['delikit]
   a. 微妙的;易碎的;清淡可口的;柔和的

9. medieval [,medi'i:vəl]
   n. 中世纪的;仿中世纪的;[贬]原始的

10. foliage ['fəuliidʒ]
    n. 植物;叶子（总称）

11. undercroft ['ʌndəkrɔft]
    n. 地下室;圆顶地下室

12. archaeological [,ɑ:kiə'lɔdʒikəl]
    a. [古] 考古学的;[古] 考古学上的

背景链接 TIPS

1. The Church of England

英国国教会（Church of England）,也称为安立甘宗或圣公宗,是基督新教的一个教派,与信义宗、归正宗同属基督新教三大主流教派。由英国国王亨利八世创始,并作为当时英国的国教,由英国国王担任教会最高首脑。

2. Biblical

圣经是亚伯拉罕诸教（包括基督新教、天主教、东正教、犹太教等各宗教）的宗教经典,由旧约全书与新约全书组成,旧约全书是犹太教的经书,新约全书是耶稣基督以及其使徒的言行和故事的纪录。

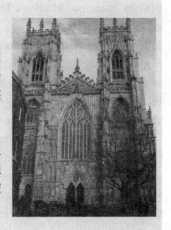

069 The British Museum

The British Museum is a museum of human history and culture in London, covering an area of over 75,000 m² of exhibition space. It is also the first national public museum in the world. Its collections, with a number of more than seven million objects, are amongst the largest and most comprehensive in the world. In addition, the collections originate from all continents, together illustrating and documenting the story of human culture from its beginnings to the present.

The British Museum was founded in 1753, largely based on the collections of the physician and scientist Sir Hans Sloane. It was first housed in a seventeenth-century mansion, Montagu House, in Bloomsbury on the site of today's building. Its expansion over the following two and a half centuries was largely a result of an expanding British colonial footprint. Some objects in the collection, most notably the Elgin Marbles from the Parthenon, are the objects of intense controversy and of calls for restitution to their countries of origin.

The core of today's building, the four main wings of the British Museum, was completed in 1852. The quadrangle building was designed in the Greek Revival style, which emulated classical Greek architecture. Greek features on the building include the columns and

【小译】

大英博物馆是一座位于伦敦的人文历史文化的博物馆，展出面积75000平方米。它也是世界上第一个国立公共博物馆。大英博物馆拥有超过七百万件的收藏品，是世界上最多、最全面的。此外，这里的收藏来自各大洲，共同描绘和记录了人类文明从发源至今的故事。

大英博物馆成立于1753年，其收藏品大都由物理学家兼科学家汉斯·斯罗纳爵士所提供。它们最先被收藏于一幢17世纪的宅邸——位于布卢姆斯伯里的蒙塔古大楼，也就是今天的博物馆所在地。接下来的两个半世纪，它追随着英国殖民扩张的脚步而不断扩建。它的一些展品，特别是来自帕台农神殿的埃尔金石雕，在是否应归还给其原产国的问题上存在巨大的争议。

今天博物馆建筑的核心——四栋主要的侧厅建成于1852年。这个四方形的建筑是模仿古希腊建筑结构，以希腊复兴式风格设计。建筑中的希腊

pediment at the South entrance. It included galleries for classical sculpture and Assyrian antiquities as well as residences for staff. In 1853, the quadrangle building won the Royal Institute of British Architects' Gold Medal.

The King's Library was a royal collection of books created by King George III and donated to the nation. A house, named after the collection, was built at the British Museum in 1827 to house them. The house on the ground floor of the East Wing, was described as one of the finest rooms in London although it was not fully open to the general public until 1857. It is now home to the permanent exhibition Enlightenment: Discovering the world in the eighteenth century.

Since its foundation, the museum granted free admission to all studious and curious persons. Visitor numbers have grown from around 5,000 a year in the eighteenth century to nearly 6 million today.

特征包括其柱子以及南门的山型墙。它包括有关古典雕塑以及亚述人文明史的画廊以及员工宿舍。1853年，这幢四方体建筑赢得了英国皇家建筑师协会金奖。

国王图书馆展出皇家收藏的书籍，它是由乔治三世国王创立并捐给国家的。这栋房子于1827年在大英博物馆建成，并以其收藏品命名。国王图书馆位于东厅的一楼，被认为是伦敦最好的房子，但是它直到1857年才向公众开放。现在这里举办了一个长期展览——启蒙运动：探索18世纪的世界。

自成立之日起，博物馆向所有勤奋好学的来访者发放免费参观券。访客人数已由18世纪的每年5000人增长到了现在的每年600万人。

词汇 VOCABULARY

1. comprehensive [ˌkɔmpriˈhensiv]
   n 综合学校；专业综合测验 a 综合的；广泛的

2. controversy [ˈkɔntrə،vəːsi]
   n 争论；论战；辩论

3. restitution [ˌrestiˈtjuːʃən]
   n 恢复；赔偿；归还

4. quadrangle [kwɔˈdræŋgl]
   n 四边形；方院

5. emulate [ˈemjuleit]
   n 仿效；仿真 v 仿真；尽力赶上；同…竞争

6. pediment [ˈpedimənt]
   n 山形墙；三角墙

7. sculpture [ˈskʌlptʃə]
   n 雕塑；雕刻；刻蚀 vt / vi 雕塑；雕刻

8. antiquity [ænˈtikwiti]
   n 高龄；古物；古代的遗物

9. permanent [ˈpəːmənənt]
   a 永久的，永恒的；不变的

10. studious [ˈstjuːdjəs]
    a 用功的；热心的；专心的；故意的

背景链接 TIPS

1. Greek Revival style

在19世纪初，在英国兴起了希腊复兴建筑。它的主要特点是使用希腊式的多立克和爱奥尼柱式，并且追求体形的单纯。

2. Royal Institute of British Architects

英国皇家建筑师学会（简称RIBA）于1834年以英国建筑师学会的名称成立，1837年取得英皇家学会资格。它的宗旨是：开展学术讨论，提高建筑设计水平，保障建筑师的职业标准。

070 Madame Tussauds

As a globally famous wax museum, Madame Tussauds is one of the most visited attractions in London. Constantly updated figures from the list of the rich and famous, ancient and modern, make a day trip to Tussaud's a memorable experience for visitors from all round the world.

Marie Tussaud (1761~1850), a native of Strasbourg, France, learned the fine art of sculpting from her mother's employer, a physician skilled in the art of wax modeling. Her first solo exhibit appeared on Baker Street in 1835 followed by her famous Chamber of Horrors collection in 1845, where Madame Tussaud displayed a collection of death masks that she had made of the victims of the guillotine during the French Revolution in Paris. In the meantime, she added many likenesses to her collection. In 1884, several decades after her death, Madame Tussaud's Wax Museum moved to its current location on London's Marylebone Road.

Tussaud and her successors have fashioned literally thousands of replicas of famous people. Visitors can view world leaders, actors/actresses like Marilyn Monroe, sports legends, famous writers and artists, religious figures, musicians like Michael Jackson, and a host of other characters. Besides those displays there are also several themed sections in the museum include the Grand Hall where you'll find royals from down the ages as well as the current Queen Elizabeth I; and the Spirit of London where you will be offered a taxi ride through the sights, sounds and smells of 400 years of London life.

【小译】

作为全球知名的蜡像博物馆，杜莎夫人蜡像馆无疑是伦敦最具吸引力的游览之所。古代与现代列表中不断更新的蜡像，对于来自全世界的前往杜莎夫人蜡像馆的游客来说都是一次值得纪念的旅行经历。

杜莎夫人（1761~1850）生于法国的斯特拉斯堡。她从她母亲的雇主——一名在制作蜡像模型方面颇具造诣的医生——那里学到了优良的雕塑手艺。杜莎夫人的第一个独立展馆于1835年在贝克大街开业，紧随其后的便是1845年创立的著名的恐怖之屋。在那里杜莎夫人展出了她制作的死亡面具，这些面具是根据法国大革命期间在巴黎被送上断头台的受害者制作的。与此同时，她又为她的收藏添加了许多逼真的作品。1884年——她逝世数十年后，杜莎夫人蜡像馆被迁至现址——伦敦的玛丽伯恩路。

杜莎夫人和她的继承者们制作了数千个世界知名人士的复刻蜡像。观众们可以看到世界上的领导人们、演员（如玛丽莲·梦露），传奇的体育人，著名的作家和艺术家、宗教人士、音乐家（如迈克尔·杰克逊）以及许许多多的其他的人物形象。除了这些展览外，博物馆中还有一些主题展览，包括"大会堂"，你可以看到与现在的伊丽莎白一世女王年龄相仿的皇室成员；还有"伦敦精神"，你将会坐上出租车穿越层层景象，亲身感受伦敦400年的历史变迁。

The current museum suffered a fire in 1925 and many statues were lost. However, the molds remained intact and several of the pieces were recreated. It is now one of London's busiest attractions and during peak tourist season, it is common to encounter long lines that stretch for blocks. The museum started an overseas expansion in 1970, when it opened a branch location in Amsterdam. Today it has expanded to many more cities including Amsterdam (The Netherlands), Berlin (Germany), Bangkok (Thailand), Hong Kong, Shanghai (China), New York, Las Vegas, Hollywood and Washington D.C. (United States). A new branch in the UK was opened in Blackpool in 2011.

1925年，一场大火毁掉了博物馆，很多作品都遗失了。但是模具依然较为完好，一些残骸也被还原。现今，它已是伦敦最为繁忙的景点。在旅游高峰期，馆前经常会排起横跨街区的长队。博物馆于1970年开始了海外扩张，在阿姆斯特丹开设了分馆。现在，它已经在很多城市开设了分馆，包括荷兰的阿姆斯特丹、德国柏林、泰国曼谷、中国的香港和上海、美国的纽约、拉斯维加斯、好莱坞和华盛顿特区。新的英国分馆于2011年在布莱克浦开业。

词汇 VOCABULARY

1. update [ʌp'deit]
   n 更新；现代化 *v* 更新；校正；使现代化

2. memorable ['memərəbl]
   a 显著的，难忘的；值得纪念的

3. sculpting
   n 雕塑法 *v* 雕刻；雕塑（sculpt的现在分词）

4. guillotine ['giləti:n, gilə'ti:n]
   n 断头台；切纸机 *v* 于断头台斩首

5. successor [sək'sesə]
   n 继承者；后续的事物

6. mold [məuld]
   n 霉菌；模子 *v* 塑造；使发霉 *v* 发霉

7. intact [in'tækt]
   a 完整的；原封不动的；未受损伤的

背景链接 TIPS

1. Marilyn Monroe

玛丽莲·梦露（1926年6月1日～1962年8月5日）是美国20世纪最著名的电影女演员之一。她动人的表演风格和正值盛年的殒落，成为影迷心中永远的性感女神性感符号和流行文化的代表性人物。1999年，她获美国电影学会选为百年来最伟大的女演员第六名。

2. Michael Jackson

迈克尔·杰克逊（1958年8月29日～2009年6月25日），是一名在世界各地极具影响力的流行音乐歌手、作曲家、作词家、舞蹈家、演员、导演、唱片制作人、慈善家、时尚引领者，被誉为流行音乐之王。他的音乐曲风完美地融合了黑人节奏蓝调与白人摇滚的独特的MJ乐风。他魔幻般的舞步更是让无数的明星效仿。因其私人医生莫里违规操作注射镇静剂过量导致心脏病突发逝世，终年50岁。

071 The Stonehenge

Stonehenge is a prehistoric, mysterious circle of upright stones in southern England. One of the most famous ancient sites in the world, Stonehenge is composed of earthworks surrounding a circular setting of large standing stones. The current site, awe-inspiring as it is, is only part of the original Stonehenge. The original construction has suffered a great deal from both weather damage and human pillage of its rock over the millennia. The site and its surroundings were added to the UNESCO's list of World Heritage Sites in 1986.

Stonehenge has been the subject of much archaeological and scientific inquiry and research, especially in the last century. The modern account of the construction of Stonehenge is based primarily on excavations done since 1919 and especially since 1950. Archaeologists believe the first stones was erected around 2500 BC and the construction was carried out in three main stages, which have been labeled Stonehenge I, Stonehenge II and Stonehenge III, spanning at least 1500 years.

The original purpose of building the Stonehenge is unclear to us, but some have speculated that it was

【小译】

巨石阵是位于英格兰南部的，是一圈神秘的、呈圆环状分布的直立的史前的石头。巨石阵是世界上最著名的古代遗迹，是由环绕在站立的石头周围的环状土方结构所组成。巨石阵的现址，虽然依然令人敬畏，但只是其最初样子的一部分。其最原始的构造在长达千年的岁月中饱经恶劣天气和人类掠夺带来的破坏。1986年，该遗址被列入联合国教科文组织的世界遗产名单。

巨石阵是众多考古学和科学的研究对象，特别是在上个世纪。在现在，对于巨石阵的描述主要是基于1919年以来，特别是1950年以来的发掘工作的成果。如今考古学家们认为，第一批巨石建于公元前2500年，整个建造过程历经三个阶段，分别被标示为巨石阵Ⅰ，巨石阵Ⅱ和巨石阵Ⅲ，前后历经1500年之久。

巨石阵建造的最初目的我们还不

a temple made for the worship of ancient earth deities. It has been called an astronomical observatory for marking significant events on the prehistoric calendar. Archaeological evidence found by the Stonehenge Riverside Project in 2008 indicates that Stonehenge served as a burial ground from its earliest beginnings. The dating of cremated remains found on the site indicate burials from as early as 3000 BC, when the initial ditch and bank were first dug. Burials continued at Stonehenge for at least another 500 years.

The astonishing scale and beauty of the stones, the great care and labor in construction, and the mystery that surrounds its original purpose make Stonehenge one of the most popular sights in England. It draws over 800,000 visitors per year, and several thousand gather on the summer solstice to watch the sunrise at this ancient and mystical site. The stones are aligned almost perfectly with the sunrise on the summer solstice.

得而知。一些人推测说，这是古代地球上为了供奉神灵而建造的庙宇。它在史前日历被称为标记重要事件的天文台。考古学家们通过2008年的巨石阵河畔项目发现的迹象表明，巨石阵最早是作为一个墓地来使用的。遗址中所发现的火葬的残留物显示，殉葬早在公元前3000年，也就是沟渠和岸堤首次开挖的时候，巨石阵的殡葬功能至少另外持续了500年。

巨石阵以其惊人的规模、漂亮的石头、建造中出色的维护和所动用的巨大劳力、以及它神秘莫测的建造初衷，成为了英格兰最受欢迎的景观之一。这里每年吸引超过80万的参观者，而夏天的时候，数千人聚集在这古老而神秘的遗址中观看日出。在夏至日出之时，石头的排列近乎完美。

词汇 VOCABULARY

1. prehistoric [ˌpriːhisˈtɔrik]
   adj. 史前的；陈旧的

2. upright [ˈʌpˈrait]
   adj. 垂直；竖立 adj. 正直的，诚实的；笔直的

3. earthwork [ˈɜːθwɜːk]
   n. [建] 土方工程；土木工事

4. pillage [ˈpilidʒ]
   n. 掠夺；掠夺物 vt./vi. 掠夺；抢劫

5. millennia [miˈleniə]
   n. 千年期（millennium的复数）；一千年

6. archaeological [ˌɑːkiəˈlɔdʒikəl]
   adj. [古] 考古学的；[古] 考古学上的

7. excavation [ˌekskəˈveiʃən]
   n. 挖掘，发掘

8. speculate [ˈspekjuˌleit]
   vi. 推测；投机；思索

背景链接 TIPS

UNESCO

联合国教科文组织，英文（United Nations Educational, Scientific and Cultural Organization），简称UNESCO。1946年成立，总部设在法国巴黎。其宗旨是促进教育、科学及文化方面的国际合作，以利于各国人民之间的相互了解，维护世界和平。为了保护世界文化和自然遗产，1976年，世界遗产委员会成立（World Heritage Sites），并建立了《世界遗产名录》。

072 Hyde Park

Hyde Park is one of four royal parks in Central London. Covering more than 360 acres (142 hectares), Hyde Park is the largest of the four royal parks which form a chain from the entrance of Kensington Palace through Kensington Gardens and Hyde Park, via Hyde Park Corner and Green Park (19 hectares), past the main entrance to Buckingham Palace and then to Saint James's Park (23 hectares). With a history of over 500 years, Hyde Park has hosted many large events like celebrations and concerts. It is also a popular place for jogging, swimming, rowing, picnicking and even horse riding.

In 1536 King Henry VIII acquired Hyde Park from the monks of Westminster Abbey. It was used primarily for hunting at that time. The park was opened to the public by King Charles I in 1637. The current park layout was planned by architect Decimus Burton in 1825.

The Serpentine, a large artificial lake, is located at the south end of the park and extends into the neighboring Kensington Gardens where the lake is called the Long Water. Constructed by Queen Caroline, wife of King George II in 1730, it is now a popular site for boating and swimming. Just southwest of the Serpentine is a memorial fountain installed in honor of Princess Diana. The memorial fountain, which resembles a small river rather than a fountain, was inaugurated in 2004 by Queen Elisabeth II.

At the south end of Hyde Park is Rotten Row, a famous bridle path. In

【小译】

英国有四大皇家公园，海德公园是其中最大的，座落于伦敦市中心，占地360多英亩（约142公顷）。四大皇家公园从肯辛顿宫的入口处开始，沿着海德公园与肯辛顿公园，通过海德公园的演讲角和格林公园（占地19公顷），途经白金汉宫的主入口，延伸到圣詹姆斯公园（占地23公顷），呈链形分布。在超过五百年的悠久历史中，海德公园曾举办了多次重大庆典和隆重的音乐会。这里也是大众慢跑、游泳、划船、野餐乃至游乐骑马的好去处。

1536年，英王亨利八世从威斯敏斯特教堂的僧侣手中得到海德公园，开始是作为狩猎场使用的。1637年英王查理一世向公众开放了海德公园。如今的公园布局是由建筑师德西默斯波顿在1825年设计建成的。

海德公园的南端蜿蜒伸展着一条人造湖泊——九曲湖，此湖一直延伸至相邻的肯辛顿公园，故名为"长水"。九曲湖1730年由国王乔治二世的妻子凯瑟琳皇后建成，现在已经成为划船和游泳的场所。

九曲湖的西南部有一座纪念喷泉，说是喷泉，其实倒更像一条小河流。这座喷泉2004年由伊丽沙白二世亲自主持落成仪式，是为了向戴安娜王妃致敬而建成。

海德公园的南面是

the 17th century the road was used by William III, who found the walk from Kensington Palace to St. James was too dangerous. So he had oil lamps installed along the route, thus creating the first public road to be lit in England. The road is almost four miles long (6.4 km) and is now used as a horse riding, cycling, rollerblading and jogging route.

In the 19th century, Hyde Park had become a popular place for meetings. In 1872, in response to riots after police tried to disband a political meeting, Speaker's Corner was established, creating a venue where people would be allowed to speak freely. Here, every Sunday people stand on a soap box and proclaim their views on political, religious or other items, sometimes interrupted and challenged by their audience.

一条著名的跑马道，罗德路。这条路是17世纪威廉三世御用，他发现从肯辛顿宫至圣詹姆斯大教堂的道路太阴暗危险，就命人在路边挂上油灯，这也开创了英格兰第一条照亮路径的公路。罗德路总长约4英里（合6.4公里），现在成为民众骑马、自行车和滑旱冰的道路。

到了19世纪，海德公园成为各种集会的场所。1872年，警察驱散一个民众的政治集会而引发了一场暴动，此后为了给民众创造一个自由表达的场所，于是"演讲者之角"应运而生。在这儿，每个周日都有人站上临时讲台宣扬他们的政治和宗教等理念，有时这些演讲者也会被听众打断和质疑。

词汇 VOCABULARY

1. layout ['lei,aut]
   n 布局；设计；安排；陈列

2. fountain ['fauntin]
   n 喷泉，泉水；源泉

3. resemble [ri'zembl]
   v 类似，像

4. riot ['raiət]
   n 暴乱；放纵 v 骚乱；放荡 vt 浪费，挥霍

5. disband [dis'bænd]
   v 解散 vt 解散；遣散

6. proclaim [prə'kleim]
   vt 宣告，公布；声明，表明；赞扬

背景链接 TIPS

1. Princess Diana

戴安娜(Diana Spencer)王妃1961年7月1日出生于英国诺福克，是爱德华斯宾塞伯爵的小女儿，1981年7月29日与威尔士亲王查理斯结婚。她是查尔斯的第一任妻子，亦是威廉王子和哈里王子的亲生母亲。

2. William III

英格兰的威廉三世（William III，1650年~1702年），即苏格兰的威廉二世、奥兰治的威廉亲王、奥兰治亲王、荷兰执政、英国国王。他是荷兰执政威廉二世与英国国王查理一世之女玛丽公主的儿子。

073　The Tower of London

Tower of London, is a historic castle on the north bank of the River Thames in central London, England. It was built at the beginning of the 11th century by William the conqueror and was expanded during the 13th century into the fortified complex that we know today. As a whole, the Tower is a complex of several buildings set within two concentric rings of defensive walls and a moat.

The oldest part of the fortress is the so-called White Tower, which was completed in 1097. It was whitewashed during the reign of Henry III, which gave the tower's facade its white appearance. Ever since the tower is known as White Tower. The White Tower was long the tallest building in London at 27.4 meter. Its walls had a width of 4.6 meter. It has four domed turrets at each corner, three of which have a square shape, the other is round, due to its spiral staircase. The round turret was long used as an observatory.

The most famous tourist attraction in the Tower of London today is the collection of Crown Jewels that has been on display here since the 17th century, during the reign of Charles II. Most of the jewels were

【小译】

伦敦塔是伦敦中部泰晤士河北岸的一座历史悠久的城堡。自11世纪征服者威廉开始建造，在13世纪又经扩建后成为今人所知的大型塔群。总体来讲，伦敦塔是好几座建筑物的复合体，处于两层同心圆防御城墙和护城河的环绕保护之下。

伦敦塔最古老的城堡被称为白塔，于1097年完工。亨利三世统治期间伦敦塔被涂成白色，拥有了白色的外表，从此白塔之名才为人所熟知。白塔高27.4米，曾是伦敦最高的建筑物。白塔城墙厚4.6米，四角耸出四座高塔，三座为方型，另一座因其内部有螺旋楼梯，故为圆形，过去长时间用作观象台。

自17世纪查尔斯二世统治期开始，全套御用珠宝就开始在伦敦塔展出，如今珍宝馆已成为伦敦塔最知名的景点。大多珠宝都在1660年君主复辟时被制成，克伦威尔统治时期毁掉

created around the year 1660, when the monarchy was reinstalled. The majority of the older crown jewels were destroyed by Cromwell. The jewels can be found in the Jewel House, located in the Waterloo Barracks just north of the White Tower.

The Tower of London has played a prominent role in English history. It was besieged several times and controlling it has been important to controlling the country. The Tower has served variously as an armoury, a treasury, a menagerie, the home of the Royal Mint, a public records office. It used to be notorious for the many political opponents of the kings that were locked, tortured and killed in there. The Tower was also a royal residence: several kings lived here, especially during turbulent times when the donjon seemed a lot safer than the palace in Westminster.

了古老珠宝中的大部分。残留下来的珠宝如今陈列于白塔北部滑铁卢军营的珍宝馆中。

伦敦塔在英国历史中扮演了非常重要的角色，历史上曾多次被围攻，要控制英国必须占领伦敦塔。该塔用途广泛，曾作为兵器库、珠宝库、动物园、皇家铸币厂以及记录档案室使用。曾有大量的国王政敌在此被关押、虐待、刑杀，伦敦塔也因此臭名昭著。此外，伦敦塔也是一处皇家宫殿，英国数代国王都曾居住在此，在时局动荡的年代，重重防护的城堡看起来要比威斯敏斯特宫殿安全多了。

词汇 VOCABULARY

1. fortify ['fɔ:tifai]
   v 加强；增强；设防于 v 筑防御工事

2. concentric [kɔn'sentrik]
   a 同轴的；同心心的

3. fortress ['fɔ:tris]
   n 堡垒；要塞 v 筑要塞；以要塞防守

4. facade [fə'sɑ:d]
   n 正面；表面；外观

5. dome [dəum]
   n 圆屋顶 v 成圆顶状 v 加圆屋顶于…上

6. turret ['tʌrit]
   n 炮塔；角楼；小塔；攻城用仰冲车

7. observatory [əb'zə:vətəri]
   n 天文台；气象台；瞭望台

8. besiege [bi'si:dʒ]
   v 围困；包围；烦扰

9. armoury ['ɑ:məri]
   n 兵工厂，军械库

10. donjon ['dɔndʒən]
    n 城堡主楼

背景链接 TIPS

1. River Thames

泰晤士河（Thames River）是英国著名的"母亲"河。发源于英格兰西南部的科茨沃尔德希尔斯，全长402公里，横贯英国首都伦敦与沿河的10多座城市，

2. Cromwell

奥利弗·克伦威尔是英国政治家、军事家、宗教领袖。17世纪英国资产阶级革命中，资产阶级——新贵族集团的代表人物、独立派的首领。

EVENTS

Part 5
英国人正在关注的现代轶事与
高频回望的历史事件

Unit 17 现代重大事件

In the past decade, the British has witnessed a lot of big events taking place in the world as well as in their own country which had also influenced the rest of the world.

Globalization, which had intensified in the post-Cold War 1990s, continued to influence the world in the 2000s. The Internet is one of the prime contributors to globalization, making it possible for people to interact with other people, express ideas, introduce others to different cultures and backgrounds, use goods and services, sell and buy online, research and learn about anything, along with experiencing the whole world without having to leave home.

The September 11 attacks in 2001 ultimately led to the United States, United Kingdom and other nations invading and occupying Afghanistan, as well as implementing various anti-terrorist measures at home and abroad in what was known as the War on Terror. The European Union saw further integration and expansion throughout much of Europe. The economic growth of the 2000s, while responsible for lifting millions out of poverty, also had considerable environmental consequences, raised demand for diminishing energy resources, and was still shown to be vulnerable as demonstrated during the Global Financial Crisis of the late 2000s.

Back in the UK, the General Election of 6 May 2010, resulted in the first hung parliament since 1974 with the Conservative Party winning the largest number of seats but falling short of the 326 seats required for an overall majority. Following this, the Conservatives and the Liberal Democrats agreed to form the first coalition government for the UK since the end of the Second World War with David Cameron becoming Prime Minister and Nick Clegg Deputy Prime Minister.

The UK also have some good occasions to celebrate: the city of London was finally elected as the host city of the 2012 Olympic Games and the whole country is preparing for the coming international sports event. What's more, on 29 April 2011, the British witnessed and celebrated the grand wedding ceremony of their beloved Prince William with a commoner – Princess Kate.

In this part, we will mainly focus on three of the most sensational events that have most influence to the British people and that are best-known to the global community – the financial crisis, the 2012 London Olympic Games and Prince William's wedding.

在过去的十年中，英国见证和发生了许多影响世界的大事。

上世纪90年代冷战之后日益加剧的全球化进程，在2000年后继续影响着世界。互联网是全球化的首要因素，它使得以下的一切在网络上成为可能：人们与其他人交流，分享想法，向其他人介绍不同的文化和背景，使用商品和服务，在线交易，足不出户体验全世界。

2001年9月11日的恐怖袭击最终使得美国、英国以及其他一些国家入侵并占领了阿富汗，以反恐战争的名义在其国内外实行多项反恐政策。欧盟看上去更加统一，并扩展到了大部分欧洲领土。21世纪头十年经济的增长，使得数百万人摆脱了贫困，同时也是很大程度上环境影响的后果。经济的增长使得对于节能减排的诉求不断升温，而近年来的全球金融危机则显示出这股经济增长的势头仍然是非常脆弱的。

回到英国。2010年5月6日的大选中,保守党赢得了最多的席位,但没有达到获胜所需的326席,导致了1974年以来的第一个无多数议会的产生。鉴于此,保守党和自由民主党同意组建自二战结束以来的第一个联合政府,由大卫·卡梅伦出任首相,尼克·克莱格担任副首相。

英国同样有很多值得庆祝的时刻:伦敦成为了2012年奥运会的主办城市,整个国家都在为这个即将到来的全球性的体育盛会做着准备。2011年4月29日,全英国人民见证了他们所爱戴的威廉王子同平民公主凯特的盛大婚礼。

在这一部分,我们重点关注三个最具轰动效应的,对英国人影响最大同时也是最广为全世界所知的事件——金融危机、2012年伦敦奥运会以及威廉王子的婚礼。

|074 The Global Financial Crisis

【小译】

The global financial crisis in the late 2000s is considered by many economists to be the worst financial crisis since the Great Depression of the 1930s. It is commonly believed to have begun in July 2007 with the credit crunch, when a loss of confidence by US investors in the value of subprime mortgages caused a liquidity crisis. This, in turn, resulted in the US Federal Bank injecting a large amount of capital into financial markets.

The collapse of Lehman Brothers on September 14, 2008 marked the beginning of a new phase in the global financial crisis. Governments around the world struggled to rescue giant financial institutions as the fallout from the housing and stock market collapse worsened. Many financial institutions continued to face serious liquidity issues. Consumer confidence hit rock bottom as everyone tightened their belts in fear of what could lie ahead.

Although the housing collapse in the United States is commonly referred to as the trigger for the global financial crisis, many experts who have examined the events over the past few years, and indeed even politicians in the United States, now agree that the financial system was poorly regulated and to some extent even encouraged unscrupulous lending.

The U.S. government proposed a $700 billion

发生在21世纪前十年末期的全球金融危机被很多经济学家看作是自20世纪30年代经济大萧条以来的最严重的经济危机。人们普遍认为这场危机始于2007年7月的信贷紧缩,那时的美国投资者们的信用下降引发了次贷危机,相应地导致了美国联邦银行向资本市场注入了大笔资金。

2008年9月14日雷曼兄弟的破产标志着新一轮全球金融危机的到来。由于次级房地产和股票市场的崩溃加剧,世界各国政府都努力地挽救其庞大的金融机构。许多金融机构继续面临着不断恶化的资金流动问题。消费者信任度降到了谷底,每个人都对未来可能发生的一切产生了恐惧。

美国房地产市场的崩盘被认为是引发全球金融危机的推手。很多专家在分析了近几年发生的事件后开始相信——甚至很多美国政治家也开始同意——金融系统调节能力低下,在一定程度上甚至鼓励了无节制的贷款。

美国政府提出了7000亿美元的救市计划,但未能通过。原因是国会中的一些议员反对动用如此巨额的纳

rescue plan, which subsequently failed to pass because some members of US Congress objected to the use of such a massive amount of taxpayer money being spent to bail out Wall Street investment bankers who had in many people's eye been the cause of the global financial crisis. By September and October of 2008, people began investing heavily in gold, bonds and US dollar or Euro currency as it was seen as a safer alternative to the ailing housing or stock market. In January of 2009 US President Obama proposed federal spending of around $1 trillion in an attempt to improve the state of the financial crisis.

Some financial commentators believe that we have now seen the worst of it, while others are now saying that the massive government spending on stimulus packages could come back to haunt future generations, as at some point in time the debt will need to be repaid.

税人的钱款用于救助华尔街的投资银行家们，这些银行家在许多人眼里已经成为了全球金融危机的产生动因。2008年9月和10月，人们开始大量投资黄金、债券、美元以及欧洲货币。相比于恶劣的房地产和股票市场，这被认为是一种较为稳妥的选择。2009年1月，美国总统奥巴提出了1万亿美元的联邦开支，用于重振金融危机下的美国经济。

有些金融评论家相信最糟糕的时期已经过去，而另有一些人说政府庞大的一揽子计划开支将困扰我们的后代，因为在某种程度上这些钱终归是要偿还的。

词汇 VOCABULARY

1. subprime [sʌb'praim]
   adj. 次级的；准最低贷款利率的

2. mortgage ['mɔ:gidʒ]
   n. 抵押 *vt.* 抵押

3. liquidity [li'kwiditi]
   n. 流动性；流动资产；偿债能力

4. unscrupulous [ʌn'skru:pjuləs]
   adj. 肆无忌惮的；寡廉鲜耻的；不讲道德的

5. subsequent ['sʌbsikwənt]
   adj. 后来的，随后的

背景链接 TIPS

1. The Great Depression of the 1930s

指1929年至1933年间的全球性的经济大衰退。这次衰退是以农产品价格下跌为起点，随后1929年10月华尔街股市暴跌，上千万人失业。这次萧条比历史上任何一次经济衰退造成的影响都更深远。

2. Lehman Brothers

雷曼兄弟公司自1850年创立以来，已在全球

范围内建立起了创造新颖产品、探索最新融资方式、提供最佳优质服务的良好声誉。北京时间2008年9月15日，在次级抵押贷款市场危机（次贷危机）加剧的形势下，作为美国第四大投资行的雷曼兄弟最终丢盔弃甲，宣布申请破产保护。

|075 Prince William's Wedding

The wedding of Prince William, Duke of Cambridge, and Catherine Middleton was held on 29 April 2011 at Westminster Abbey in London. Prince William, second in the line of succession to Queen Elizabeth II, first met Catherine Middleton in 2001, when both were studying at the University of St Andrews. On 16 November 2010 their engagement was announced. The prince had proposed while the pair were on holiday in Kenya. The occasion attracted much media attention and is broadcast live around the world, with much of the attention focused on Kate Middleton's status as a commoner marrying into royalty.

It was a public holiday in the United Kingdom and over 5000 street parties were held to mark the Royal wedding throughout the United Kingdom and one million people lined the route between Westminster Abbey and Buckingham Palace. Hours before the service, the Queen conferred the titles Duke of Cambridge upon William. Upon her marriage, Middleton therefore became Her Royal Highness The Duchess of Cambridge.

As Prince William was not the heir apparent to the throne, the wedding was not a full state occasion and many details were decided by the couple, such as much of the guest list of about 1,900. The ceremony was attended by most of the Royal Family, as well as many foreign royals, diplomats, and personal guests the couple had chosen.

【小译】

剑桥公爵威廉王子与凯瑟琳·米德尔顿的婚礼于2011年4月29日在伦敦威斯敏斯特大教堂举行。威廉王子在伊丽莎白二世女王的王位继承权排行中排名第二，他与凯瑟琳·米德尔顿初次相识是在2001年，那时二人都在圣安德鲁斯大学学习。2010年11月16日，他们订婚的消息被公之于众，威廉王子是于二人在肯尼亚度假时提出求婚的。婚礼吸引了众多媒体的关注，向全世界现场直播。很多舆论的焦点聚焦于凯特·米德尔顿以平民身份嫁入皇室。

这是一个英国的公众假期，为庆祝皇室婚礼，英国举行了超过5000场街区集会，超过100万人在威斯敏斯特大教堂和白金汉宫之间排起了长龙。婚礼前一小时，女王授予了威廉剑桥公爵称号。而因为这场婚姻，米德尔顿成为了剑桥公爵夫人殿下。

由于威廉王子不是王位的法定继承人，所以婚礼并不是一个完全的官方场合，所以婚礼的许多细节得以由夫妇二人自行决定，比如1900人的宾客名单。大部分的皇室家族参加了婚礼，还有很多外国皇室、外交官以及夫妇二人自己挑选的私人贵宾。

新娘身着一件由英国设计师莎拉·伯顿设计的白色婚纱，头戴女王借给她的皇冠。威廉王子身

The bride wore a white dress by British designer Sarah Burton, as well as a tiara lent to her by the Queen. Prince William wore the uniform of his honorary rank of Colonel of the Irish Guards. Prince Harry, William's brother acted as his best man, while the bride's maid of honor was her sister, Pippa. The wedding ceremony began at 11:00 am, local time. The ceremony lasted just over an hour and included vows and a sermon delivered by the Bishop of London, private clergyman to the queen. After the ceremony, the newly married couple departed Westminster Abbey, by carriage, and processed to Buckingham Palace for the traditional appearance on the balcony.

Despite reports that the couple would leave for their honeymoon the day after their wedding, Prince William immediately returned to his work as a search-and-rescue pilot. The location of the honeymoon was initially kept secret, with not even Catherine knowing where they would be heading. However, it was later revealed that the couple ultimately decided to honeymoon for 10 days on a secluded villa on a private island in the Seychelles.

穿象征他爱尔兰卫队上校名誉的制服。威廉王子的弟弟哈里王子充当他的伴郎，而新娘的伴娘则是她的姐姐皮帕。婚礼于当地时间上午11点开始，持续了超过一个小时，包括新人许愿以及女王的私人牧师——伦敦主教的布道。婚礼结束后，新婚夫妇乘马车离开了威斯敏斯特大教堂，前往白金汉宫传统的皇室成员亮相的阳台。

尽管有报道说这对新婚夫妇于婚礼后去度了蜜月，威廉王子在蜜月后很快回到他的工作岗位上，他的职务是一名救援机飞行员。度蜜月的地点最初是保密的，甚至连凯瑟琳都不知道。但据事后透露，夫妇俩最终在偏远的塞舌尔岛上的一栋私人别墅里度过了为期10天的蜜月。

词汇 VOCABULARY

1. engagement [inˈgeidʒmənt]
   n. 婚约；约会；交战；诺言

2. commoner [ˈkɔmənə]
   n. 自费学生；平民；下议院议员

3. royalty [ˈrɔiəlti]
   n. 王权；皇室；版税；专利税

4. diplomat [ˈdipləmæt]
   n. 外交家，外交官；有外交手腕的人

5. tiara [tiˈɑ:rə]
   n. 女式冕状头饰；（罗马教皇的）三重冕

6. colonel [ˈkə:nl]
   n. 陆军上校

背景链接 TIPS

Sarah Burton

莎拉·伯顿，英国服装设计师，是亚历山大·麦昆在中央圣马丁学院的同门师妹。1996年，刚从圣马丁毕业一年的莎拉·伯顿，就加入了亚历山大·麦昆旗下，14年来一直追随亚历山大·麦昆，成为他在世时的挚爱密友和第一助理。2000年起，莎拉·伯顿被任命为亚历山大·麦昆女装设计总管，3月的亚历山大·麦昆2010秋冬秀，也正是在她的主持下完成。2010年5月27日她被GUCCI集团正式任命为亚历山大·麦昆的掌门人。

076 2012 London Olympic Games

London was elected as the host city of the 2012 Summer Olympic Games on 6 July 2005 during the 117th IOC Session in Singapore, defeating Moscow, New York City, Madrid and Paris after four rounds of voting. The successful bid was headed by former Olympic champion Sebastian Coe. The Games are scheduled to take place from 27 July to 12 August 2012. London will become the first city to officially host the modern Olympic Games three times, having previously done so in 1908 and in 1948.

The handover ceremony, which marked the moment when the previous games in Beijing in 2008 handed over the Olympic Flag to the new host city of London, took place on the closing ceremony of the 2008 Beijing Olympic Games on 24 August 2008. Mayor of London Boris Johnson received the flag from Mayor of Beijing Guo Jinlong, on behalf of London. The handover ceremony also featured the urban dance group ZooNation, the Royal Ballet and Candoco, a disabled dance group, all dressed as typical London commuters waiting for a bus by a zebra crossing. A double-decker bus drove around the stadium to music composed by Philip Sheppard eventually stopping and

【小译】

在2005年7月6日于新加坡举行的国际奥委会第117次全体会议上，经过了4轮投票，伦敦击败了莫斯科、纽约、马德里和巴黎，被选为了2012年夏季奥运会的主办城市。这次成功的申办是由前奥运冠军塞巴斯蒂安·科所领导。本次奥运会计划于2012年7月27日至8月12日举行。伦敦也成为了有史以来第一个三次举办现代奥运会的城市，前两次分别是在1908年和1948年。

2008年8月24日，在北京奥运会的闭幕式上举行了交接仪式。仪式上，北京将奥运会的会旗正式交给了新一届的主办城市伦敦。伦敦市市长鲍里斯·约翰逊代表伦敦从北京市市长郭金龙手中接过旗帜。交接仪式上表演的还有ZooNation城市舞团、皇家芭蕾舞团以及一个残疾人舞蹈组合Candoco。所有来往于人行横道上斑马线的等待巴士的人们穿着传统的伦敦服饰。一辆双层巴士在菲利普·谢

transforming into a privet hedge featuring famous London landmarks such as Tower Bridge, The Gherkin and the London Eye. Jimmy Page and Leona Lewis then performed the Led Zeppelin classic Whole Lotta Love and David Beckham kicked a football into the crowd of athletes accompanied by violinist Elspeth Hanson and cellist Kwesi Edman.

The logo for the 2012 London Olympic Games was unveiled on 4 June 2009 and is a representation of the number 2012, with the Olympic Rings embedded within the zero. The official mascots for the 2012 Summer Olympic and Paralympic Games were unveiled on 19 May 2010. Wenlock and Mandeville are animations depicting two drops of steel from a steelworks in Bolton. They are named Wenlock, after the Shropshire town of Much Wenlock, which held a forerunner of the current Olympic Games, and Mandeville, after Stoke Mandeville, a village in Buckinghamshire where a forerunner to the Paralympic Games were first held.

波德的音乐下绕着体育场行驶，最终停了下来并转化为了水腊树，上面有伦敦著名地标，例如伦敦塔桥、"小黄瓜"大楼和伦敦眼。吉米·佩吉和莱昂纳·刘易斯率领齐柏林飞艇乐队合唱《全部的爱》。大卫·贝克汉姆将一个球踢向了人群和运动员们，伴着他一起出现的还有小提琴家埃尔斯佩思·汉森和大提琴家科威斯·艾德曼。

2012年伦敦奥运会会徽于2007年6月4日公布，它象征数字2012，并在数字0中嵌入了奥运五环。2012年夏季奥运会及残奥会的吉祥物于2010年5月19日公布。文洛克和曼德维尔是由来自博尔顿钢铁厂的两个钢块绘制成的卡通形象。文洛克来自于马齐文洛克的施普罗维尔村，那里曾经举办的奥林匹克运动会是现代奥运的先驱。曼德维尔则来自白金汉郡的斯托克曼德维尔村，那里曾举办了第一个残疾人运动会。

词汇 VOCABULARY

1. privet ['privit]
   n. 女贞；水蜡树

2. hedge [hedʒ]
   n. 树篱；障碍 *vt.* / *vi.* 用树篱笆围住

3. mascot ['mæskət]
   n. 吉祥物；福神

4. steelworks ['sti:lwɜ:ks]
   n. 炼钢厂

5. forerunner ['fɔ:,rʌnə]
   n. 先驱；先驱者；预兆

背景链接 TIPS

1. IOC Session

国际奥林匹克委员会全体会议（简称国际奥委会全会）是国际奥林匹克委员会的最高权力机构，奥林匹克运动中一切重大问题的决策权均由全会掌握。譬如通过、修改和解释《奥林匹克宪章》，挑选主办奥运会的城市等。全会每年至少举行一次会议。

2. Sebastian Coe

塞巴斯蒂安科是上世纪80年代英国优秀的中长跑运动员，曾称霸于800m和1500m两个项目。伦敦申奥时任伦敦奥申委主席，并帮助伦敦夺得了2012年的奥运会主办权。

Unit 18 战争篇

The British history is a history of wars. Wars of different kinds with different aims permeated the whole British history. However, there is one thing in common in all the wars, that is, to fight either for power or land.

The Roman Conquest was the first important ancient wars took place in Britain. After the conquest, England was subjected to the Roman ruling. As soon as the Romans gone in the early 5th century, Germanic people invaded Britain in the middle of the century, which was known as the Germanic Invasions. They were the ancestors of Anglo-Saxon people. By the end of the 9th century, England suffered from another invasion from Danish Vikings, generally referred to as the Danish Invasion and met the resistance of Alfred the Great. That was the end of the major ancient British wars.

Different from the ancient wars, the Hundred Years' War was more about conquest instead of being conquest. The war was fought between England and France during 1337 and 1453, lasting for over one hundred years, as was indicated by the name.

The Wars of Roses was another kind of war in that it occurred between two different royal houses struggling for the throne. The war took many people's life, especially members from royal families.

Also struggling for power, the Civil War differentiates the Wars of Roses in the nature of the country. The two sides of the war were "Ironsides" led by Oliver Cromwell and the royalist led by King Charles I. The war resulted in the establishment of a commonwealth.

Although the monarchy was restored in 1660, the power of the monarchy was limited by the Bill of Rights signed by William the Orange and Mary owning to the Glorious Revolution and the constitutional monarchy was created.

Britain has also been involved in many other wars such as The Seven Years' War with France, The War against Napoleon and of course the First and Second World War. Except for the Glorious Revolution, all the other wars deprived numerous lives.

英国的历史就是一部战争史。英国历史上充满了不同种类、不同目的的战争。然而，这些战争都有一个共同点，那就是为权力或土地而战。

这部战争史以罗马征服为起点。被征服后的英格兰被罗马统治了5个世纪。罗马人5世纪初刚撤退，英格兰就在世纪中期遭到日耳曼人的入侵。日耳曼人就是盎格鲁-萨克逊人的祖先。到了9世纪末，英格兰再次遭到丹麦维金人的侵略，阿尔弗雷德大王坚决抵御。古代战争基本告终。

与古代战争不同，英法百年战争更像是一场侵略战争，而不是受侵略战争。这场战争从1337年一直打到1453年，持续了一百多年，因此得名。

玫瑰战争又是另一种性质的战争。它是两个王室家族争夺权力之战。战争中无数人牺牲，尤其是王室家族的成员。

同是权力的争夺，内战与玫瑰战争有着大不相同的性质。战争双方分别是奥利弗·克伦威尔领导的"铁军"和国王领导的王党。内战以王党的失败告终，英国也进入了短暂的共和国时期。

1660年虽然王朝被复辟，但是在1688年光荣革命胜利后，1689年奥伦治的威廉和玛丽签署了限制国王的权力的《权利法案》，英国形成了君主立宪制的政体。

英国经历过的另一些比较重大的战争有英法七年战争，拿破仑战争和两次世界大战。在英国战争史上，除了光荣革命，其他的战争都夺取了无数无辜的性命。

077 The Hundred Years' War

This is a war between England and France lasted for over one hundred years from 1337 to 1453 on and off.

Before Edward III came to the throne, England has already got a series of quarrels with France. In the 1330s, Edward III invaded the Scots. Before succeeded in making himself the king of Scotland, the Scots received assistance from France who broke their promise not to interfere English rights to territories on the mainland again and again. The war between England and France was eventually triggered when the French King Philip VI demanded Edward to return the French land held by Edwards. In response, Edward claimed that he was the legal heir to the French throne because the mother of Edward was the sister of three French kings, all of whom died without a son. King Philip VI was only the son of a French Duke instead of a member of royal family.

The war started in 1337 and had a 6-year break after the English fleet destroyed a French fleet in 1340. In 1346, the war broke again in which English won the first important battle at Crecy. Son of Edward III, Edward, the Black Prince became famous for his excellent command in the battle, although he was only 16 years old. In the following year, Edward III seized Calais and the two parties came to another truce lasted for 8 years until 1355 when the Black Prince won the second

【小译】
这是1337到1453年之间英国和法国进行的一系列战争。战争打打停停一直持续了100多年，因此得名。

在爱德华三世即位之前，英国和法国就有争执。14世纪30年代，爱德华三世入侵苏格兰。苏格兰人得到法国的支持奋起反抗，阻止了爱德华称王。法国一直打破不在英国领土内进行干涉的承诺，激怒了爱德华三世。而战争的导火索是法国国王腓力六世向英王索要英国持有的法国领地。爱德华反过来向腓力六世索要本属于爱德华的法国王位。原来，爱德华的母亲是法国三任国王的妹妹，而这三位国王死时都无子。腓力六世只不过是法国一位公爵的儿子，不属于王室成员。

战争持续到1340年英国舰队挫败法国舰队后停战6年。1346年，战争再次爆发，英国在克雷西取得了百年战争的第一次大捷。该战争中最大的英雄是爱德华的儿子黑太子，当时只有16岁。次年，英国夺取加莱后，双方再次停战。8年后，黑太子在普瓦提埃战役中取得了第二次大捷。法国通过加莱条约把整个阿基坦划给英国，条件是爱德华不得再索要

important battle at Poitiers. The Peace of Calais gave all of Aquitaine to Edward in exchange of the French throne. However, in his late years, Edward forged another war resulting in the loss of most of the French territory upon failure.

There was a long break of the war after Edward III's death until Henry V took the throne. Henry V was an innate soldier and military commander. Like Edward III, he again claimed a right to the French throne and renewed the Hundred Years' War. Henry won the third most English victory in the Hundred Years' War at Agincourt, which was also one of the most famous victories in the England history. Henry won many other battles and captured more territories until his death. However, during the reign of his son Henry VI, France took back most of the territories by continuously defeating English army. When the war finally ended in 1453, only Calais was left in the hands of England.

法国王位。然而，爱德华晚期又发动了一次对法战争，结果失掉了以前获得的大部分法国领土。

爱德华三世死后，几任国王都没有再次发动对法战争，直到亨利五世继位。亨利五世天生骁勇善战，是个优秀的军事统领。亨利五世再次向法国索要法国王位，重开百年战争。在他的领导下，英国在阿让库尔战役中获得了百年战争的第三次大捷，也是本国史上最有名的大捷之一。一系列的战役让英国再次占领了法国大多数地区。然而在他的儿子亨利六世继位后，法国不断打败英国军队夺回领地。到战争1453年结束时，英格兰在法国只剩了加莱一个据点。

1. interfere [ˌintəˈfiə] vt 干涉；打扰；妨碍 vi 冲突；介入	2. trigger [ˈtrigə] n 触发器；扳机 vt 松开扳柄 vi 触发；引发
3. fleet [fliːt] n 舰队；小河 a 快速的 vi 疾驰；飞逝	4. truce [truːs] n 休战；休战协定 vi 以休战结束；停止争执
5. innate [ˈineit] a 先天的；固有的；与生俱来的	

背景链接 TIPS

百年战争起因

法国力图把英国人从法国西南部（基思省）驱逐出去，从而消除英在法境内的最后一个堡垒，而英国则力图巩固它在基恩的地位，夺回早先失去的诺曼底、曼恩、昂茹和法国的其他一些地区。英法两国对佛兰德的争夺，加深了它们之间的矛盾。佛兰德形式上是处于法国国王的统治之下，但实际上却是独立的，并且与英国有密切的贸易关系（英国的羊毛是佛兰德毛纺织业的主要原料）。战争的导火线是英国国王爱德华三世觊觎法国王位。德国封建主和佛兰德站在英国一方，苏格兰和罗马教皇则支持法国。英军主要由雇佣兵组成，由国王指挥，其主体是步兵（弓箭兵）和雇佣骑士部队。法军主要由封建骑士武装（见骑士军）组成。

078 The War of the Roses

The wars of the Roses refer to a series of wars fought between two royal families, House of Lancaster and House of York struggling for power. The wars were called so because the badge of the House of Lancaster was a red rose while the badge of the House of Lancaster was a white rose.

The last king of the House of Lancaster was Henry VI who was very weak. His weakness provided opportunities for many people to take advantage. During Henry VI's ruling, the power of English nobles expended to a large extent and France used this opportunity to free itself from English control. By 1453, France had taken back all the land they had lost to England except Calais. Even his wife, Queen Margaret of Anju was much powerful than him. The English people were dissatisfied with Henry VI's weakness.

On account of Henry's weakness, the nobles of the House of York decided to overthrow him. Richard, an ambitious duke of York claimed the throne with a reason that he was the descendent of the third son of King Edward III while Henry was the descendent of Edward III's fourth son. Therefore, he had a better right to the throne. The parliament accepted his justification and it was decided that Edward III would be the king after Henry VI died. However, this decision was refused by Queen Margaret who wanted her son to succeed his father. The wars broke out between the two families and by 1459; Richard won the victory with the support of a nobleman Earl of the Warwick and forced Henry to promise passing the throne to him after death. However, the persistent Queen Margaret forged another war and killed Richard in the following year. In 1461, Warwick declared Richard's first son Edward IV to be the king who was the first king of the House of York and defeated the Lancaster army together resulting in the former king and queen's escaping to Scotland. Three years later,

【小译】

玫瑰战争指的是兰开斯特家族和约克家族为争夺王权展开的一系列战争。之所以称之为玫瑰战争是因为兰开斯特家族的徽章是一支红色的玫瑰，而约克家族是白色玫瑰。

兰开斯特家族最后一任国王亨利六世是一位非常软弱的君主。很多人伺机谋求利益。亨利六世统治期间，贵族势力膨胀，法国乘机夺回了大部分领地。到1453年，英国在法国占领的领土只剩下了加莱。连他的妻子安茹·玛格丽特也比他权力大。英国人民对软弱的国王产生了强烈的不满。

约克家族的贵族伺机企图把亨利六世赶下台。约克家族的一个雄心壮志的贵族理查德提出了王位要求，理由是他是爱德华三世第三个儿子的后代，而亨利六世是爱德华四世第四个儿子的后代，因此，他理应获得王位。议会认为理查德里理由正当并宣布理查德在亨利六世之后继位。亨利的妻子玛格丽特对此坚决反对，她认为王位理应由儿子继承。1459年，两个家族开战。爱德华在得到势力强大的沃里克伯爵的支持下取得胜利并迫使亨利六世保证死后传王位给他。然而，玛格丽特仍不甘心并在次年发动战争杀死了理查德。1461年，沃里克把理查德的长子爱德华四世推上了王位，成为约克家族第一位国王。晚些时候，被爱德华和沃里克打败的亨利六世和玛格丽特逃亡苏格兰。三年后亨利返回英格兰参加推翻爱德华的叛乱，结果被关入伦

Henry came back to rebel Edward IV but was captured and imprisoned in the Tower of London.

However, splitting between the winners occurred as Edward and Warwick had quarrels. In 1470, Warwick drove Edward into exile and put Henry and Margaret back to the throne. Edward fought against Warwick in 1471 and killed him. Henry was sent back to the tower by Edward died in the same year. Henry's only son Edward was also killed, marking the end of the ruling of the House of Lancaster. Edward IV ruled the country until 1483 when he passed the throne to his 12 years son who was later imprisoned by the boy's uncle Richard, Duke of Gloucester who crowned himself as King Richard III. Eventually in 1485, Henry Tudor, Earl of Richmond defeated Richard III in a war and claimed the throne on the grounds that he was relative of the House of Lancaster. Henry Tudor was known as King Henry VII and the first king of the House of Tudor. He connected the House of Lancaster and York by marrying Edward IV's daughter Elizabeth.

敦塔。

　　然而，爱德华四世和沃里克产生了分歧。1470年，沃里克迫使爱德华流亡国外并把亨利和玛格丽特再次送回了王位。一年后，爱德华征战沃里克并杀死了他。亨利再次被送入伦敦塔并在同年内死亡。他的儿子也惨遭杀害。兰开斯特家族的直系从此断绝。爱德华四世统治英国直到1483年死亡，他的12岁的儿子继位。不久后，幼王的叔父格罗斯特公爵理查德夺取了王位，称号理查德三世。1485，理查德三世被亨利·都铎打败后取代了王位。亨利登基为亨利七世，成为都铎王朝的第一位国王。亨利娶爱德华四世的女儿伊丽莎白为妻，把斗争了几十年的两个家族联合了起来。

词汇 VOCABULARY

1. badge [bædʒ]
   n. 徽章；标记；证章 v. 授给…徽章

2. overthrow [ˌəuvə'θrəu]
   n. / v. 推翻；倾覆；瓦解

3. ambitious [æm'biʃəs]
   a. 有雄心的；野心勃勃的；热望的；炫耀的

4. descendent [di'sendənt]
   n. 后裔；派生物 a. 派生的；降落的；世袭的

5. justification [dʒʌstifi'keiʃ(ə)n]
   n. 理由；辩护；认为有理，认为正当；释罪

6. persistent [pə'sistənt]
   a. 固执的，坚持的；持久稳固的

7. exile ['eksail, 'egz-]
   n. 流放，充军 v. 放逐，流放；使背井离乡

背景链接 TIPS

Plantagenet Family

　　金雀花王朝（Plantagenet）是12～14世纪统治英国的封建王朝。王朝名称的由来，一说亨利二世的父亲安茹伯爵杰弗里经常在帽子上饰以金雀花枝，故有此名。除英国本土外，该王朝在法国的安茹、诺曼底、布列塔尼等地拥有大量领土。兰开斯特家族和约克家族是金雀花王朝的两个分支。

079 The Glorious Revolution

When Queen Victoria died, her cousin James VI of Scotland became King of England, known as James I and ushered the ruling of House of Stuart.

King James I was an unwise king in that he believed that the power of the King came from God, not from the power so that he had the absolute power to do anything he liked. Therefore, he spent the royal spending lavishly and raised taxes. He had many disagreements with the Parliament. Besides, he supported the Church of England but treated Roman Catholic improperly. His son Charles I was a worse king. He not only believed the divine right of the king and the authority of the Church of England, but also dismissed the Parliament several times. The conflict between King Charles I and the Parliament eventually led to the Civil War in which Charles I was defeated and beheaded in 1649.

From 1649 to 1660, England became a commonwealth presided by Oliver Cromwell in which there was no monarch. But in 1660, the monarchy was restored with Charles II taking the throne. However, when his brother James II took charge after his death in 1685, James II hurt the feelings of his supporters for his cruel behaviors. With his permission, three hundred people were hanged or burned and a thousand more ware sent to American farms as slaves for revolt. As a Roman Catholic, he put Roman Catholics in the government, army and other important places. When the British people put all their hopes on his Protestant daughter Mary to succeed him after his death, James's wife gave birth to a son and destroyed people's dream.

In 1688, James II's opponents invited William of Orange, the ruler of Netherlands and Mary back to take the throne. James II fled when they arrived. The event

【小译】

维多利亚女王去世后，王位由他的表亲苏格兰的詹姆斯六世继承，他就是英国历史上的詹姆斯一世，开始了斯图亚特王朝对英国的统治。

詹姆斯一世不是一个明智的国王。他相信君权神授，而不是来自于臣民，因此为所欲为。他增加王室开支，并加大征收赋税力度，和议会产生争执。他的儿子查理一世同样不聪明。除了笃信君权神授和英国国教的权威，不断与议会发生冲突。他甚至几次解散议会，最终引发了内战，结果在1649年被送上了断头台。

从1649到1660年，英国在奥利弗·克伦威尔的领导下经历了短暂的共和国时期。1660年，查理二世继位，英国再次被置于君主制统治下。查理二世死后，王位由弟弟詹姆斯二世继承。詹姆斯二世在位时遭遇叛乱。叛乱被镇压后，詹姆斯二世用极其残暴的方式对叛乱者实施报复。经他的许允，叛乱者中有三百人被处以绞刑或火刑，还有一千多人被送往美国的庄园当奴隶。结果，他很快失去了人心。加之他信仰天主教，并试图把天主教恢复为国教，因此在重要的部门都安置了天主教徒。英国人民把全部希望寄托于他信仰新教的女儿玛丽身上，希望她的继位能扭转局面。无奈詹姆斯二世再添一子，使人们的希望破灭。

1688年，詹姆斯二世的反对者们邀请玛丽的丈夫威廉和玛丽回国夺取

was called the Glorious Revolution because it was successful and bloodless.

In the following year, William of Orange and Mary were given the throne after they affirmed the Bill of Rights. Bill of Rights was a very important document that protected the basic right of the people and put limitations on the power of monarchy. From then on, Britain became a constitutional monarchy country in which the monarch was under the control of Parliament.

王位。詹姆斯二世在他们到达前逃亡法国。这一事件被成为光荣革命，因为这次王位的更迭没有引起任何流血冲突。

1689年，威廉和玛丽在签署《权利法案》之后继位。权利法案保障了人民的一些基本权利，限制了君主的权力。从此，英国形成了君主立宪制的政体。

词汇 VOCABULARY

1. lavishly ['lævi∫li] *ad.* 浪费的；丰富的；大方的	2. improperly [im'prɔpəli] *ad.* 错误的；不适当的
3. dismiss [dis'mis] *vt.* 让…离开；开除；解散；解雇 *vi.* 解散	4. commonwealth ['kɔmənwelθ] *n.* 共和国；联邦；国民整体
5. revolt [ri'vəult] *n.* 反抗；叛乱 *vt.* 反抗；反叛 *vi.* 使恶心	6. fled [fled] *v.* 消逝；逃走（flee的过去分词）
7. affirm [ə'fə:m] *vt.* 断言；肯定 *vi.* 断言；确认	8. constitutional [,kɔnsti'tju:∫ənəl] *a.* 宪法的；体质上的 *n.* 保健散步；保健运动

背景链接 TIPS

英国君主立宪制的世界历史意义

英国在1688年"光荣革命"后建立起来的议会权利超过君主的君主立宪制度以及两党制度等，不仅对英国以后的历史、而且对欧美许多国家都产生了重要影响。在17世纪的西欧以及世界其他地区，君主专制是一种普遍的政体形式。西欧的法国、西班牙、奥地利以及丹麦、瑞典、德意志的一些公国，都建立了中央集权的君主专制制度。在这些国家中占统治地位的政治思想是君权神授。至于东欧的俄国以及东方的中国等，则等级森严，绝对专制君主制更为强固。1688年后，英国的政治制度及由此而萌发的政治思想，对欧洲绝对君主专制制度和君权神授、君主万能、臣民必须无条件服从等思想，都是一个沉重的打击，而对一些民主、进步的思想家，如18世纪法国的启蒙思想家孟德斯鸠、伏尔泰等则起了巨大的鼓舞作用。虽然对东欧、俄国及东方的中国等国未发生直接影响，但当这些国家的改革运动兴起的时候，英国的"巴力门"（议会）、"君民共治"（君主立宪制）就成了鼓舞他们进行斗争的现实源泉和效法的榜样。19世纪末，中国的维新派在为改革而奋斗的时候，就常常引用英国的民主政治制度作为楷模。

080　The First World War

The First World War (1914-1918) was one of the most destructive wars in the world which involved many of the European countries and America, with nearly 10 million people being deprived of life.

The World War I involved two sides named the Allies and the Central Powers respectively. The Allies included countries like Britain, France, Russia, Serbia and later Italy, Rumania, Greece, Japan and America etc. The Central Powers were Germany, Austria-Hungary, the Ottoman Empire and Bulgaria.

The direct cause of WWI was the death of Archduke Francis Ferdinand, heir to the throne of Austria-Hungary. When he and his wife paid a visit to Sarajevo, the couple was shot by a Serbian nationalist and died. The Austria Hungary accused Serbia government of murdering and brought up the war. Serbia was backed by the Allies to combat the Central Powers Austria-Hungary and Germany.

In the beginning, Germany won victories on most of the European battlefields. It wanted to take France quickly but was strongly fought back in the battle of Marne on 6 September1914. In early 1916, Germany decided to take the French city of Verdun. The Germany army met with strong resistance and till the end of the year, Germany still didn't get the upper hand. To relieve Germany's pressure on Verdun, the Allies waged a war near the Somme River in France. Although the Allies won a narrow victory, the battle was considered the turning point for the Allies. On the eastern front, a Russian army attacked Austria in 1914 and won a victory. America declared war on Germany on 6 April, 1917 after Germany sank several American ships and American troops won their first decisive victory at Chateau-Thierry. On 26 September, 1918 the Allies launched the last great attack in the WWI – the Battle of the Meuse-Argonne. In the battle, the Allies defeated Germany troop.

In the end, Bulgaria, Turkey and Austria surrendered one by one and Germany demanded an agreement. On

【小译】

第一次世界大战（1914-1918）是历史上最具有摧毁力的世界战争之一。欧洲很多国家和美国都被卷入这场战争，约1000万人在战争中遇难。

一战的交战双方分别为协约国和同盟国。协约国包含的国家有英国、法国、俄国、塞尔维亚以及后来加入的意大利、罗马尼亚、希腊、日本和美国等。同盟国由德国、奥匈帝国、奥斯曼帝国和保加利亚组成。

一战的直接起因是奥匈帝国王储弗朗西斯·斐迪南的死亡。当王储携妻子在萨拉热窝进行访问时被一名塞尔维亚民族主义分子枪击身亡。奥匈帝国认为这场谋杀是由塞尔维亚政府策划的，并因此向塞宣战。塞尔维亚得到协约国的支持，与同盟国奥匈帝国和德国抗争。

起初，德国在欧洲战场赢得了大部分战争并妄图在法国取得迅速的胜利。但是德国在1914年9月6日的马恩河战役中受到法国激烈的反击，使得德国的计划受挫。1916年年初，德国决定攻取法国凡尔登。法国军队拼死守城，直到年底德国都没有占领凡尔登。为了缓解德国对凡尔登的压力，协约国在索姆河附近发动了反攻。虽然战果不显著，索姆河战争依然被视为战争的转折点。在东线，俄国军队1914年袭击奥地利并赢得了胜利。1917年4月6日，在德国先后数次击沉美国船只后，美国向德国宣战并在蒂耶里堡战役中取得大捷。1918年9月26日，协约国发动了一战最后一次

11 November 1918, the agreement was signed by the Germans and the WWI was finally ended.

On 28 June, 1919, the Treaty of Versailles was signed in which Germany was asked to give up territories and overseas colonies to the Allies countries. The Allied army force was to occupy the west bank of the Rhine River for 15 years. Germany was also responsible for the loss caused by the war. The Treaty of Versailles provided opportunity for Adolf Hitler to gain power in Germany and eventually led to the next world war.

大规模战役——默兹-阿尔贡战役并粉碎了德国的抵抗。

保加利亚、土耳其和奥地利先后投降，德国要求议和。1918年11月11日，德国签署合约，一战结束。

战争结束后，于1919年6月28日协约国迫使德国签订了凡尔赛合约。合约规定德国割让领土和殖民地给协约国。协约国军队占领莱茵河东岸15年。德国赔偿战争造成的一大笔赔款。这些为阿道夫·希特勒执掌政权提供了条件，并最终促成第二次世界大战的爆发。

词汇 VOCABULARY

1. destructive [dis'trʌktiv]
   adj. 破坏的；毁灭性的；有害的，消极的

2. Allies ['ælaiz, ə'laiz]
   n. （第一次世界大战时的）协约国

3. Serbia ['sə:bjə]
   n. 塞尔维亚（南斯拉夫成员共和国名）

4. Rumania [ru(:)'meinjə]
   n. 罗马尼亚（等于Romania）

5. Austria-Hungary
   n. 奥匈帝国（1918年解体）

6. Ottoman ['ɔtəumən]
   n. 土耳其人 adj. 土耳其人的；土耳其民族的

7. Bulgaria [bʌl'gɛəriə]
   n. 保加利亚

8. Sarajevo [ˌsærə'jeivəu]
   n. 萨拉热窝（位于南斯拉夫中部）

9. nationalist ['næʃənəlist]
   n. 民族主义者；国家主义者
   adj. 民族主义的（等于nationalistic）

10. launch [lɔ:ntʃ, lɑ:ntʃ]
    n. 发射；下水；汽艇；发行，投放市场
    vt. 发射（导弹、火箭等） vi. 下水；开始

11. treaty ['tri:ti]
    n. 条约，协议；谈判

12. Versailles [vɛə'sai, və'seilz]
    n. 凡尔赛（法国城市）

背景链接 TIPS

萨拉热窝事件

这次事件为在欧洲爆发全面战争的直接原因。1914年6月28日上午9时正，奥匈帝国皇太子斐迪南大公参加指挥一次军事演习，演习结束后，塞尔维亚一个秘密组织成员，17岁的普林西普向斐迪南夫妇开枪射击，斐迪南夫妇毙命，普林西普被捕。这一事件被称为萨拉热窝事件，被认为是第一次世界大战的导火线。普林西普的行动是热爱民族的一种伟大表现，但是这一事件被奥匈帝国当做了对塞尔维亚发动战争的口实。1914年7月23日奥国在获得德国无条件支持下向塞尔维亚发最后通牒，包括拘捕凶手、镇压反奥活动和罢免反奥官员等，塞国除涉及内政项目外悉数同意。不过，奥国依然将行动升级。与此同时，德国知悉俄国的军事动员，德皇要求俄国停止并迅速备战。鉴于各国的强硬外交和对国家军事力量的自骄，战争已无可避免。

081 The Second World War

The Second World War was the most destructive war in the world which involved 1700 million people in and took over 17 million lives. The far-reaching destructive power of this war is greater than any other wars in the history.

The World War I ended in1918 but left many problems unsolved and caused other new problems. The first problem was the dissatisfaction aroused by the Treaty of Versailles. Many countries thought the treaty was unfair and was too harsh on the defeated countries, especially Germany. Even some winning nations were unhappy because they didn't get what they wanted. Besides, the war damaged the European countries to such an extent that most of the countries were struggled in poverty. The situation was aggravated by the Great Depression in the early 1930s. Under this circumstance, nationalisms in some countries grew rapidly and dictatorships came to power in several countries, such as Nazi Party in Germany. With the ambition to conquer more territories, Germany and Italy formed alliance in 1936 and added Japan in 1940, known as the Rome-Berlin-Tokyo Axis. The countries fought against the Axis were the Allies included over 50 countries by the end of the war.

On 1 September 1939, Germany invaded Poland and started the WWII. In May 1940, Germany attacked Belgium, Luxembourg, and the Netherlands and advanced toward France. When France was captured by Germany, Britain stood against Hitler. In August 1940, Italy invaded North Africa with the aim to cut Britain off from oil fields in the Middle East and was driven out by the British army. In the Battle of El Alamein in the following year, Italian army was defeated by British army, marked the turning point of the war in North Africa. On 7 December 1941, Japanese planes attacked Pearl Harbor in Hawaii and involved America in the war. With the US, Canada and Britain declared war on

【小译】

第二次世界大战是世界上破坏力最大的战争之一。全球17亿人被卷入战争并有1700万人丧生。战争造成的深远的负面影响是任何战争都无法企及的。

1918年结束的一战造成了很多遗留问题，同时也引起了很多新问题。首先就是很多国家对凡尔赛合约的不满。战败国认为合约对他们的惩罚过于苛刻，尤其是德国。而一些战胜国也因没有获得自己想得到的而耿耿于怀。其次，一战严重破坏了欧洲国家的经济，很多国家因此陷入穷困境地。30年代席卷全球的大萧条更是雪上加霜。如此境况下，一些国家的民族主义势力迅速增长。几个国家建立独裁统治体系，例如德国的纳粹党。带有扩张领土野心的德国、意大利独裁统治者在1936年结成联盟，1940年日本也加入，形成了罗马-柏林-东京轴心。与轴心国作战的联盟被称为同盟国。到战争结束时，同盟国成员增加到50个国家。

1939年9月1日，德国入侵波兰，二战开始。次年5月，德国占领了比利时、卢森堡与荷兰并向法国推进。当法国沦陷后，英国成为唯一与希特勒对抗的国家。1940年8月，意大利入侵北非意图切断英国与中东油田的关系，结果被英军驱逐出埃及。在阿拉曼战争中，英国打败意军，成为北非战场上的一个转折点。1941年10月7日，日本袭击夏威夷的珍珠港，将美国卷入战争。随着美国、加拿大和英国向日本宣战、中国向轴心国宣战以及德国和意大利向美国宣战，二战逐

Japan, China declared war on the Axis and Germany and Italy declared war on the America, World War II turned into a global war. The turning point of the war came in February 1943 at the Battle of Stalingrad. After the battle in Tunisia in May 1943, the last Axis forces in Northern Africa surrendered. Italy surrendered after American and Britain's invasion in September. The war eventually ended with Germany government signed a statement of unconditional surrender on 8 May 1945 after Hitler committed suicide.

渐演变成了一场全球战争。1943年2月斯大林格勒战役成为战争的决定性的转折点。同年5月盟军在突尼斯的战争彻底肃清了轴心国在北非的势力。9月，英美联军入侵意大利，意军投降。1945年5月8日，德国政府在希特勒自杀后签署了无条件投降声明，二战到此结束。

词汇 VOCABULARY

1. unsolved [ʌnˈsɒlvd]
   adj. 未解决的；未解答的

2. aggravated [ˈæɡrəveitid]
   adj. 加重的；恶化的
   v. 加重；刺激（aggravate的过去分词）

3. depression [diˈpreʃən]
   n. 沮丧；忧愁；洼地；不景气

4. nazi [ˈnɑːtsiː]
   n. 纳粹党人 *adj.* 纳粹党的；纳粹主义的

5. alliance [əˈlaiəns]
   n. 联盟，联合，联姻

6. axis [ˈæksis]
   n. 轴；轴线；轴心国

7. Belgium [ˈbeldʒəm]
   n. 比利时（西欧国家，首都布鲁塞尔Brussels）

8. Luxembourg [ˈluksəm,bəːg]
   n. 卢森堡公国；卢森堡（卢森堡公国首都）

9. Alamein [ˌæləˈmein]
   n. 阿拉曼（埃及北部村庄，第二次世界大战战场；=El Alamein）

10. harbor [ˈhɑːbə]
    n. 海港；避难所 *v.* 庇护，怀有
    v. 入港停泊；躲藏；居住，生存

11. Stalingrad [ˈstɑːlingræd]
    n. 斯大林格勒（苏联城市名，是现在的伏尔加格勒）

12. Tunisia [tjuː(ː)ˈniziə]
    n. 突尼斯（非洲国家）

13. unconditional [ˌʌnkənˈdiʃənəl]
    adj. 无条件的；绝对的；无限制的

背景链接 TIPS

第二次世界大战爆发的根本原因

二战是由帝国主义经济政治发展的不平衡加剧引起的。经济上，一战后德国不甘心《凡尔赛条约》对其严惩和限制，由于希特勒政府干预经济政策，经济再度超过了英法；意大利在一战后经济衰落；日本侵略亚洲国家的同时，美英等国禁止

向日本输送石油战略物资，导致日本经济发展受到阻碍。政治上，1929~1933年资本主义世界严重的经济危机引起了政治危机，德国和日本建立了法西斯专政，而英、法、美继续坚持资产阶级民主制度。世界大战彻底严重爆发。

Unit 19 工业革命

The Industrial Revolution refers to the mechanization of industry and the consequent changes in social and economic organization in the late eighteenth and early nineteenth century. It began in the United Kingdom, then subsequently spread throughout Europe, North America, and eventually the world. The Industrial Revolution symbolizes a major turning point in human history; almost every aspect of daily life was influenced in some way. Most notably, average income and population began to exhibit unprecedented sustained growth. In the two centuries following 1800, the world's average per capita income increased over 10-fold, while the world's population increased over 6-fold.

The economy of the UK started to be transferred from manual-labour-based towards machine-based manufacturing in the later part of the 18th century. It started with the mechanization of the textile industries, the development of iron-making techniques and the increased use of refined coal. Trade expansion was enabled by the introduction of canals, improved roads and railways.

Without the new technology and inventions in the textile industries, there would not have been as drastic a rise in economy, nor would the UK be considered the first instance of modern capitalism. Several inventions including fly shuttle and Spinning Jenny were essential to speeding up the textile industry.

The steam engine was arguably the most important technology of the Industrial Revolution. During the Industrial Revolution, steam power began to replace water power and muscle power (which often came from horses) as the primary source of power in use in industry. Its first use was to pump water from mines. The early steam engines were not very efficient, but a double-acting rotative version created by James Watt gave engines the power to become a driving force behind the Industrial Revolution.

In this unit we will mainly lay our focus on two important inventions during the Industrial Revolution, namely the invention of Spinning Jenny in the textile industry and the invention the steam engine and importnat further improvement made on it.

工业革命指的是18世纪晚期到19世纪早期发生的工业机器化进程。工业革命由英国开始，随后扩散到欧洲其他国家、北美，最终到整个世界。工业革命象征着人类历史的一个重要转折点。人类日常生活的每一个方面都或多或少地受到工业革命的影响。最显著的影响莫过于平均收入与人口数量展现出来的前所未有的持续增长。在1800年接下来的两个世纪中，全球平均人口增长10倍，人口增长了超过六倍。

从18世纪后期起，英国的经济开始由手工生产转向机器生产。这种转变始于纺织业机械化、炼铁技术的发展与精煤使用的增长。而运河开通、公路与铁路运输改进之后，英国的贸易也开始扩张。

如果纺织业没有引进新技术、出现新发明的话，就不会出现经济的急速增长，英国也不会成为现代第一个资本主义国家。一些发明，像飞梭与珍妮纺纱机是使纺织业加速发展的关键。

蒸汽机可以说是工业革命中最重要的发明。在工业革命期间，蒸汽动力开始取代水动力与肌肉动力（常常来自马匹），成为工业的主要力量来源。蒸汽机的第一次应用是在煤矿中。早期的蒸汽机并不是很有效，直到詹姆斯·瓦特发明了双动回转型蒸汽机，蒸汽机才成为驱动工业革命的重要力量。

在这一单元中我们将重点介绍工业革命中的两项重要发明，即纺织业中珍妮纺纱机的发明与蒸汽机的发明，以及对其所作的一些重要改进。

082 The Invention of Spinning Jenny

The Spinning Jenny was invented in 1764 by an inventor named James Hargreaves (1720~1778) in Lancashire, England. This device greatly improved the production rate of yarn, from one string of yarn created at a time to eight, and later 120 as the technology improved. At the same time, the invention also minimized the human hands needed to create the yarn at that time.

At the beginning of the eighteenth century in England, the use of machines in manufacturing was already widespread. But the textile industry had some special problems. It took four spinners to keep up with one cotton loom, and ten persons to prepare yarn for one woolen weaver. Spinners were busy, but weavers often had to be idle for lack of yarn. In 1733, the invention of the flying shuttle by John Kay increased the demand for yarn tenfold by doubling the cotton being produced, which was still delayed by the seriously low yarn producing efficiency. A machine was needed to increase the yarn production and so Spinning Jenny was invented in 1764 on which one operator could spin many threads simultaneously. Now the weaver did not have to wait for yarn to be spun and could create more woven goods at a time, which consequently resulted in the opening of a large number of cotton mills in the UK.

The idea of the Spinning Jenny came from when James Hargreaves saw an overturn spinning wheel (producing one string of yarn) still working as normal, with the originally

【小译】

珍妮纺纱机于1764年由英国兰夏郡的一位名叫詹姆斯·哈格里夫斯（1720年～1778年）的发明家发明。这个发明大大提高了纱线生产效率，由原来一次纺一根纱线提高到八根，技术改进之后可以一次纺120根。同时，这个发明也在当时将纺纱所需人力降到最低。

十八世纪初期，英国制造业已广泛使用机械。然而，纺织工业有其特殊的问题。一台织布机需要四名纺纱工，而一名羊毛织布工需要十名纺纱工为其备纱线。因而导致了纱工繁忙、而羊毛织布工因缺纱线而闲散的情形。1733年，约翰·凯发明了飞梭织布机，织布速度加快，但是由于纺纱效率低下，纱线依然缺乏，纺织过程依然迟缓。纱线产量需要通过新的机器继续提高，因此1674年，珍妮纺纱机问世，这样，一个工人同时就可以纺多根纱线。现在织布工不需要等待纱线被纺出，可以一次生产出更多的纺织品，从而最终导致英国出现大量的纺织厂。

詹姆斯·哈格里夫斯发明珍妮纺纱机的灵感来自于他偶然看到的一台打翻的纺车（当时一次只能纺一根纱线），虽然原来水平放置的纺锤已经竖立了起来，但是纺车依然可以正常工作。这一幕让他意识到纺锤不一定非要水平旋转才可以正常工作，而且如果一组纺锤紧挨

horizontal spindle pointed upright. This made him realize that there was no particular reason the spindles had to be horizontal and if a number of spindles were placed upright and next to each other, several strings could be spun at once. His idea worked perfectly.

It is said that the "Jenny" part of the name is an abbreviation of "engine". Another explanation is that the name "Jenny" supposedly comes from James Hargreaves' daughter who knocked over the spinning wheel giving him the idea, although this is not a proven fact. One thing is for sure, if was not for James Hargreaves and his spinning jenny then the textile industry would not be where it is today. Friedrich Engels notes that it was "the first invention which gave rise to a radical change in the state of the English workers."

着竖立放置的话，就可以同时纺多根线了。他的想法完美地实现了。

据说珍妮纺纱机中"珍妮"的叫法来自"engine"的缩写，另一种说法称"珍妮"事实上是詹姆斯·哈格里夫斯的女儿，是她将纺车撞翻，从而给了他灵感。虽然这个说法并未被证明。但是我们有一点可以确信，那就是如果没有詹姆斯·哈格里夫斯和他的珍妮纺纱机，那就不会有今天的纺织业。弗里德里希·恩格斯称珍妮纺纱机是"使英国工人的状况发生根本变化的第一个发明"。

词汇 VOCABULARY

1. yarn [jɑːn]
   n 纱线；奇谈；故事 v 用纱线缠 v 讲故事

2. spinner ['spinə]
   n 纺纱机；纺纱工人；旋床工人；旋式诱饵

3. cotton ['kɔtn]
   n 棉花；棉布 vi 一致；理解 a 棉的；棉制的

4. weaver ['wiːvə]
   n 织工；织布者

5. tenfold ['tenfəuld]
   n 十倍 a 十倍的；十重的 ad 十倍地；成十倍

6. abbreviation [əˌbriːviˈeiʃən]
   n 缩写；缩写词

背景链接 TIPS

1. James Hargreaves

詹姆斯·哈格里夫斯（1721～1778年），英国兰开郡工人，珍妮机发明者。詹姆斯·哈格里夫斯是一位纺纱工人，同时又是一个木工，他在1765年成功地制造出能够同时纺出多根棉纱的纺纱机，大大提高了纺纱机的功率（大概提高了八倍），传说他用自己女儿的名字把这种纺纱机命名为"珍妮机"（Spinning Jenny）。

2. Friedrich Engels

弗里德里希·冯·恩格斯（Friedrich Von Engels，1820年11月28日～1895年8月5日），德国哲学家，马克思主义的创始人之一。恩格斯是卡尔·马克思的挚友，被誉为"第二提琴手"，他为马克思创立马克思主义提供了大量经济上的支持，在马克思逝世后，帮助马克思完成了未完成的《资本论》等著作，并且领导国际工人运动。

083 The Invention of the Steam Engine

A steam engine is a heat engine that performs mechanical work using steam as its working fluid. In the history of the invention for the steam engine, there are three key figures. Thomas Savery patented the first crude steam engine in 1698. Thomas Newcomen improved on this design by inventing the atmospheric steam engine. However, it wasn't until Scotsman James Watt improved on the steam engine in the second half of the 18th century that it became a truly viable piece of machinery that helped start the Industrial Revolution. Therefore, the inventor of the steam engine is constantly referred to as James Watt in modern history.

James Watt was a Scottish inventor and mechanical engineer, born in Greenock in 1736. In 1765, James Watt, while working for the University of Glasgow, was assigned the task of repairing a Newcomen engine, which was deemed inefficient but the best steam engine of its time. That started the inventor to work on several improvements to Newcomen's design. In 1769, Watt patented his most notable discovery for a separate condenser connected to a cylinder by a valve. Unlike Newcomen's engine, Watt's design had a condenser that could be cool while the cylinder was hot. Watt's engine soon became the dominant design for all modern steam engines and helped bring about the Industrial Revolution.

【小译】

蒸汽机是一种以蒸汽为燃料，将热能转化为机械能的装置。托马斯·萨佛里的世界上第一台简单的蒸汽引擎于1698年获得专利。1705年，托马斯·纽科门通过他发明的大气式蒸汽引擎改进了这一设计。但它还不能真正得以普遍应用，直至18世纪下半叶詹姆斯·瓦特对它作出了改进，并由此引发了工业革命。因此，在现代历史中瓦特通常被认为是蒸汽机的发明者。

詹姆斯·瓦特于1736年出生在格林诺克，是一名苏格兰发明家和机械工程师。1765年詹姆斯·瓦特在格拉斯哥大学工作时，被指派去维修纽科门蒸汽机，虽然它的效率很低，但在当时被认为是最好的蒸汽引擎。他对纽科门机的设计做了一些改进工作。1769年，瓦特最引人注目的发明，即设有分离的凝汽器并通过阀门与汽缸相连的蒸汽机获得了专利。与纽科门机不同的是，瓦特的设计中有一个冷凝器，可以在汽缸发热的时候起到降温作用。瓦特的机器很快便成为了现代蒸汽机设计的主流，并且引发了工

James Watt came up with the term "horsepower" as a way to help explain how much work his steam engines could do for a potential buyer. A unit of power called the Watt was named after James Watt, whose symbol is W.

The importance of the steam engine invention can hardly be underestimated – it gave us the modern world. A key feature of it was that it brought the engine out of the remote coal fields into factories where many mechanics, engineers, and even tinkerers were exposed to its virtues and limitations. It was a platform for generations of inventive men to improve. It was clear to many that higher pressures produced in improved boilers would produce engines having even higher efficiency, and would lead to the revolution first in transportation that was soon embodied in the locomotive and steamboat and later to the farm field and the Traction Steam Engine.

业革命。

詹姆斯·瓦特提出了术语"马力"用以为其潜在客户解释他的蒸汽机可以做多少功。瓦特的名字被用来命名一个能量单元，它的符号是"W"。

蒸汽机这项发明的重要性是不可低估的——它给予了我们现代世界。它的一个显著特征就是将引擎从遥远的煤矿领域带入到了工厂，在那里，很多的技师、工程师甚至小生产者可以享受蒸汽带来的长处，发现蒸汽机的局限。从而为一代又一代的发明者提供了改进的平台。很明显改进锅炉而使其产生的更高的压力会使引擎更加高效，最终导致首先出现在交通运输领域的变革——将蒸汽机安装到机车和轮船上，这种变革随后将体现在农田以及蒸汽牵引车上。

词汇 VOCABULARY

1. steam [sti:m] n. 蒸汽；精力 v. 蒸，散发 vi. 冒水汽 a. 蒸汽的	2. crude [kru:d] n. 原油；天然的物质 a. 粗糙的；天然的
3. viable ['vaiəbl] a. 可行的；能养活的；能生育的	4. condenser [kən'densə] n. 冷凝器；[电] 电容器；[光] 聚光器
5. cylinder ['silində] n. 圆筒；汽缸；[数] 柱面；圆柱状物	6. underestimate ['ʌndər'estimeit] vt. 低估 n. 低估；看轻
7. tinker ['tiŋkə] n. 补锅匠 vi. 做焊锅匠 vt. 修补；粗修	8. embody [im'bɔdi] vt. 体现，使具体化；具体表达
9. locomotive [ˌləukə'məutiv] n. 机车；火车头 a. 火车头的；运动的	

背景链接 TIPS

Thomas Savery

托马斯·萨弗里（1650～1715），英国发明家，生于英格兰的德文郡。萨弗里制成的世界上第一台实用的蒸汽提水机，在1698年取得标名为"矿工之友"的英国专利。萨弗里的提水机依靠真空的吸力汲水，汲水深度不能超过六米。为了从几十米深的矿井汲水，须将提水机装在矿井深处，用较高的蒸汽压力才能将水压到地面上，这在当时无疑是困难而又危险的。

PEOPLE

Part 6

英国人正在关注的英国人

Unit 20　皇室成员

The beginning of the monarchy in Britain could be traced back to the 9th century. In the following thousands of years, altogether 12 royal houses have ruled the country. Chronically speaking, there were Normans, Plantagenet family, House of Lancaster, House of York, House of Lancaster, House of York, House of Tudor, House of Stuart, Commonwealth, House of Stuart, House of Hanover, House of Sax-Cobourg-Gotha and House of Winsor.

The throne was hereditary, that is, only the members of royal family could became the monarch. If the throne is passed on to a male member of the royal family, the name of the royal house will remain the same; however, once the throne is given to the female member of the royal family, the name of royal house will change with the family name or land. The only exception is the current royal house the House of Winsor.

The originally name of the House of Winsor was House of Saxe-Coburg-Gotha, a German name coming from Queen Victoria's husband Prince Albert of Saxe-Coburg-Gotha. The name was carried on by Queen Victoria's son Edward VII. However, when Edward VII's son George V was on the throne, the First World War broke out in which Germany was the enemy of Britain. Under this circumstance, George V renounced all the German title inherited from his grandfather and changed the name of the royal house to Winsor. The present Elizabeth II is the fourth monarch of House of Winsor.

The current royal family includes Queen Elizabeth II and her husband Prince Philip and their four children Prince Charles, Princess Anne, Prince Andrew and Prince Edward. Prince Charles had two sons Prince William and Prince Henry lining behind him to take the throne. Since April 2011, the British royal family received a new member Princess Kate.

英国君主制最早可以追溯到公元9世纪。在接下来的十几个世纪中，共有12家皇室家族统治过英国。英国历代朝代依次是诺曼王朝、金雀花王朝、兰开斯特王朝、约克王朝、兰开斯特王朝、约克王朝、都铎王朝、斯图亚特王朝、共和国时期、斯图亚特王朝、汉诺威王朝、萨克斯·科堡·哥达王朝和温莎王朝。

英国皇位是世袭的，因此只有皇室成员才有权利继承皇位。如果皇位传给男性皇室成员，那么朝代名称保持不变；而如果皇位传给女性皇室成员，那么新的朝代通常是根据执政王的家族姓氏或封地来命名，然而，英国目前的朝代——温莎王朝是唯一不是这样命名的朝代。

根据以上规定，温莎王朝最初叫做"萨克斯·科堡·哥达"王朝，这是继承了他母亲维多利亚女王的王位后根据他父亲德国萨克斯·科堡·哥达家族王子艾尔伯特的封号"萨克斯·科堡·哥达"命名的。爱德华七世在位时，第一次世界大战爆发。德国成为英国的死敌。1901年继位的英王乔治五世居然还保持着具有浓厚德国色彩的朝代名称——萨克斯·科堡·哥达王朝，引起英国人民强烈的愤怒和不满，因此乔治五世决定放弃"萨克斯·科堡·哥达"这个德国姓氏并更改为温莎王朝。现在的伊丽莎白二世女王是温莎王朝第四代君主。

当今温莎王朝的皇室成员包括伊丽莎白二世女王和丈夫菲利普王子以及四个子女查尔斯王子、安娜公主、安德鲁王子和爱德华王子。王储查尔斯王子生有两个儿子威廉王子和哈里王子，两人排在父亲之后依次继承皇位。2011年4月英国皇室迎来了新成员凯特王妃。

084 Mary I

Mary I was the first English queen in the history of England whose ruling lasted from 1553 to 1558. During the reign of Mary I, the economy of England declined sharply and the Protestants were cruelly oppressed and England lost its last continental territory, Calais, in the war with France.

Mary I was born on 18 February 1516 as the only surviving child of Henry VIII and Catherine of Aragon. When Henry VIII intended to divorce Catherine and was rejected by Roman Pope, he built up the Church of England and allowed himself to settle his own affair, that is to divorce Catherine. Mary I suffered a lot from the divorce. At the time when Ann Boleyn was the new queen, Mary I was deprived of her title and made into a maid for Ann's daughter Elizabeth.

Mary was a devout Catholic all though her life despite that her father spent most of his time breaking with the Roman Catholic Church. Because of her religious belief, when she was due to become the queen of England, a faction of Protestants made her cousin Lady Jane Grey queen instead of her. However, with the support of most English people who favored her more, Mary replaced Jane Grey only nine days after her crowning.

However, once queen, Mary I's ruling disappointed English people one time after another. First, she denied all the effort her father and her half-brother Edward made in establishing Church of England and conformed to Roman Catholic again. In order to seek obedience, she made laws against Protestants beliefs. In the following years, Mary's persecution of Protestants was extremely bloody. Within only 3 years, near 300 hundred Protestants were burnt at the stake and earned Mary the title "Bloody Mary". None of her measures

【小译】

玛丽一世是英国历史上第一位女王，在位时间为1553到1558年。玛丽一世统治下的英国经济迅速衰退、新教徒遭受迫害，并在与法国的交战中失去了在欧洲大陆最后一片领地加莱。

玛丽一世出生于1516年2月18日，是亨利八世与阿拉贡的凯瑟琳唯一存活的孩子。在亨利八世提出与凯瑟琳离婚遭到教皇反对后，他创建了英国教会并以教会首领的身份赋予自己独立解决自身问题的权利，之后与凯瑟琳离婚。父母的离异使玛丽吃了很多苦。新王后安妮·博林剥夺了玛丽的公主封号，并迫使她做了自己女儿伊丽莎白的侍女。

玛丽是个虔诚的天主教徒，就在父亲想方设法与罗马天主教会决裂之时，玛丽也没有改变自己的信仰。也正因此，在她继位之即，一群极端新教徒把简·格雷拥上了王位，取代了理应属于玛丽的位置。仅仅9天后，受人拥戴的玛丽便在人民的帮助下夺回王位。

然而，继位后的玛丽一再让拥护她的臣民失望。首先，玛丽否定了他父亲和哥哥的努力，恢复了已不再得人心的天主教。她颁布了很多对新教徒不利的法令，并以此来巩固天主教的地位。玛丽对付新教徒的手段非常血腥。在短短的三年内，将近300名新教徒都被玛丽活活烧死。人们都叫她"血腥玛丽"。这些措施让玛丽大

were popular. Then, she married Philip II of Spain which irritated her subjects because English people have long considered Spain as their biggest enemy. What's more, Philip was also a Catholic; it added more negative feelings on English people towards Philip. It was Philip who coerced Mary to enter war with France, which resulted in the loss of Calais, England's last possession in France.

Deserted by Philip, Mary I died childless on 17 November 1558 owning to sickness and was succeeded by her Protestant half-sister Elizabeth I.

失人心。其次，她与西班牙腓力二世的结合引起了强烈的民愤，因为英国人一直都把西班牙当做最大的敌人。不仅如此，腓力二世也是一名天主教徒，这增加了人们对他的憎恨。玛丽在腓力二世的怂恿下与法国交战，结果丢掉了英国在法国的最后一块领地加莱。

最终，被腓力二世抛弃的玛丽于1558年11月17人病逝，死后无嗣。王位由她的妹妹伊丽莎白继承。

词汇 VOCABULARY

1. continental [ˌkɔntiˈnentlə]
   n. 欧洲人 *a.* 大陆的；大陆性的

2. devout [diˈvaut]
   a. 虔诚的；衷心的

3. faction [ˈfækʃən]
   n. 派别；小集团；内讧；纪实小说

4. crowning [ˈkrauniŋ]
   n. 加冕 *a.* 最高的 *v.* 加冕（crown的现在分词）

5. obedience [əˈbi:djəns, -diəns]
   n. 顺从；服从；遵守

6. persecution [ˌpə:siˈkju:ʃən]
   n. 迫害；烦扰

7. bloody [ˈblʌdi]
   a. 嗜杀的，残忍的；血腥的 *vt.* 使流血 *ad.* 很

8. coerce [kəuˈə:s]
   vt. 强制，迫使

背景链接 TIPS

女性——英国最高权力斗争的受害者

在英国古代，卷入最高权力争战的女性，大多下场都悲惨。英格兰的玛丽一世由于母亲被父亲抛弃，在她继位之前一直着很悲惨的生活，甚至被沦为仆人。即使继位后，也并没有很幸福，与小她11岁的腓力二世的结合主要出于政治原因，最终还被遗弃。"童贞女王"伊丽莎白一世为了国家和民族放弃了婚姻，孑然一生。而"九日女王"简·格雷纯粹就是政治斗争的牺牲品，在17岁就丢了性命。

PEOPLE

085 Elizabeth I

When Queen Mary I died, Elizabeth took the throne and became the Queen of England and Ireland. She was the first Queen in the history that ruled the country for as long as nearly half a century from 1558 to 1603.

Elizabeth was born on 7 September 1533 as the daughter of Henry VIII and his second wife Anne Boleyn and half-sister of Mary I. Like Mary, Elizabeth also had a painful childhood. When she was only two years old, her mother was accused of being unfaithful to her father and was beheaded, then Elizabeth was declared not the daughter of Henry VIII. As a Protestant, when Mary was listed the next monarch after Edward, Elizabeth was brought out to prevent Mary becoming Queen. In addition, listed second in line behind Mary I, Elizabeth has been long considered as a big threat by Mary and even put in prison for some time. These experiences taught Elizabeth how to avoid unnecessary risks and she tried to keep away from any political involvement.

When Elizabeth took the throne from Mary I, the country was in chaos. The English people suffered a lot from Mary's ruling and expected little from another woman ruler. Elizabeth soon proved them wrong with her intelligence and sophisticated handling of religious issues. Elizabeth accepted the existence of different religious worship and embraced them. As a protestant, Elizabeth broke away from the Catholic Pope as was wished and reestablished the Church of England as her father did. However, the Church of England followed a middle course

【小译】

玛丽一世死后，伊丽莎白一世继承了王位成为英格兰和爱尔兰的新女王。她是英国历史上第一位在位时间将近半个世纪的女王。她的统治从1558年开始一直延续到1603年。

伊丽莎白一世出生于1533年9月7日，是亨利八世与第二任妻子安妮·博林的女儿，和玛丽一世是同父异母的姐妹。伊丽莎白一世的童年并没有比玛丽快乐多少。在她仅仅2岁的时候，他的父亲亨利八世就以安妮不忠为由杀死了她，并与伊丽莎白断绝了父女关系。身为一名新教徒，当玛丽被宣布在爱德华之后继承王位的时候，新教徒们试图利用新教徒伊丽莎白阻止玛丽继位。玛丽继位后，一直把伊丽莎白作为最大的隐患，加之伊丽莎白排在她之后继位，玛丽一直在寻找机会除掉她并曾把她关进监牢。所有这些经历教会了伊丽莎白如何避免不必要的冒险，同时她也学会了怎样躲避政治牵连。

伊丽莎白从玛丽手中接过的英国一片混乱。英国人民在玛丽的统治下过着水深火热的日子，自然也不会对另一个女人的统治报太大期望。伊丽莎白很快用自己的睿智和高超的处事方式赢得了人们的肯定。伊丽莎白一世实行宽容的宗教政策。作为一名清教徒，伊丽莎白顺应民意，切断了与罗马教皇的关

so that it could be accepted by both Catholics and Protestants. Meanwhile, she had to fight with a small group of conservative Catholics and radical Protestants. Elizabeth's religious measures on the whole satisfied different religious groups and held them together.

Elizabeth I devoted all her life to the nation and never got married, thus gaining the title "Virgin Queen". In her ruling, great achievements were made. Britain defeated the Spanish Armada and became the No. 1 on the sea. The comprehensive national strength enhanced steadily. Therefore, Elizabeth I's reign is also referred as the Golden Age or the Elizabethan Age which is considered to be one of the most glorious in English history. The legendary Elizabeth I died on 24 March 1603, leaving no heir to succeed her crown. Her cousin James VI of Scotland became the next monarch, known as King James I of England.

系，重新建立英国国教。新的英国国教奉行中庸政策，以此消除天主教徒和新教徒的反对。与此同时，伊丽莎白一世与一部分顽固的天主教徒和激进的新教徒展开坚决的斗争。

伊丽莎白一世终身未婚，她的全部精力都给了国家，赢得了"童贞女王"的称号。在她的统治期间，英国取得了很大的成就。英国打败了西班牙的海上舰队，成为海上霸主，综合国力稳步提升。因此，伊丽莎白的统治也被称作"黄金时代"或"伊丽莎白时代"。这一时期普遍被认为是英国历史上最辉煌的时期之一。富有传奇色彩的伊丽莎白一世女王在1603年去世。死后无嗣，王位由她的表亲苏格兰的詹姆斯六世继承，史称英格兰詹姆斯一世国王。

词汇 VOCABULARY

1. accuse [ə'kju:z]
    vt 控告，指控；谴责；归咎于 vi 控告，指责

2. behead [bi'hed]
    vt 砍头；[地质]使河流被夺流

3. involvement [in'vɔlvmənt]
    n 牵连，混乱；包含；财政困难

4. sophisticated [sə'fistikeitid]
    a 久经世故的；富有经验的；精致的
    v 使变得世故（sophisticate的过去分词形式）

5. radical ['rædikəl]
    n 激进分子；原子团 a 根本的；激进的

6. virgin ['və:dʒin]
    n 处女 a 处女的；纯洁的；未经利用的

7. legendary ['ledʒəndəri]
    n 传说集；圣徒传 a 传说的，传奇的

背景链接 TIPS

与伊丽莎白一世有关的影视作品

在由BBC主持的民众公选的"最伟大的100名英国人"中，伊丽莎白列前十名。她经常在话剧或小说中出现。1971年格伦达·杰克逊拍摄的《伊丽莎白女王和苏格兰玛丽女王》深受欢迎。1998年凯特·布兰切特在《伊丽莎白》中扮演女王年轻的时候，朱迪·登奇在《莎翁情史》中扮演年老的女王。米兰达·理查森在电视连续剧《黑蝰蛇》中表演了一个超现实主义的女王。同性恋先驱昆汀·克利斯普在《奥兰多》中扮演她。本杰明·布里顿在他为伊丽莎白二世的加冕作的歌剧赞美中描绘了她与罗伯特·德弗罗的关系。

PEOPLE

|086 Queen Victoria

Queen Victoria became the Queen of England in 1837 at the age of 18 and ruled the country till her death in 1901. Reigning England for 63 years, she was the longest reigning British monarch. Queen Victoria ushered the glorious "Victorian Era" in Britain during which period the British Empire reached its height and became the leading power of the world.

Born on 24 May 1819, Victoria was the only child of Edward, Duke of Kent, and Victoria Maria Louisa of Saxe-Coburg. Her father died when she was only eight months old and she was raised by her mother. At the age of 18, upon her uncle King William IV's death, Victoria inherited the crown and became the British Queen since William IV had no legitimate children. Victoria married her cousin Prince Albert on 10 February 1840 and they had nine children. The couple was very happy together and set a very good example for the whole empire. Albert was Victoria's secret secretary and Victoria relied on him heavily. It was during Albert's lifetime that Queen Victoria was the most active in ruling. However, the death of Albert in 1861 left Victoria heart-broken. She had never recovered from her husband's death. Gradually, she withdrew from public life and even missed the state opening of Parliament which made her unpopular among her subjects. Her focus was on her family. All of her nine children got married and eight of them had children of their own. Many of Victoria's children or grandchildren

【小译】

维多利亚女王于1837年成为英国女王，当时只有18岁。她的统治一直持续到1901年去世，成为英国历史上统治时间最长的君王。她的统治长达63年。维多利亚女王统治时期，也就是历史上辉煌的"维多利亚时代"，堪称英国发展的鼎盛时期。维多利亚时代的英国成为世界上最强大的国家，被称为"日不落帝国"。

维多利亚女王出生于1819年5月24日，是爱德华王子——肯特和斯特拉森的公爵和德国萨克森·科堡维多利亚公主的独生女。父亲在她八个月大时就去世，她由母亲抚养成人。18岁那年，她的叔父威廉四世国王去世，死后没有合法子女。维多利亚继承皇位成为英国女王。1840年2月10日，维多利亚与艾尔伯特王子结婚，婚后生有9个孩子。他们美满的婚姻为英国人民树立了好榜样。艾尔伯特成为女王的私人秘书，给她很大的帮助。这一时期维多利亚的统治最活跃。然而，艾尔伯特1861年去世，维多利亚深受打击，此后一直都没有从丧夫的阴影中走出来。此后，维多利亚无心打理朝政并逐渐淡出政治生活，甚至不出席议会开幕。她把重心转移到子女身上。她的9个子女都结婚并且8个都有了自己的孩子。维多利亚女王的儿孙们很多都与欧洲皇室联姻，比如西班牙、俄国、瑞典等。维多利亚女王也被称为"欧洲的祖母"。

eventually married into the European royal families, such as Spain, Russia, Sweden and etc. Victoria was thus known as the "Grandmother of Europe".

By the late 1870 and 1880s, Victoria gradually returned to public life and regained favor. In 1877, she became the Empress of India. During her reign, the British took up a quarter of the world's territory and the British Empire included Canada, Australia, India, New Zealand and most parts of Africa. The expansion in industry and trade turned Britain into the workshop of the world. Every aspect of Britain and British people's life was improved and developed.

After witnessing the prosperity she brought to Britain, Queen Victoria died on 22 January 1901.

到了十九世纪七八十年代，维多利亚的重心回到治理国家，也再次受到人民的爱戴。1877年，维多利亚女王成为印度女皇。维多利亚统治时期的英国拥有世界上四分之一的领土，英联邦国家囊括了包括加拿大、澳大利亚、印度、新西兰和大部分非洲国家。工业贸易的快速发展使英国成为了世界工厂。英国的方方面面和英国人民的生活都得到了很大的改善和提高。

在见证了英国繁荣之后，维多利亚女王于1901年1月22日辞世。

词汇 VOCABULARY

1. era ['iərə]
   n 时代；年代；纪元

2. usher ['ʌʃə]
   n 引座员，带位员 vt 引导，招待；迎接
   vi 作招待员；当引座员

3. legitimate [li'dʒitimit]
   a 合法的；合理的；正当的；正统的
   vt 使合法；认为正当（等于legitimize）

4. withdraw [wið'drɔ:]
   vt 撤消，收回；撤退，拉开
   vi 撤退；离开

5. regain [ri'gein]
   n 取回，收复 vt 恢复；收回 vi 上涨

6. empress ['empris]
   n 皇后；女皇

7. prosperity [prɔs'periti]
   n 繁荣，成功

背景链接 TIPS

英国皇家遗传病——血友病

1840年2月，21岁的维多利亚女王和她的表哥（舅舅的儿子）艾尔伯特结婚，当时谁也没有想到，这场婚姻会给她的个人生活带来巨大的不幸。他们一共生下了9个孩子，四男五女，4个男孩子有3个患有遗传病——血友病，女孩子也是血友病基因的携带者。所幸5位公主都美丽健康，于是不少国家的王子都前来求婚，他们都为能得到维多利亚女王的女儿而感到无上的光荣和自豪。然而当她们先后嫁到了西班牙、俄国和欧洲的其他王室后，她们所生下的小王子也都患上了血友病。这件事把欧洲许多王室都搅得惶恐不安，所以当时把血友病称为"皇室病"。

087 Elizabeth II

Elizabeth II is the fifth monarch of the House of Winsor and the present Queen of the United Kingdom of Great Britain and Northern Ireland. She is also one of the longest monarchs on the throne. Elizabeth II is highly respected for her rich experience in political issues since she has worked with six governments and eleven ministers. In her weekly meeting with the prime minister, she could always offer good advice to handle the public affairs.

Born in 21 April 1926 as the first daughter of Albert, duck of York and Lady Elizabeth Bowes-Lyon, Elizabeth didn't expect too much from becoming the British Queen because her father was the second son of King George V and the throne should be given to her uncle King Edward VIII. However, King Edward VIII gave up the throne to marry a divorced American woman Wallis Warfield Simpson and became the first king in the British history to give up the throne. Elizabeth II's father Albert succeeded the throne and became King George VI which made Elizabeth the next in line to become a queen. Elizabeth married Philip Mountbatten, a member of the Greek and Danish royal families and

【小译】

当今大不列颠及北爱尔兰联合王国的女王伊丽莎白二世是温莎王室的第五位君主。她也是英国在位时间最长的君主之一。伊丽莎白二世经历了6届政府的更迭，与11位首相打过交道，她丰富的政治经验为她赢得很高的威望。在每周一次与首相的会面中，她总能提出值得借鉴的建议。

伊丽莎白二世生于1926年4月21日，是约克公爵艾尔伯特与妻子伊丽莎白·鲍斯·莱昂的长女。父亲是国王乔治五世的次子，按理说是没有继承王位的可能的。然而，在她十岁时发生了一件改变她命运的事情。她的叔父，乔治五世的长子爱德华八世为了与一个美国离婚女人辛普森夫人结婚而主动放弃了王位，成为英国历史上第一位主动放弃王位的国王。如此一来，王位由他的父亲乔治六世继承并最终传给了长女伊丽莎白二世。1947年，伊丽莎白嫁给了希腊和丹麦

a British naval lieutenant in 1947 and her husband became Prince Philip, Duke of Edinburgh. Their first son Prince Charles was born in 1948 and they have three other children Princess Anne, Prince Andrew and Prince Edward.

Queen Elizabeth made effort to shorten the distance between common people and royal families. She allowed the public to have more information about the royal families so that the life of royal family became less mysterious. Queen Elizabeth even met her subjects informally and invited people of all walks of life to lunch at Buckingham Palace. In 1992, the Winsor Castle caught fire and caused some damage. In order to raise money to repair Winsor Castle, the Buckingham Palace was partly opened to the tourists in the following year. Consequently, the British public had a closer access to the royal family.

Prince Charles, the first son of Queen Elizabeth will be the next king of Britain, followed by his son Prince William and Prince Harry.

皇家成员、英国海军上尉菲利普·蒙巴顿。他的丈夫被封受为菲利普亲王，爱丁堡公爵。1948年，他们的长子查尔斯王子出生。女王还有其他三个孩子：安娜公主、安德鲁王子和爱德华王子。

伊丽莎白二世努力使王室平民化，缩短与大众的距离，揭下长期以来皇室在人们心中神秘的面纱。她让人们有机会获得更多有关王室的信息。她还在白金汉宫举行午餐会接待来自各行各业的人们。1992年温莎城堡遭遇火灾。为了筹款修缮温莎城堡，白金汉宫部分区域开始对游客开放。英国民众也多了一条了解王室的途径。

目前，伊丽莎白二世的长子查尔斯王子是下一位王位继承人，排在他之后的依次是查尔斯王子的长子威廉王子和次子哈里王子。

词汇 VOCABULARY

1. respected [ris'pektid]
   a 受尊敬的
   v 尊敬；重视（respect的过去式和过去分词）

2. divorced [di'vɔ:sd]
   a 离婚的

3. succeed [sək'si:d]
   v 成功；继承 v 继承；接替；继…之后

4. lieutenant [lef'tenənt; le'tenənt; lju:'tenənt]
   n 中尉；助理人员；副官

5. subject ['sʌbdʒikt]
   n 主题；科目 v 使…隶属；使屈从于…
   a 服从的；易患…的；受制于…的

6. castle ['kɑ:sl]
   n 城堡；象棋中的车
   v 置…于城堡中；筑城堡防御

背景链接 TIPS

英国为什么屡现女性君主？

在以下两种情况下，女性都可能出任英国君主：

1. 男嗣死亡或放弃王位，而他又没有继承人的情况下，则由君主的女儿出任国王；

2. 国王没有男嗣，只有女儿。

而这两种情况在英国历史上恰恰反复地出现，所以英国会屡屡出现女性君主。

088 Prince Charles

Born the eldest son of present Queen Elizabeth II and Prince Philip, Duke of Edinburgh on 14 November 1948 at Buckingham Palace, Prince Charles is destined to become the next monarch of Britain. After Queen Elizabeth II's accession in 1952, Prince Charles was made Duke of Cornwall and was also granted titles as Duke of Rothesay, Earl of Carrick and Baron Renfrew, Prince and Great Steward of Scotland as well as Lord of the Isles. At the age of nine, Charles became Prince of Wales and Earl of Chester.

Prince Charles studied in Hill House School in 1956 and the Cheam School in 1957. He also went to study in Scotland and Australia and then received his university education at Trinity College of the University of Cambridge starting from 1967, studying in archaeology, anthropology and history. Upon graduation in 1970, Charles began his military career and joined the Royal Navy in 1971. His military life finished in 1976.

Prince Charles knew Lady Diana Spencer since his was young but the two of them were reintroduced in the early 1980s. The British people favored Lady Diana very much. The couple became engaged in 1981 in spite of the 13-year age difference, which was warmly congratulated by the public. Their grand marriage ceremony took place in St Paul's Cathedral on 29 July 1981 which drew the attention of millions of people all over the world. Their wedding was regarded as the wedding of the century by most British people. From then on, Lady Diana became The Princess of Wales. The Prince and Princess of Wales had two sons, Prince William and Prince Harry. However, their love fairytale didn't last forever due to huge responsibilities, pressures and infidelities. On 9 December 1992, their

【小译】

查尔斯王子是当今英国女王伊丽莎白二世和菲利普亲王、爱丁堡公爵的长子。这位出生于1948年11月14日的王子注定要成为母亲之后的下一位英国君主。1952年被封为康沃尔公爵、卡里克伯爵、伦弗鲁男爵、苏格兰诸岛和大斯图尔德勋爵。九岁时,查尔斯被封为威尔士亲王(英国王位继承人在储位期间的专用封号)和切斯特伯爵。

查尔斯王子1956年就读于Hill House学校并于次年就读于Cheam学校。在从苏格兰和澳大利亚学习回来后,他从1967年开始进入剑桥大学三一学院,主修考古学、人类学和历史。1970年毕业后接受了军事教育并于1971年加入皇家海军,1976年军事生涯结束。

查尔斯王子和戴安娜王妃自小认识,但是两人正式被引荐并开始交往是在1980年以后。英国人民非常爱戴查尔斯王子的这位妻子。虽然两人年龄相差13岁,但最终走到了一起。1981年,两人宣布订婚并受到了英国人民的祝福。他们盛大的婚礼于1981年7月29日在圣保罗大教堂举行。全球亿万人观看了他们的婚礼。他们的婚礼被英国国民称之为世纪婚礼。婚后的戴安娜受封为威尔士王妃。查尔斯王子和戴安娜王妃有两个儿子,威廉王子和哈里王子。然而,他们的爱情童话并没有持续到永久。巨大的责任、来自各方面的压力和对彼此的不忠诚把他们的婚姻推向了尽头。1992

separation was officially announced by then Prime Minister John Major and their divorce took place on 28 August 1996.

When Princess Diana was killed in a car accident on 31 August 1997 in Paris, Prince Charles went to Paris and brought her body back to London. On the day of Princess Diana's funeral, Prince Charles accompanied his two sons to Westminster Abbey to attend the funeral.

After keeping their relationship for years, Prince Charles eventually married Camilla Parker Bowles on 9 April 2005 and made her the Duchess of Cornwall.

年12月9日，首相约翰·梅尔正式宣布两人离婚的决定。最终，两人于1996年8月28日正式离婚。

1997年8月31日，戴爱娜王妃遭遇车祸在巴黎去世。查尔斯王子飞往巴黎把王妃的遗体接回英国，并在她的葬礼上陪伴两个儿子到威斯敏斯特教堂送她最后一程。

查尔斯王子和卡米拉长期以来的感情终于在2005年4月9日修成正果。婚后的卡米拉王妃受封为康沃尔公爵夫人。

词汇 VOCABULARY

1. destined ['destind]
   a 命定的；注定的；去往…的
   v 注定（destine的过去式和过去分词）

2. accession [æk'seʃən]
   n 增加；就职；到达 v 登记入册

3. archaeology [,ɑ:ki'ɒlədʒi]
   n 考古学

4. anthropology [,ænθrə'pɒlədʒi]
   n 人类学

5. congratulate [kən'grætjuleit]
   v 庆贺；恭喜；祝贺

6. infidelity [,infi'deliti]
   n 无信仰，不信神；背信

7. abbey ['æbi]
   n 大修道院，修道院中全体修士或修女

背景链接 TIPS

卡米拉王妃殿下

威尔士亲王查尔斯的第二任妻子卡米拉的官方头衔全称为查尔斯·费力普·阿瑟尔·乔治王妃殿下，威尔士王妃，切斯特伯爵夫人，康沃尔公爵夫人，罗斯西公爵夫人，卡里克伯爵夫人，雷佛来男爵夫人，爱斯勒斯女士，苏格兰王妃。

卡米拉与查尔斯在查尔斯、戴安娜婚后藕断丝连，这段婚外情令王储的婚姻在五年内迅速败坏，卡米拉亦受不少英国人指责为王储这段童话式婚姻的破坏者。2005年4月9日卡米拉与相恋35年的情人查尔斯王子在温莎市政厅以民事注册的方式低调举行了婚礼，英国女王伊丽莎白二世出席了在温莎城堡圣乔治礼拜堂的赐福仪式。

|089 Princess Diana

Princess Diana was one of the best loved royal members in her life time and even till today; Princess Diana is remembered by the people as a beautiful, philanthropic and genial Princess. She was selected as one of the "Ten Greatest People" by British subjects.

Born on 1 July 1961, Diana Spencer was the daughter of Edward John Spencer, then Viscount Althorp. Diana became Lady Diana Spencer in 1975 when her father inherited the title of Earl Spencer. Diana was very fond of children and after finishing school, she became a kindergarten teacher at the Young England School till her marriage.

Diana was no stranger to the royal family. When she was a child, her family rented Park House that was owned by Queen Elizabeth II. However, it was in the 1980s when Charles started to treat Diana as the potential bride. On 6 February 1981, The Prince proposed to Diana and was accepted. The news of their engagement surprised the British public since the two were of different types of people and had an age difference of 13 years. Besides, their interests varied a lot. However, they were still blessed by the people as Diana was strongly loved by the people. On 29 July 1981, the 20-year Diana married Prince Charles at St Paul's Cathedral instead of Westminster Abbey where royal weddings usually took place because St Paul's Cathedral contained more people than Westminster Abbey. At the wedding, 600,000 people lined the streets to catch a glimpse of Diana and the wedding was

【小译】

　　戴安娜王妃是英国王室中最受欢迎的成员之一。直至今天，人们仍然不断缅怀这位美丽、博爱、和善的英国王妃。她被人民选为英国的"十大伟人"之一。

　　戴安娜·斯宾塞出生于1961年7月1日。她是爱德华·约翰·斯宾塞伯爵的女儿。1975年爱德华继承了伯爵头衔，戴安娜也成为了戴安娜·弗兰西斯·斯宾塞小姐。戴安娜非常喜欢孩子，于是在毕业后成为了一名幼儿园教师。

　　戴安娜对皇室来说并不陌生。在她很小的时候，父亲就租下了属于伊丽莎白女王的公园屋。但到了上世纪80年代，查尔斯王子才开始正式追求戴安娜。1981年2月6日，查尔斯王子向戴安娜求婚并被接受。他们订婚的消息令很多英国民众吃惊，因为在他们印象中，二人性格迥异，而且年龄相差13岁，兴趣爱好也各不相同。但是，他们还是得到了人们的祝福因为民众非常喜欢这位准王妃。1981年7月29日，20岁的戴安娜嫁入了皇室。婚礼地点从往日的皇室婚礼举行地威斯敏斯特教堂改到了圣保罗大教堂，因为后者能够容纳更多的人。婚礼当天，60万英国市民走上街头一睹王妃的风采，还有7.5亿人通过电视收看了这场盛大的婚礼。这场婚礼被称为"世纪婚礼"。

　　然而，并不是所以童话都有幸福的结局。查尔斯王子与戴安娜王妃童

broadcast on television around the world and watched by 750 million people. The wedding was considered to be the wedding of the century.

However, the fairytale wedding didn't bond the couple forever. Over their married years, infidelities were reported on both parties. Diana was also troubled with depression and bulimia. Their marriage was finally ended in 1996. Diana devoted herself to her sons and did more charity works. Even after their divorce, Diana still received high popularity. At the night of 31 August 1997, trying to escape from the paparazzi, Diana and the Egyptian film producer and Dodi Al-Fayed had a car crash. Diana left the world at a Paris hospital owning to her injuries. The following investigation found that the driver had drunk alcohol and the pursuing paparazzi were also to be blamed.

The news of Princess Diana's death shocked the world. People all over the world paid tribute to the "people's princess" in various ways.

话般的婚礼也没有把他们永远绑在一起。结婚后，双方都曾被曝光不忠。戴安娜还受到抑郁和厌食折磨。最终在1996年，他们的婚姻走到了尽头。离婚后的戴安娜把精力都放在了儿子和慈善事业上。离婚后的戴安娜仍然受到人民的爱戴。1997年8月31日，为了躲避狗仔队的追踪，戴安娜和埃及电影制片人多迪·法耶兹在巴黎遭遇车祸。由于受伤过重，戴安娜在巴黎的一家医院离开了人世。调查证实司机属于酒后驾车，而且追踪的狗仔队也有大的责任。

戴安娜王妃辞世的消息震惊了全球。世界各地的人们通过不同的方式缅怀这位"平民王妃"。

词汇 VOCABULARY

1.	philanthropic [filən'θrɔpik] a. 博爱的；仁慈的	2.	genial [dʒi'naiəl] a. 亲切的，友好的；和蔼的；适宜的
3.	potential [pə'tenʃ(ə)l] n. 可能性；潜能 a. 可能的；潜在的；[物]势的	4.	glimpse [glimps] n. 一瞥，一看 vi./vt. 瞥见
5.	bond [bɔnd] n. 结合；粘合剂 vt. 结合 vi. 以…作保	6.	paparazzi [,pɑːpɑːˈrɑːtsi] n. 狗仔队（paparazzo的复数）
7.	tribute ['tribjuːt] n. 贡物；颂词；礼物			

背景链接 TIPS

英国"十大伟人"：

英国广播公司评选出了英国的"十大伟人"。入选"十大伟人"的名人有大文豪莎士比亚、二战时期的英国首相丘吉尔、提出生物进化论的生物学家达尔文和英国前王妃戴安娜、提出万有引力定律的物理学家牛顿、大英帝国鼎盛时期在位的伊丽莎白一世、曾于19世纪初率英远洋舰队战胜西班牙和法国联合舰队并立下赫赫战功的纳尔逊将军、前"甲壳虫"乐队主唱约翰·列侬、英国资产阶级革命时期著名人物奥列弗·克伦威尔等。

090 Prince William

Prince William, the eldest son of Prince Charles and the late Princess Diana, is the second in line behind current Queen Elizabeth and his father Prince Charles, the Prince of Wales. William was born on 21 June 1982 in London with the full name of Prince William Arthur Philip Louis. His wedding with Catherine Middleton was held on 29 April 2011 and then was conferred the title The Duke of Cambridge by Queen Elizabeth.

Prince William studied in Eton College upon graduation from junior high school in 1995. In the school, he was an excellent student and also good at sports. William took a break to visit South America and Africa after graduated from Eton and then went to Scotland's St Andrew's University for Art and then Geography. In 2006, William joined the Royal Military Academy Sandhurst. Besides receiving military training, Prince William also devoted to charity works. He has been president or patron to a lot of charities and organizations. In 2007, along with his brother Prince Harry, William held a special concert to raise funds for charities their mother has supported during her life.

Prince William grew up under the observation of

【小译】

威廉王子是查尔斯王子和已故戴安娜王妃的长子，是英国王位第二号继承人，排在其父之后。威廉王子全名威廉·亚瑟·菲利普·路易斯·蒙巴顿·温莎，出生于1982年6月21日。2011年4月29日，29岁的威廉王子迎娶了凯特·米德尔顿，并被伊丽莎白女王封受为剑桥公爵。

威廉王子1995年初中毕业后进入伊顿公学学习。学校里的威廉王子是一名成绩优异的好学生，而且很擅长体育。伊顿公学毕业后，他到过南美和非洲，然后进入苏格兰的圣安德鲁斯大学主修艺术和地理。2006年，威廉进入桑赫斯特皇家军事学院学习。除了接受军事训练之外，威廉王子还参加了慈善工作并成为很多慈善机构的领导或资助人。在2007年，威廉王子曾和弟弟哈里王子组织一场特殊的慈善音乐会，为母亲在世时资助过的慈善机构筹款。

the media despite of his parents' protection. Disturbed by his parents' divorce in 1996 and his mother's tragic death in 1997, Prince William once publicly stated his dislike for the press. The overall impression Prince William left to the public is a responsible, mature and well-behaved gentleman conscious of the role he will be playing in the future Britain.

As the future king, Prince William's life received huge public attention, including his romance with Kate Middleton. Prince William met Kate when he was at St Andrew's University in 2001. When people were busy predicting the possible engagement, the news came out that they broke up in April 2007. However, Middleton still accompanied Prince William in several public occasions after the news. In October 2010, Prince William proposed to Kate Middleton with his mother's engagement ring and was accepted. Their engagement was finally announced on 16 November. Their wedding ceremony was held on 29 April 2011 at Westminster Abbey, an event that attracted more attention than the wedding of Prince Charles and the late Princess Diana.

威廉王子是在公众目光中成长起来的，虽然父母尽力保护他们不受媒体的烦扰，但他特殊的身份使得这种保护不太可能。父母1996年的离异和母亲1997年被媒体追踪不幸身亡使得威廉王子对媒体产生强烈的厌恶感。他从未公开表达过这种情绪。然而，威廉王子留给民众的整体印象是一个有责任心、举止优雅的绅士，深知自己将来的角色。

这位未来的王位继承者的恋爱史也备受关注。他和凯特·米德尔顿的罗曼史也曾一度是公众的焦点。威廉王子与凯特邂逅于圣安德鲁斯大学。正当人们忙于猜测他们何时订婚时，2007年4月传出他们分手的消息。但之后，凯特依然陪同威廉王子出席过公共场合。2010年10月，威廉王子把母亲的订婚戒指戴在了凯特手上。订婚的消息在次月正式宣布。威廉王子与凯特的婚礼于2011年4月29日举行于威斯敏斯特教堂。婚礼受到的关注度远远超出当年查尔斯王子与戴安娜王妃的婚礼。

词汇 VOCABULARY

1. confer [kən'fə:]
   vt 授予；给予 vi 协商

2. patron ['peitrən, 'pæ-]
   n 赞助人，保护人；主顾

3. overall ['əuvərɔ:l]
   a 全部的；全体的 ad 总的说来 n 工装裤

4. predict [pri'dikt]
   vt 预报，预言；预知 vi 作出预言；作预料

背景链接 TIPS

Eton College

伊顿公学是英格兰最大和最有名望的私立寄宿学校，1440年由亨利四世创建，位于伦敦以西20英里的温莎镇。伊顿公学素以管理严格著称，学生成绩大都十分优异，也是英国王室、政界、经济界精英的培训之地，被公认是英国最好的中学。长久以来，英国王室成员都会把男孩子送到伊顿公学。许多英国皇室子弟，都曾经在伊顿公学就读过。王储查尔斯王子、威廉王子和哈里王子也是该校毕业生。

091 Princess Kate

Catherine Elizabeth Middleton or Kate Middleton was born on 9 January 1982 into a middle class family to be the eldest children of Michael and Carole Middleton. Her mother was an airline hostess when she met Michael Middleton, a dispatcher and then married soon. In order to send her children to private schools, Kate's parents set up their own company specialized in delivering mail-order goods and it was a big success that made the Middleton family multi-millionaires.

Kate Middleton studied at St. Andrew's School in Pangbourne till 1995 and went on to Marlborough College in Wiltshire to study Chemistry, Biology and Art. She excelled in her study and was also a good sports player. From 2001, Kate became a student at the University of St Andrews and shared several classes with Prince William. They became friends but not quite close. It was in 2002 when Kate participated in a fashion-show that Prince William looked at her in a new way. Their romance began in 2003 after Middleton ended the former relationship. In avoidance of the press's attention, the couple kept their relationship in secret and showed no intimacy in public. This situation didn't last long as Kate was caught by paparazzi on a royal family skiing trip in 2004. The whole year after this, Kate was a favorite on the tabloids. In December 2006, Kate again caught the public attention by attending Prince William's being commissioned as an army officer and joined the Household Cavalry as a Second Lieutenant. In spite of their short split in 2007,

【小译】

凯瑟琳·伊丽莎白·米德尔顿，也叫凯特·米德尔顿，出生于1982年1月9日，是迈克尔·米德尔顿和卡罗尔·米德尔顿的长女。母亲以前是一名空姐，父亲曾是一名调度员。为了能够把孩子送到私立学校，父母创办了自己的公司，经营邮购业务。公司发展很顺利并使米德尔顿家成为百万富翁。

凯特曾就读于威尔特郡的马尔堡学院，主修化学、生物和艺术。她成绩优秀而且擅长体育。2001年进入圣安德鲁斯大学并和威廉王子同上几门课程。他们成为朋友，但并不很亲密。2002年，威廉出席了凯特作为模特的一场慈善时装秀，从此开始追求凯特。2003年凯特与前男友分手后，两人正式开始交往。为了避免媒体的跟踪，他们一直没有公开恋情，并在公共场合保持距离。然而，狗仔队对他们穷追不舍并在2004年拍摄凯特和威廉王子一家在滑雪胜地度假的照片。此后的一年，凯特一直都是各类小报的新闻头条。2006年12月，凯特再次成为焦点。26日，威廉王子从桑德赫斯特皇家军事学院毕业，正式成为皇家骑兵团的一员，军衔少尉。英国女王伊丽莎白二世及凯特·米德

the couple finally announced their engagement on 16 November 2010. On 29 April 2011, Prince William married Kate Middleton at Westminster Abbey. Their wedding ceremony received more public attention than ever. The wedding was frequently related to the wedding of Prince Charles and Princess Diana 30 years ago.

Besides the wedding, Kate Middleton, now the Duchess of Cambridge herself is compared to Princess Diana from time to time. The public raise a lot of question concerning Kate Middleton, such as will she follow the example of Princess Diana to devote herself to charity work? Can she receive the same popularity as Princess Diana did? All of the questions will be answered with time.

尔顿都盛装出席，成为全场最受瞩目的两个女性。虽然2007年爆出分手新闻，两人最终走到了一起，于2010年11月16日宣布订婚，于2011年4月29日举行婚礼。婚礼受到全世界的瞩目，也被不停地拿来与30年前查尔斯王子和戴安娜王妃婚礼进行比较。

不仅婚礼如此，凯特·米德尔顿，如今的剑桥公爵夫人，也不断地被媒体和民众与戴安娜王妃比较。民众对这位王室的新成员有着太多的疑问，她是否会以戴安娜王妃为榜样投身于慈善事业呢？她能否能赢得戴安娜王妃那般的爱戴呢？人们所有的疑问都会随着时间的推移而得到答案。

词汇 VOCABULARY

1. hostess ['həustis]
   n 女主人，女老板；女服务员；女房东

2. dispatcher [dis'pætʃə]
   n 调度员；调度程序；分配器

3. millionaire [,miljə'nɛə]
   n 大富豪；百万富翁 n 100万以上人口的

4. tabloid ['tæbloid]
   n 小报；药片；文摘 a 小报式的；缩略的

5. lieutenant [lef'tenənt; le'tenənt; lju:'tenənt]
   n 中尉；助理人员；副官

6. duchess ['dʌtʃis]
   n 公爵夫人；女公爵；雍容华贵的妇女
   vt （澳）盛情款待；[口]讨好 vi 热情款待

背景链接 TIPS

威廉王子与女友凯特恋爱史：

2001年9月 在苏格兰圣安德鲁斯大学同修读艺术史，因而认识

2003年9月 二人连同室友从学生宿舍搬出，租下学校旁边的别墅

2004年3月 二人被拍到在瑞士克洛斯特斯一起滑雪

2005年6月 女王伊丽莎白二世出席威廉和凯特的毕业典礼，媒体纷纷称"女王见未来孙媳"。

2006年12月 凯特见证威廉毕业成为军官，女王也在场

2007年4月 传媒指二人已经分手

2007年6月 二人出席纪念戴妃的音乐会，但相隔两行

2007年年尾 传媒指二人复合

2008年4月 凯特出席威廉的皇家空军毕业礼

2010年10月 两人在肯尼亚度假订婚

2011年4月29日 世纪婚礼大典

092 Prince Harry

Prince Harry or Prince Henry Charles Albert David was born on 15 September 1984. As the second son of Prince Charles and Princess Diana and the third in line to take the throne behind his father Prince Charles and his brother Prince William, Prince Harry also received excess public attention since birth.

Prince Harry's followed his elder brother's step in receiving education. He studied at the Wetherby School and Ludgrove School in sequence, both of which were attended by Prince William. In order to be accepted to Eton College, Prince Harry spent an extra year at Ludgrove School and be accepted in 1998. Upon graduation, Prince Harry spent a gap year in Australia and Lesotho where he was involved in some charity works. Prince Harry's military career began in 2006 at Royal Military Academy Sandhurst and was commissioned as an army officer in April 2007. Joined the Household Cavalry, Prince Harry served more than two months in Afghanistan from the end of 2007 to early 2008 and is now training to become a pilot in the Army Air Corps.

Prince Harry is also involved in the romance with Chelsy Davy. They have been dated on and off

【小译】

哈里王子全名亨利·查尔斯·阿尔伯特·大卫·蒙巴顿·温莎，出生于1984年9月15日，是当今英国王储威尔士亲王查尔斯和威尔士王妃戴安娜的次子。哈里王子现是英国王位第三继承人，排在其兄长威廉王子之后。他的特殊身份使他注定从出生就备受公众瞩目。

哈里王子的学业，几乎是踏着其兄威廉王子的印记走过的。他先后就读于哥哥读过的Wetherby学校和Ludgrove学校。为了能被伊顿公学录取，哈里王子复读了一年并最终在1998年顺利进入伊顿。自伊顿公学毕业后，哈里王子在澳大利亚和莱索托度过了一个间隔年（gap year），并在此做了些慈善活动。哈里于2006年5月自动请缨，进入桑赫斯特学院受训，于2007年4月被授阶陆军少尉。进入皇家骑兵团后的哈里王子在2007年底到2008年初曾赴阿富汗前线服役两个月，与塔利班部队作战。如今，哈里王子在接受飞行员训练。

几年来，哈里王子和切尔西保持着一段曲折的恋情。在哈里王子21岁生日的时候，他曾公开承认切尔西是他的女友。然而，几年来，他们不断被爆出分分合合的消息。2011年4月29日哥哥威廉王子大婚之日，切尔西以哈里王子女朋友的身份出现在婚礼和晚宴上。

哈里王子也有当今年轻人反叛的一面，曾多次因为他好奇贪玩的举动

for several years. At Prince Harry's 21th birthday, he admitted Chelsy as his girlfriend. However, in the following years, the news of their breaking up and getting back together came out several times. On 29 April 2011, Chelsy attended the wedding ceremony as the girlfriend of Prince Harry and the following dinner.

Like many youngsters, Prince Harry liked to play and became the subject of numerous reports for his insensitive behaviors. However, as Prince Harry reaching his maturity, he is more and more conscious of his position and responsibility. A survey on the comparison of Prince Harry and his peers indicated that Prince Harry is getting more and more credit from the public. Besides, he is highly regarded for his strong determination to fight for the country.

受到公众指责。随着他逐渐成熟，现在的哈里已经不再是过去那个顽皮、爱惹事的男孩，而是越来越意识到自己的身份和责任。英国媒体通过拿他和同龄的英国年轻人比较发现人们对哈里王子的综合评价不断提高，这证明哈里如今更受欢迎了。而哈里王子誓效国家的坚定决心更是倍受称赞。

Unit 21 政治家

As is known to all that Britain is a constitutional monarchy with a king or queen as the head of the country and the Prime Minister, the head of government, is assigned by the monarch from the political party that wins the most seats in the General Election. The Prime Minister then chooses around 20 Members of Parliament to form government ministers in the Cabinet. The monarchy meets the prime minister and Cabinets minister on a regular basis to discuss state issues. However, this division of labor in Britain didn't exist until King George I's ruling.

King George was the famous English king who didn't speak English. When Queen Ann died in 1714, her half-brother James should have been the succeeding King. However, James was a Catholic and the British law prevented Catholic to take the throne. Therefore, Princess Sophia, a Protestant assessed to the throne. When she died in 1714, her son George became King George I after Queen Anne.

However, George I didn't speak England well and had little knowledge of British politics, so he chose his council ministers from the Whig party to discuss state issues with. The most prominent of the ministers was Sir Robert Walpole who took the role of the chief minister; a position that was later called the Prime Minister and the council ministers are now known as the Cabinet ministers.

众所周知，英国是一个君主立宪制国家。在君主立宪制中，国王或女王是国家的首领，而政府的首领、首相是由君主从大选中赢得最多席位的政党中指定的。被指定后，首相才能从该政党中选择20名左右议员组成内阁。君主定期与首相和内阁大臣会面商讨国家事务。然而，这样的政府构成并不是一开始就有的，首相和内阁是在乔治一世统治时期形成的。

乔治一世因不懂英语而闻名。当安妮女王在1714年去世之际，王位本应由她同父异母的弟弟詹姆士继承。然而，詹姆士是一名天主教徒，英国法律规定天主教徒不能继承王位，因此王位被新教徒索菲娅公主继承。索菲娅公主于1714年去世，王位传承给她的儿子乔治，成为乔治一世。

但是，乔治一世不通英语而且对英国政治了解甚少。因此，他从辉格党中挑选拔出部分议会大臣与之商议国事。其中最出名的大臣是罗伯特·沃波尔爵士。沃波尔爵士担当首席大臣的职位。首席大臣演变为后来的首相，而这些议会大臣就是现在的内阁大臣。

093 Oliver Cromwell

Oliver Cromwell (1599~1658) is best remembered as a freedom fighter who put Charles I on the guillotine and who built up a commonwealth in England. Many think that Cromwell is a better fighter than a ruler because his ruling was not satisfactory enough and eventually failed to maintain the commonwealth.

Cromwell was born in 1599 in a poor family. When he studied at Sidney Sussex College, Cambridge, he converted into a Puritan and became a pious Puritan ever since. Elected in the Short Parliament in 1840 and then Long Parliament, Cromwell became known for his commending voice and his enthusiasm. However, what made Cromwell famous was his good performance in the wars.

When Charles I declared a war against the Parliament, the Civil War broke out. Cromwell fought for the Parliament and became a very important general. Cromwell was a military genius. He saw the well-trained king's army and realized that if the Parliament's army wanted to win, it must be well trained or even better trained. Therefore, he chose soldiers of great strength and courage and imbued them with strong religious conviction and strict discipline. This army came to known as "Ironsides". With this army, Cromwell won a series of wars. However, Cromwell gave all the glory of victories to God and believed that they were fighting for God.

In 1646, Charles I was forced to surrender. There was divided opinion as to how to handle Charles I between Cromwell's army and the Parliament, Cromwell and his supporters won the upper hand and put Charles on trial and sentenced him to death in 1649.

After Charles I was beheaded, England transformed from a monarchy country into a republic

【小译】

奥利弗·克伦威尔（1599～1658）之所以被人民铭记是因为他是一个为自由而战的战士，他不仅把查理一世送上了断头台，而且在英国成立了共和国。很多人认为克伦威尔是一个优秀的战士，但不是一个很好的统治者，因为他的统治并没有令人们满意，最终，共和国还是被君主制取代。

克伦威尔于1599年出生于一个贫苦家庭。他曾就读于一所清教徒创办的学校并成为虔诚的清教徒。在1840年被选入短期议会，之后进入长期议会。在议会中的克伦威尔以他权威性的口气和热情引起大家注意。然而，克伦威尔被人们所熟知是因为他在战争中的卓越表现。

随着查理一世向议会宣战，内战爆发。克伦威尔为议会而战并晋升为一位重要的将军。克伦威尔可以说是一位军事天才。他意识到如果想要打败训练优良的王军就必须要有更优秀的军队。于是，他挑选了强壮勇敢，并具有强烈宗教情感的士兵并加以严格训练。他培养出的这只钢铁般的军队被称为"铁军"。在克伦威尔的带领下，铁军赢得了多次胜利。虔诚的将军和士兵们把他们的荣耀归于上帝，坚信他们是"为上帝而战"。

1646年查理一世被迫投降。克伦威尔的军队与议会在如何处置查理一世的问题上产生了分歧。在其拥护者的支持下，克伦威尔获得决定权，查理一世接受审判并被处以死刑。

country called the Commonwealth of England. After defeating two powerful enemies of the commonweath, namely Scotland and Ireland, Cromwell was regarded as the savior of the Commonwealth. According to a constitution named Instrument of Government in 1653, Cromwell was given the tile of Lord Protector and was given the chief power of the country. Cromwell was actually became a dictator instead of a commonwealth leader. Eventually, Charles II returned and restored the monarchy from Cromwell's son's hands after Cromwell's death in 1658.

查理一世被砍头之后，英国由君主制转变为共和国，称为英格兰共和国。克伦威尔为共和国打败苏格兰与威尔士两大劲敌，赢得人民的拥护，被视为共和国的拯救者。1653年的一项法律《政府约法》册封克伦威尔护国公的称号，并赋予其国家大权。至此，克伦威尔从共和国的领导转变为一个独裁者。克伦威尔1658年死后，他的儿子接管了大权却无法控制政府。最终，查理二世复辟，英国恢复君主制。

词汇 VOCABULARY

1. guillotine ['giləti:n, gilə'ti:n]
   n. 断头台；切纸机；截止辩论以付表决法
   v. 于断头台斩首；终止辩论将议案付诸表决

2. imbue [im'bju:]
   v. 使感染；灌输；使渗透

3. Ironside ['aiənsaid]
   n. 克伦威尔的铁军

4. trial ['traiəl]
   n. 试验；磨炼；审讯 *a.* 审讯的；试验的

5. behead [bi'hed]
   v. 砍头；[地质]使河流被夺流

6. dictator [dik'teitə]
   n. 独裁者；命令者

背景链接 TIPS

长期议会和短期议会来历

苏格兰在16世纪已经完成了宗教改革，长老派的宗教信仰占据了统治地位。詹姆士成为英国国王之后，苏格兰和英格兰共有一个国王，但是苏格兰仍是一个独立的国家，有自己独立的议会和教会组织。然而1637查理一世根据大主教劳德的建议，命令苏格兰采用英国国教的稍加修改的祈祷书和国教祈祷仪式。消息传来，引起苏格兰的普遍不满并组织了一只军队攻入了英国国境。查理一世不得不在1640年4月召开停止11年的议会，企图要议会通过他所需要的经费，以便组织军队。然而议会的许多代表不但拒绝了，而且提出了议会的权利问题。查理一世在5月初解散了议会。这届议会存在不到一个月，历史上称为"短期议会"。

在英国国内，伦敦和其他城市的手工业工人和平民发生了暴动，农民运动也在英国东部爆发。各地人民纷纷递交请愿书，要求召开议会。10月，查理一世与苏格兰人签定了停战协议，但被迫答应每天付给苏格兰850镑的费用，直到最后和约的签定。对于这笔款项无处筹集，他不得不在11月召开了新的议会。这届议会断断续续，一直存在到1660年，历史上称为"长期议会"。

094 Winston Churchill

Winston Churchill (1874~1965) is generally regarded as greatest British leader of the 20th century and one of the greatest politicians in the world history because he led Britain through one of the darkest times in the British history, the World War II. Besides, he is also a good writer and a painter as well as an excellent orator.

Winston Churchill was born as the descendent of John Churchill, one of the greatest British military commanders of the 17th century. Churchill entered Royal Military College at Sandhurst at the age of 18 and was appointed a second lieutenant in a proud cavalry regiment. From 1896, Churchill travelled to many countries as a journalist and wrote books and reports, such as Cuba, India, and Sudan. During the Boer War, Churchill was hired by a newspaper to report the war but was captured. He escaped from prison and walked 480 kilometers of enemy territory before reached safe place. He became famous for this experience. After the Boer War, Churchill entered politics. His early political career was full of ups and downs. Before the World War II began, Churchill was appointed first lord of the admiralty. In the following year, Chamberlain was forced to resign; Churchill took his place as the prime minister of the Great Britain at the age of 66. Churchill made many wise critical decisions in the WWII to resist Hitler's invasion, which enabled Britain to become the last fort to defend Germany. Churchill made many stirring war speech that inspired the British people greatly. Everywhere he went; he held up two fingers and made the victory gesture which became the symbol for final victory for British people as well as people of the Allied nations.

In 1953 Queen Elizabeth II made Churchill Sir Winston Churchill by made him a knight of the Order of the

【小译】

温斯顿·丘吉尔是20世纪英国一位伟大的领袖，也被认为是全球最伟大的政治家之一。他带领着英国人走过了英国历史上最黑暗的二战时期。除此之外，他还是一位作家、画家以及卓越的演讲家。

温斯顿·丘吉尔是17世纪英国伟大军事领袖约翰·丘吉尔的后裔，18岁进入桑德赫斯特的皇家军事学院学习，1895年在一个荣誉骑兵团任少尉。从1896年开始，丘吉尔以记者身份去过很多国家并写出相关的书籍或报道，比如古巴、印度、苏丹等地。在布尔战争期间，丘吉尔受派于一家报社到南非进行报道。在被俘虏之后，他逃出监狱并穿过480公里敌占区到达安全地带，这一经历使他名噪一时。布尔战争之后，丘吉尔决定从政。他的早期政治生涯较为坎坷。在二战即将爆发之际，丘吉尔被任命为海军大臣。1940年张伯伦被迫下台后，66岁的丘吉尔接任成为英国首相。丘吉尔以其杰出的领导才能在战时做了很多抵抗希特勒的正确决策，使英国成为欧洲战场上抗德的最后一个堡垒。丘吉尔在战时发表了很多精彩的演讲，极大地鼓舞了英国人民的斗志。无论丘吉尔到哪里，他都会高举两个手指做出胜利的"V"字，象征着英国人民、乃至同盟军最终的胜利。

为了表彰丘吉尔的卓越功勋，伊丽莎白二世女

Garter, the highest honor of knighthood. Churchill also won the Nobel Prize for literature for his works and his oratory. In 1963 Churchill was made an honorary citizen of the United States.

Two months after the celebration of his 90th birthday, Winston Churchill died peacefully at his home.

王授予他最高荣誉嘉德勋章。丘吉尔还因他的著作和演讲获得诺贝尔文学奖。1963年，美国国会授予丘吉尔美国荣誉公民的称号。

在度过他90岁生日的两个月后，丘吉尔在家中安详辞世。

词汇 VOCABULARY

1. orator ['ɔrətə]
   n 演说者；雄辩家；演讲者；[法]原告

2. cavalry ['kævəlri]
   n 骑兵；装甲兵；装甲部队

3. regiment ['redʒimənt]
   n 团；大量　vt 把…编成团；严格地管制

4. admiralty ['ædmərəlti]
   n [英]海军部；[律]海事法庭；海军上将的职位

背景链接 TIPS

Excerpt from "This was Their Finest Hour"

…What General Weygand called the Battle of France is over. I expect that the Battle of Britain is about to begin. Upon this battle depends the survival of Christian civilization. Upon it depends our own British life, and the long continuity of our institutions and our Empire. The whole fury and might of the enemy must very soon be turned on us. Hitler knows that he will have to break us in this Island or lose the war. If we can stand up to him, all Europe may be free and the life of the world may move forward into broad, sunlit uplands. But if we fail, then the whole world, including the United States, including all that we have known and cared for, will sink into the abyss of a new Dark Age made more sinister, and perhaps more protracted, by the lights of perverted science. Let us therefore brace ourselves to our duties, and so bear ourselves that, if the British Empire and its Commonwealth last for a thousand years, men will still say, "This was their finest hour."

……魏刚将军所说的法兰西之战已告终结，不列颠之战即将揭幕。基督教文明的生死存亡在此一战。我们英国人、我们的制度和我们的帝国的存亡续绝也都在此一战。敌人全部的凶狂和残暴很快就会转向我们。希特勒懂得，必须把我们粉碎在这个岛上，否则他就输了这场战争。如果我们能顶得住，全欧洲都将获得解放，全世界的人民就能进入一个阳光普照的辽阔高地。但是，如果我们失败了，全世界，包括美国和所有我们熟悉和关怀的国家，都将坠入一个新的黑暗时代的深渊、一个由某种扭曲了的科学所造成的更加凶险或者可能更加漫长的黑暗时代的深渊。那么就让我们振作精神，承担起自己的责任来，让我们干出名堂来——倘若英联邦和英帝国再生存一千年，到那时人们还会说"这是他们最光辉的时刻"。

095 Margaret Hilda Thatcher

Margaret Hilda Thatcher is known as the Iron Lady of British politics who served the most consecutive terms as a prime minister in the 20th century. She changed the general opinion about woman and proved to the world that women could achieve as much as men do and women could even undertake what might be impossible for most men.

Thatcher was born on 13 October 1925 in England. Graduated from Oxford University with a Science bachelor degree and then a Master of Arts degree, Thatcher worked as a barrister before being selected into the House of Commons and elected the leader of her party. When the Conservative Party defeated the Labour Party in 1979 election, Thatcher became the first woman prime minister of the Britain. Her service as the prime minister lasted from 1979 to 1990 made her the longest prime minister in the 20th century.

The Thatcher government was dedicated to reduce the government control over the economy. The private ownership was encouraged for many government interests were sold to the private citizens or businesses, namely, privatization. The government also adopted monetarist policies to control inflation which involved controlling the money supply to reduce inflation. With the implementation of these policies, inflation was reduced; however, the unemployment rate increased greatly and many British enterprises were on the edge of bankruptcy. Many people began to doubt or even criticize the government. But Thatcher stuck to her policies all along and won herself the nickname of "Iron Lady".

With the revival of the world economy, British economy was also improved. Many of Thatcher's policies gained her popularity such as her sensible and decisive handling of Britain's conflict with Argentina; the government under Thatcher attached great

【小译】

玛格丽特·希尔达·撒切尔，人称"铁娘子"，是英国20世纪连续执政时间最长的首相。她改变了人们对女性的普遍看法，向世人证明，女性不仅能够完成和男性一样的工作，而且能做到很多男性无法做到的事情。

撒切尔出生于1925年10月13日。先后获得牛津大学理学学士和文学硕士学位，毕业后成为一名律师直到被选入下议院。之后成为保守党领袖。1979年，保守党在大选中战胜工党成为执政党，撒切尔夫人也成为了英国历史上第一位女首相。她的执政时间从1979年持续到1990年，这也使她成为20世纪执政时间最长的英国首相。

撒切尔夫人领导下的政府致力于减少政府对经济的控制力度。政府支持个体和私营经济的发展，同时政府把很多国有的所有权出售给私人或企业。这就是英国的私有化。为了控制通货膨胀，撒切尔政府推行以控制通货膨胀为主的货币主义政策，包括减少货币供应。随着这些政策的实施，通货膨胀受到抑制；然而，失业率猛增，很多企业面临破产。人们开始对撒切尔夫人的领导产生质疑甚至批判，但撒切尔毫不动摇。她的坚定为她赢得了"铁娘子"的称号。

随着世界经济的复苏，英国经济也得到了改善。撒切尔夫人的很多决策开始赢得人们的肯定，尤其是她果断处理了英国与阿根廷的冲突为她获得了无数的好评。撒切尔夫人执政期间英国保持了与美国的友好关系，并重视加强西欧防务体系。一切撒切

importance to its relationship with US as well as its defense system with Western Europe. All of Thatcher's polices were named Thatcherism.

Thatcher's service as a prime minister ended in 1990, succeeded by John Mayor due to her disagreement with several Cabinet ministers. Thatcher submitted her resignation on 28 October 1990. In 1992, she was made a baroness for her contribution to the country and also became a member of the House of Lords.

Till now, Thatcher is still regarded as one of greatest statesmen in the history of Britain and many of her policies still have great influences on their country.

尔夫人做出的政策被称为"撒切尔主义"。

由于与几位内阁大臣在经济外交政策出现分歧，撒切尔夫人于1990年10月28日辞去首相职位，由约翰·梅杰继任。1992年，撒切尔夫人因其对国家做出的突出贡献被册封为女男爵并成为上院议员。

时至今日，撒切尔夫人仍被人们认为是英国历史上最伟大的政治领袖之一。她实施的很多政策对今天的英国依然有着重大的影响。

词汇 VOCABULARY

1. barrister ['bærɪstə]
   n [美口]律师；（英）（有资格出席高等法庭并辩护的）专门律师

2. privatization [,praɪvətaɪˈzeɪʃ ən]
   n 私有化

3. nickname ['nɪkneɪm]
   n 绰号；昵称 vt 给…取绰号；叫错名字

4. Argentina [,ɑːdʒənˈtiːnə]
   n 阿根廷（位于拉丁美洲）

5. Thatcherism
   n 撒切尔主义

6. baroness ['bærənɪs]
   n 男爵夫人；（欧洲某些国家）女男爵

背景链接 TIPS

英国私有化

国有化是英国两党"共识政治"的产物。从1945年到1979年英国经过两次国有化浪潮，国有企业在英国国民经济上占有了相当重要的地位。为了管理好这些国有企业，英国政府制定了种种措施，形成了一套对国有企业的管理体制，但这一体制存在着严重的弊端，导致国有企业政企不分，效率低下。这成为英国私有化的一个重要原因。上世纪70年代面对资本主义世界严重的滞胀危机，西方社会涌现出形形色色的社会思潮，其中对英国影响最大的是新右派思潮。新右派思潮主张："自由的经济，强大的国家。"为英国撒切尔夫人为首的保守党右翼在英国的改革提供了关键的理论基础和意识形态上的动力。撒切尔政府执政期间，推行以新右派思想为理论基础的私有化政策，加大对政府管制体制的改革力度，成功实现了政企分开，提高了企业效率。撒切尔政府的私有化政策，不仅使80年代以来的英国经济、政治和社会产生根本性的变化，在世界上也有深远影响。

096 Tony Blair

 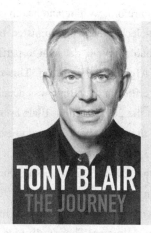

Born in 5 May 1953, Tony Blair is the youngest leader of the British Labour Party and the youngest prime minister since Lord Liverpool in 1812. He was also the first prime minister from Labour Party who served 3 terms continuously. In 2000, Blair made another first in the British history for being the first prime minister who got a child when he was in service since 1849.

Tony Blair studied law in St. John College of Oxford University. Upon graduation, he became a lawyer. His political career started in 1983 when he was elected into House of Commons. By 1994, he became the leader of the Labour Party. Blair brought some changes in the Labour party and named his policies "New Labour" to distinguish from the former Labour Party. It was Tony Blair who moved the Labour Party to the center of the British politics. The Labour party's successful election in 1997 made Blair the youngest prime minister since the 19th century. After taking office, Blair continued the Conservative's policies to stimulate economy but made some changes nationwide. Blair made the Bank of England independent of the government and gave permission to Wales' and

【小译】

生于1953年5月5日，托尼·布莱尔是英国工党历史上最年轻的领导人，也是自1812年利物浦伯爵以来英国最年轻的首相。他同时还是工党历史上连任时间最长的首相，共担任3届首相。2000年，布莱尔又成为自1849年以来第一位在任期内得子的首相。

托尼·布莱尔毕业于牛津大学圣约翰学院法律系。毕业后成为一名律师。1983年，布莱尔进入下议院，开始了他的政治生涯，并于1994年成为工党的领导人。布莱尔对工党进行了一系列的改革并将他的政策命名为"新工党"，并以此与之前的工党进行区别。布莱尔将英国工党推上了政治中心。工党1997年的大选胜利使布莱尔成为1812年以来最年轻的首相。执政以来，布莱尔继续施行保守党制定的刺激经济增长的计划，同时在全国范围内进行了一些调整。布莱尔使英格兰银行脱离了政府控制，下放权力给苏格兰和威尔士进行自治。

Scotland's self-government. Blair also deprived many hereditary peers' title in the House of Lords. He also made effort to reform welfare and health care. In 2001, Blair was re-elected the prime minister. But this time, Blair was troubled by his decision to participate in the invasion of Afghanistan and Iraq. This decision met with public criticism and Blair was accused of being dishonest. In the 2005 election, Blair broke the record and became the first Labour prime minister to run the government 3 terms in a row.

In October 2004, Blair stated he would not serve a fourth term as Prime Minister and in June 2007, he stepped down and was succeeded by Gordon Brown as the Prime Minister. There's divided opinions in evaluating Tony Blair as the leader of Labour Party and Prime Minister. However, it is undeniable that Blair brought changes to the British society.

同时，他剥夺了许多上议院世袭议员的头衔并在福利和医疗保健方面做出努力。2001年，布莱尔再次当选为首相。然而在此任期中，布莱尔参加阿富汗战争和伊拉克战争的决定让他深陷被指责的泥潭。2005年布莱尔大选再次获胜，成为工党历史上第一个三次蝉联首相职位的领导人。

布莱尔2004年10月声称不再任选第四个任期并于2007年6月离职，首相职位由乔登·布朗接替。人们对布莱尔作为工党领导人甚至首相的评价高低不一。无论如何，不可否认的是布莱尔为英国带来了诸多改变。

词汇 VOCABULARY

1. distinguish [dis'tiŋgwiʃ]
   vt. 辨别；区分；使杰出 vi. 区别，区分；辨别

2. hereditary [hi'reditəri]
   n. [数]遗传类 a. 遗传的；世袭的

3. peer [piə]
   n. 贵族；同等的人 vi. 凝视，盯着看；窥视
   vt. 封为贵族；与…同等

4. divided[di'vaidid]
   a. 分开的；分裂的；有分歧的
   v. 分离；分开（divide的过去分词）

5. undeniable ['ʌndi'naiəbl]
   a. 不可否认的；公认优秀的；无可争辩的

背景链接 TIPS

Lord Liverpool

第二代利物浦伯爵（1770～1828, Liverpool, Earl）原名罗伯特·班克斯·詹金逊，英国首相（1812～1827）。1790年进入下院，不久成为重要的托利党员。先后担任外交大臣（1801～1804）、内务大臣（1804～1806、1807～1809）和陆军暨殖民大臣（1809～1812）。在他任首相期间，发生了1812年与美国的战争以及拿破仑战争的最后几场战役。1814～1815年间他在维也纳会议上竭力主张废除奴隶买卖。尽管有时会被笼罩在他的同事们以及威灵顿公爵军事威猛的阴影下，但他还是执行了坚强可靠的行政管理。

Unit 22　文学家

In the British history, numerous literary pieces have been produced and more and more are still producing and will be produced. We usually use the word "canon" to describe the literature pieces written by great British writers. What is the literary Canon?

The word "canon" was originated from a Greek word "Kanon", meaning "measure" or "a basis for judgment; standard; criterion". It was primitively a religious word adopted to label those books of the Bible considered to be both authentic and authoritative. Later on, it extended to contain much wider meanings. The literary canon nowadays refers to a collection of books and authors that gained general approval from academic and cultural fields. The books and authors are respected throughout the history as classics. Besides their serious academic value, they also gain universal popularity and are supposed to be read and respected by everyone. When a work is referred to as a canon, it is thus canonized and is widely studied and respected. However, there is no definite standard as to which work is a piece of canon and which is not. It is a matter of subjective decision.

Owing to its ancient history, the British literature is flourished with excellent literary pieces; many of them are widely regarded as canons. The major plays of William Shakespeare; the major poems of William Wordsworth, George Gordon Byron, Percy Bysshe Shelley and John Keats' as well as famous novels written by the Bronte Sisters and Jane Austen, Charles Dickens, Thomas Hardy and Oscar Wilde and to name a few.

In order to appreciate a literary canon better, one needs to understand the circumstance in which the work was written; a glimpse of the background knowledge of the author's thoughts and experiences will also help the readers to grasp the essence of the work. A good literary work deserves repeated reading.

在英国历史上，无数文学作品被创造出来，而且越来越多的作品正在被谱写。我们用"经典"来形容很多英国作家的作品。那么什么是文学经典呢？

"canon"这个词来自于希腊单词"Kanon"，意思是"测量"或者"一种评判的依据、标准、准则"。该词最初属于宗教词汇，用来描述那些忠实于《圣经》且比较权威的书籍。之后词义被扩大。现在所说的文学经典指的是一系列在学术界和文化领域都受到普遍认可的作品和作者的集合。这些作品和作家在任何历史时期均受到推崇。除了其严肃的学术价值，经典作品作家还受到普通大众的欢迎并且被认为是人人必读必知的。当一部作品被认为是经典时，它就被经典化并被广泛地研究和推崇。然而，对于一部作品是否经典没有固定的衡量标准，这个问题见仁见智。

得益于其悠久的历史，英国拥有繁荣的文学，大量优秀的文学作品出自英国。其中很多都被广泛誉为经典作品。例如：莎士比亚的戏剧；威廉·华兹华斯、乔治·戈登·拜伦、珀西·比西·雪莱和约翰·济慈的诗歌；勃朗特姐妹、简·奥斯汀、查尔斯·狄更斯、托马斯·哈代和奥斯卡·王尔德的小说。这里只是几个例子，还有更多。

要想更好地欣赏文学经典，读者需要了解作品的写作背景。对作家的思想和生活经历的了解也会有助于把握作品精髓。一部文学作品总是值得反复品味。

097 William Shakespeare

William Shakespeare is generally considered as the greatest playwright of all time. However, the life of the great man is still a mystery for us.

William Shakespeare was born on 23 April 1564 in Stratford-upon-Avon in a wealthy family. However, his family met with financial crisis when he was 13, so he went for London and did odd jobs to earn money, such as stable boy, servant at the theater, actor, and playwright and finally became stockholder of the theatre. However, all of these were inferred from the existed documents and without accurate evidence. The next sure thing was Shakespeare's marriage with Anne Hathaway in 1582 followed by the birth of his twin daughters three years later. From the year 1585 to 1592 was a period of "lost years" for Shakespeare because there's no sign of any kind as to where Shakespeare was and what did he do. Shakespeare reappeared in 1592 in a London theatre. Shakespeare's acting career was in the Lord Chamberlain's Company where he became a partner later. The theatre was quite popular at the time and renamed the King's Company in 1603 when James came to power. It was the original form of the renowned the Royal Shakespeare Theatre. According to various documents and records, Shakespeare gradually grew richer in London and bought a house in London's wealthiest parts as well as the biggest house in his hometown.

Shakespeare's writing career could be divided into three phases: the early phase was from 1590 to 1600 in which historical plays and comedies were produced, such as Richard III, Henry III and A Midsummer Night's Dream, The Merchant of Venice and Twelve Night. The famous tragedy Romeo and Juliet was also produced in this period; in the middle phase of 1601-1607, Shakespeare's works were mainly tragedies. Shakespeare's four tragedies Hamlet, Othello, King

【小译】

威廉·莎士比亚任何时候都被公认为最伟大的剧作家，然而，这个伟人的生活对于我们来说依然是个谜。

威廉·莎士比亚于1564年4月23日生于英国中部埃文河畔斯特拉特福的一位富裕的市民家庭。但是他13岁的时候家里遭受了经济危机，他被迫离家到伦敦做一些零活来赚钱。他曾做过马倌，在剧院做服务生、演员和剧作家，最终成为了剧院的股东。但是这些都是从现有的资料推断出来的，并没有确凿的证据证明这些。但是可以确定的是莎士比亚在1582年与安妮·海瑟薇结婚，他们的双胞胎女儿在1585年出生。从1585到1592这段时间，关于莎士比亚的信息是缺失的，没有任何证据来提示我们那段时间他在哪里在做什么。1592年莎士比亚重新出现在伦敦剧院中。莎士比亚的演出是附属于Lord Chamberlain剧院的，后来他也成为了这个剧院的一个合伙人。这个公司在当时非常受欢迎，在1603年吉姆斯加盟之后更名为国王公司，它是皇家莎士比亚剧院的前身。根据史料记载，莎士比亚在伦敦逐渐富裕起来，在伦敦最繁华的地方买了房子，在当时是他家乡最大的房子。

莎士比亚的写作生涯可以分成三个阶段：早期，从1590到1600，主要作品是历史剧和喜剧，比如：《理查三世》，《亨利三世》，《仲夏夜之梦》，《威尼斯商人》，《第十二夜》等。著名的悲剧《罗密欧和朱丽叶》也是在那个时期完成的。中期，

Lear, and Macbeth were all written in this period. The late phase lasted from 1608 to 1612 when tragicomedies, also known as romances were created such as Cymbeline, The Winter's Tale and The Tempest and etc..

Most scholars agree that Shakespeare was the person who was born in Stratford-upon-Avon and who later became an actor. However, there were divided opinions as to whether Shakespeare wrote all the works known presently or they were created by a group of people instead of one, there are even doubts about the existence of Shakespeare the person. These days, the study of the ownership of Shakespeare's works has developed into a serious academic research topic.

1601到1607，莎士比亚的作品主要是悲剧，莎士比亚四大悲剧《哈姆雷特》、《奥赛罗》、《李尔王》、《麦克白》均出现于这一时期。晚期，1608到1612，莎士比亚作品主要是悲喜剧（即浪漫主义作品）。例如《辛白林》、《冬天的故事》、《暴风雨》等。

绝大部分的学者认为莎士比亚是出生在埃文河畔斯特拉特福，后来成为了一个演员。然而，也有不同的意见质疑目前的这些知名作品都出自莎士比亚一人之手还是集体智慧的结晶，甚至有人也怀疑是否存在莎士比亚这个人。目前，莎士比亚的作品的出处问题也成为了一个非常重要的学术研究领域。

词汇 VOCABULARY

1. playwright ['pleirait] n 剧作家	2. crisis ['kraisis] n 危机；决定性时刻 adj 用于处理危机的
3. stockholder ['stɔkhəuldə(r)] n 股东；股票持有人	4. phase [feiz] n 相；位相 vt 使定相 vi 逐步前进
5. tragicomedies [trædʒi'kɔmidi] n 悲喜剧	

背景链接 TIPS

名人名言

Frailty, thy name is woman! (Hamlet 1.2)

脆弱啊，你的名字是女人！——《哈姆雷特》

This above all: to thine self be true. (Hamlet 1.3)

最重要的是，你必须对自己忠实。——《哈姆雷特》

Nothing will come of nothing. (King Lear 1.1)

一无所有只能换来一无所有。——《李尔王》

Fair is foul, and foul is fair. (Macbeth 1.1)

美即是丑，丑即是美。——《麦克白》

Beauty! Where is thy faith? (Troilus and Cressida 5.2)

美貌！你的真诚在何方？——《特洛伊罗斯与克瑞西达》

|098 William Wordsworth

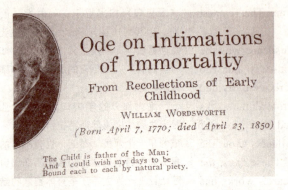

【小译】

威廉·华兹华斯是英国浪漫主义运动的领军人物以及英国最伟大的诗人之一。也是湖畔诗人之一。

威廉·华兹华斯1770年4月7日生于北部昆布兰郡科克茅斯的湖边区域。他很小的时候父母就去世了，由亲戚抚养长大，并且被送到了寄宿学校。1787年他进入剑桥大学的圣约翰学院读书。毕业之后，他去了法国，与法国姑娘阿内特·瓦隆恋爱，后生有一女卡罗琳。由于经济拮据，加之英法两国的紧张关系，华兹华斯后来被遣送回英国。

回国后华兹华斯从一位朋友那里接受了一笔900英镑的遗产。后来他遇到了塞缪尔·泰勒·柯勒律治，并且与他的妹妹多萝西搬到了湖区的乡下。在那里他和柯勒律治共同完成了英国浪漫主义文学的开山之作《抒情歌谣集》(1798)。《抒情歌谣集》并没有为华兹华斯赢得好名声，相反，一些评论家对他进行了激烈的抨击。1798～1799年间与柯勒律治以及多萝西一同到德国游历期间，华兹华斯创作了他的自传体诗《序曲》以及其他的一些知名的作品组诗《露西》。从德国回来之后，他们三人定居到湖区的多佛村舍，在这里华兹华斯在1802年与玛丽·哈钦森结婚，在1804年创作了他最

William Wordsworth was the leading figure of the British Romantic movement and one of the greatest poets in the British poetry history. He was also one of the Lake Poets.

William Wordsworth was born on 7 April 1770 at Cockermouth in Cumberland, part of the Lake District. With his parents died when he was young, Wordsworth was raised by his relatives and was sent to a boarding school. In 1787, Wordsworth entered St. John College, Cambridge University. Upon graduation, he went for France and met Annette Vallon who gave birth to a daughter Caroline. Due to the shortage of money and tension between France and Britain, Wordsworth was forced back to England.

Receiving a legacy of 900 pounds upon a friend's death, Wordsworth met Samuel Taylor Coleridge and moved to countryside with his sister Dorothy in Lake District where he and Coleridge composed Lyrical Ballads (1798), the manifesto of British Romanticism. The publication of Lyrical Ballads didn't win Wordsworth reputation; instead, he was criticized fiercely by critics. During a trip with Dorothy to Germany in 1798 and 1799, Wordsworth created the autobiographical poem The Prelude and some other famous pieces like "The Lucy Poems". Back from Germany, the three of them settled at Dover Cottage in the Lake District where Wordsworth married Mary Hutchinson in 1802 and created his most famous poem "I Wandered Lonely as a Cloud" in 1804.

It is generally believed that the summit of Wordsworth's poetry writing career was between 1797 and 1807. Received widely recognition from the public in the 1830s, Wordsworth was appointed Poet Laureate. Wordsworth and Coleridge and another important Romantic poet Robert Southey all spent most of their lives in the Lake District and wrote poems about the beautiful sceneries of the district. Therefore, they were named Lake Poets.

William Wordsworth emphasized spontaneity, intuition and imagination in poetry writing. According to Wordsworth, "all good poetry is the spontaneous overflow of powerful feeling recollected in tranquility". This became a criterion for good poetry during the British Romantic period. Wordsworth's poems had great influence on many later poets.

著名的诗《漫游》。

通常认为华兹华斯创作的顶峰是在1797到1807年之间，他的作品在18世纪30年代获得了广泛的认可，他也被称为"桂冠诗人"。华兹华斯和柯勒律治以及另外一个重要的浪漫主义诗人罗伯特·骚赛绝大部分时光都是在湖区度过的，同时也描述了这一地区的美丽风景，因而，他们都被称为"湖畔诗人"。

威廉·华兹华斯在诗作中强调自然情感、直觉以及想象。华兹华斯认为"优秀的诗作体现的应该是在平静中一点一点积累起来的有波澜的一些自发情感"，这也成为了英国浪漫主义时期优秀诗作的一个标准。华兹华斯的诗作对后来的一些诗人也产生了深远的影响。

词汇 VOCABULARY

1. boarding['bɔ:diŋ] n 木板；寄膳宿；上船 a 供膳的 v 用木板遮住（board的ing形式）	2. ballad ['bæləd] n 歌谣，民谣；叙事歌谣；流行抒情歌曲
3. prelude['prelju:d] n 前奏 vt 成为…的序幕 vi 作为序曲	4. laureate['lɔ:riit] n 桂冠诗人 a 戴桂冠的 vt 使戴桂冠
5. spontaneity [,spɒntə'ni:iti] n 自发性；自然发生	6. tranquility [trɑːnˈkwiliti] n 宁静；平静

背景链接 TIPS

I Wandered Lonely as a Cloud	
I wandered lonely as a cloud	我好似一朵流云独自漫游
That floats on high o'er vales and hills,	越过山谷飘过天边
When all at once I saw a crowd,	木然间我看见
A host, of golden daffodils;	一大片，金黄的水仙
Beside the lake, beneath the trees,	在湖畔，在树下
Fluttering and dancing in the breeze.	随微风摇曳起舞

Continuous as the stars that shine	如银河繁星
And twinkle on the milky way,	不停歇地闪亮连绵
They streched in never-ending line	连绵不断
Along the margin of a bay:	沿着水湾的岸边
Ten thousand saw I at a glance,	一眼瞥见一万朵
Tossing their heads in sprightly dance.	枝头摇曳轻盈起舞
The waves beside them danced; but they	粼粼波光也跳着舞,
Outdid the sparkling waves in glee;	水仙的欢欣却胜过水波;
A poet could not but be gay,	与这样快活的伴侣为伍,
In such a jocund company;	诗人怎能不满心快乐!
I gazed–and gazed–but little thought	我久久凝望, 却想象不到
What wealth the show to me had brought:	这奇景赋予我多少财宝。
For oft, when on my couch I lie	每当我躺在床上不眠,
In vacant or in pensive mood,	或心神空茫, 或默默沉思,
They flash upon that inward eye	它们常在心灵中闪现,
Which is the bliss of solitude;	那是孤独之中的福;
And then my heart with pleasure fills,	于是我的心便涨满幸福,
And dances with the daffodils.	和水仙一同翩翩起舞。

| 099 The Bronte Sisters

The Bronte's Sisters are widely admired for producing a cast of unforgettable characters such as the devoted governess Jane Eyre, the lovers Heathcliff and Catherine and Agnes. Moreover, the sisters' fragile lives also appealed readers of all generations. The lives of the Brontes were full of suffering. All of the three sisters were short-lived and lived their lives combating diseases.

Charlotte Bronte was born on 21 April 1816 as the eldest of the three siblings and shouldered the responsibility to take care of the younger sisters and brothers. Her writings were neat and tender and full of imagination. Unlike her sister Emily whose Wuthering Heights received immediate popularity, Charlotte's first

【小译】

由于塑造了一系列难忘的人物角色，比如有献身精神的女家庭教师简爱、情人希斯克利夫、凯瑟琳以及阿格尼丝等，勃朗特姐妹赢得了大家的尊敬。此外，三姐妹波折的命运也吸引了一代代的读者。勃朗特姐妹的生活充满了磨难。三姐妹的寿命都比较短而且一直与疾病进行着斗争。

夏洛蒂·勃朗特出生于1816年4月21日，她是三个姐妹中最大的，承担起了照顾弟妹的重任。她的作品工整而敏感，充满想象。不像她的妹妹艾米丽的《呼啸山庄》一出版就受

SELECTED WORKS OF
The Brontë Sisters

JANE EYRE • VILLETTE • WUTHERING HEIGHTS •
AGNES GREY • THE TENANT OF WILDFELL HALL

novel The Professor was rejected by the editor. Despite of the rejection, Charlotte continued to write Jane Eyre and eventually became famous with this book. As a romanticist in love, Charlotte spent most of her life searching for an ideal husband and finally married his father's assistance Arthur Bell Nicholls in 1854 and died one year later while she was still working on the her novel Emma. Although Charlotte only created four complete novels in her lifetime, Jane Eyre, Shirley, Villette and The Professor, she has secured a very important position in the British literature for modeling women with strong aspiration for independence.

Emily Bronte was said to be the greatest writer of the three siblings although Wuthering Heights was her only novel, but she led a shorter life than her elder sister. Emily died of tuberculosis at the age of 30. Emily was interested in mysticism and her writing was more passionate and rougher. Beautiful as she was, she never got married. Her novel Wuthering Heights was regarded as "one of the most intense novels ever written in the English language".

Anne Bronte was the youngest of the three and so was her achievement in the British literature. Her novel Agnes Grey was frequently compared with The Pride and Prejudice written by Jane Austen because

到广泛欢迎，夏略特的第一部小说《教授》遭到了出版社的拒绝。尽管如此，夏略特坚持写了《简爱》，出版后赢得了极大的成功。在爱情中，夏洛特是一个浪漫主义者，她花费了很长的时间来寻找自己的白马王子，最终她在1854嫁给了她父亲的助手亚瑟·贝尔尼·可拉斯，一年后在创作《爱玛》的过程中去世。尽管夏洛特在有生之年只完成了四部小说《简爱》《雪莉》《维莱特》《教授》，她却因为追求自由的女性模范而在英国文学史上占据了很重要的位置。

尽管《呼啸山庄》是她唯一的作品，但是艾米丽·勃朗特被认为是三姐妹中最杰出的作家，但是她的寿命比她的姐姐都要短。艾米丽30岁时死于肺结核。艾米丽对神秘主义比较感兴趣，她的作品更有激情。尽管她很漂亮，但是一直未婚。她的作品《呼啸山庄》被认为是最扣人心弦的英文小说。

安妮·勃朗特是姐妹三个中年龄最小的一个，在英国文学方面的成就也是最小的一个。她的小说《阿格尼

they shared a great deal of similarity in writing styles. Her work was simple and earnest. Anne lived the shortest life among the three and died at the age of 29. When she was dying, she anchored her hope for living on Charlotte and said "Be brave, Charlotte" and she was missed the most by Charlotte in her later years.

At present, there is an institution in England called The Bronte Society. Every year, the society publishes a volume of the studies on the Brontes to commemorate the Bronte Sisters.

斯·格雷》经常被用来与简·奥斯汀的《傲慢与偏见》拿来做比较，因为两者在写作风格上有很大的相似之处。她的作品都比较简单和真挚。安妮是三个姐妹中寿命最短的，29岁就去世了。在她重病期间，夏洛特是她唯一的生存希望，她也曾对夏洛特说过"勇敢点，夏洛特"，她也是夏洛特有生之年最思念的人。

现在，在英国有一个称为"勃朗特社区"的机构，该机构每年都会出版大量的研究勃朗特的出版物来纪念勃朗特三姐妹。

词汇 VOCABULARY

1. combat ['kɔmbət]
   n 战斗；争论 a 战斗的；为…斗争的
   v 与…战斗；反对 v 战斗；搏斗

2. tuberculosis [tju,bə:kju'ləusis]
   n 肺结核；结核病

3. mysticism ['mistisizəm]
   n 神秘主义

4. earnest ['ə:nist]
   n 定金；认真；诚挚 a 认真的，热心的

5. commemorate[kə'meməreit]
   v 庆祝，纪念；成为…的纪念

背景链接 TIPS

《阿格尼斯·格雷》简介

《阿格尼斯·格雷》是安妮·勃朗特的代表作，有很强的自传性，全书以女主人公第一人称的叙述语气写成。该书讲述一个自幼受人宠爱的娇弱英国少女格雷因家道中落被迫外出，担任富人家的家庭教师。她怀着美好的理想和满腔的热忱踏上社会，然而势利的主人和调皮的学生使她尝尽人间辛酸。格雷小姐并不因此而消极颓废，凭着坚定的信念和百折不回的毅力，终于赢得纯真的爱情，开拓了成功的事业。本书系安妮·勃朗特的代表作，文笔细腻，曲折动人，与《简爱》和《呼啸山庄》有异曲同工之妙。这是英国维多利亚时期一部很有深度的优秀现实主义小说，作者站在那个时代的进步立场上，揭示了社会的不平等与不合理，对于"世胄蹑高位，英俊沉下僚"的社会现实，表现出强烈的不满和抗议。

100 Jane Austen

Jane Austen was born on 16 December 1775 at the rectory in the village of Steventon in Hampshire. As the seventh child of a clergyman, Jane was educated at home because her father taught several live-in children. Spending most of her time with her brothers and sisters as well as her father's students, Jane had a very happy childhood. Jane loved reading very much and thanks to her father's library, she read extensively which provided materials for her own writing. Jane spent most of her life at home and her life was quiet and uneventful. She never married and died when she was only 41 years old.

Jane Austen started her writing career at the age of 14 and produced six well-received novels throughout her life: Sense and Sensibility, Pride and Prejudice, Northanger Abbey, Mansfield Park, Emma and Persuasion. All of Jane Austen's novels were published anonymously. In her works, Jane drew many realistic and vivid pictures of everyday life of the ordinary people in the country society and her focus was on the relationship between family members and neighbours. Though Jane never married her life, her perception of marriage was widely accepted. For Jane, there were three kinds of marriage; marriage for money, marriage out of passion as well as marriage based on love with the consideration of economic and social status.

Jane Austen's novels have always been the favorites of the film makers. All of her six famous novels have been adapted in films before. In recent years, some of them were re-adapted into films, such as Sense and Sensibility (1995) starred by Emma Thompson and Kate Winslet and Emma (1996) with the leading actor of Gwyneth Paltrow

【小译】

简·奥斯汀1775年12月16日生于罕布什尔乡村小镇斯蒂文顿的一个牧师家庭。她是七个孩子中最小的一个。父亲是当地的教区牧师,他与父亲的学生一起接受了家庭式教育。她与兄弟姐妹和父亲的学生一起度过了非常愉快的童年。简非常喜欢阅读。得益于她父亲的大量藏书,她涉猎了大量书籍,这也为她后来的创作积累了大量素材。简的一生几乎是在家中度过的,而且生活一直都很平静,没有波澜壮阔的经历,她一生未婚,41岁去世。

简·奥斯汀14岁时开始了她的写作生涯,一生创作了6部受到广泛认可和欢迎的作品:《理智与情感》《傲慢与偏见》《诺桑觉寺》《曼斯菲尔德花园》《爱玛》《劝导》。简·奥斯汀的所有作品都是匿名发表的。在她的作品中,简刻画了很多逼真形象的普通人日常生活的场景,她描绘的重点是亲人以及邻里直接的关系。尽管简自己一生未婚,但是她在作品中对婚姻的深刻认识却被大家广泛认同。在简看来,基于经济因素和社会地位考虑,婚姻可以分为三种:为了金钱的婚姻、平淡无奇毫无激情的婚姻以及基于爱情的婚姻。

简·奥斯汀的作品一直以来都是电影制作者的最爱。她的6部作品之前就已经全部被改编成电影。近些年来,她的部分作品被再次改编成电影,《理智与情感》(1995)由艾玛·汤普森和凯特·温斯莱特出演,《爱玛》由顶级演员格温妮丝·帕特洛出演,此外《傲慢与偏见》(2005)由凯拉·奈特利加盟。同时,

as well as Pride and Prejudice (2005) starred by Keira Knightley. There were also films on the author Jane Austen, The Jane Austen Book Club (2007) co-stared acted by Emily Blunt and Hugh Dancy as well as Becoming Jane (2007) co-starred by Anne Hathaway and James Andrew McAvoy.

也有关于简·奥斯汀本人的电影问世，《简·奥斯汀的书吧》（2007）由艾米莉·布朗特和休·丹西共同出演，此外《成为简·奥斯汀》由安妮·海瑟薇和詹姆斯·麦卡沃伊共同出演。

词汇 VOCABULARY

1. clergyman ['klə:dʒimən]
   n 牧师；教士

2. eventful [i'ventful, -fəl]
   a 多事的；多变故的；重要的；重大的

3. anonymous [ə'nɔniməs]
   a 匿名的，无名的；无个性特征的

4. adapted [ə'dæptid]
   a 适合的 *v* 使适应，改编（adapt的过去式）

5. prejudice ['predʒudis]
   n 偏见；侵害 *vt* 使有偏见；损害

背景链接 TIPS

《成为简·奥斯汀》精彩对白：

Mrs. Austen: Affection is desirable. Money is absolutely indispensable!

爱情至关重要，金钱同样必不可少。

Jane: If our love destroys your family , it will destroy itself.

如果爱情毁了你的家庭，它就会毁掉自己。

Jane: Could I really have this?

你觉得我能拥有吗？

Lefroy: What, precisely?

拥有什么？确切点？

Jane: You.

你。

Lefroy: Me, how?

我？如何拥有？

Jane: This life with you.

今生与你共度。

Mr. Wisley: Sometimes affection is a shy flower that takes time to blossom.

有时爱情是朵含蓄的花，需要时间才能怒放。

101 Charles Dickens

Charles Dickens was born on 7 February 1812 at Portsmouth. His family was wealthy at first but was running in debts when he was only nine and his father was put in prison for debts. At the age of twelve, Dickens was sent to work in a blacking factory and led an extremely harsh life which became an indelible scar in his heart. When 15 years old, he started to work as a law clerk and later a journalist.

Dickens' writing career started in the 1830s when he used the pen name Boz and his first publication was a short story collection named Sketches By Boz in 1836. However, it was The Pickwick Papers (1837) that gained him widely popularity.

Generally speaking, Dickens' writing career can be divided into three periods. All the work finished before 1841 were included into the first period including The Pickwick Papers (1837), Oliver Twist (1838), The Old Curiosity Shop (1839) and Nicholas Nickleby (1841). In this period, Dickens' works were featured by gentle social criticism and fantastic optimism. The second period of Dickens' writing career was from 1842 to 1847 during

【小译】

查尔斯·狄更斯1812年2月7日出生于朴次茅斯市郊。他很小的时候家境还比较富裕，但是9岁那年，家庭陷入债务危机，他的父亲也因为无力偿还大量的外债而被迫入狱。12岁那年，狄更斯就被送去鞋油厂打工，从此开始了艰辛的生活，这段经历也在他的心里留下了无法磨灭的伤痕。15岁的时候他开始做法务助理，后来又担任采访记者。

19世纪30年代狄更斯用笔名鲍兹开始创作，这也是他写作生涯的开始，1836年他发表了短篇小说集《鲍兹随笔》这也是他的第一份出版物。然而让他大受追捧的却是1837年发表的《匹克威克外传》。

通常来说，狄更斯的写作生涯可以划分为三个时期。1841年之前完成的作品可以归为第一个时期，包括《匹克威克外传》（1837），《孤雏泪》（1838），《老古玩店》（1839）以及《尼古拉斯·尼克贝》（1841）。这一时期狄更斯的作品的特点是带有温和的社会批判，同时满怀幻想。从1842到1847，可以说是狄更斯写作生涯的第二个时期，这期间《美国纪行》（1842），《小气财神》（1843），《马丁·翟述伟》（1843）等陆续出版。这一时期的作品中，他对社会问题

which American Notes (1842), A Christmas Carol (1843) and Martin Chuzzlewit(1843) were published. In this period, there was a more fierce criticism towards the society and the plots and structures of the novels were more unified and sophisticated. Dickens' writing career arrived at its prosperity at the time between 1850 and 1870. Most of Dickens' greatest works were created in this period such as David Copperfield (1852), Bleak House (1853), Hard Times (1854), Little Dorrit (1857), A Tale of Two Cities, Great Expectations (1861), and Our Mutual Friend (1865). In the late period, Dickens' criticism of the society was extremely poignant and his mastery of works also reached the highest level.

Charles Dickens was at his best in writing using critical realism and his protagonists were mostly from the lower class. It was his critically realistic description of the lower class people that made him one of the greatest writers in the British literary history.

的批判更尖锐了，小说的情节和结构也更加紧凑和复杂。狄更斯的写作生涯在1850～1870之间达到了巅峰，狄更斯最伟大的作品也是在那个时期问世的，比如《大卫·科波菲尔》（1852），《荒凉山庄》（1853），《艰难时世》（1854），《小杜丽》（1857），《双城记》，《远大前程》（1861），《我们共同的朋友》（1865）。这一时期的作品中，狄更斯对社会的批判极其深刻而且他对作品的驾驭能力也达到了新的高度。

狄更斯是杰出的批判现实主义小说家，他的作品的主人公绝大部分来自社会底层。也正是他对社会底层人民生活的采用批判现实主义手法的描述使得他成为英国历史上一位杰出的作家。

词汇 VOCABULARY

1. indelible [in'delibl]
   a. 擦不掉的；难忘的

2. fantastic [fæn'tæstik]
   n. [古]古怪的人 *a.* 奇异的；极好的；空想的

3. unified ['ju:nifaid]
   a. 统一的 *v.* 统一（unify的过去分词）

4. prosperity [prɔs'periti]
   n. 繁荣，成功

5. protagonist [prəu'tægənist]
   n. 主角，主演；主要人物，领导者

背景链接 TIPS

《远大前程》电影版：

《远大前程》前后拍了4个版本,如下：

1.Great Expectations （1946英国黑白版）

2.Great Expectations （1974英国彩色版）

3.Great Expectations （1998美国现代版）

4.Great Expectations （1999英国彩色版）

Unit 23 科学家

The UK has been a world leader in science and technology, discoveries and innovations, and since the Industrial Revolution the nation has been a pioneer in the use of machinery. British scientists have won more Nobel Prizes, over 70, than those of any other country except the United States. With about 1 percent of the world's population, Britain conducts about 5 percent of the world's scientific research.

Science and technology in the United Kingdom has a long history, producing many important figures and developments in the field. Major theorists from the UK include the 17th-century physist Isaac Newton whose laws of motion and illumination of gravity have been seen as a keystone of modern science, 19th-century biologist Charles Darwin whose theory of evolution by natural selection was fundamental to the development of modern biology and 20th-century physist and cosmologist Stephen Hawking whose theory of exploding black holes redefined the structure of the universe.

Major scientific discoveries include hydrogen by Henry Cavendish in the 18th century, penicillin by Alexander Fleming in the 20th century, and the structure of DNA, by Francis Crick and others in the 20th century. Major engineering projects and applications pursued by people from the UK include the steam engine improved by Scottish Inventor James Watt in the 18th century, the jet engine by Frank Whittle and the World Wide Web by Tim Berners-Lee. Scientists from the UK continue to play a major role in the development of science and technology and major technological sectors include the aerospace, motor and pharmaceutical industries.

In this unit, we will mainly focus on four of the leading figures in the history of British science and technology, namely, one of the key inventors during the Industrial Revolution James Watt, major theorists Isaac Newton, Charles Darwin and Stephen Hawking.

英国在科学技术、发明创造方面领先于全世界。从工业革命开始，英国就是机械化应用方面的先锋。英国的科学家获得了超过70个诺贝尔奖，是除美国外最多的。英国以占全世界1%的人口，完成了全世界5%的科学研究。

科学技术在英国有着很长的历史，并在该领域涌现出了很多重要的人物和发明。英国最重要的理论学家包括17世纪的物理学家艾萨克·牛顿，他的万有引力定律被认为是现代科学的基石；19世纪的生物学家查尔斯·达尔文，他的革命性的自然选择理论是现代生物学的基础；还有20世纪的物理学家和宇宙论学者史蒂芬·霍金，他的黑洞爆炸理论重新定义了宇宙的结构。

重要的科学发现包括由18世纪亨利·卡文迪许发现的氢气，20世纪亚历山大·佛莱明的盘尼西林，20世纪佛朗西斯·克里克等人的DNA的结构。重要的工程项目及应用包括18世纪苏格兰发明家詹姆斯·瓦特的蒸汽机，佛兰克·惠特尔的喷气式引擎以及蒂姆·伯纳斯李的万维网。英国科学家将继续在科学研究及重要的科技领域内扮演重要角色，包括航空航天业、汽车以及医药工业。

在这个单元，我们将主要聚焦四位英国科学技术史中的领军人物，他们是：工业革命期间重要的发明家詹姆斯·瓦特，伟大的理论家艾萨克·牛顿，查尔斯·达尔文和史蒂芬·霍金。

102 James Watt

James Watt, Scottish inventor and mechanical engineer, renowned for his improvements of the steam engine. Watt was born on January 19, 1736, in Greenock, Scotland. He worked as a mathematical-instrument maker at the University of Glasgow from the age of 19 and soon became interested in improving the steam engines, invented by the English engineers Thomas Savery and Thomas Newcomen, which were used at the time to pump water from mines.

In 1763, a model of Thomas Newcomen's steam pumping engine was brought into Watt's shop for repairs. Watt set up the model and watched it in operation. He noted how the alternate heating and cooling of its cylinder wasted power. He concluded, after weeks of experimenting, that in order to make the engine practical, the cylinder had to be kept as hot as the steam which entered it. Yet in order to condense steam there should be some cooling taking place. That was challenge the inventor faced.

Watt came up with the idea of the separate condenser. In his journal the inventor wrote that the idea came to him on a Sunday afternoon in 1765, as he walked across the Glasgow Green. If the steam was condensed in a separate vessel from the cylinder, it would be quite possible to keep the condensing vessel cool and the cylinder hot at the same time. The next morning Watt built a prototype and found that it worked. He added other improvements and built his now famous improved steam engine.

Watt attempted to commercialize his invention, but

【小译】

詹姆斯·瓦特是苏格兰发明家及机械工程师，因对蒸汽机的改良而闻名于世。瓦特于1736年1月19日出生于苏格兰格里诺克。他从19岁起就开始为格拉斯哥大学制作数学仪器，很快就对改进蒸汽机产生了兴趣。蒸汽机是由英国工程师托马斯·萨佛里和托马斯·纽科门发明的，当时被用于从矿井中抽水。

1763年，一台现代的托马斯·纽科门蒸汽抽水引擎被送到瓦特的作坊进行维修。瓦特对它进行了建模并在操作中对它进行观察。他注意到了汽缸在进行冷热转化时的能量浪费。经过了数周的实验，他得出结论：为使得引擎更加耐用，汽缸必须在蒸汽进入时始终保持是热的。而为了压缩蒸汽，需要发生冷却。这是摆在发明家面前的挑战。

瓦特提出了分离冷凝器的设想。他在日记中写道，在1765年的一个周日下午，他在格拉斯哥的一片绿地上散步时想出了一个主意：如果蒸汽能在一个分离于汽缸的容器中被压缩，那么就很有可能实现在保持压缩容器是冷的同时将汽缸保持为热的。第二天早晨他做出了雏形，发现它运转良好。他又为它做了一些改进，造出了如今已非常有名的改良型的蒸汽机。

瓦特尝试着将他的发明用于

experienced great financial difficulties. In 1775, he entered a partnership with Matthew Boulton and their firm achieved enormous commercial success. In retirement, Watt continued to develop new inventions though none were as significant as his steam engine work. Watt lived until August 19, 1819 at the age of 83, long enough to see his steam engine become the greatest single factor in the upcoming new industrial era. Watt has been described as one of the most influential figures in human history, who radically transformed the world from an agricultural society into an industrial one. Through Watt's invention of the first practical steam engine, our modern world eventually moved from a 90% rural basis to a 90% urban basis.

商业，但却经历了巨大的财政困难。1775年，瓦特与马修·博尔顿及其公司达成了合作伙伴关系，并取得了巨大成功。瓦特在退休后继续着他的发明工作，尽管再也没有哪样发明像他的蒸汽机那样引人瞩目。瓦特逝世于1819年8月19日，享年83岁，在有生之年看到了他的蒸汽机成为即将到来的新的工业时代中最伟大的单个因素。瓦特被描述为人类历史中最具影响力的人物，他将世界由农耕社会彻底转变为工业社会。由于瓦特发明的第一台实用的蒸汽机，我们的现代世界已经从农村占90%变为了城市占90%。

词汇 VOCABULARY

1. renown [ri'naun]
   n 声誉；名望　v 使有声望

2. alternate [ɔ:l'tə:nit]
   n 替换物　v / vi 交替；轮流　a 交替的

3. cylinder ['silində]
   n 汽缸；圆筒；圆柱状物；柱面

4. condenser [kən'densə]
   n 冷凝器；[电] 电容器；[光] 聚光器

5. commercialize [kə'mə:ʃəlaiz]
   vt 使商业化；使商品化

6. upcoming ['ʌp,kʌmiŋ]
   a 即将来临的

背景链接 TIPS

1. Thomas Savery

公元1698年，托马斯·萨弗里第一个利用蒸汽排水，使蒸汽通入密闭容器，然后在容器上喷冷水，使其中的蒸汽冷凝，从而产生真空。他利用这种真空从矿井抽水，又利用锅炉蒸汽将容器中的水排空。这个循环过程反复进行。

2. Thomas Newcomen

纽科门（Thomas Newcomen）是英国工程师，蒸汽机发明人之一。他发明的常压蒸汽机是世界上第一台实用的蒸汽机，瓦特蒸汽机的前身。他为后来蒸汽机的诞生和发展奠定了基础。

103 Charles Robert Darwin

Charles Robert Darwin (1809~1882) was a British scientist who laid the foundation of modern evolutionary theory with his concept of the development of all forms of life through the slow-working process of natural selection. His work was of major influence on the life and earth sciences and on modern thought in general.

Charles Robert Darwin was born on 12 February 1809 in Shrewsbury, Shropshire into a wealthy and well-connected family. Darwin himself initially planned to follow a medical career, and studied at Edinburgh University but later switched to divinity at Cambridge. In 1831, he was recommended as a naturalist on HMS Beagle, which was bound on a long scientific survey expedition to South America and the South Seas (1831~36). His zoological and geological discoveries on the voyage resulted in numerous important publications and formed the basis of his theories of evolution.

Seeing competition between individuals of a single species, he recognized that within a local population the individual bird, for example, with the sharper beak might have a better chance to survive and reproduce and that if such traits were passed on to new generations, they would be predominant in future populations. He saw this natural selection as the mechanism by which advantageous variations were passed on to later generations and less advantageous traits gradually disappeared. He worked on his theory for more than 20

【小译】

查尔斯·罗伯特·达尔文（1809～1882），英国科学家。他提出了所有形式的生命都要通过缓慢的自然选择而发展的概念，奠定了现代进化理论的基础。他的学说主要影响着生命及地球科学以及现代人的普遍思维。

查尔斯·罗伯特·达尔文于1809年2月12日诞生在希罗普郡什鲁斯伯里的一个富裕而有名望的家庭。达尔文自己最初打算从事医科职业并就读于爱丁堡大学，但随后他转入了剑桥大学的宗教学专业。1831年，他被推选为英国政府公务皇家舰艇比格尔号上的一名自然学家，参加了对南美及南部海域的长途科学考察工作（1831～1836）。他在航行中发表了很多重要的动物学和地质学的发现，从而奠定了他的进化理论的基础。

观察了单个种群个体之间的竞争后，他认识到，比如说一个地区性的鸟类种群，有着尖锐的喙的可能会有更好的机会幸存和繁衍。如果这种特质被传递给了下一代，那么它们就将在未来的种群中占据优势。达尔文认为自然选择是一种有利的变化被传递给后代而无益的变化逐渐消失的一种机制。他在研究了他的理论20多年

years before publishing it in his famous On the Origin of Species by Means of Natural Selection (1859).

The book was immediately in great demand, and Darwin's intensely controversial theory was accepted quickly in most scientific circles; most opposition came from religious leaders who held that the world was created by God in seven days as described in the Bible. However, his ideas soon gained currency and have become the new orthodoxy. Though Darwin's ideas were modified by later developments in genetics and molecular biology, his work remains central to modern evolutionary theory.

For the remainder of his life Darwin studied, researched, and made many important contributions to geology, zoological geography, taxonomy, ecology and animal breeding. He died on 19 April 1882, at the age of seventy-three and was honored by a major ceremonial funeral in Westminster Abbey, where he was buried close to John Herschel and Isaac Newton. Darwin has been described as one of the most influential figures in human history.

后，于1859年出版了他著名的著作《物种起源》。

这本书很快便供不应求，而达尔文的具有强烈争议的理论也很快被科学界的大多数所接受。反对声来自于宗教领袖们，他们坚持《圣经》里的说法，认为世界是上帝在七天时间里创造出来的。但是达尔文的想法很快占据主流，成为了新的正统理论。虽然达尔文的理论随后在遗传学以及分子生物学中被改进，但他的工作仍然是现代进化理论的中心。

在余生中达尔文继续学习研究；并在地质学、动物学、地理学、分类学、生态学和动物繁殖学中做出了很多重要贡献。达尔文逝世于1882年3月19日，享年73岁。威斯敏斯特大教堂为他举行了盛大的葬礼。在那里，他葬在约翰·赫舍尔和伊萨克·牛顿旁边。达尔文被视为人类历史上最有影响的人物之一。

词汇 VOCABULARY

1. evolutionary [ˌiːvəˈluːʃənəri]
   a 进化的；发展的；渐进的

2. divinity [diˈviniti]
   n 神；神学；神性

3. zoological [ˌzəuəˈlɔdʒikəl]
   a 关于动物的；动物学的

4. geological [dʒiəˈlɔdʒikəl]
   a 地质的，地质学的

5. orthodoxy [ˈɔːθədɔksi]
   n 正统说法；正统；正教

6. molecular [məuˈlekjulə]
   a 由分子组成的；分子的

7. taxonomy [tækˈsɔnəmi]
   n 分类学；分类法

8. ecology [i(ː)ˈkɔlədʒi]
   n 生态学；社会生态学

背景链接 TIPS

natural selection

自然选择：生物在生存斗争中适者生存、不适者被淘汰的现象。最初由达尔文提出。"选择"这个词只是一种比喻，并非说有超自然的力量在进行选择。按照达尔文的意见，自然选择不过是生物与自然环境相互作用的结果。

104 Isaac Newton

Sir Isaac Newton (1642~1727) was an English physicist, mathematician, astronomer, natural philosopher, alchemist, and theologian of all time.

Born at Woolsthorpe, near Grantham in Lincolnshire, where he attended school, Newton entered Cambridge University in 1661. Since 1669, Newton had held the prestigious post of Lucasian Professor of Mathematics unitl 1696 when he was appointed warden of the Royal Mint, settling in London. He took his duties at the Mint very seriously and campaigned against corruption and inefficiency within the organization. In 1703, he was elected president of the Royal Society, an office he held until his death. He was knighted in 1705.

Newton has been regarded for almost 300 years as the founding exemplar of modern physical science, his achievements in experimental investigation being as innovative as those in mathematical research. With equal, if not greater, energy and originality he also plunged into chemistry, the early history of Western civilization, and theology.

His monograph Philosophiæ Naturalis Principia Mathematica, published in 1687, lays the foundations for most of classical mechanics. In this work, Newton showed how a universal force, gravity, applied to all objects in all parts of the universe. This book is generally considered to be one of the most important scientific books ever written.

Widely regarded as one of the most influential people in human history, Newton built the first practical reflecting telescope and developed a theory of color based on the observation that a prism decomposes white light into the many colors that form the visible spectrum. He also formulated an empirical law of

【小译】

艾萨克·牛顿爵士（1642～1727）是一位英国物理学家、数学家、天文学家、自然哲学家、神学家，同时热衷于炼金术。

牛顿出生于林肯郡格兰瑟姆附近的伍兹索普，并在那里开始了求学生涯。牛顿于1661年进入剑桥大学。从1669年开始，牛顿担任了颇具名望的卢卡斯数学教授一职，一直持续到1696年他被任命为皇家造币厂督察员。他在造币厂严格地履行着他的职责，并在体制内与腐败和低效作斗争。1703年他被选举为皇家学会主席，并担任此职直至去世。1705年，他被授予爵士爵位。

近300年来，牛顿一直被认为是现在物理学的奠基人。他在科学实验方面的成就与他在数学领域的研究同样具有创新性。他在能量学，以及早期他投入的化学、早期西方文明史和神学方面就算称不上伟大，也是同样有创新性的。

他的著作《自然哲学的数学原理》出版于1687年，奠定了经典力学的绝大部分基础。在这部作品中，他展示了宇宙中普适的力——重力——是如何作用于宇宙中各部分的所有实体的。这本书普遍被认为是史上最重要的科学著作之一。

在人类历史上，牛顿被公认为的最具影响力的人之一，他制造了第一台实用型反射式望远镜。他用棱镜把白色的光分解成多种不同的颜色，形

cooling and studied the speed of sound.

In mathematics, Newton shares the credit with Gottfried Leibniz for the development of differential and integral calculus. He also demonstrated the generalized binomial theorem, developed Newton's method for approximating the roots of a function, and contributed to the study of power series.

Newton was a difficult man, prone to depression and often involved in bitter arguments with other scientists, but by the early 1700s he was the dominant figure in British and European science. He never married and lived modestly, but was buried with great pomp in Westminster Abbey.

成可见光谱，从而提出了颜色理论。他还建立了冷却定律，并研究了声音的速度。

数学方面，牛顿与莱布尼兹共同发明了微积分。他还论证了二项式定理，建立了用于求方程近似的根的牛顿方法。他还致力于幂级数的研究。

牛顿是一个难以捉摸的人，容易抑郁，经常卷入与其他科学家的争论之中。但一直到17世纪早期，他在英国和欧洲科学界地位都非常重要。牛顿终生未婚，为人谦逊，但死后却以盛况空前的葬礼葬于威斯敏斯特大教堂。

词汇 VOCABULARY

1. alchemist ['ælkimist]
   n. 炼金术士

2. theologian [ˌθiːəˈləudʒjən]
   n. 神学者；空头理论家

3. mint [mint]
   n. 薄荷；造币厂，巨款　*v.* 铸造，铸币

4. inefficiency [ˌiniˈfiʃ ənsi]
   n. 效率低；无效率；无能

5. exemplar [igˈzemplə]
   n. 模范，榜样；标本

6. telescope ['teliskəup]
   n. 望远镜　*v.* 压缩；使套叠　*vt.* 套叠；变短

7. spectrum ['spektrəm]
   n. [物]光谱；[电信]频谱；[心]余象；范围

8. calculus ['kælkjuləs]
   n. 微积分学；结石

9. binomial [baiˈnəumiəl]
   n. [数]二项式；二种名称　*a.* 二项式的

10. theorem ['θiərəm]
    n. 定理；原理

背景链接 TIPS

1. Lucasian Professor of Mathematics

卢卡斯数学教授是英国剑桥大学的一个荣誉职位，授予对象为数理相关的研究者，这一席位要具有极为高深学术造诣的学者才能担负。同一时间只授予一人。

2. Gottfried Leibniz

戈特弗里德·威廉·莱布尼茨（1646年～1716年），德国哲学家、数学家。涉及的领域有法学、力学、光学、语言学等40多个范畴，被誉为十七世纪的亚里士多德。和牛顿先后独立发明了微积分。

105 Stephen William Hawking

Stephen William Hawking is an English theoretical physicist and cosmologist who is world famous for his theory of exploding black holes. Stephen Hawking is generally considered as one of the most celebrated scientists and greatest minds of the present time. His work helped to reconfigure models of the universe and to redefine what's in it. In addition to being a brilliant scientist, Hawking is a great popularizer of science.

Stephen Hawking was born on 8 January 1942 in Oxford, England. When he was eight, his family moved to St. Albans. At the age of eleven, Stephen went to St. Albans School and then on to his father's old college, University College, Oxford. Stephen wanted to study Mathematics, which was not available at University College, so he pursued Physics instead. After getting his degree in 1962, Hawking moved to Cambridge University. In 1973 he joined the Applied Mathematics and Theoretical Physics department at Cambridge, where in 1977 he became Professor of Gravitational Physics. Since 1979, Hawking has held the post of Lucasian professor of mathematics at Cambridge University.

Hawking's key scientific works to date have included providing, with Roger Penrose, theorems

【小译】

史蒂芬·威廉姆·霍金是英国理论物理学家和宇宙学家，以其黑洞爆炸理论而闻名于世。史蒂芬·霍金被普遍认为是当今最著名的科学家以及最伟大的智者之一。他的研究重塑了宇宙的模型，重新定义了宇宙的内容。他不但是一位杰出的科学家，还是一位伟大的科学普及者。

史蒂芬·霍金于1942年1月8日出生于英格兰的牛津。8岁时，举家迁往圣奥尔本斯。11岁时进入圣奥尔本斯学校学习，之后霍金打算进入他父亲的母校——牛津大学学习数学专业未果，于是转而学习物理学，1962年取得学位，后到剑桥大学继续学习。1973年，他加入了牛津大学应用数学与理论物理系，并在那里于1977年成为了引力物理学教授。从1979年开始，霍金担任了剑桥大学卢卡斯数学教授的职务。

霍金最为关键的研究包括与罗杰·彭罗斯一起在广义相对论框架内证明了奇性定理，以及关于黑洞辐射

regarding gravitational singularities in the framework of general relativity, and the theoretical prediction that black holes should emit radiation, which is today known as Hawking radiation. He has also achieved success with works of popular science in which he discusses his own theories and cosmology in general; these include the best seller A Brief History of Time, which stayed on the British Sunday Times best-sellers list for a record-breaking 237 weeks.

At the age of 21, Hawking was diagnosed with ALS (amyotrophic lateral sclerosis) or Lou Gehrig's disease, a neuromuscular disease that progressively weakens muscle control. Doctors gave him about two years to live. He not only exceeded their estimate, but also earned his doctorate, married, had three children, was appointed an Honorary Fellow of the Royal Society of Arts, a lifetime member of the Pontifical Academy of Sciences, and in 2009 was awarded the Presidential Medal of Freedom, the highest civilian award in the United States.

的预测理论，也就是我们今天所知的霍金辐射。他的科普著作也取得了巨大成功。在他的著作中，他讨论了自己的理论以及大众化的宇宙知识。这些著作包括他的最畅销的《时间简史》，该书创下了连续237周登上《星期日泰晤士报》上的最畅销书籍排行榜的记录。

在霍金21岁的时候，他被诊断出患上了肌肉萎缩性脊髓侧索硬化症，或者叫做卢加雷综合症，这是一种能够逐渐导致全身肌肉瘫痪的神经肌肉疾病。当时医生预言他最多还有2年寿命。但他不仅延长了这一估计，还取得了博士学位，结了婚，有了3个孩子，并被推选为皇家学会荣誉会员，梵蒂冈教皇科学学会终身成员，并于2009年被授予总统自由勋章。这是平民在美国所能获得的最高荣誉。

词汇 VOCABULARY

1. cosmologist [kɔz'mɔlədʒist]
   n. 宇宙论者，宇宙学家

2. reconfigure [ˌri:kən'figə(r); -gjuə(r)]
   vt. 重新配置

3. popularizer ['pɔpjuləri'z-]
   n. 大众化的人；普及读物；普及者

4. cosmology [kɔz'mɔlədʒi]
   n. 宇宙论，宇宙学

5. neuromuscular [njuərəu'mʌskjulə, nuər-]
   a. [解剖] 神经肌肉的

6. doctorate['dɔktərit]
   n. 博士头衔；博士学位

背景链接 TIPS

A Brief History of Time

《时间简史》是一本包含了非常多文字的书，连霍金自己都说，这是一本很长很长的书，长到几乎要把整个时间都包含进去，然而，时间又是根本没有尽头的，它不可能被任何空间所包含，所以，时间的无始无终也就成了霍金教授在整本书结束的时候要表达的终极意图。《时间简史》这本书可以说是一部写给普通人看的物理学著作，用最简单的语言阐述最深奥的宇宙原理，同时，它也是一本当代青年不可不读的经典名著。

Unit 24 哲学家

The British philosophy is a part of the western philosophy that has a very long history. The history of western philosophy could trace back to early Greeks who literally modeled the western philosophy.

The history of western philosophy could be chronologically divided into many stages, including Ancient philosophy, Medieval philosophy, Renaissance philosophy, Early modern philosophy and Modern philosophy.

The philosophy in ancient times focused on the understanding of the universe with its fundamental causes and principles and nature as well as abstract things such as numbers and concepts. The most representative of ancient philosophers were Socrates, Plato and Aristotle. Socrates was the father of the western philosophy, Plato introduced the concept of "The Idea" and Aristotle built the classic logic. The medieval philosophy was dominated by Catholic religious and served its ends as it provided explanations for the reliability of religion and the problems discussed were the existence of God, the object of theology and metaphysics and etc. The Renaissance philosophy functioned as transition between the Medieval philosophy and modern philosophy and shift the emphasis from logic, metaphysics into morality and philology. Bruno, Copernicus, Newton, Bacon and Hobbes were all the most prominent representatives. The early modern philosophy in the west covered both 17th and 18th centuries. Philosophy at this time was more independent from traditional authorities and focused again on the foundations of knowledge. Locke, Kant and Hegel were all renowned philosophers in this period. The modern western philosophers' supported the scientific method of understanding such as Russell.

Two of the most important British philosophers will be discussed in this chapter to serve as the guidance to the British philosophy.

英国哲学史作为西方哲学史的一个组成部分,拥有很长的一段历史。西方哲学史的历史可以追溯到早期希腊人。希腊人可以说是西方哲学史的先驱。

西方哲学史根据时间顺序可以分为以下几个阶段:古代哲学史、中世纪哲学史、文艺复兴时期哲学、早期现代哲学和现代哲学。

古代哲学侧重于对世界及其起源的思考,对自然的理解和对抽象概念,如数字和概念的认识。苏格拉底、柏拉图和亚里士多德都是古代哲学的代表。苏格拉底被誉为西方哲学之父;柏拉图引入了"意念"这一概念;亚里士多德构建起了经典逻辑。中世纪哲学受到基督教的操控,成为宗教证实其可靠性的幌子。该阶段的哲学主要讨论上帝存在问题、神学的研究对象和玄学等。文艺复兴时期哲学是中世纪哲学和现代哲学的过渡阶段,这时期的哲学重点从逻辑和玄学转移到道德和语言学。布鲁诺、哥白尼、牛顿、培根和霍布斯都是这一时期的代表。西方早期现代哲学主要指17世纪和18世纪西方哲学。这一时期的哲学脱离了传统权威的束缚,再次将重点回归到知识的基础。洛克、康德和黑格尔都是这一时期的杰出代表。现在西方哲学强调科学的理解方法,罗素就是这样的一位现代哲学家。

本部分旨在通过两位英国哲学家来介绍西方哲学的发展及主要观点。

106 Francis Bacon

Francis Bacon was a famous British politician, philosopher, scientist and essayist. His contribution to the world most lied in his role as the founder of materialism in philosophy and science. Carl Marx once commented on Bacon was "The real progenitor of English materialism"

Bacon was born in January 1561 in London. His family held high position in court. His father Sir Nicholas Bacon was the Lord Keeper of the Privy Seal for Elizabeth I and his mother was the daughter of Edward VI's tutor. Born in such a well-connected family, Bacon was naturally expected to pursuit a political career.

Bacon received early education at home and entered Trinity College; Cambridge in 1573 when he was only twelve and was admitted to Gray's Inn to study law and later became a big lawyer. At the age of 23, Bacon was elected as a MP in House of Commons. However, his opposition of certain new taxes offended Elizabeth I and didn't come to a high position at her reign. When James I came to power, Bacon was greatly favored and ascended from one post to another until he became Lord Chancellor. In the course of rising, he made many enemies who later charged him of bribery, an accepted custom of the time and there's not necessarily evidence of his deeply corrupt behavior and was admitted by himself. Consequently, he was deprived of office, fined and banished from London in 1621 and died five years later.

Bacon's major works on philosophy included The Proficiency and Advancement of Learning (1605),

【小译】

弗兰西斯·培根是英国一个有名的政治家、哲学家、科学家和散文家。他对世界最大的贡献在于他是哲学和科学中唯物主义的创始人。培根被卡尔·马克思称为"英国唯物主义的创始人"。

培根1561年1月出生于伦敦。他的家人都是高官。父亲尼古拉斯·培根爵士是伊丽莎白一世在位时的玉玺大臣，负责保管玉玺。母亲是爱德华六世私人教师的女儿。出生在如此显赫家庭的培根自然也会走上政治舞台。

培根的早期教育在家中完成。1573年进入剑桥三一学院学习，当时他只有12岁，后来被格雷律师学院录取，毕业后成为一名律师。23岁的培根被选入下议院成为议员。然而，由于不满于伊丽莎白一世征收的一项新税收，培根在伊丽莎白一世统治时期一直没有得到过高的提拔。詹姆士一世掌管政权之后，培根倍受器重，官路亨通直到坐上大法官的职位。在晋升过程中，培根树敌无数，他的敌人最终以当时很普遍的受贿罪控告他，虽然并没有证据证明培根受贿很严重，但培根也没有否认。结果，培根在1621年不仅被罢了官，而且被处以罚款并驱逐出伦敦。五年后，培根去世了。

培根的主要哲学著作包括《论学术的进展》（1605）、《伟大

Magna Instauratio (1620) and The New Atlantis (1626) and etc. His works advocated the scientific revolution and established an inductive methodology for scientific inquiry. Bacon was also the inventor of a method involving collecting data and interpreting them judiciously as well as carrying out experiments to learn the secrets of nature by organized observation of its regularities. This idea had a great influence on the scientific research in the 17th Europe.

的复兴》（1620）和《新西特兰提斯岛》（1626）。培根在著作中提出科学革命，并建立了科学研究的推衍方法。培根还发明了一种收集数据、进行缜密的分析、并通过有组织的实验观察其规律来了解事物本质的方法。这种方法对17世纪欧洲的科学研究产生了巨大影响。

词汇 VOCABULARY

1. materialism [mə'tiəriəlizəm]
   n 唯物主义；唯物论；物质主义

2. progenitor [prə'dʒenitə]
   n 祖先；原著；起源

3. inn[in]
   n 旅馆；客栈 v 住旅馆

4. deprive [di'praiv]
   vt 使丧失，剥夺

5. proficiency [prə'fiʃənsi]
   n 精通，熟练

6. inductive [in'dʌktiv]
   a [电]感应的；[逻]归纳的；诱导的

背景链接 TIPS

1. Knowledge is Power. 知识就是力量。

2. Histories make men wise; poets witty; the mathematics subtile; natural philosophy deep; moral grave; logic and rhetoric able to contend. Abeunt studia in mores. 读史使人明智，读诗使人灵秀，数学使人周密，科学使人深刻，伦理学使人庄重，逻辑修辞使人善辩；凡有所学，皆成性格。

3. Crafty men contemn studies, simple men admire them, and wise men use them; for they teach not their own use; but that is a wisdom without them, and above them, won by observation. 有一技之长者鄙读书，无知者羡读书，唯明智之士用读书，然书并不以用处告人，用书之智不在书中，而在书外，全凭观察得之。

4. Virtue is like a rich stone, best plain set; and surely virtue is best in a body that is comely, though not of delicate features; and that hath rather dignity of presence than beauty of aspect. 德行犹如宝石，朴素最美；其于人也：则有德者但须形体悦目，不必面貌俊秀，与其貌美，不若气度恢宏。

5. In beauty, that of favor is more than of color; and that of decent and gracious motion more than that of favor. 美不在颜色艳丽而在面目端正，又不尽在面目端正而在举止优雅合度。

107 Bertrand Arthur William Russell

Bertrand Arthur William Russell was a British mathematician, essayist, logician and social activist and one of the greatest philosophers in the 20th century.

Bertrand Russell was born on 18 May 1872 in Wales to a prominent aristocratic family in Britain. His grandfather John Russell had once been prime minister. His parents died when he was only four years old and Russell was brought up by his grandmother whose liberal spirit had great influence on him. Instead of being sent to public schools, Russell received education at home and read extensively in his grandfather's library. From very early age, Russell showed interest in mathematics, history and literature.

In 1890, Russell was admitted by Trinity College, University of Cambridge studying Mathematics, philosophy and economics. Upon graduation he was made a 6-year researcher in Trinity College. In collaboration with British mathematician Alfred North Whitehead, Russell composed a monumental work Principia Mathematica.

Apart from his achievement in mathematics, Russell also made contribution on philosophy.

His ideas on philosophy found expression in almost every area of philosophy. His work The Problems of Philosophy (1912) covered many of his basic philosophical ideas and Our Knowledge of the External World as a Field for Scientific Method in Philosophy (1914) which contained most of his speeches delivered in Harvard University branded him the successor of John Locke, David

【小译】

伯兰特·阿瑟·威廉·罗素是一位英国数学家、散文家、逻辑学家，也是20世纪最伟大的哲学家之一。

伯兰特·罗素1872年5月18日出生于威尔士一个有名望的贵族家庭。他的爷爷约翰·罗素曾经做过英国首相。他的父母在他4岁的时候就去世了，罗素由奶奶抚养成人。罗素深受奶奶的自由精神的影响。罗素并没有上公学，而是在家中接受家庭教师的教育，并在爷爷的图书馆里广泛阅读。从很小起，罗素就显示出对数学、历史和文学的极大兴趣。

1890年，罗素进入剑桥三一学院学习数学、哲学和经济学。毕业后在三一学院做了为期六年的研究员。罗素和英国数学家怀特海合作写出了一部巨著《数学纲要》。

除了在数学方面的成就，罗素还对哲学做出了很大的贡献。

他的哲学涉及贯穿哲学的方方面面。他的很多哲学观点都在《哲学的问题》（1912）里都有涉及，《我们关于外部世界的知识》（1914）包含他在哈佛大学的多数演讲稿，罗素也因此被提升到约翰·洛克和大卫·休谟的继承者的位置。罗素还被冠以"分析哲学创始人之一"的头衔。

作为一个社会积极主义者，罗素不仅有影响力，也备受争议。

Hume. Russell was also regarded as one of the founders of analytic philosophy.

As a social activist, Russell was an influential but controversial figure. During the First World War, he once was put in prison and lost his job in Cambridge University for criticizing both sides of the war. After visiting Soviet Union, he expressed his disappointment with the socialism in Soviet directly in one of his book. When he was teaching in the College of City of New York, he was for another time fired for attacking religion in his book What I Believe.

Bertrand Russell was a man of great talent. His achievements rested in more areas than one. Apart from mathematics and philosophy, he was known in other subjects like education, history, political theory and religious studies as well. He was also awarded the Nobel Prize for Literature in 1950.

一战期间，他因批判交战双方被投入监狱，也被剑桥解雇。在一次访问苏联之后，他在自己的一本书中公开表示他对苏联的社会主义很失望。在纽约大学任职时，他因在《我的信仰》一书中抨击宗教再次被解雇。

伯兰特·罗素是一位极具天赋的人才。他在很多领域都取得了突出的成绩。除了数学和哲学，他在其他学科也享有盛名，包括教育、历史、政治学说和宗教研究，他还在1950年获得了诺贝尔文学奖。

词汇 VOCABULARY

1. aristocracy [ˌærisˈtɔkrəsi]
   n. 贵族；贵族统治；上层社会；[法]贵族政治

2. trinity [ˈtriniti]
   n. 三位一体；三人一组；三个一组的东西

3. monumental [ˌmɔnjuˈmentl]
   adj. 不朽的；纪念碑的；非常的

4. philosophical [ˌfiləˈsɔfikəl]
   adj. 哲学的（等于philosophic）；冷静的

5. controversial [ˌkɔntrəˈvəːʃəl]
   adj. 有争议的；有争论的

背景链接 TIPS

罗素悖论

一天，萨维尔村理发师挂出了一块招牌："村里所有不自己理发的男人都由我给他们理发，我也只给这些人理发。"于是有人问他："您的头发由谁理呢?"理发师顿时哑口无言。

因为，如果他给自己理发，那么他就属于自己给自己理发的那类人。

但是，招牌上说明他不给这类人理发，因此他不能自己理。

如果由另外一个人给他理发，他就是不给自己理发的人。但是，招牌上明明说他要给所有不自己理发的男人理发，因此，他应该自己理。由此可见，不管作怎样的推论，理发师所说的话总是自相矛盾的。

这是一个著名的悖论，称为"罗素悖论"。这是由英国哲学家罗素提出来的，他把关于集合论的一个著名悖论用故事通俗地表述出来。

Unit 25 经济学家

The classical economics is considered to be the first modern economic school. It came to historical stage in the middle of the 18th century, a time when capitalism was rising from feudalism and industrial revolution was taking place. At that time, the handcraft industry was gradually replaced by the modern machinery industry and mercantilism was no longer a possible option for the development of the capitalist class, thus a new theory for capitalism was in dire need.

In 1776, Adam Smith made a stir in the economics by publishing The Wealth of Nations. The Wealth of Nations is generally considered to be the beginning of classical economics, a school emphasized on economic freedom such as laissez-faire and free competition as a reaction against mercantilism. The theories of the classical economists were marked with their concerning with the dynamics of economic growth which gained favor from the capitalists. The British classical economics is considered beginning with Adam Smith and came to maturity at the hands of David Ricardo and John Stuart Mill. The term "classical economics" was originally proposed by Carl Marx to apply to David Ricardo's theories, or Ricardian economics but was later expended to refer to the school.

The Wealth of Nations contains many essential principles of classical economics. Adam put forward two ways to increase nation wealth, namely, to improve labor productivity by division of labor; to increase capital accumulation by reducing consumer spending and increasing production spending. Adam also developed the idea of economic liberalism on the basis of self-interest "economic man", with "invisible hand" as its core. David Ricardo, with his On the Principles of Political Economy and Taxation (1817), developed classical economics by his comparative advantage proposing each country should specialize in producing products that it has comparative advantage and then trade. Mill made contribution to relate the theories to the contemporary social situations.

古典经济学被认为是现代经济学的第一个流派。它于十八世纪中后期登上了历史舞台。在该时期，资本主义正在从封建主义中滋生出来，工业革命也刚刚展开，大机器工业正在逐渐取代了手工业，重商主义并不符合资产阶级发展的要求。因此，一个顺应资本主义发展的理论被迫切期待。

1776年，亚当·斯密发表了《国富论》，在经济学界引起了轩然大波。《国富论》被认为是开启了古典经济学的大门。古典经济学强调经济自由，比如自由放任政策和自由竞争。这与重商主义截然相反。以经济的动态发展为标志的古典经济学赢得了资产阶级的青睐。一般认为，古典经济学开始于亚当·斯密，并在大卫·李嘉图和约翰·斯图亚特·穆勒手中达到了成熟。"古典经济学"这个词起初是卡尔·马克思用来形容李嘉图主义经济学，但后来被用来指代整个流派。

《国富论》囊括了古典经济学的很多核心原理。亚当提出了两种增加国家富裕的方式，一是通过劳动分工提高劳动生产率，二是通过减少消费型支出，增加生产型支出来积累资本。亚当还在利己的"经济人"基础上提出了经济自由学说，学说的核心是"看不见的手"的概念。大卫·李嘉图撰写了《政治经济学及赋税原理》（1817），用以各国生产具有比较优势的产品然后进行贸易为主要思想的比较优势理论推动了古典经济学的发展。穆勒最大的贡献是把古典经济学的理论与当时社会现状结合了起来。

108 Adam Smith

The Theory of
Moral Sentiments

Adam Smith

Adam Smith is a worldly known economist whose greatest contribution was the publication of his book The Wealth of Nations. Smith is thus generally regarded as the founder of modern economics.

The exact birth date of Adam Smith is unknown. He was born in Kirkcaldy of County Fife in Scotland and was baptized on 5 June 1723. His father was a local customs officer and died a few months before his birth. Adam lived with his mother, the daughter of a landlord in Strathendry, all of his life and never got married. His mother died in May 1754 and Adam died on 17 July 1790 at the age of 67.

Adam studies in University of Glasgow in 1737 and after finishing classes like Latin, Greek, Math and Ethnics three years later, he entered Oxford University where he read extensively. After that, he delivered a series of lectures at Edinburgh and met David Hume. In 1751, Adam went back to University of Glasgow to teach logic and later moral philosophy till 1764. At this period, Adam published The Theory of Moral Sentiments and acquired favorable receptions among the academia. Adam spent 5 years writing his most important work The Wealth of Nations and finished the

【小译】

亚当·斯密是一名享誉全球的经济学家，他对经济学的最大贡献是他的著作《国富论》。亚当·斯密被普遍誉为"现代经济学之父"。

亚当·斯密的准确出生日期还是个谜。他出生于苏格兰法夫郡的寇克卡迪，于1723年受洗。父亲原为一名海关官吏，在他出生前几个月去世。母亲是法夫郡斯一位大地主的女儿。亚当终身未婚，与母亲相依为命直到母亲1754年5月去世。亚当本人去世于1790年7月17日，享年67岁。

亚当1737年进入格拉斯哥大学，用3年完成拉丁语、希腊语、数学和伦理学等课程。毕业后又求学于牛津大学，在此阅读了大量的书籍。之后，他在爱丁堡进行了一系列的讲座并结识了大卫·休谟。1751年，亚当回到格拉斯哥大学任教，先后教授逻辑和哲学课程直到1764年。此间出版了《道德情操论》，获得学术界极高评价。亚当用了5年的时间撰写他的巨著

first draft in 1773. In March 1776, the book was finally published after 3 years' of revision. The publication of The Wealth of Nations was an instant success and made Adam Smith incredibly well known. The first edition was emptied in only 6 months. Adam and his mother settled in Edinburgh from 1778 after being appointed a commissioner of customs in Scotland and stayed there until his death.

The Wealth of Nations or An Inquiry into the Nature and Causes of the Wealth of Nations is the most influential book in the economics field. In the book, Adam stated that social order is formed when all individuals in the society pursued their own interests and the freedom in buying and selling created social harmony because on one hand, people will voluntarily produce goods that others need and on the other hand, people are willing to spend money on things they want. Adam believed it were those business entities who seek their own interests that organize the society best. Government control will do harm to free competition.

《国富论》，1773年完成了第一稿。经过3年的修改，该书终于在1776年3月出版。《国富论》一经出版就引起了巨大反响，亚当也因此名声大作。第一版在短短6个月售罄。亚当于1778年接受了爱丁堡海关专员职位，与母亲定居苏格兰直到去世。

《国富论》，全称《国家康富的性质和原因的研究》，是经济学领域最重要的一本著作。书中，亚当指出，当个人追求自身利益时，社会秩序自然形成。自由买卖又创造了社会和谐。这是因为，一方面，人们会主动生产符合其他人需要的产品，另一方面，人们又愿意花钱买自己想要的东西。亚当认为社会在那些追求自己利益的商业实体的驱使下会达到最佳。政府干预会破坏自由竞争。

词汇 VOCABULARY

1. baptize [bæp'taiz]
   vt 给…施浸礼；命名；使经受考验（等于baptise）*vi* 施行洗礼（等于baptise）

2. customs ['kʌstəms]
   n 海关；关税；习惯（custom的复数）

3. academia[ˌækə'di:mjə]
   n 学术界；学术生涯

4. incredibly [in'kredəbli]
   ad 难以置信地；非常地

5. commissioner [kə'miʃənə]
   n 理事；委员；行政长官；总裁

背景链接 TIPS

亚当·斯密思想总结

1. 追求财富增加是每个人和社会的目标。

2. 利己是个人从事经济活动的动力，即人是经济人。

3. 市场机制这只"看不见的手"把个人利己的行为引导向有利于整个社会，即主张经济中的自由放任。

109 David Ricardo

David Ricardo was one of the representatives of British economists and a successful businessman. His huge contribution to the economics made him one of the most influential classical economists in Britain and even in the world. Carl Marx called Ricardo "the last great representative of British classic economist". His most representative work is On the Principles of Political Economy and Taxation (1817).

David Ricardo was born on 18 April 1772 in London in a Jewish immigrant family. His father was a successful stockbroker. Ricardo started to work in his father's Exchange at a young age of 14 after studying in a business school in Netherland for two years. By 16, he already became personage in this area. However, Ricardo's marriage with a non-Jewish girl Priscilla Wilkinson and renounced by his family at 21 years old and set up his own company which turned out to be successful and earned him a fortune of £40 million equivalence today.

Ricardo's interested in economist ignited as he read The Wealth of Nations by Adam Smith at the age of 27 and then started to publish articles analyzing current economic problems, the first one being the High Price of Bullion (1809) which sparked a hit debate. His another article Essay on the Influence of a Low Price of Corn on the Profits of Stock (1815) opposed the Corn Laws generated another debate that lasted until the annulment of law. From 1814 on, Ricardo retired from the business world and dedicated to the economics. His monumental work On the Principles of Political Economy and Taxation appeared in 1819. This book was an instant success and made Ricardo the most prominent economist as well as the consummator of British classical economics.

Among many of Ricardo's important theories, the theory of rent and the concept of comparative advantage

【小译】

大卫·李嘉图是英国经济学家的杰出代表，同时也是成功的商人。他在经济学方面的出色表现使他在英国乃至世界上产生了巨大的影响力。卡尔·马克思称他为英国古典政治经济学最后一位伟大的代表。他的代表作是《政治经济学及赋税原理》。

大卫·李嘉图于1772年4月18日出生于一个犹太移民家庭。他的父亲是一名成功的证券交易人。在荷兰读了两年商业学校后，李嘉图从14岁就开始在父亲的交易所工作。16岁的时候就已经是行业里的名人了。然而，21岁的时候他与一个非犹太女孩普丽拉·威尔金森结婚，由于信仰问题和家里关系僵化，也因此离开了父亲的公司，自己开办公司并取得了不小的成功，赚得了相当于现在4000万英镑的资产。

李嘉图对经济学产生兴趣要归功于亚当·斯密。27岁，李嘉图读了《国富论》之后产生了兴趣，于是开始发表文章分析现实经济问题。他的第一篇文章《黄金的价格》（1809）在发表之后引起了一场论战。而他的另一篇反对谷物法的文章，《论低价谷物对资本利润的影响》在发表之后又引发了一场论战，这场论战一直持续到该法令被废除。从1814年起李嘉图退出商界并开始致力于经济学，他的丰碑式的作品《政治经济学及赋税原理》在1819年发表后引起了强烈的社会反响。他本人也成为当时英国最著名的经济学家，并且成为了英国古典经济学的完成者。

are his most important contributions. Ricardo defined rent as "that portion of the produce of the earth which is paid to the landlord [by the tenant farmer] for the use of the original and indestructible powers of the soil." It is the surplus above the average profit. Rent arises from the advantages that one site has over another due to differing degrees of soil fertility and location. Ricardo developed his comparative advantage based on Adam Smith's absolute cost difference. For him, each country should specialize in producing products that it has comparative advantage and then trade. Such kind of international trade would benefit all countries.

In 1819, Ricardo made himself a member of the House of Commons and died four years later for ear infection at the age of 51.

在李嘉图众多的理论中，他的地租理论和比较优势理论贡献最突出。李嘉图把地租定义为"为使用土地原有和不可摧毁的生产力而付给地主的那一部分土地产品，是投入土地的劳动产品价值一部分。"他认为地租是平均利润以上的超额利润，产生于土地在肥沃程度和位置上的差别性。李嘉图基于亚当·斯密的绝对成本理论，形成了比较优势理论。他认为，每个国家都应该集中生产该国成本优势最大的商品，然后进行交易。这样的国际贸易才能使各国都受益。

1819年李嘉图取得了下议院中的一个席位。四年之后，他因患耳疾去世，享年51岁。

词汇 VOCABULARY

1. personage ['pɜ:sənidʒ]
   n. 要人；角色；名士

2. equivalence [i'kwivələns]
   n. 等值；相等

3. ignite [ig'nait]
   vt. 点燃；使燃烧；使激动 *vi.* 点火；燃烧

4. annulment [ə'nʌlmənt]
   n. 取消；废除

5. consummate ['kɔnsʌmeit]
   a. 至上的；完美的 *vt.* 完成，作成；使达到极

6. surplus['sɜ:pləs]
   n. 过剩；盈余；剩余；顺差 *a.* 剩余的；过剩的

背景链接 TIPS

斯密与李嘉图比较

相同点：

（1）古典政治经济学的杰出代表，反映新兴资产阶级的利益和要求；

（2）朴素的劳动价值论者，马克思劳动价值论的思想来源；

（3）经济自由主义者；

（4）由流动转向生产领域，着重于物质财富的增长和生产力的发展；

不同点：

（1）劳动价值论上，斯密处于摇摆之中，而李嘉图则更坚决，并接近于劳动创造价值一元论，马克思的许多思想来源于李嘉图；

（2）研究范围上，斯密着重本国财富的创造，李嘉图还对国际贸易及其作用有较多论述；（3）价值范畴上，斯密较模糊，李嘉图较具体，李嘉图对三种收入决定价值的批判；

（4）斯密试图构建古典政治经济学的体系，李嘉图是古典政治经济学的完成者。

110 John Maynard Keynes

【小译】

John Maynard Keynes was such an influential economist that all of his successors paid tribute to him and his theory on economics functions as a benchmark for all the later economists. Together with Freud's psychoanalysis and Einstein's relativity theory, Keynes's macroeconomics was regarded as one of the three intellectual revolutions in the 20th century.

John Keynes was born in Cambridge, England on 5 June 1883. His father John Neville Keynes was a famous Cambridge economist at the time and his mother Florence Ada Keynes was mayor of Cambridge. He entered Eton College at 14 years old studying mathematics and attended King's College, Cambridge with scholarship and received Master's Degree in Literature. Keynes prolonged his study there another year for Economics. Upon graduation, he became a civil servant in Britain in India Office and collect material for his first book Indian Currency and Finance describing India's monetary system procedures. Bored by the job, he went back to lecture in Cambridge and was called to work for the British Treasury. In 1919, Keynes presented at Versailles as the Treasury's principal representative for peace conference and later published another book The Economic Consequences of the Peace predicting the consequences of the treaty: Germany would be thrown into perpetually poverty and eventually become a threat to all Europe. The book became instant success and made Keynes a celebrity. However, Keynes' fame reached highest after the publication of his The General Theory of Employment, Interest and Money in 1936 amid the Great Depression.

The basic idea of The General Theory was that when economy is slowing down, the government should run deficits in order to secure the employment because

约翰·梅纳德·凯恩斯在经济学界享有非凡的影响力，这使得他受到他之后所有经济学家的尊敬。凯恩斯的宏观经济学理论和佛洛伊德的心理分析理论，以及爱因斯坦的相对论一同被誉为"二十世纪人类知识界的三大革命"。

凯恩斯1883年6月5日出生于英格兰剑桥。父亲约翰·内文斯·凯恩斯是剑桥一位出名的经济学家，他的母亲弗洛伦斯·艾达·凯恩斯是当时的剑桥市长。他14岁进入伊顿公学学习数学之后带奖学金进入剑桥大学国王学院，获得文学硕士学位。之后凯恩斯留校一年攻读经济学。毕业后成为公务员，进入印度事务部。任职期间为其第一部经济著作《印度通货与金融》作了大量研究准备工作。因不甘于单调的工作，凯恩斯返回剑桥任教并应征入英国财政部。1919年，凯恩斯以财政部首席代表的身份出席了凡尔赛会议。回国后出版了《和平的经济后果》一书对会议后果做出预测，即致使德国长期处于贫困状态并最终威胁欧洲的安全。这本书的出版引起了极大的反响，凯恩斯因此出名。然而，真正把凯恩斯的知名度提到最高的还是他在大萧条期间出版的《就业、利息和货币通论》一书。

《就业、利息和货币通论》的基本思想是在经济减退之时，政府应该通过赤字来保证就业率。这是因为随着经济的衰退，私营企业自然会缩

in such a circumstance, private enterprises would naturally reduce their investments. Less investment leads to fewer job opportunities which results in less consumption. With less consumption comes even less investment which generates another similar cycle. Therefore, the government ought to run deficits in order to prevent lower unemployment and social problems.'

The General Theory overturned the economists' way of thinking laid foundation for the later macroeconomics and Keynes is widely considered to be the father of modern macroeconomics and the most influential economist of the 20th century. Keynes was also entered the list of 100 most influential people of the 20th century.

减投资。投资减少导致就业岗位的减少，进而导致消费水平降低。消费水平降低又会引发私营企业投资的进一步减少。引起下一轮的恶性循环。因此，英国政府通过实行赤字来保证就业率的下降以及其引发的社会问题。

《就业、利息和货币通论》彻底改变了经济学家的思维方式，也为后来宏观经济学打下基础。凯恩斯被誉为现代宏观经济学之父，同时成为20世纪最重要的经济学家。在20世纪全球最具影响力的100位名人列表中榜上有名。

词汇 VOCABULARY

1. tribute ['tribjuːt] n. 贡物；颂词；礼物	2. psychoanalysis [ˌsaikəuə'næləsis] n. 心理分析；精神分析
3. relativity [ˌrelə'tiviti] n. 相对性；相对论；相关性	4. prolonged [prə'lɔŋd] a. 延长的；拖延的；持续很久的
5. currency ['kʌrənsi] n. 货币；通货	6. deficit ['defisit] n. 赤字；不足额
7. consumption [kən'sʌmpʃən] n. 消费；消耗；肺痨	

背景链接 TIPS

凯恩斯名言

1. It is Enterprise which builds and improves the world's possessions. Thrift may be the handmaid and nurse of Enterprise. But equally she may not. For the engine which drives Enterprise is not Thrift, but Profit.

进取精神建造和增加了世界上的财富。节俭可以是进取精神的仆人和护理人，同样地也可以不是。因为进取精神的动力不是节俭，而是利润。

2. Jovons saw the kettle boil and cried out with the delighted voice of a child; Marshal too had seen the kettle boil and sat down silently to build an engine.

杰文斯看见壶开了，高兴得像孩子似地叫了起来；马歇尔也看见壶开了，却悄悄地坐下来造了一部蒸气机。

Unit 26 电影明星

The U.K has cultivated many world-famous film artists. The British directors Alfred Hitchcock and David Lean are among the most critically acclaimed of all time. Hitchcock pioneered many techniques in the suspense and psychological thriller genres and he is widely regarded as one of cinema's most significant artists. Other important directors including Charlie Chaplin, Michael Powell, Carol Reed and Ridley Scott. Charlie Chaplin is one of the most famous film stars in the world before the end of World War I best known for his comic work during the silent film era which entertains audience of one generation after another.

British actors and actresses have always been significant in international cinema. Many British actors have achieved international fame and critical success, including Julie Andrews, Michael Caine, Richard Burton, Sean Connery, Laurence Olivier, Vivien Leigh and Anthony Hopkins. Global audience have been deeply impressed Vivien Leigh who bring to life Scarlett O'Hara in the time-honored love legend Gone with the Wind (1939). Anthony Hopkins is generally considered as one of the greatest living actors known for his portrayal of cannibalistic serial killer Hannibal Lecter in The Silence of the Lambs (1991).

There are also a great number of world-renowned British performers of younger generation currently active in international cinema like Catherine Zeta-Jones, Jude Law, Kate Winslet, Hugh Grant, Colin Firth, Keira Knightley, Ralph Fiennes, and Orlando Bloom and so on. These younger actors and actresses undertake the responsibility of demonstrating to contemporary audience the everlasting charm of British film as well as the unique temperament of British artists. Therefore, these performers of younger generation will be the main focus of our present part.

英国哺育了许多世界著名的电影艺术家。英国导演阿尔弗雷德·希区柯克与大卫·里恩是世界电影史上广受好评的导演。希区柯克开创了许多悬疑心理恐怖电影的拍摄技巧，他被广泛尊称为电影史上最重要的艺术家之一。其他重要导演还包括查理·卓别林、迈克尔·鲍威尔、卡罗尔·里恩与雷德利·斯科特。查理·卓别林是第一次世界大战结束之前世界上最重要的电影明星，他最著名的作品莫过于在默片时代的那些喜剧作品，让一代又一代的观众忍俊不禁。

英国电影演员也一直在国际影坛上享有盛誉，包括朱丽·安德鲁丝、迈克尔·凯恩、理查德·伯顿、查理、肖恩·康纳利、劳伦斯·奥利弗、费雯·丽与安东尼·霍普金斯。费雯·丽将久享盛名的爱情经典《乱世佳人》中的斯嘉丽·奥哈拉演活了，给世界观众留下了深刻的印象。安东尼·霍普金斯被公认为最伟大的在世演员，他在《沉默的羔羊》中扮演的食人魔最为观众所熟识。

英国还有大量的正活跃于国际影坛的英国影星，如凯瑟琳·泽塔琼斯、裘德·洛、凯特·温斯莱特、休·格兰特、科林·费斯、凯拉·奈特莉、拉尔夫·费因斯、奥兰多·布鲁姆等等。这些年轻演员肩负着将英国电影恒久魅力与英国艺人的独特气质展示给当代观众的重任，因此，这些年轻演员将成为我们这一部分的主要介绍对象。

111 Colin Firth

Colin Firth is an English film, television, and stage actor. He was appointed Commander of the Order of the British Empire (CBE) in the 2011 Birthday Honors for services to drama. In April 2011, Time magazine included Firth in its list of the world's 100 Most Influential People.

The son of two university lecturers, Firth was born in England's Hampshire county on 10 September 1960. While playing Hamlet in a school production, the actor was discovered, and he went on to make his London stage debut in Julian Mitchell's Another Country in 1984. Despite such an auspicious beginning to his career, Firth spent the rest of the decade and half of the next working in relative obscurity. It is not until he played Mr. Darcy in the 1995 BBC television adaptation of Jane Austen's Pride and Prejudice that Firth gained wide public attention, for which he was further rewarded with a BAFTA award.

In 1997, Firth had a supporting role in The English Patient (1996) and since then, has excellent performance in films such as Shakespeare in Love (1998), Bridget Jones's Diary (2001), Love Actually (2003), What a Girl Wants (2003), Girl with a Pearl Earring (2003), Bridget Jones: The Edge of Reason (2004) and the film adaptation of Mamma Mia! (2008).

In 2010, Firth got his first Academy Award

【小译】

科林·费斯是一位英国电影、电视、舞台演员。由于他对戏剧艺术卓越的贡献，他在2011年英国女王生日的时候被授予英国二等勋位爵士。2011年4月，他被《时代》杂志选为世界上最有影响力的100人之一。

1960年9月10日，费斯出生于英格兰的汉普郡，他父母都是大学老师。在学校参演《哈姆雷特》的时候，他的演戏天分崭露头角。1984年，他在伦敦首次登台，出演朱利安·米歇尔执导的舞台剧《另一个城市》。尽管费斯的电影生涯有着很好的开始，但是在接下来的10年里，他所参与演出的电影和电视剧并没有令他成为真正的巨星。1995年BBC改编的电视剧版《傲慢与偏见》中扮演达西先生，这个角色才让他获得广泛的公众关注，并为他赢得了英国电影学院奖。

1997年，费斯在《英国病人》（1996）中饰演男配角，并且之后在诸如《莎翁情史》（1998）、《BJ单身日记》（2001）、《真爱至上》（2003）、《父女大不同》（2003）、《戴珍珠耳环的少女》（2003）、《BJ单身日记：理性边缘》（2004）以及电影版的《妈妈咪呀》（2008）中均有精彩演出。

2010年，费斯凭借自己在《单身男人》中饰演的主角获得了他职业生涯的第一个奥斯卡提名，该片也为他赢得了英国电影学院奖，并在威尼斯电影节中获得最佳男演员奖。2011年，费斯凭借

nomination for his leading role in A Single Man, a performance that won him a BAFTA Award as well as the Best Actor Award in the Venice International Film Festival. In the following year, Firth received the Academy Award for his portrayal of King George VI in The King's Speech, a performance that also earned him the Golden Globe, BAFTA, and Screen Actors Guild Award for Best Actor. He received a star on the Hollywood Walk of Fame in 2011.

In 1989, he entered into a romantic relationship with Canadian-American actress Meg Tilly and she gave birth to a son. In 1994, after he and Tilly had separated, Firth became involved with British-American actress Jennifer Ehle, his co-star in Pride and Prejudice; the two eventually broke up. Since 1997, Firth is married to Italian film producer/director Livia Giuggioli who gave birth to two sons for him and they live in both London and Italy currently.

在《国王的演讲》饰演的乔治六世国王获得了奥斯卡奖、金球奖、英国电影学院奖、美国演员工会奖中的最佳男演员奖。2011年他在好莱坞星光大道上获得一颗星形奖章。

1989年，费斯与加裔美籍女演员梅格·提利开始恋爱，他们育有一子。1994年，与提利分手之后，费斯又与他在《傲慢与偏见》中的搭档——英裔美籍女演员詹妮佛·艾利擦出爱情火花，但最终劳燕分飞。1997年，费斯与意大利电影制片人兼导演利维亚·格吉沃利喜结连理，两人育有两子，两人现在居住于伦敦和意大利。

词汇 VOCABULARY

1. influential [ˌinfluˈenʃəl]
   adj. 有影响的；有势力的

2. auspicious [ɔːˈspiʃəs]
   adj. 吉兆的，吉利的；幸运的

3. obscurity [əbˈskjuəriti]
   n. 阴暗；身份低微；不分明；朦胧；晦涩

4. Venice[ˈvenis]
   n. 威尼斯（意大利港市）

背景链接 TIPS

Golden Globe

美国电影电视金球奖始自1943年，由好莱坞外国记者协会主办，是美国影视界最重要的奖项之一。金球奖共设有24个奖项，金球奖的被提名者名单通常是在圣诞节前公布，颁奖晚会则选在一月中旬举行。作为每年第一个颁发的影视奖项，金球奖被许多人看作是奥斯卡奖的风向标。

112 Orando Bloom

Orlando Bloom is one of the most popular British movie stars in Hollywood as well as in the world. In 2004, Bloom was on People (USA) magazine's "50 Most Beautiful" list and "Hottest Bachelors" list. Website Ananova.com chose him as the sexiest actor in Britain in the same year. On 12 October 2009, Bloom was named a UNICEF Goodwill Ambassador.

Orlando Bloom was born in Canterbury, Kent, England on 13 January 1977. He attended St. Edmunds School in Canterbury but struggled in many courses because of dyslexia. At the age of 16, he moved to London and attended the Guildhall School of Music and Drama to study acting. It was there, in 1998, that Orlando fell three stories from a rooftop terrace and broke his back. Although the doctor said that he would be permanently paralyzed, he quickly recovered and returned to the stage. As fate would have it, seated in the audience one night in 1999 was a director named Peter Jackson. After the show, he met with Orlando and asked him to audition for his new set of movies – the Lord of the Rings trilogy. Orlando succeeded in the audition and after graduating from Guildhall, Orlando began work on the Lord of the Rings trilogy, spending 18 months in New Zealand bringing to life "Legolas", a part which made him a household name.

Bloom next starred opposite Keira Knightley and Johnny Depp in Pirates of the Caribbean: The Curse of the Black Pearl, which was a blockbuster

【小译】

奥兰多·布鲁姆是在好莱坞以及世界上最受欢迎的英国电影明星之一。2004年，布鲁姆被美国《人物》杂志评选为"最美丽的50人"以及"最受欢迎的单身贵族"之一。Ananova.com网站同年评选他为英国最性感的男演员。2009年10月12日，联合国儿童基金会任命布鲁姆为亲善大使。

1977年1月13日，奥兰多·布鲁姆出生于英格兰肯特郡的坎特伯雷市。由于患有阅读障碍症，他在坎特伯雷的圣埃德蒙学校上学时有很多课程成绩不佳。16岁的时候，他搬到伦敦居住，并开始在伦敦市政厅音乐戏剧学校学习演戏。在那所学校就读期间，奥兰多在1998年从一个三层楼顶的露台上摔了下来，摔伤脊背。尽管医生说他有可能一辈子瘫痪，奥兰多还是很快地康复，并重返舞台。也许是命运的安排，1999年的一个晚上，一个名叫彼得·杰克逊的导演去观看了奥兰多的表演。演出结束后，他与奥兰多见面，并邀请他去参加他即将执导的电影——《指环王》三部曲的面试。奥兰多成功地通过了面试，从市政厅学校毕业后，奥兰多就在新西兰开始了为期18个月的《指环王》三部曲拍摄工作。他成功地将"莱格拉斯"这个角色活灵活现地呈现给观众，而这个角色也让他家喻户晓。

布鲁姆紧接着在《加勒比海盗之黑珍珠的诅咒》扮演主要角色，和约翰尼·德普以及凯拉·奈特利演对手戏，这部电影成为了2003年暑期的票房巨作。《海盗》大获成功之后，布鲁姆又接出演了2004年春季的票房巨

hit during the summer of 2003. After the success of Pirates, Bloom subsequently established himself as a lead in Hollywood films starring in the 2004 Spring blockbuster – Troy as well as Kingdom of Heaven and Elizabethtown (both 2005). Bloom then starred in sequels Pirates of the Caribbean: Dead Man's Chest (2006) and At World's End (2007). Bloom was the most searched male on Google News in 2006. As of May 2007, Bloom has appeared in four of the top 15 highest grossing films of all time. In 2007, Bloom stated that he would to like to leave films for a time and instead appear in stage roles. Bloom made his professional stage debut in West End's In Celebration in London from July to September in 2007.

In late 2007, Bloom began dating Australian model Miranda Kerr. Kerr released a statement on 22 July 2010 announcing that she and Bloom had married in "an intimate ceremony". Kerr gave birth to a son, Flynn Bloom, on 6 January 2011 in Los Angeles.

制《特洛伊》，随后在2005年接拍了《天国王朝》与《伊丽莎白镇》，这些影片最终确立了布鲁姆在好莱坞一线影星的身份。布鲁姆随后又出演了《加勒比海盗——决战魔盗王》（2006）与《加勒比海盗——世界的尽头》（2007）。布鲁姆在2006年是谷歌新闻搜索量最高的男性。截止2007年5月，在史上票房最高的15部电影中，布鲁姆参演了4部。2007年，布鲁姆称他将息影一段时间，专注于舞台剧表演。布鲁姆的舞台剧是由伦敦西区制作的《辉煌人生》，于2007年7月到9月在伦敦上映。

2007年后半年，布鲁姆开始与澳大利亚模特米兰达·克尔恋爱，克尔于2010年7月22日发表声明称她与布鲁姆已举行"私人仪式"结婚。他们的儿子弗林·布鲁姆于2011年1月6日在洛杉矶出生。

词汇 VOCABULARY

1. ambassador [æmˈbæsədə]
   n 大使；代表；使节

2. dyslexia [disˈleksiə]
   n 诵读困难；阅读障碍；难语症

3. rooftop [ruːftɔp]
   n 屋顶 a 屋顶上的

4. household [ˈhaushəuld]
   n 家庭；一家人 a 家庭的；日常的

5. terrace [ˈterəs]
   n 平台；梯田；阳台 a （女服）叠层式的
   v 使成梯田，使成阶地 成阶地，成梯田

6. intimate [ˈintimit]
   a 亲密的；私人的；精通的；有性关系的
   n 知己；至交 v 暗示；通知；宣布

7. blockbuster [ˈblɔkˈbʌstə]
   n 轰动；巨型炸弹；一鸣惊人者

背景链接 TIPS

Peter Jackson

彼得·杰克逊是上世纪80年代和90年代新西兰电影界颇有声望的导演，随着编导的《群尸玩过界》、《罪孽天使》等影片受到世人的肯定，他也成了为数不多的赢得主流媒体尊重的恐怖片导演之一。他的早期作品以恐怖成份居多，但也不乏幽默搞笑，擅长使用电脑特技呈现出奇特的视觉效果。美焕绝伦的《指环王》三部曲推出，令世人震叹，使这位魔幻导演的事业迈进了一个新的辉煌天地。

113 Hugh Grant

Hugh Grant, is an English actor and film producer. As one of Britain's best known faces, he has received a Golden Globe Award, a BAFTA, and an Honorary César. His movies have earned more than $2.4 billion from 25 theatrical releases worldwide. He is best known for his roles in Notting Hill (1999), opposite Julia Roberts, and in Music and Lyrics (2007), opposite Drew Barrymore, among his other works.

Grant was born on 9 September 1960, in Hammersmith, London. Young Grant was fond of literature and acting. He won a scholarship to Oxford, going up to New College in 1979 where he starred in his first film, Privileged, produced by the Oxford University Film Foundation in 1982. After Oxford, he turned down a scholarship to do postgraduate studies in Art History at the Courtauld Institute in London, and focused on his acting career.

Grant's breakthrough came with the leading role in Richard Curtis's sleeper hit Four Weddings and a Funeral (1994), a role which won him a Golden Globe Award, as well as a BAFTA Film Award for Best Actor. During the 1990s Grant established himself as a very original and resourceful actor. He played a string of characters projecting a positive mindset, showing how to stay optimistic when you are actually worried about a cascade of troubles. In 1995, Grant played a leading role as Emma Thompson's suitor in Ang Lee's Academy

【小译】

休·格兰特是一位英国演员、电影制片人。作为英国最知名的演员之一，他到目前获得一次金球奖、一次英国电影学院奖、一次凯撒荣誉奖。他共有25部影片在世界各地的影院上映，共获得24亿美元的票房收入。他最著名的电影有《诺丁山》（1999，与朱莉娅·罗伯茨对戏）与《K歌情人》（2007年，与德鲁·巴里摩尔对戏）等等。

格兰特于1960年9月9日出生于伦敦的哈默史密斯市。年轻的时候，格兰特喜欢文学与演戏。他获得了牛津大学的奖学金，于1979年开始就读于牛津大学新学院。他在牛津大学出演了自己的第一部电影——由牛津大学电影基金会于1982年制作的《牛津之爱》。从牛津大学毕业之后，格兰特放弃了伦敦考陶尔德学院提供的艺术历史研究生学位奖学金，专注于发展自己的演艺事业。

格兰格的演艺突破来自于理查德·科蒂斯的一部票房黑马电影《四个婚礼一个葬礼》（1994），他凭借在该片中的表演获得了金球奖以及英国电影学院奖最佳男主角。20世纪90年代期间，格兰特将自己定位为一个独创而善于随机应变的演员。他扮演了一系列积极向上的角色，这些角色展现了如何在有许多烦心事的时候依然能保持乐观。1995年，格兰特在李安根据简·奥斯汀的同名小说改编的奥斯卡获奖电影《理智与情感》中扮演了主

Award-winning adaptation of Jane Austen's Sense and Sensibility. In 1999, he paired with Julia Roberts in Notting Hill, which was a commercial as well as relative critical success. Indeed, the romantic comedy seemed to be simply the most natural fit for the actor, and he found more success in new millennium with returns to this genre in Bridget Jone's Diary (2001), Two Weeks Notice (2002), About a boy (2002), Love Actually (2003), Bridget Jones: The Edge of Reason (2004) and Music and Lyrics (2007).

Outside of his acting profession, Grant has been a good athlete, he played cricket and football in his younger years. He currently enjoys playing golf, frequently taking part in Pro-Am tournaments. He has been an avid art lover since his younger years, and has been collecting fine art, a passion he inherited from his father.

角——艾玛·汤普森的追求者。1999年, 他与茱莉娅·罗伯茨搭档出演了《诺丁山》, 这部电影不仅获得了商业成功, 也受到了评论界的好评。

事实上, 浪漫爱情喜剧似乎是最适合休·格兰特的电影类型。跨入21世纪, 格兰特在类似的电影如《BJ单身日记》(2001)、《双周情人》(2002)、《单亲插班生》(2002)、《真爱至上》(2003)、《BJ单身日记·理性边缘》(2004)和《K歌情人》(2007)中获得了更多的成功。

在演艺事业之外, 格兰特还是一个不错的运动员, 他在年轻的时候曾玩过板球和足球。现在他喜欢玩高尔夫球, 并经常参加职业选手和业余选手混合锦标赛。受其父的影响, 格兰特从少年时代起就对艺术有着狂热的热爱, 有收藏艺术作品的习惯。

词汇 VOCABULARY

1. resourceful [ri'sɔ:sful]
   a 资源丰富的; 足智多谋的; 机智的

2. mindset ['maindset]
   n 心态; 倾向; 习惯; 精神状态

3. cascade [kæs'keid]
   n 层叠; 小瀑布; 喷流 v 使瀑布似地落下
   vi 像瀑布般冲下或倾泻

4. suitor ['sju:tə]
   n 求婚者; 请愿者; [法] 起诉

5. millennium [mi'leniəm]
   n 千年期, 千禧年; 一千年, 千年纪念

6. genre [ʒɑːŋr]
   n 类型; 流派; 风俗画 a 风俗画的

7. tournament ['tuənəmənt]
   n 锦标赛, 联赛; 比赛

背景链接 TIPS

Courtauld Institute

考陶尔德艺术学院是在艺术历史和收藏领域中集教学与研究为一体的世界领先的学院之一。考陶尔德艺术画廊中收藏了世界上著名的艺术品, 是英国最重要的收藏画廊之一。学院招收本科生和研究生, 并设有春季班和暑期班。学院有雄厚的师资力量, 有很多著名的教授、高级讲师。

114 Kate Winslet

Kate Winslet is a renowned English actress who amassed a career full of exquisite performances of which most of her contemporaries could have only dreamed. She has received multiple awards and nominations. She is the youngest person to accrue six Academy Award nominations so far, and won the Academy Award for Best Actress for The Reader (2008). Winslet has been acclaimed for both dramatic and comedic work ranging from period to contemporary films, and from major Hollywood productions to less publicized indie films.

Born on 5 October 1975 and raised in Berkshire, as the daughter of stage actors and the granddaughter of a repertory theater manager, Winslet inherited the acting talent from her family. She commenced her formal dramatic training at the age of 11 and debuted cinematically in Heavenly Creatures (1994) when she was 19. She next appeared in international megahits such as Ang Lee's Sense and Sensibility (1995), as the willful, passionate Marianne; and James Cameron's Titanic (1997), as the object of Leonardo Di Caprio's affections, Rose. She received dual Oscar nominations for the two roles, but, surprisingly, failed to neither one.

Titanic had the potential for locking Kate into a steady string of Hollywood blockbusters, but Winslet wisely chose to retreat into the independent world, where she had a successful start in acclaimed films like Hideous Kinky (1999) and Quills (2000). But what she was best at was always playing free-spirited women tinged with sexuality – sometimes with a comic flare, as she did in Eternal Sunshine of the Spotless Mind (2004); other times, with deeply tragic undertones like

【小译】

凯特·温斯莱特是一位著名的英国女演员，她的演艺生涯充满了精湛的表演，让许多同龄艺人自愧不如。她获得了许多奖项以及提名。她是目前为止获得六次奥斯卡提名的最年轻的演员。她凭借《生死朗读》（2008）获得了最佳女演员。无论是戏剧还是喜剧电影，无论是古装剧还是现代剧，无论是好莱坞大片还是宣传较少的独立电影，温斯莱特的演出均受到赞赏。

温斯莱特出生于1975年10月5日，童年在伯克郡度过，她的父母都是舞台剧演员，而她的祖父是剧院经理。温斯莱特从她的家庭继承了演戏天分，她11岁开始接受正式的戏剧训练，19岁的时候推出了她的电影处女作《梦幻天堂》（1994）。她接下来参演了一些国际巨片，如在李安的《理智与情感》（1995）扮演了任性热情的玛丽安，在詹姆斯·卡梅隆的《泰坦尼克号》（1997）中扮演了莱昂纳多·迪卡普奥的挚爱——罗丝。她凭借这两个角色获得了两项奥斯卡提名，但是出人意料，并没有获奖。

《泰坦尼克号》本来很有可能将温斯莱特的戏路限制在好莱坞大片上，但是她作出了一个明智的选择——转战独立电影，她在诸如《北非情人》（1999）与《鹅毛笔》（2000）为她开创了一个良好的开端。而她最擅长的始终是扮演略带性感的自由女性 ——有时还略带喜剧色彩，像《美丽心灵的永恒阳光》（2004）；有时又有着深刻的悲剧色彩，像《身为人母》（2006）——这

in Little Children (2006) – making Winslet one of the most accomplished and highly regarded actresses of her generation. After finally winning an Oscar for her tragic role in The Reader (2008), Winslet charted a new course on the small screen with her critically acclaimed role in the cable miniseries, Mildred Pierce (HBO, 2011), which helped stake her claim as being one of the most accomplished and versatile actresses of her generation.

Winslet married assistant director Jim Threapleton in 1998; the pair had a daughter, Mia, in 2000 and divorced in 2001. On 9 June 2003, Winslet married Sam Mendes, the Oscar-winning director of American Beauty (1999). Their son, Joe, was born in 2003; the couple separated in 2010. She lives in New York City.

些影片让温斯莱特跻身同辈中成就最高、评价极高的女演员之列。2008年，温斯莱特终于凭借在《生死朗读》中的悲情角色获得了奥斯卡奖，之后，她开始向电视事业进军，她在由HBO制作的迷你电视剧集《欲海情魔》（2011）中的角色广受好评，从而进一步稳固了她在同辈人中成就颇高、多才多艺的女演员地位。

温斯莱特与副导演吉姆·薛瑞登于1998年结婚；他们的女儿米亚于2000年出生，而他们也于2001年离婚。2003年6月9日，温斯莱特与导演萨姆·门德斯结婚，萨姆曾凭借《美国丽人》（1999）获得奥斯卡奖。他们的儿子乔出生于2003年。这对夫妇于2010年离婚。温斯莱特目前居住于纽约市。

词汇 VOCABULARY

1. amass [ə'mæs]
   v. 积聚，积累

2. exquisite ['ekskwizit]
   a. 精致的；细腻的 n. 服饰过于讲究的男子

3. accrue [ə'kru:]
   vi. 自然增长或利益增加 vt. 积累；获得

4. indie ['indi]
   n. 独立经营的电影院等 a. 独立的

5. megahit ['megə]
   n. (电影、戏剧等艺术)佳作，特别成功的作品

6. hideous ['hidiəs]
   a. 可怕的；丑恶的

7. kinky ['kiŋki]
   a. 奇形怪状的，怪癖的；稍微变态的

8. flare [flɛə]
   vt. 使闪耀；使张开；用发光信号发出
   n. 闪光，闪耀；爆发 vi. 闪耀，闪光；燃烧

9. undertone ['ʌndə,təun]
   n. 低音；浅色；小声；潜在的含意

背景链接 TIPS

Leonardo Di Caprio

莱昂纳多·迪卡普里奥，演员。1974年11月11日出生在美国洛杉矶。曾获柏林电影节最佳男主角和奥斯卡最佳男主角提名。1997年担当《泰坦尼克号》男主角之后，莱昂纳多因在此片中的完美表演而成了"世纪末的票房炸弹"。2006年的《无间道风云》和《血钻》给他带来了一个金球奖最佳男主角的双提名，莱昂纳多也是历史上首个获得最佳男主角双提名的演员，同时在次年奥斯卡上凭借《血钻》获得最佳男主角提名。2010年他与名导克里斯托弗·诺兰合作了票房大片《盗梦空间》。

Unit 27 音乐人

Throughout its history, the United Kingdom has been a major exporter and source of musical innovation in the modern and contemporary eras. Britain has had an enormous impact on popular music disproportionate to its size, due to its linguistic and cultural links with many countries and its great capacity for invention, innovation and fusion, which has led to the development of many of the major trends in popular music.

In the early-20th century, influences from the United States became most dominant in popular music, which led to the explosion of the British Invasion, since the early 1960s, led by The Beatles. Large number of rock and pop performers from the United Kingdom became popular in the United States. The British Invasion helped to secure British performers a major place in development of pop and rock music. Since then, folk music, jazz, pop and rock music, have particularly flourished in Britain.

The United Kingdom has one of the world's largest music industries today, with many contemporary British musicians having had a great impact on modern music. In this part we will focus on the leading figures in British music industry during the 50 decades since the 1960s, including legendary rock band The Beatles, The Rolling Stones, Queen, Oasis, Coldplay as well as pioneer pop band like Spice Girls and Take That and the most prominent British solo artists in the recent decades – Robbie Williams.

在历史上，英国一直都在不断进行或接受着现当代音乐改革的洗礼。由于与其他国家的语言、文化联系，以及自身强大的发明、改革及吸收能力，英国对流行音乐做出了与其本身的规模并不成比例的巨大影响力，引领了流行音乐的许多发展趋势。

20世纪早期，美国对流行音乐有着主导性的影响，然后自从上世纪60年代起，由披头士乐队引领的"英国入侵"暴发了，大批的英国摇滚与流行音乐艺术家在美国大受欢迎。"英国入侵"使得英国音乐家在流行音乐与摇滚乐的发展史上占据主要地位。从那时起，民谣、爵士、摇滚和流行音乐在英国一直蓬勃发展。

英国现在有世界上最大的音乐产业，许多当代英国音乐家对现代音乐有很大影响力。在这一部分我们将主要介绍自20世纪60年代起的50年来在英国音乐产业中起领军作用的音乐人。其中包括传奇摇滚乐队披头士、滚石、皇后、绿洲、酷玩，和包括辣妹、接招组合在内的先锋流行组合以及近20年来最重要的英国独唱艺人——罗比·威廉姆斯。

115 The Beatles

The Beatles, the most famous English rock band of the 20th century, are widely recognized as the most commercially successful band in the history of pop music. The band was founded in 1960 in Liverpool and broke up in 1970. From 1962, the group consisted of John Lennon (rhythm guitar, vocals), Paul McCartney (bass guitar, vocals), George Harrison (lead guitar, vocals) and Ringo Starr (drums, vocals).

Initially the band made their reputation by playing clubs in Liverpool and Hamburg over a three-year period from 1960. Later they are mounded into a professional group with great music potential by their manager Brian Epstein and their producer George Martin. Their first single "Love Me Do" helped them to achieve mainstream success in the United Kingdom in late 1962. After they gained international popularity with the single of "I want to hold your hand" over the next year, they went on extensive tours until 1966. Then the band devoted their music career mainly to the recording studio until their break-up in 1970. Each was successful in independent musical professions. Lennon was murdered outside his home in New York City in 1980, and Harrison died of cancer in 2001. McCartney and Starr remain active.

Based on skiffle and rock & roll in the 1950s, the band developed their own music style by integrating different music genres like psychedelic rock, pop ballads and classical music in creative ways. Such unique music style had profound impact on the later development of the Western music. As their songwriting

【小译】

披头士组合（又称甲壳虫乐队）是英国20世纪最著名的乐队，也被公认为全球商业上最成功与最伟大的乐队。乐队于1960年成立于英国利物浦，1970年解散。从1962年起，乐队成员包括约翰·列侬（节奏吉他、主唱、作词作曲）、保罗·麦卡特尼（贝斯、主唱、作词作曲）、乔治·哈里森（主音吉他、主唱）及林格·斯塔（鼓手）。

自1960年组建以来，该乐队在开始的三年主要在利物浦和汉堡的一些俱乐部表演，逐渐在业内小有名气。之后他们遇到了一位伟大的经理人，布莱恩·斯普坦恩，将他们打造成一支专业的乐队，而他们的音乐潜能也被乐队制作人乔治·马丁发掘了出来。1962年下半年他们发行了首支单曲《我愿意》，这首单曲在英国大获好评。1963年，随着单曲《我想要握你的手》的发行，披头士风潮席卷全球，乐队同时也开始大规模世界巡演。直到1966年，乐队结束世界巡演，重返录音棚，开始专注唱片录制事业。1970年，乐队宣布解散。而乐队成员在各自的音乐生涯中也取得了不斐的成绩。1980年列侬在纽约家门外被谋杀，哈里森2001年死于癌症，麦卡特尼与斯塔依然健在。

在噪音爵士乐与上世纪50年代的摇滚的基础上，披头士乐队将诸如迷幻摇滚、流行民谣与古典音乐等不同的音乐风格创造性地结合起来，开创了他们自己的音乐风格。这种独特的

grew more and more sophisticated, their influence was extended to the realm of the social and cultural revolutions of the 1960s.

The Beatles is the best-selling band in the history of popular music and four decades after their break-up, their recordings are still in demand. According to the RIAA, the Beatles have sold more albums in the United States than any other artist selling over 170 million copies. It is believed that their global sales have exceeded 1 billion. They have had 15 number one albums on the UK charts and 19 on the U.S. Billboard, more than any other artists in the world. The group was inducted into the Rock and Roll Hall of Fame in 1988. They were collectively included in Time magazine's compilation of the 20th century's 100 most influential people.

音乐风格对后来欧美音乐的发展有着深远的影响。随着他们歌曲作品更多地关注社会问题，他们的影响力也延伸到了60年代的社会文化改革方面。

披头士是流行音乐史上销量最好的乐队，即使在他们解散四十多年之后，他们的唱片依然很受欢迎。据美国唱片工业协会统计，披头士是在美国国内销量最高的音乐人，总销量1.7亿，全球销量超过10亿。他们在英国有15张冠军专辑，在美国有19张，皆为史上最高。1988年披头士进入了摇滚名人堂。他们被《时代》杂志评选为20世纪最具影响力的100人之一。

词汇 VOCABULARY

1.	Liverpool ['livəpu:l] 利物浦（英格兰西北城市及港口）	2.	bass guitar [beisgi'ta:] 低音电吉他（贝斯）
3.	vocal ['vəukl] 声乐表演	4.	lead guitar [li:dgi'ta:] 主音吉他
5.	extensive [iks'tensiv] 广阔的，广泛的；大量的，大规模的	6.	skiffle ['skif(ə)l] 噪音爵士乐（英国的一种摇滚乐）
7.	integrate ['intigreit] 使结合成为整体 / （使）融入	8.	psychedelic [,saiki'delik] （指药物）引起幻觉的，致幻觉的
9.	sophisticated [sə'fistikeitid] 老练的，老于世故的；精密的，尖端的			

背景链接 TIPS

RIAA（Recording Industry Association of America）

美国唱片工业协会是一个代表美国唱片业的贸易团体，成员由多家制作与发行、约90%美国音乐唱片的私有公司实体如唱片公司与分销商组成。RIAA为高销量的专辑举行了一个奖励计划，该计划最初始于1958年，销售额达到100万美元的单曲与专辑唱片会获得"金奖"。该计划于1975年更改为以唱片的销量为基础，销量达50万的单曲与专辑唱片会获得金奖，1976年为销量达100万的唱片增加"白金奖"，1999年为1,000万销量的唱片增加"钻石奖"。

116 The Rolling Stones

The Rolling Stones are a legendary British rock band known for many popular hits, such as "Paint it Black", "Lady Jane", "Ruby Tuesday", and "(I Can't Get No) Satisfaction". Its original members were Mick Jagger (lead vocals, harmonica, guitar), Keith Richards (guitar, vocals), Brian Jones (guitar, harmonica), Bill Wyman (Bassist), and Charlie Watts (drummer).

The band was formed in London in April 1962 when Jagger, Richards, and Jones, who had been performing sporadically in a blues band, recruited Wyman and formed their own group. Watts joined the band in 1963. By 1966 a series of outstanding songs had made the band second in popularity only to the Beatles. During 1966-1969 they toured the world, and constantly updated their song-list with many great hits like "Lets Spend the night together" (1967), "Sympathy for the Devil" (1968) and "Honky tonk woman" (1969). The group reached the height of its popularity with albums such as Beggar's Banquet (1968) and Exile on Main Street (1972).

The Rolling Stones grew out of the fertile British blues scene when the meteoric rise of the Beatles expanded the boundaries of what was possible for a British rock group. The Rolling Stones were shrewd enough to capitalize on the dichotomy between the two bands – while The Beatles were likable mop-tops who played upbeat pop music nearly anyone could enjoy, The Stones played much grittier blues-based rock & roll that came to define hard rock and assumed a tough, rebellious image that made them scary to grown-ups but appealing to teens.

First popular in Europe, the Rolling Stones quickly became successful in North America

【小译】

滚石乐队是一支具有传奇色彩的英国摇滚乐队，他们创作了很多受欢迎的歌曲，像《染成黑色》、《简女士》、《红宝石星期四》和《（我无法）满足》。滚石的原始成员有米克·贾格尔（主唱、口琴手、吉他手）、基斯·理查德（吉他手、主唱）、布莱恩·琼斯（吉他手、口琴手）、比尔·怀曼（贝司手）、查利·沃茨（鼓手）。

滚石乐队于1962年4月在伦敦成立，当时贾格尔、理查德、琼斯在一个布鲁斯组合中偶尔表演，后来他们又招募了怀曼，成立了自己的组合。沃茨于1963年加入了乐队。到1966年乐队创作出了一系列仅次于披头士的杰出歌曲。1966年到1969年期间，他们在世界各地巡演，并不时地创作出诸如《让我们一起过夜》（1967）、《同情恶魔》（1968）和《钢琴女郎》（1969）。随着包括《乞丐的宴会》（1968）和《大街上的放逐》（1972）等在内专辑的发行，滚石乐队迎来了他们的巅峰时刻。

滚石乐队产生于英国布鲁斯盛行的大背景之下，当时披头士的火速窜红扩大了英国摇滚组合可能实现的音乐梦想。滚石乐队很聪明地利用了两个乐队之间的不同——披头士乐队梳着蘑菇头，招人喜欢，他们创作流行音乐乐观向上，朗朗上口；而滚石乐队的布鲁斯摇滚音乐节奏更加有力，后被定义为硬摇滚，乐队本身也展现了一种坚忍反叛的形象，这种形象让成年人害怕，却让青少年着迷。

during the British Invasion of the mid 1960s. Their worldwide sales are estimated at more than 200 million albums. Sticky Fingers (1971) began a string of eight consecutive studio albums reaching number one in the United States. In 1989 the Rolling Stones were inducted into the Rock and Roll Hall of Fame, and in 2004 they ranked number 4 in Rolling Stone magazine's "100 Greatest Artists of All Time". In 2008, Billboard magazine ranked the Rolling Stones at number ten on "The Billboard Hot 100 Top All-Time Artists", and as the second most successful group in the "Billboard Hot 100 Chart".

在20世纪60年代"布列颠入侵"时期，滚石乐队开始先在欧洲走红，后来很快在北美获得成功。据统计，他们的全球销量超过了2亿张。从《偷盗习惯》（1971）开始，连续有8张录音棚专辑在美国获得销量第一。1989年，滚石乐队进入摇滚名人堂，2004年，他们在《滚石》杂志评选的"史上最伟大的100位艺术家"排名中位列第4。2008年，《公告牌》杂志将滚石乐队排在"公告牌史上最热门的100位艺术家"的第4位，并且是"公告牌最热门100首单曲"中第二成功的组合。

词汇 VOCABULARY

1. sporadical [spəˈrædikəl] 🔲 零星的	2. blues [bluːz] 🔲 忧郁布鲁斯歌曲
3. honky [ˈhɔŋki] 🔲 白鬼子（黑人对白人的贬称）	4. tonk [tɔŋk] 🔲 轻易获胜；强打
5. exile [ˈeksail, ˈegz-] 🔲 流放，充军；流犯 🔲 放逐，流放	6. shrewd [ʃruːd] 🔲 精明的；机灵的 🔲 精明（的人）
7. dichotomy [daiˈkɔtəmi] 🔲 二分法；两分；分裂；双歧分枝	8. upbeat [ˈʌpbiːt] 🔲 兴旺；上升；弱拍 🔲 乐观的；上升的
9. gritty [ˈgriti] 🔲 坚韧不拔的；有砂砾的；多沙的；像砂的	

背景链接 TIPS

British Invasion

"布列颠入侵"出现在上世纪60年代中期，当披头士在美国取得成功性突破时，一拨英国摇滚乐队横渡到美国市场。尽管不是所有的乐队演奏都有所雷同，但在从滚石乐队的硬摇滚到深受美国摇滚、布鲁斯和R＆B影响的Gerry和the Pacemakers、Hermans Herimts的范围内变

化。"布列颠入侵"乐队的风格是用吉他演奏迷人的韵律，配以布鲁斯、摇滚和流行乐。在1964年到1966年间，英国乐队垄断了美国和英国联合王国的乐队。在那时候，又涌现出第二拨"布列颠入侵"的乐队——比如the Who和"蟆神"乐队——它们又吸收了美国摇滚和"英国入侵"流行的优点。在60年代后期，许多乐队成为摇滚中的偶像，但更多的却逐渐消失。

117 Spice Girls

The Spice Girls were a British pop girl group whose sexy charisma, modest musical talent, and "girl power" philosophy made them the major British pop music phenomenon of the mid 1990s. The group consisted of Victoria Beckham (Posh Spice), Melanie Brown (Scary Spice), Emma Bunton (Baby Spice), Melanie Chisholm (Sporty Spice) and Geri Halliwell (Ginger Spice).

The Spice Girls came into being in early 1994, when the various members responded to an advertisement in the Stage magazine which was looking for "streetwise, ambitious, and dedicated" young women to form a female version of the popular British boy pop band Take That. They were signed to Virgin Records and released their debut single, "Wannabe" in 1996, which hit number-one in more than 30 countries and helped establish the group as a "global phenomenon". Credited for being the pioneers that paved the way for the commercial breakthrough of teen pop in the late 1990s, their debut album, Spice, sold more than 23 million copies worldwide, becoming the best-selling album by a female group in music history.

The Spice Girls hit the peak of their fame in 1997 with the release of a second album, Spiceworld, plus a jovial feature film of the same name. Halliwell left the Spice Girls in 1998 to go solo. The group continued on as a quartet, with the individual members also pursuing

【小译】

辣妹是一个英国女子流行音乐组合，她们拥有迷人的魅力，朴实无华的音乐天赋，提倡"女孩力量"的理念，她们是英国20世纪90年代中期流行音乐的主力军。辣妹组合由维多利亚·贝克汉姆（时髦辣妹）、梅兰尼·布朗（疯狂辣妹）、艾玛·巴顿（宝贝辣妹）、梅兰尼·奇泽姆（运动辣妹）和洁芮·哈利维尔（姜汁辣妹）组成。

辣妹组合于1994年早期成立，当时《舞台》杂志发布了一个招募广告，想要寻找一些"了解城市文化、有雄心壮志而又有专注精神的"年轻女孩来成立女子版的"接招乐团"（英国男子流行组合），而辣妹的各个成员因为这个广告而聚集到了一起。她们与维京唱片公司签约之后在1996年发行了首支单曲《我想要》，这支单曲在30多个国家登上了排行榜冠军，让辣妹组合在国际上红得一发不可收拾。辣妹组合被看作在20世纪90年代后期使青春流行音乐在商业上取得突破的探索先锋。她们的首张专辑《香料》在全球销量超过2亿3千万张，成为了音乐史上由女子组合发行的最畅销专辑。

1997年，辣妹组合发行了他们的第二张专辑《辣妹世界》，并且还拍摄了一部明快的同名电影，使得辣妹的名气达到了巅峰状态。哈利维尔于1998年单飞离开辣妹组合。剩下的四个人依然保持组合形式，但是同时也各自开拓个人事业。1999年，维多利亚因与足球巨星大卫·贝克汉姆结

solo careers; Victoria gained extra fame in 1999 when she married soccer star David Beckham. After releasing the album Forever in 2000, the Spice Girls disbanded in 2001. But all five original Spice Girls reunited late in 2007 for an eight-country world concert tour and released their Greatest Hits album.

The Spice Girls go down in history as one of the most commercially successful acts in contemporary pop music history. They have sold over 75 million records worldwide, making them the best-selling female group of all time. The Union Jack dress that Halliwell wore has been identified with iconic status, becoming one of the most prominent symbols of 1990s pop culture. The iconic symbolism of the Spice Girls in the 1990s is also attributed to their merchandising and willingness to be a part of a media-driven world. Because of their regular appearances in ads and the media, the band solidified themselves as a phenomenon – an icon of the decade and for British music.

婚而增加了额外的名气。辣妹组合于2000年发行了专辑《永远》之后，于2001年解散。2007年，辣妹组合的五个成员再次团聚，开始了八国巡演，并于同年12月发行了《精选辑》。

辣妹组合是现代流行音乐史上最成功的商业音乐人之一。她们是音乐史上最畅销的女子组合，全球专辑销量达7亿5百万张。哈利维尔身穿的英国国旗裙成为了一个20世纪90年代流行音乐文化最重要的标志之一。辣妹组合在90年代的象征意义还在于她们的商业性，和对媒体追逐的配合。由于在广告和媒体上频繁露面，更加坚固了辣妹音乐现象的地位——她们是90年代和英国音乐的标志。

词汇 VOCABULARY

1. charisma [kəˈrizmə]
   n 魅力；神授的能力；非凡的领导力

2. streetwise [ˈstriːtwaiz]
   a 熟悉民间疾苦的；在现代化城市的生存能力

3. jovial [ˈdʒəuvjəl, -viəl]
   a 天性快活的；主神朱庇特的

4. quartet [kwɔːˈtet]
   n 四重奏；四重唱；四件一套

5. disband [disˈbænd]
   vt 解散 vi 解散；遣散

6. merchandise [ˈmɜːtʃəndaiz]
   n 商品；货物 vt 买卖；推销 vi 经商

7. solidify [səˈlidifai]
   v 团结；凝固

背景链接 TIPS

Union Jack

英国国旗，俗称"米字旗"，正式称呼是"the Union Flag"，也常常称为"the Union Jack"。Jack是海军用语，指悬挂在舰首的旗帜。Union Flag是意为"联合旗帜"。综合了原英格兰（白地红色正十字旗）、苏格兰（蓝地白色交叉十字旗）和爱尔兰（白地红色交叉十字旗）的旗帜标志。国旗形状：长方形，长宽之比为2：1。

118 Coldplay

Coldplay are an English alternative rock band formed in 1996 comprising vocalist Chris Martin, guitarist Johnny Bucklan, bassist Guy Berryman and drummer Will Champion. They are one of the greatest bands of the new millennium, exploring a mix of introspective Brit-pop and anthemic rock that landed the British quartet a near-permanent residence on record charts worldwide.

Coldplay was formed in 1996 at the University College of London (UCL) with the four members all being students from the university. The band achieved worldwide fame with the release of the single "Yellow" in 2000, followed by their debut album released in the same year, Parachutes, which was nominated for the Mercury Prize. They released their second album, A Rush of Blood to the Head in 2002, which was hailed by critics as one of the best records of 2002. Their next release, X&Y, the best-selling album worldwide in 2005, was initially met with mixed reviews upon its release. However, the band's fourth studio album, Viva la Vida or Death and All His Friends (2008), was released again to largely favorable reviews, earning several Grammy nominations and wins at the 51st Grammy Awards.

The band has won a number of music awards throughout their career, including six Brit Awards—winning Best British Group three times, four MTV Video Music Awards, and seven Grammy Awards from

【小译】

酷玩乐队是一支英国另类摇滚组合，他们成立于1996年，由主唱克里斯·马汀、吉他手强尼·巴克兰、贝司手盖伊·贝瑞曼和鼓手威尔·查平组成。他们是千禧年以来最伟大的乐队之一，他们开创了一种内省式英国流行音乐与圣歌式摇滚相混合的曲风，这种曲风也让他们长期雄踞全球专辑排行榜上。

酷玩乐队于1996年在伦敦大学学院成立，四位成员均是该大学学生。乐队在2000年发行了单曲《黄色》之后扬名国际乐坛，同年他们发行了处女专辑《降落伞》，获得了水星音乐奖提名。接着他们于2002年发行了第二张专辑《血气上涌》，被评论家称赞为2002年最好的专辑之一。第三张专辑《X&Y》虽然刚发行时受到了褒贬不一的评价，但成为了2005年全世界最畅销的专辑。然而乐队的第四张录音棚专辑《生命万岁》（又名《死神和他的兄弟们》，2008）获得了大量好评，为他们在51届格莱美颁奖典礼上赢得了几项音乐奖以及提名。

酷玩乐队的音乐生涯中获得了许多音乐奖项，包括六项全英音乐奖——其中三次获得最佳英国组合，四项MTV音乐电视大奖，七项格莱美奖（20项提名）。作为世界上最畅销的音乐艺人，酷玩乐队的全球专辑销量超过了5亿张。

twenty nominations. As one of the world's best-selling music artists, Coldplay have sold over 50 million records worldwide.

Coldplay's soulful, haunting, intelligent songs have set them apart from bubblegum pop stars, aggressive rap artists. Much has been made in Britain's music press of lead singer Chris Martin's clean-living ways and general distaste for alcohol—a far cry from the lifestyle of a stereotypical rock star. The band has shied away from corporate endorsements, choosing to promote causes that address world poverty or environmental issues. In spite of—or perhaps because of—the ways in which they differ from their peers, Coldplay has become a sensation, selling millions of records, earning numerous major awards, and garnering praise from music critics all over the world. Chris Martin married Oscar-winning actress Gwyneth Paltrow in December of 2003.

酷玩乐队的歌曲充满精神、睿智，常常萦绕于听者耳畔，与摇滚舞曲流行乐和充满攻击性的饶舌音乐形成鲜明的对比。英国的音乐媒体也常常报道主唱克里斯·马汀不酗酒的严谨的生活方式——与摇滚歌星固有的形象形成了相差甚远。酷玩乐队也常常回避企业邀请，以促进解决世界贫困与环境问题为音乐主题。他们与同辈音乐人有着很大不同，也许正是这些不同，使得他们红遍乐坛，专辑销量数以百万计，获得大大小小的各种奖项，得到了世界各地音乐评论家的赞赏。克里斯·马汀于2003年12月与奥斯卡影后格温妮丝·帕特洛结婚。

词汇 VOCABULARY

1. introspective [ˌintrəu'spektiv]
   adj 内省的；反省的

2. hail [heil]
   vt 致敬；招呼，向…欢呼 vi 招呼；下雹

3. bubblegum ['bʌbl,gʌm]
   n 泡泡糖；摇滚舞曲 adj 七至十三岁年龄儿童的

4. distaste ['dis'teist]
   n 厌恶；讨厌 vt 厌恶；不喜欢 vi 不喜欢

5. stereotypical ['stiəriəu'tipikəl]
   adj 老一套的；陈规的

6. corporate ['kɔ:pərit]
   adj 法人的；共同的，全体的；社团的

7. endorsement [in'dɔ:smənt]
   n 认可，支持；背书；签注（文件）

8. sensation [sen'seiʃən]
   n 感觉；轰动；感动

背景链接 TIPS

Grammy Awards

格莱美音乐奖系美国唱片行业里最具影响力的音乐大奖。因其奖杯形状酷似一架老式的留声机而得名并流传至今。首届格莱美奖于1958年诞生，奖项宗旨是献给那些在录音艺术和技术方面做出突出贡献的音乐人。格莱美奖与其他大奖不同之处在于所有奖项的评比都不受销售和排行榜的影响，完全取决于参赛者在技术和艺术方面的贡献，故饮誉音乐界之"奥斯卡奖"。格莱美奖已涵盖105个奖项，音乐类型达到30种，每年从10月1日起开始启动评选，吸引了全球10多亿乐迷的关注，使之成为全球最具影响力的音乐大奖之一。

Unit 28 艺术家

According to many scholars, there was no English school of painting before the 18th century. Although medieval English painting, mostly religious, had a strong national tradition and was at times influential on the rest of Europe, it was in decline from the 15th century. In the 16th and 17th centuries, the artists of the Tudor court in the Renaissance and their successors until the early 18th century were mostly imported talents, often from Flanders in France.

During the 18th century British arts began once again to take the leading place it had had in European art during the Middle Ages, being especially strong in portraiture and landscape art. Increasing British prosperity led to a greatly increased production of both fine art and the decorative arts, the latter often being exported. The late 18th century and the early 19th century characterized by the Romantic movement in British art produced the very diverse talents of William Blake, J. M. W. Turner, John Constable and Samuel Palmer. The Victorian period saw a great diversity of art, and a far larger quantity created than before. Much Victorian art is now out of critical favour, with interest concentrated on the Pre-Raphaelites and the innovative movements at the end of the century.

Stepping into the 20th century, the British arts continues to exhibit diversified fashion, cultivating world famous artists like print maker Paul Nash and Eric Ravilious who favored a return to pastoral subjects as their subjects as the reaction to the horrors of the First World War, and Henry Moore emerged after World War II as Britain's leading sculptor as well as outstanding woman wood engraver Joan Hassall.

In this unit, we will mainly put our focus on the artists of the 19th and 20th century, choosing some representative artists of the two centuries to offer a glimpse of the British arts of modern times.

许多学者认为，英国画派直到18世纪才形成。中世纪的英国绘画以宗教绘画占大多数，虽然有很强的民族历史传承，并不时地对欧洲其他地区造成影响，但是从15世纪就开始衰败。从16和17世纪到18世纪早期，文艺复兴时期的都铎王朝的艺术家们，以及他们的后来人都来自外国，通常来自法国的佛兰德斯。

在18世纪期间，英国艺术家开始重拾中世纪时对欧洲艺术的领导地位，尤其是在肖像画与风景画方面取得了很高的造诣。英国艺术的繁荣也大大增加了美术艺术品与装饰艺术品的制作，后者还经常出口。而18世纪晚期到19世纪早期的浪漫主义时期还出现了许多多才多艺的艺术家，如威廉·布莱克、约瑟夫·玛罗德·威廉·透纳、约翰·康斯坦堡与塞缪尔·帕尔默等。维多利亚时期，英国的艺术风格也非常多样化，艺术品数量也大大超过以前。许多维多利亚时期的艺术品现在多受批评审美艺术家的青睐。维多利亚时期的拉斐尔前派画派与19世纪末的改革运动多受后世关注。

进入20世纪，英国艺术继续呈现多样化的风格，培养出了一些世界著名的艺术家，像在一战期间出现的保罗·纳什与艾里克·拉斐留斯，出于对一战造成的恐惧情绪，他们的作品重新回归田园主题。此外还有二战之后出现的亨利·摩尔，是英国最主要的雕塑家之一，以及杰出的女木刻家琼·海塞尔。

在这一单元，我们主要将重点放在19世纪与20世纪的艺术家，选择其中一些有代表性的艺术家进行介绍，让大家对世界现代艺术有一个初步的了解。

119 Eric Ravilious

Eric Ravilious (1903~1942) was an English painter, wood-engraver and designer. He was a leading exponent of wood engraving in the 1920's.

Born in Acton in southeast England, Ravilious was educated at Eastbourne School of Art and then at the Royal College of Art (1922~1925), where he was taught by Paul Nash and became close friends with Edward Bawden. He began teaching part-time at Eastbourne School of Art in 1925 and later that year was elected to the Society of Wood Engravers, having been proposed by Paul Nash. In 1930 he married the artist Tirzah Garwood.

Ravilious was appointed Official War Artist in 1940. His watercolors during this period document the setting up of coastal defenses at, amongst other places, Newhaven in Sussex; he also worked on a series of lithographs which record life as a submariner patrolling the Channel waters. In 1942, aged 39, Ravilious was posted to Iceland, and in September he participated in an air/sea rescue on board a Hudson plane in search of an aircraft that had disappeared on the previous day. The Hudson itself, however, was lost and Ravilious, along with four others, never returned from this

【小译】

艾里克·拉斐留斯（1903～1942）是英国著名的油画家、木雕家和设计师。他在上世纪二十年代极力倡导木雕艺术。

拉斐留斯出生于英国东南部，就学于伊斯特本艺术学校，后在皇家艺术学校（1922～1925）受教于保罗那什，并于爱德华·保登成为挚友。1925年拉斐留斯开始在伊斯特本艺术学校兼职教书，随后保罗·那什推荐他选入了木雕社。1930年，他与艺术家蒂尔扎·哥伍德结为夫妻。

1940年，拉斐留斯被任命为官方战时艺术家。在这个时期，他的水彩画记录了纽黑文州苏塞克斯以及其他地区海岸防御线的建立。他还创作了一系列石版画，描述了巡逻在英吉利海峡水下一名潜艇兵的生活。1942年，39岁的拉斐留斯被派往冰岛，同年9月份，他登上哈登森号飞机，参加了一艘失事飞机的营救行动。然而，哈登森号自己也杳杳无踪，拉斐留斯

mission.

Ravilious began his working life as a muralist, first coming to notice as an artist in 1924. He went on to become one of the best-known artists of the 1930s. His watercolors, painted with a fine stippling technique within compositions that give light or dark features a telling role, are thought by some to have an almost uncanny loveliness. He was the leading light of wood-engraving in England at that time and undertook ceramic designs for Wedgwood who, in 1937, brought out the George VI commemorative Coronation Mug, and in the same year the Alphabet Mug and Nursery Ware designs. He also designed graphics for London Transport.

Ravilious's sensitive and accomplished watercolors, drawings, book illustrations and ceramic designs for Wedgwood have continued to influence a generation of British design. The Imperial War Museum in London organized a major retrospective in 2004.

和其他四人也在任务中失踪。

拉斐留斯最开始以壁画家为职业，1924年他才以艺术家的身份引起注意。到30年代，他成为最知名的艺术家之一。他在创作水彩画时应用了非常精致的点画技法，赋予了作品光与暗的效果，使作品更为生动，很多人认为其作品拥有一种魔魅的吸引力。拉斐留斯是当时木雕界的领军人物，他为伍吉伍德公司设计了一系列陶器，包括1937年发行的乔治六世加冕纪念杯，字母表杯以及苗圃制品。另外，伦敦运输局的图标也是他设计的。

拉斐留斯的作品细腻成熟，他创作的水彩画、手绘画、书本插图、以及为伍吉伍德公司设计的陶瓷作品，影响了一代英国艺术家的设计思路。2004年伦敦的帝国战争博物馆还为他举办了一场专题回顾展览。

词汇 VOCABULARY

1. engraver [in'greivə(r)]
   n 雕刻师；雕工

2. exponent [eks'pəunənt]
   n 说明者，说明物；典型；指数 a 说明的

3. watercolor ['wɔ:tə'kʌlə]
   n 水彩画，水彩颜料 a 水彩的，水彩画的

4. lithograph ['liθə,grɑ:f]
   n 平版印刷 v 用平版印刷术印刷

5. muralist ['mjuərəlist]
   n 壁画家

6. uncanny [ʌn'kæni]
   a 可怕的；离奇的；神秘的

7. ceramic [si'ræmik]
   a 陶器的；陶瓷的；制陶艺术的 n 陶瓷

8. retrospective [,retrəu'spektiv]
   a 回顾的；怀旧的；可追溯的 n 回顾展

背景链接 TIPS

The Imperial War Museum

英国皇家战争博物馆是一所位于英国大曼彻斯特地区特拉福德的战争纪念博物馆，是解构主义建筑的代表作品之一。2002年7月5日开馆，设计师是世界知名的建筑师丹尼尔·利伯斯金，整个建造花费约为2800万英镑。负责公司为麦卡宾爵士建筑公司和英国营建和环境顾问公司奥雅纳。曾获得2003年英国营造业建筑奖。

120 Joan Hassall

Joan Hassall, (1906~1988) was an English wood engraver, book illustrator and typographer. Her subject matter ranged from natural history to illustrations for English literary classics. In 1964 she was elected the first woman master member of the Art Workers Guild and in 1987 was awarded an OBE (Order of the British Empire).

Born in Notting Hill, London, Joan Hassall was the daughter of illustrator John Hassall. She attended The Royal Academy Schools from 1928 to 1933. In 1931 she began evening classes in engraving at the London Central School of Photo-engraving and Lithography in Fleet Street, where her teacher was R. John Beedham who taught her the skills and techniques which she used for the rest of her life.

By the late 1930s the quality of Joan's wood engraving was widely recognized. Her first commissioned engraving was for her brother Christopher's poetry book for which she painted his portrait in 1936. She subsequently illustrated works by Jane Austen, Trollope, Mrs. Gaskell and Mary Russell Mitford and The Saltire Chapbooks, published by the Saltire Society in the 1940s. During World War II, Kingsley Cook, a tutor of Book Illustration and Drawing at Edinburgh College of Art, suggested that Joan Hassall act as his replacement, a post that she accepted. In 1950 she designed an edition of Robert Burns poems and created a series of illustration that are among her most delightful small prints, especially the one of a tiny mouse rolling in the glass.

Hassall's talents as a wood engraver did not mean that she did not possess a delicate hand, as the exquisite watercolor invitation for the Queen's coronation in 1953 demonstrates. The queen commissioned Joan to create

【小译】

琼·海赛尔（1906～1988）是英国著名木雕家、插图画家和出版商人。她的作品涵盖了从博物学到英语经典文学作品插图的多个领域。1964年她被选举为艺术家协会的首位大师级会员，1987年获大英帝国勋章。

琼·海赛尔生于伦敦诺丁山，父亲约翰·海赛尔是一位插图画家。1928至1933年，琼就读于皇家艺术学院。1931年，琼在佛里特街伦敦中央学校雕刻系和石刻系的夜校学习雕刻，师从R·约翰·毕德汉姆，并学到了终身受用的绘画技巧。

上世纪30年代末，琼的木雕艺术水平受到广泛公认。她收到的第一个订单是为她哥哥克里斯托弗的诗集绘制作者的肖像油画。之后她又为简·奥斯汀、特洛普，加斯克尔夫人、玛丽·拉塞尔·米特福德等作家的著作绘制了插图，并为上世纪40年代由圣安德鲁教会出版的诗集绘制插图。第二次世界大战期间，琼接受了导师金斯利库克的建议并接替了他的职位，就职于爱丁堡艺术学院的书本插图绘画系。1950年琼为罗伯特伯恩斯的诗集设计了一个新的版本，创作了一系列优美的插图，这些小插画是琼最优秀的作品，尤其是一幅绘制了一只小老鼠在玻璃上打滚的作品更是脍炙人口。

海塞尔在木雕方面的天赋毋庸置疑，同时她还拥有一双灵巧的手。1953年女王命琼·哈塞尔为查尔斯王

an invitation especially for Prince Charles, who was only five years old at the time. The watercolor invitation is still proudly displayed in the royal collection.

Hassall's health was frail, and as early as 1943 she asked to be relieved of teaching at Edinburgh College of Art on medical grounds. She died in Malham, Yorkshire, in 1988, highly regarded as one of the foremost wood-engravers of the 20th century.

子制作一份独特的请帖，当时王子仅有五岁，于是琼为女王加冕礼制作了一份精致的水彩画请帖，直到现在这张请帖还傲然陈列于皇家展览室。

海塞尔体弱多恙，早在1943年她就因身体原因请求辞去了爱丁堡艺术学院的教师工作。1988年，海塞尔在约克郡的马尔哈姆市与世长辞。她被公认为是20世纪最顶尖的木雕艺术家之一。

词汇 VOCABULARY

1. typographer [ti'pɒgrəfə]
   n 印刷商；印刷工人

2. guild [gild]
   n 协会，行会；同业公会

3. illustrator ['iləstreitə(r)]
   n 说明者；插图画家；图解者

4. commission [kə'miʃən]
   n 委员会；佣金；犯 vt 委任；使服役

5. replacement [ri'pleismənt]
   n 更换；代替者；补充兵员；复位

6. coronation [kɒrə'neiʃ(ə)n; (US) kɔːrə'neʃ(ə)n]
   n 加冕礼

7. frail [freil]
   n 灯心草篓；少妇；少女 adj 虚弱的；脆弱的

背景链接 TIPS

Robert Burns

罗伯特·彭斯（1759～1796）苏格兰农民诗人，在英国文学史上占有特殊重要的地位。他复活并丰富了苏格兰民歌；他的诗歌富有音乐性，可以歌唱。彭斯生于苏格兰民族面临被异族征服的时代，因此，他的诗歌充满了激进的民主、自由的思想。诗人生活在破产的农村，和贫苦的农民血肉相连。他的诗歌歌颂了故国家乡的秀美，抒写了劳动者纯朴的友谊和爱情。

121 Samuel Palmer

Samuel Palmer (1805~1881) was one of Britain's greatest artists. He was a landscape painter, etcher and printmaker and also a prolific writer. Palmer was a key figure in Romanticism in Britain and produced visionary pastoral paintings. He painted familiar scenes – trees, villages, the night sky – but using rich forms and vivid colors. Many are surprised that works that look so bold and modern were painted nearly two centuries ago.

Palmer was born in London on 27 January 1805. He was delicate as a child, but in 1819 he exhibited both at the Royal Academy and the British Institution; and shortly afterwards he became intimate with John Linnell, who introduced him to William Blake, whose strange and mystic genius had the most powerful effect on Palmer's art. An illness led to a residence of seven years at Shoreham in Kent, and the characteristics of the scenery of the district are constantly recurrent in his works. Among the more important productions of this time are the "Bright Cloud" and the "Skylark", paintings in oil, which was Palmer's usual medium in earlier life.

In 1839 he married a daughter of Linnell. The

【小译】

塞缪尔·帕尔默（1805～1881）是英国最伟大的艺术家之一，他是一位风景画家、蚀刻师、制版工人，同时也是一位多产的作家。帕尔默是英格兰浪漫主义画派的关键人物，创作了大量的幻想风格的田园油画。他用丰富的形式和活泼的色彩描绘那些似曾相识的场景：树林、村庄、夜空，许多现在看来都非常大胆和现代的作品，却是他在两个世纪前绘制的。

帕尔默生于1805年1月27日，出生在伦敦。孩提时他非常羞怯，但1819年他却在皇家艺术学院和不列颠研究院有过表演。不久之后，他与约翰·林内尔结为至交，林内尔把他引荐给了威廉·布莱克，后者奇异而神秘的才华对帕尔默的作品产生了重要的影响。因为一场疾病，帕尔默在肯特郡的肖勒姆渡过了七年，这个地区的景色在他之后的作品中屡屡重现。这时期比较重要的作品是"亮云"和"云雀"，是帕尔默早期少见的油画作品。

wedding tour was to Italy, where he spent over two years in study. After returning to London from Italy, he worked in watercolor and took up etching. In 1843, he was elected an associate and in 1854 a full member of the Society of Painters in Water Colors. In 1853 the artist was elected a member of the English Etching Club. In his later years, Palmer suffered a series of personal hardships – including the death of his favorite son – and ended his life living as a recluse.

In 2005 the British Museum collaborated with the Metropolitan Museum of Art to stage the first truly major retrospective of his work – Samuel Palmer: Vision and Landscape. The show ran from October 2005 – January 2006, and from March – May 2006 at The Metropolitan Museum of Art, New York. It marked the 200th anniversary of Palmer's birth and brought together his finest pictures from collections around the world.

1839年帕尔默与林内尔的女儿结为夫妻。蜜月旅行去的是意大利，他曾在那儿学习了两年时间。回到伦敦后，他开始绘制水彩画，并吸纳了蚀刻画的特点。1843年，他成为油画和水彩画协会的准会员，并于1854年成为正式会员。1853年，帕尔默选举为英国蚀刻画俱乐部成员。帕尔默在晚年遭遇了一系列的不幸，他最爱的儿子和他的夫人相继去世，于是他开始避世不出。

2005年大英博物馆与大都会艺术博物馆联合起来，第一次真正地为帕尔默的作品举办了一场主题回顾展览，名为《塞缪尔·帕尔默：视野与风景》。这次展出从2005年10月持续到2006年1月，随后从2006年5月到6月在纽约的大都会艺术博物馆进行。这次展览纪念了帕尔默的200年诞辰，并将其最优秀的作品展现给全世界。

词汇 VOCABULARY

1. printmaker ['print,meikə(r)]
   n. 版画复制匠

2. prolific [prə'lifik]
   a. 多产的；丰富的

3. characteristic [,kæriktə'ristik]
   n. 特征；特性；特色 a. 典型的；特有的

4. recurrent [ri'kʌrənt]
   a. 周期性的，经常发生的；复发的

5. etching ['etʃiŋ]
   n. 蚀刻术；蚀刻版画 a. 蚀刻的

6. recluse [ri'klu:s]
   n. 隐士；隐居者 a. 隐居的

背景链接 TIPS

Metropolitan Museum of Art

大都会艺术博物馆，是美国最大的艺术博物馆，也是世界著名的博物馆。位于美国纽约5号大道上的82号大街，与著名的美国自然历史博物馆遥遥相对。占地13万平方米，它是与英国伦敦的大英博物馆、法国巴黎的卢浮宫、俄罗斯圣彼得堡的列宁格勒美术馆（也称冬宫音译艾尔米塔什博物馆）齐名的世界四大美术馆之一，共收藏有300万件展品。现在是世界上首屈一指的大型博物馆。

Unit 29 体育明星

As the origin of many major sports in the world like soccer, cricket, snooker, tennis, golf and boxing, the UK ranked fourth in the medal table in the 2008 Beijing Olympic Games behind only China, USA and Russia. The huge success can mainly be attributed to some of the world-famous British sports starts.

As the most popular sports in UK, the sports of soccer has cultivated both athletically and commercially famous football stars David Beckham and Michael Owen. The sports of tennis which was in decline in the last 80 years was ignited again by the young Scottish player Andy Murray who is currently a World No. 4. As for snooker, the Great Britain also attracts the world's attention by former world champions Stephen Gordon Hendry and Ronnie O'sullivan. Hendry has won the World Championship a record seven times and was snooker's world No. 1 for eight consecutive years between 1990 and 1998, and again in 2006/2007. O'sullivan has been World Champion on three occasions and has been the world's No. 1 player on five occasions.

Lewis Hamilton is a British Formula One racing driver from England. He won the 2008 Formula One World Champion at the age of 23, becoming the youngest driver to win the tilte, as well as the first black driver. Hamilton is widely regarded as the new focus in the F1 sports after the retirement of Michale Schumacher.

Other famous sports stars in the UK also include the English diver Thomas Daley who specialises in the 10 metre platform event and was the 2009 FINA World Champion in the individual event at the age of 15 and one of the world's greaterst boxer Joe Calzaghe – the longest-reigning world champion in recent years, having held the WBO super middleweight title for over ten years.

Due to limited space, we will only focus on two of the most popular British sports stars around the world in the field of tennis and soccer, namely Andy Murray and David Beckham.

作为世界上很多重要体育项目的发源地，诸如足球、板球、斯诺克、网球、高尔夫以及拳击，英国在2008年北京奥运会的金牌榜上位列第四名，仅次于中国、美国和俄罗斯。这个巨大的成功主要归功于英国的那些闻名于世的体育明星。

作为英国最受欢迎的体育运动，英国足球培养出了集竞技水平与商业价值于一身的足球明星大卫·贝克汉姆和迈克尔·欧文。近80年来处于衰退中的网球也因年轻的苏格兰运动员安迪·穆雷而重新点燃了人们的热情，穆雷目前排名世界第4。斯诺克方面，英国也因前世界冠军史蒂芬·戈登·亨德利和罗尼·奥沙利文而吸引着全世界的目光。亨德利曾经创记录的7次夺得世界冠军，并于1990至1998年间连续八年排名世界第一，并于2006至07年再次荣登榜首。奥沙利文曾经3次夺得世界冠军，并5次成为世界排名第一。

刘易斯·汉密尔顿是来自英格兰的英国一级方程式赛车运动员。他于2008年23岁的时候夺得一级方程式世界冠军，成为获得这一荣誉的最年轻的赛车手和第一名黑人运动员。汉密尔顿被广泛认为是继迈克尔·舒马赫退役后F1领域内最受瞩目的焦点。

其他著名的英国体育明星包括跳水运动员托马斯·戴利，他的专长是10米台，并于2009年以15岁的年龄获得国际泳联单项冠军。还有世界上最伟大的拳击运动之一员乔·卡尔扎合，他是近年来独霸世界拳坛时间最长的拳手，超过10年保持了世界拳击理事会超中量级拳王称号。

由于篇幅限制，我们在这一单元将主要介绍两位在世界上最受欢迎的英国运动明星，即网球与足球领域的安迪·穆雷与大卫·贝克汉姆。

122 Andy Murray

Andy Murray is a Scottish professional tennis player and current British No. 1.He is also the best British player in almost 80 years since Fred Perry. He prefers to play on clay courts but seems more than comfortable on grass. Murray is 190 cm tall and generally uses a double-handed backhand.

Andy Murray was born in Glasgow, Scotland on 15 May 1987. His mother is Scottish tennis coach Judy Murray. Murray's brother, Jamie, is also a professional tennis player. Murray was born with a bipartite patella, where the kneecap remains as two separate bones instead of fusing together in early childhood. He was diagnosed at the age of 16 and had to stop playing tennis for six months. Murray is seen frequently to hold his knee due to the pain caused by the condition and has pulled out of events because of it, but manages it through a number of different approaches.

A native of Dunblane, Scotland, Murray attended Dunblane Primary School and was in attendance on the day of the notorious Dunblane massacre, when a gunman shot and killed16 children and one adult before killing himself. Murray was eight years old at the time.

Murray reached a career-high ranking of No. 2 on

【小译】

安迪·穆雷是苏格兰职业网球运动员，目前在英国排名第一。他也是自佛雷德·佩里以来的近80年中英国最好的网球运动员。他喜欢在红土场进行比赛，但是看上去似乎对草场更加适应。穆雷身高190公分，习惯用双手反拍打法。

安迪·穆雷于1987年5月15日出生在苏格兰的格拉斯哥。他的母亲朱迪·穆雷是苏格兰网球教练。穆雷的哥哥杰米也是一名职业网球运动员。穆雷有天生的二分髌骨症，在他童年的早期他的膝盖骨仍然是两边分开的。他16岁的时候被确诊，并因此停止了网球训练6个月之久。人们经常可以看到穆雷由于外在条件导致的疼痛而捂着膝盖，并因此退出训练。但他通过多种方法克服了这个问题。

作为一名土生土长的苏格兰邓布兰人，穆雷在邓布兰小学经历了那个臭名卓著的邓布兰惨案。在那一天，一名枪手射杀了16名儿童和一名成年

August 17, 2009, and finished that year ranked No. 4 again. Murray achieved a top-10 ranking by the Association of Tennis Professionals for the first time on 16 April 2007. He has been runner-up in three Grand Slam finals: the 2008 US Open, the 2010 Australian Open and the 2011 Australian Open, and has reached the semi-finals of all four Grand Slam tournaments. He has won four career ATP Masters Series titles, winning in Madrid and Cincinnati in 2008 and in Miami and Montreal in 2009. In 2008, Murray became the first British player in the history of the ATP rankings to finish the season ranked in the Top 4. (The previous best year-end ranking for a British man had been No. 6, achieved by both Greg Rusedski and Tim Henman.)

人之后自尽，那时的穆雷年仅8岁。

　　穆雷于2009年8月17日达到了他职业生涯的最高排名——第2名。并在年终排在了第4。穆雷首次进入世界职业网球协会排名前10位是在2007年4月16日。他三次夺得大满贯赛事亚军，分别是在2008年的美网以及2010和2011年的澳网。在所有四大满贯赛事中穆雷都进入过半决赛。他4次获得职业ATP大师系列赛冠军，分别是在2008年的马德里和辛辛那提，以及2009年的迈阿密和蒙特利尔。2008年，穆雷以年终排名世界第4成为了ATP历史上的英国选手第一人。（此前英国选手的年终最佳排名是第6，选手分别是格利格·鲁塞德斯基和蒂姆·亨曼）

词汇 VOCABULARY

1. clay [klei]
   n. 泥土；粘土；肉体 v. 用黏土处理

2. bipartite [bai'pɑ:tait]
   a. 双边的；由两部分构成的；一式两份的

3. patella [pə'telə]
   n. [解剖] 膝盖骨

4. kneecap ['ni:kæp]
   n. 膝盖骨；护膝

5. diagnose ['daiəgnəuz]
   vt. 诊断；断定 vi. 诊断；判断

6. massacre ['mæsəkə]
   n. 大屠杀 vt. 残杀；彻底击败

7. Madrid [mə'drid]
   n. 马德里（西班牙首都）
   real madrid 皇家马德里队

8. Cincinnati [,sinsi'næti]
   n. 辛辛那提（美国俄亥俄州西南部城市）

9. Miami [mai'æmi]
   n. 迈阿密（美国佛罗里达州东南部港市）
   miami beach 迈阿密海滩（位于美国佛罗里达州）

10. Montreal [,mɔntri'ɔ:l]
    n. 蒙特利尔（加拿大东南部港市）

背景链接 TIPS

ATP Masters Series

ATP（Association of Tennis Professional）职业男子网球协会，是世界男子职业网球选手的"自治"管理组织机构。ATP在1972年美国公开赛上成立，其主要任务是协调职业运动员和赛事之间的伙伴关系，并负责组织和管理职业选手的积分、排名、奖金分配，以及制定比赛规则和给予或取消选手的参赛资格等工作。

123 David Robert Joseph Beckham

David Beckham is an English professional football midfielder as well as one of the most influential and favorite football players in the world. He currently plays for and captains Los Angeles Galaxy in Major League Soccer. He is also member of the England national team, for whom he holds the all-time appearance record for an outfield player. He is widely known for his crossings, long-range free kicks and corner hits.

David Beckham is born on 2 May 1975, in Leytonstone, England. As a student in Essex, Beckham won the Bobby Charlton Soccer Skills Award at the age of 11, making his football talent evident at an early age. Beckham's career began when he signed a professional contract with Manchester United, making his first-team debut in 1992 aged 17. During his time United won the Premiership title six times, the FA Cup twice and the UEFA Champions League in 1999. He left Manchester United to sign for Real Madrid in 2003, where he remained for four seasons. In January 2007, Beckham left Real Madrid and signed a five-year contract with the MLS team Los Angeles Galaxy. His new contract with the Galaxy, effective 1 July 2007, gave him the highest salary of any MLS team Los Angeles Galaxy player in history.

In international football, Beckham made his England debut on 1 September 1996, at the age of 21. He was made captain from 15 November 2000 until the 2006 FIFA World Cup finals, during which he played 58 times. He earned a much-publicised hundredth cap against France on 26 March 2008, and became the all-time outfield player appearance

【小译】

大卫·贝克汉姆是英格兰职业中场球员，世界上最有影响力和最受欢迎的球员之一。他现在效力于美国职业足球大联盟的洛杉矶银河队，同时也是英格兰国家队的成员，并保持着外场球员出场时间记录。他广为人们所知的是他传中、远距离任意球和角球的技巧。

贝克汉姆于1975年5月2日出生于英格兰莱顿斯通。在学生时代，他11岁就在埃塞克斯获得了博比查尔顿足球技巧奖，使得他的足球天份在很小的时候就得以显现。贝克汉姆的职业生涯始于与曼彻斯特联队签约，1992年，17岁的他首次代表球队亮相。效力于曼联期间，他代表球队获得了6次英超联赛冠军，2次英格兰足总杯冠军，并在1999年夺得了欧洲冠军杯冠军。2003年，他离开曼联，加盟了皇家马德里，并在那度过了4个赛季。2007年1月，他离开了皇家马德里，与美国职业大联盟的洛杉矶银河队签订了5年的合约，新合约于2007年7月1日正式生效。在合约中，洛杉矶银河队给予了他联盟历史上的最高工资。

在国家队，贝克汉姆于1996年9月1日首次代表国家队亮相，时年21岁。他于2000年11月15日至2006年国际足联世界杯决赛阶段期间担任英格兰队队长，在此期间共为国家队出场58次。2008年

record holder on 28 March 2009 when he surpassed Bobby Moore's total of 108 caps.

He has twice been runner-up for FIFA World Player of the Year and was awarded the Order of the British Empire (OBE) by Queen Elizabeth II in June 2003. He is third in the Premier League's all time time assist provider chart, with 152 assists in 265 appearances. He was Google's most searched-for of all sports topics in both 2003 and 2004. Such global recognition has made him an elite advertising brand and a top fashion icon. He has been married to singer and fashion designer Victoria Beckham since 1999 and they have given birth to four children.

3月26日与法国队的比赛是他第100场国家队比赛。2009年3月28日，他创造了新的外场球员出场纪录，超越了博比·摩尔的108场。

贝克汉姆两次获得年度世界足球先生亚军，并于2003年6月荣获伊丽莎白二世女王颁发的不列颠帝国勋章。他在英超联赛总助攻榜上排在第3名，在他265次出场中总共送出了152个助攻。2003年和2004年，他是谷歌上运动主题中被搜索次数最多的。这样的国际影响力使得他成为了精英品牌的广告宠儿和顶级的时尚商标。1999年，他与歌手兼时装设计师维多利亚·贝克汉姆结婚，并育有4个孩子。

词汇 VOCABULARY

1. midfielder ['midfi:ld] n 中场队员	2. galaxy ['gæləksi] n 银河；[天] 星系；银河系；一群显赫的人
3. outfield ['autfi:ld] n 外场；边境；偏远的田园	4. effective [i'fektiv] a 有效的，起作用的；实际的，实在的
5. surpass [sə'pɑ:s] v 胜过，优于；超越；非…所能办到或理解	6. elite [ei'li:t] n 精英；精华；中坚分子

背景链接 TIPS

1. Manchester United

曼彻斯特联队是英国足坛的一支老牌劲旅，成立于1878年，当时是由英格兰开夏和约克夏铁路公司工人组成的一支业余球队，取名为牛顿赫斯队。1885年转为职业队，1892年加入英国足球联盟，1902年改名为曼彻斯特联队。曼联队的第一次鼎盛时期出现在20世纪初期，在1908年到1911年四年期间，曼联队在主教练查普曼的带领下夺得两次联赛冠军和1次足总杯冠军。成为当时英国足坛最受人们欢迎的一支球队，因球队队服为红色，球迷们给曼联队取了一个绰号，称之为"英国足坛的红魔"。

2. Order of the British Empire (OBE)

大英帝国最优秀勋章（Most Excellent Order of the British Empire），简称大英帝国勋章，或译为不列颠帝国勋章，是英国授勋及嘉奖制度中的一种骑士勋章，由英王乔治五世于1917年6月4日所创立。

Unit 30 商界精英

In the business world, fortune is a way to evaluate the success of a businessman. All over the world, there are many kinds of fortune lists or charts ranking businessmen according to their fortune. Forbes' Fortune 500 is regarded as one of the most authoritative fortune lists in the world. In the UK, the annually Rich List released by Times is one of the most influential fortune list in which the richest businessmen are listed in sequence.

According to the 2011 Rich List, the richest people in Britain are getting wealthier compared with last year. The combined fortune of Britain's top 1000 rich people reaches £396 billion, 18% up from that of the last year. The names of Ten Top rich people draw the whole country's attention.

According to the list, the richest British person is Lakshmi Mittal and Family. Lakshmi Mittal, the Indian-born steel tycoon with a net worth of £17.5 billion, is no stranger to the British people because Mr. Mittal has been topping the list for 7 consecutive years. He is the owner of AcelorMittal Company, the largest steel company in the world.

Russian tycoon Alisher Usmanov is the owner of Metalloinvest. Metalloinvest is the richest person in Britain next only to Mr. Mittal with a fortune of £12.4 billion. Last year, he was the sixth richest British.

The £10.3 billon worth Russian businessman Roman Abramovich ranks the third in the Rich List. His fame and wealth increased simultaneously after becoming the boss of Chelsea football team. He made his way to one of the richest by selling Russian oil products in early 1990s. He is also famous for his many properties purchased in several different countries.

The fourth to tenth richest people in Britain in 2011 are The Duke of Westminster, Ernesto and Kirsty Bertarelli, Leonard Blavatnik, John Fredriksen and his family, David and Simon Reuben, Gopichand and SRI Hindujas, Galen and George Weston and family.

The above top ten rich people are currently regarded as the most successful businessmen in Britain. However, fortune, however important, isn't the only measurement for success. In this part, 3 other successful businessmen will be introduced who become successful owning to their unique operation philosophies.

在商界，财富是衡量一个商人成功的一个指标。基于商人的财富，全世界现在有各种各样的财富排行榜。福布斯财富500强被认为是世界上最有权威性的一个财富排行榜之一。在英国，每年时代期刊发布的富人榜单是最具影响力的财富排行榜之一，在这个榜单中，最富有的人根据所有的财富情况在榜单中按顺序排列。

根据2011年的富人榜，上榜的富人与上一年相比，财富又有所增长。英国前1000个最富的人的财富总额达到了3960亿英镑，与上一年相比增加了18%。排名前十的富豪受到了举国的关注。

根据排名榜的信息，最富有的英国人是拉克希米·米塔和其家族。拉克希米·米塔，出生于印度的钢铁商业巨头，净资产175亿英镑，对英国人来说再熟悉不过了，因为拉克希米先生已经连续7年位居榜首。他拥有全球最大钢铁生产公司——阿塞洛米塔尔。

俄罗斯最大的铁矿石生产商Metalloinvest的掌控者阿利舍尔·奥斯曼诺夫以124亿英镑的资产额在榜单中紧跟着拉克希米先生，成为了英国富人。去年，他被评为英国第六富翁。

俄罗斯商人罗曼·阿布拉莫维奇以103亿英镑位居榜单的第三位，他的名声和财富的积累是在他在担任英格兰球会切尔西足球俱乐部老板的同时积累起来的。早在90年代初他就通过出售俄罗斯石油产品成为最富有的人之一。他也同样因为喜欢从很多不同的国家购买私人物品而闻名。

2011英国富豪榜排行从第四到第十位分别是威斯敏斯特公爵、内斯托和柯丝蒂·贝尔塔雷利、莱纳德·布拉瓦尼克、约翰·弗雷德里克森及家人、大卫·鲁本和西蒙·鲁本、Hindujas两兄弟以及盖伦·维斯顿和乔治·威斯顿及家人。

上述的10个人目前被认为是在英国最成功的商业人士。然而，财富尽管重要却不是衡量成功的唯一标尺。在这一部分，我们将介绍另外3位成功的商业人士，他们的成功归功于他们独特的运作理念。

124 Philip Green

Philip Green is a successful British businessman who is known for his fast speed in accumulating wealth. As the owner of Bhs retain store, Philip not only saved it from bankruptcy, but also acquired the biggest profit in Bhs's 74 years long history, with 100 million pound in only two years. According to Times' Rich List in 2002, Philip jumped from the 149th place to the 16th place with the net worth of 1.2 billion.

Born in a Jewish family on 15 March 1952 in London, Philip Green went to a Jewish boarding

【小译】

菲利普·格林是一位成功的英国商人，他迅速的财富积累速度使得他被广泛知晓。作为Bhs零售连锁店的接管人，菲利普不仅使得它免于破产，并且在Bhs零售连锁店74年的经营历史上获得了最大的盈利，在短短两年之内盈利1亿英镑。根据2002年时代杂志发布的最富有的人的统计表中，菲利普以12亿英镑（172亿美元）资产从富豪榜之149位跃至第16位。

菲利普·格林于1952年3月15日出生

school from 9 years old and left school without receiving a graduation certificate. From the age of 16, Philip already started to fight in the business world.

His first business was importing jeans from the Far East and sold to the retailers in London with the capital of £20,000 loan from the bank. In the mid-1980s, Philip bought JeanJeanie, a jeans chain store for £65,000 when it experienced difficult times and sold one year later at 33 million pounds. Later, Philip became chairman and chief executive of a discount retailer Amber Day but resigned 4 years later without reaching the company's profit forecast. Philip made his name in the retaining area in 1999 when he bought the Sears group for £548 million and sold it a few months later at a price of £729 million, gaining a profit of £181 million and became an instant celebrity.

In March 2000, Philip risked 220 million on purchasing Bhs when it was on the verge of bankruptcy, which was an unwise deal according to many people. This time, instead of selling it instantly, Philip decided to operate it himself. Within two year, Philip not only rescued Bhs from 1.6 million deficits, but also made it extremely profitable. The secret for Philip to make such a miracle was his excellent management. Take the hangover for example. As soon as Philip taking charge, he reduced the cost of hangovers for 1 penny each and subsequently saved £400, 000 each year. Besides saving cost, Philip took other effective measures as well, such as fixing the target clients on women between 40 and 55; keeping a strict eye on the work of purchase department to make sure Bhs had the newest style faster than other retailers and etc.

于伦敦的一个犹太家庭，他从9岁开始就生活在犹太人的一个寄宿学校中，后来离开学校时都没有获得毕业证。他16岁便开始在商业世界中摸爬滚打了。

菲利普最初的生意是凭借从银行获得的20,000英镑的借款从远东进口牛仔裤，然后卖给伦敦当地的零售商。上世纪80年代中期，他在牛仔时装连锁店JeanJeanie生意萧条之时以65000英镑买下这家连锁店，一年后将其转手倒卖，卖了300万英镑。之后，菲利普来到折扣店AmberDay担任主席和首席执行官，但是因为没有实现利润目标，他于四年之后辞职。让菲利普在零售业声名鹊起的是1999年他以5.48亿英镑收购了西尔斯集团，几个月后逐一转手卖出，总共卖了7.29亿英镑，获利1.81亿英镑中风靡一时。

2000年3月，菲利普筹齐2.2亿英镑买下了危在旦夕的Bhs百货公司。当时，这在很多人看来并非明智之举。这次，菲利普并没有立刻卖掉它，而是打算自己经营。在两年的时间里菲利普不仅仅将Bhs 公司从160万赤字的情况中挽救了出来，而且还取得了巨大的盈利。菲利普之所以能创造这个奇迹，应该归功于他杰出的管理才能。以衣架为例，菲利普从接管公司的那刻开始，他就将每个衣架的生产费用降低了1个便士，但是商场的年销售成本却因此而节省了40万英镑。除了节约成本，菲利普同时也采取了其他有效的措施，例如将顾客群体定在40到50岁的中年妇女，密切关注购买市场确保Bhs与其他的零售商相比，可以提供最新款的服装样式。

1. asset ['æset] _n._ 资产；财产；有利条件	2. retailer [ri:'teilə] _n._ 传播的人；零售商
3. chain [tʃein] _n._ 链；束缚；枷锁 _vt._ 束缚；囚禁；用铁练锁住	4. forecast ['fɔ:kɑ:st] _n._ 预想；预测 _vt._ 预报 _vi._ 进行预报，作预测
5. deficit ['defisit] _n._ 赤字；不足额	6. hangover ['hæŋ,əuvə] _n._ 宿醉；遗物；残留物

背景链接 TIPS

飞利浦·格林的致富秘诀

1. 定位准确。格林准确地把顾客群体定位为40～55岁的女性，将目光瞄准中档品牌。

2. 品牌维护。格林对供应商要求很严，还让采购人员对商品的质量和销售负起责任。格林能够在短短几周时间里使全部新款商品摆满货架，比所有竞争对手都快。

3. 数里淘金。格林对商店的销售情况、营业额、赢利以及每平方英尺的销售量、租金收费等无不牢记在心，随时随地信手拈来。

4. 加强团队。催生成功的因素还包括强大的管理团队。

5. 减员增效。格林被称为"杀人不眨眼"。Bhs的复兴所带来的不仅仅是令人惊叹的利润，还有成千上万的失业大军。

125 Richard Branson

【小译】

Richard Branson, the founder of the Virgin group, is a renowned British business magnate. Virgin Group is the largest private enterprise in the UK owning 350 companies and providing services covering 224 areas. According to a survey in the UK, 96% of the respondents are familiar with the Virgin brand and 95% of them have the name of the founder. Richard Branson is the 5th richest person in Britain and the 254th in the world according to Forbes' 2011 List of Billionaires, with a net worth of £2.58 billion.

Born in 1950, Richard Branson received his education at Stowe School where he established a

作为维京品牌的创始人，理查德·布兰森是英国著名的商业巨头。维京集团是英国最大的私人企业，拥有350家公司提供的服务，覆盖224个领域。英国的调查结果显示，96%的受访者称熟悉维京品牌，而且95%的受访者可以说出创始人的名字。根据2011年福布斯亿万富翁排名榜显示，理查德·布兰森以净资产25.8亿英镑在英国排名第五，在世界排名254。

理查德·布兰森出生于1950年，曾在斯多中学接受过教育，在校期间创建了校园杂志《学生》，这个杂志在后来发展成

campus magazine Student which became a national magazine later. With the capital acquired from the magazine, Branson opened a small mail company in collaboration with his friend and named the company Virgin. A strike broke out the next year affected the company and Branson changed it into a record retailer which was a big success. In 1972, Branson built a recording studio and established the record label "Virgin Records" with Mike Oldfield as the first Virgin artist. Over the years, Richard attracted superstars like Genesis, Phil Collins, Peter Gabriel, Simple Minds, The Human League and The Rolling Stones and etc. In 1992, Branson sold Virgin Music Group to EMI for $1 billion and used it as capital to expend the Virgin Group into international "Megastore". Besides record and retailing industries, Branson also entered a wide range of other industries and achieved success such as Virgin Atlantic Airways, Virgin Mobile, Virgin Trains, Virgin Cola, Virgin Fuels, Virgin Media, Virgin Comics and Virgin Animation, Virgin Health Bank and Virgin Healthcare to name a few.

Branson is a legendary leader with enormous personal charm. As a "transformational leader", he

为了一个全国性杂志。之后他利用创办杂志的赢利与朋友一起创立了一个小的邮递公司，命名为维京。就在第二年，英国爆发了邮政工人大罢工，邮递公司当然受到了影响，布兰森被迫将公司转为以经营唱片为主的折扣零售商店，但是大获成功。1972年，布兰森成立了一个唱片工作室，与维京的第一位艺术家麦克·欧德菲尔德建立了"维京唱片"，并且陆续吸引了一些巨星的注意，包括珍尼希斯、菲尔·柯林斯、彼得·盖布瑞尔、简单头脑合唱团、人类联盟合唱团、滚石等。1992年，布兰森将维京音乐集团以10亿美元卖给了百代唱片，并且用这笔资金将维京集团扩展成为一个国际化的集团。除了唱片和零售业，布兰森也将业务拓展到了更广阔的工业领域，并且取得了成功，例如维京亚特兰大航空、维京通信、维京铁路、维京可乐、维京燃料、维京媒体、维京动画、维京健康银行以及维京护理等。

布兰森是一位充满个人魅力的传奇领袖，作为一个变革领袖，他提倡工人之间的平等。集团中的每个人都可以直呼其名，而且每个雇员都有布兰森的地址和电

advocates equality among workers. Everyone in the Group calls him on the first name basis and in the early stage, every employee had the number of Branson's residence and was encouraged to call or dropped by if they had creative ideas or complaints. When Branson won the lawsuit against British Airways and got £610,000 compensation fee, he divided it among the staff and every employee got £166 so-called "BA bonus".

Apart from being a successful businessman, Richard Branson is also an adventure-lover and made several world record-breaking attempts and guest starred in several TV shows and films. His high public profile and his unconventionality gained himself both praise and criticism among the public.

话号码，他鼓励员工如果有任何创新性的建议或者是抱怨，都可以打电话给他或者直接拜访他。当巴莱森在与英国航空的官司中获胜之后，他将赢得的赔偿金额61万英镑分成若干份分发给了员工，每个雇员得到了166英镑的"英国航空公司奖金"。

除了是一位成功的商人，理查德·布兰森还是一个冒险家，他曾经有过很多破世界记录的尝试，他也曾在一些电视节目和电影中客串一些角色。他极高的社会知名度以及他不同寻常的行为让他在赢得一些赞扬的同时也受到了很多的批评。

词汇 VOCABULARY

1. respondent [ris'pɔndənt]
   n 被告；应答者 a 回答的；应答的

2. collaboration [kə,læbə'reiʃən]
   n 合作；通敌；勾结

3. healthcare [helθkɛə]
   n 医疗保健；卫生保健；健康护理

4. transformational [,trænsfə'meiʃənəl,,trænz-]
   a 改变的；转换生成的；转换的

5. bonus ['bəunəs]
   n 奖金；红利；额外津贴

6. unconventionality ['ʌnkən,venʃə'næliti]
   n 非常规；异常

背景链接 TIPS

维京（Virgin）品牌效应：

在布兰森的自传《失去处女之身》（Losing My Virginity）中提到，19岁时，一本杂志的记者访问他时，问他为何将他的新公司取名为"Virgin"（处女）时，他解释说因为"处女"这个名字比较性感，易让人产生联想而过目不忘。其次，维京不止是一个品牌的名字，它更意味着一种生活态度：自由自在的生活方式、叛逆、开放、崇尚自由以及极度珍贵的浪漫。维京鲜明而独特的品牌个性和文化为其品牌延伸提供了基础。大多数消费者把维京看成品质、价值、创新、娱乐、挑战的代名词。维京品牌在战略上绝不将品牌等同于某一项产品或服务，所以这样就不会限制它向跨行业的延伸。不像一些著名的品牌如IBM意味着电脑，柯达表示胶卷，而福特则是轿车等等，品牌名称已成定势。虽然在各个行业里维京集团都不是行业老大，但是维京却早已成为了年轻人心目中的"品牌领先者"（Brand Leading）。

126 Anita Roddick

Anita Roddick is a widely known businesswoman in Britain for her famous brand The Body Shop and was one of the richest women in Britain before she died.

Anita Roddick was born on 23 October 1942 in London in an Italian immigrant family. Anita attended the Maude Allen Secondary Modern School and was trained as a teacher at Bath Spa University before travelled to many countries. When returning, Anita was introduced to Gordon Roddick and married him in 1970. They had two daughters after marriage.

Anita opened the first Body Shop in 1976 as a means of livelihood when her husband was in South Africa. The original idea was to produce quality skin care products. With the knowledge she accumulated when travelling, she produced 15 natural cosmetic products and packaged them in recyclable plastic bottles. Her products received wide popularity and within half a year, she already opened a second shop. Anita didn't advertise because she believed the high quality products sell themselves and it was proved be her selling records. In 1984, the company went public and spread franchises all over England. Today, the Body Shop has developed into a multi-national company with thousands of stores over 50 countries. Anita was listed one of the five richest women in England in 1993.

The Body Shop had a totally different concept with many other cosmetic companies. It uses natural

【小译】

安妮塔·罗迪克是英国知名的女性商业家，凭借着自己的知名品牌美体小店（The Body Shop），她生前是英国最富有的女性之一。

安妮塔·罗迪于1942年10月23日出生于伦敦的一个意大利移民家庭。安妮塔曾经就读于莫德阿伦现代中学，在巴斯泉大学深造时，被培养的就业方向是老师。后来，她曾游历过很多国家，当她游历结束之后被介绍给了戈登·罗迪克，他们在1970年举行了婚礼，婚后生有两女。

1976年，当她的丈夫在南非的时候，安妮塔开了第一家美体小店店面用以谋生，最初的想法是生产质量还比较好的护肤品。借助她曾经游历各国时积累的经验，她生产了15种天然的化妆品并且把她们装在可重复使用的塑料瓶中。她的产品大受欢迎，半年之后她就开了第二家店面。安妮塔不做广告，因为她相信自己出售的产品的品质，这点也被产品的销售量所证实。1984年，公司规模进一步扩大化，在整个英格兰地区获得了特许经营权。今天，美体小店已经发展成了跨国公司，在全球50个国家有上千家店铺，安妮塔也在1993年被评为全英格兰最富有的五个女性之一。

与其他的化妆品公司不同，Body Shop有完全不同的理念，它采用天然元素来保护和提高皮肤状况，不会对皮肤造成任何伤害。除此之外，罗迪克推崇生态可持续的理念即"在满足当今需求的同时不会影响未来的需求

ingredients to protect and improve skin condition without causing any damages to the skin. Besides, Anita promotes ecological sustainable ideology to "meet the needs of the present without compromising the future."

Besides, Anita had a strong sense of social responsibility and thus earned a reputation for supporting social and environment activities. She supported human rights and devoted in several activities to protect human rights. She worked on environmental issues and founded Children on the Edge to help disadvantaged children and strongly against the exploitation of workers.

Anita Roddick died of acute brain hemorrhage on 10 September 2007, leaving her estate to charities.

的满足"。

此外，安妮塔有强烈的社会责任感，在资助社会活动和环保活动中赢得了很高的声望。她也支持人权，在保护人权的活动中做出了她自己的贡献。她自身致力于环境问题同时她建立了困难儿童机构来帮助残疾儿童。她也强烈反对剥削工人的行为。

安妮塔·罗迪克于2007年9月10日死于急性脑出血，死后将她的财产留给了慈善机构。

词汇 VOCABULARY

1. brand [brænd]
   n 商标，牌子
   vt 打烙印于；印…商标于；铭刻于，铭记

2. franchise ['fræntʃaiz]
   n 特权；公民权；经销权；管辖权
   vt 给…以特许（或特权）；赋予公民权

3. ecological [,ekə'lɔdʒikəl]
   a 生态的，生态学的

4. sustainable [sə'steinəbl]
   a 可以忍受的；足可支撑的；养得起的

5. hemorrhage ['heməridʒ]
   n 出血（等于haemorrhage）vt / vi 出血

背景链接 TIPS

"美体小店"（The Body Shop）正品鉴别小常识

1. 生产批号及产地

The Body Shop的产品批号一般为5到6位，由一位英文字母+三位数字+一或两位英文字母组成，其中第一位的英文字母代表产品的生产年份，按照TBS厂家的规则，B代表2006年，C代表2007年，以此类推；接下来的三位数字代表该产品是在第几天生产的，比如069代表第69天生产的，也是就三月份；产品批号最后的一到两位英文字母代表的是生产批次。需要注意的是：因为The Body Shop还有部分海外（非英国）生产商，因此也可能会有一些特殊的批号的情况。

2. 产品保质期

很多网站介绍The Body Shop产品保质期时，都说是3年，实际上The Body Shop产品是3年SHELF LIFE（就是说货架陈列寿命）及3年HOME LIFE（就是说从商店买回家,如果没有使用，至少还能保存3年）。因此The Body Shop有时会将即将下架的产品做打折特价产品，只要密封未使用，那么该产品还可以在家保存或使用3年。另外，包装上印有6M或12M的字样是表示开封后要在6月内或是12个月内用完。